studysync®

Reading & Writing Companion

GRADE 12 UNITS 4–6

Sculpting Reality

Fractured Selves

Times of Transition

studysync.com

ISBN 978-1-97-016270-7
MHID 1-97-016270-8

6 LWI 24 23 22

C

Contents

Sculpting Reality

What is the power of story?

UNIT 4

xi

Fractured Selves

What causes individuals to feel alienated?

UNIT 5

161

Times of Transition

How are we shaped by change?

UNIT 6

331

Please note that excerpts and passages in the StudySync® library and this workbook are intended as touchstones to generate interest in an author's work. The excerpts and passages do not substitute for the reading of entire texts, and StudySync® strongly recommends that students seek out and purchase the whole literary or informational work in order to experience it as the author intended. Links to online resellers are available in our digital library. In addition, complete works may be ordered through an authorized reseller by filling out and returning to StudySync® the order form enclosed in this workbook.

Reading & Writing Companion   iii

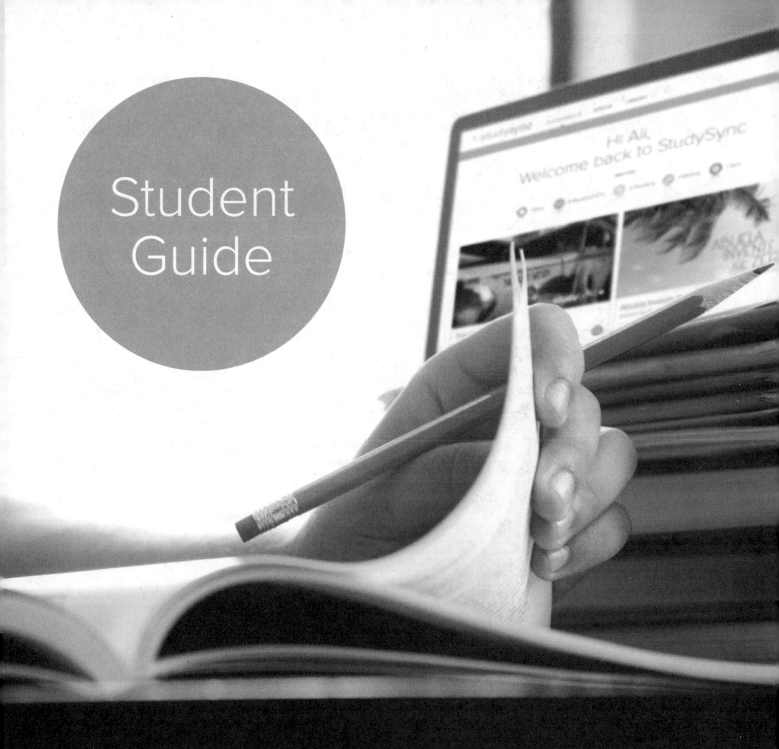

Student Guide

Getting Started

Welcome to the StudySync Reading & Writing Companion! In this book, you will find a collection of readings based on the theme of the unit you are studying. As you work through the readings, you will be asked to answer questions and perform a variety of tasks designed to help you closely analyze and understand each text selection. Read on for an explanation of each section of this book.

Close Reading and Writing Routine

In each unit, you will read texts that share a common theme, despite their different genres, time periods, and authors. Each reading encourages a closer look through questions and a short writing assignment.

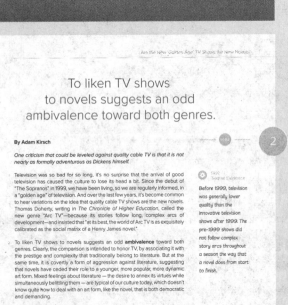

1 Introduction

An Introduction to each text provides historical context for your reading as well as information about the author. You will also learn about the genre of the text and the year in which it was written.

2 Notes

Many times, while working through the activities after each text, you will be asked to **annotate** or **make annotations** about what you are reading. This means that you should highlight or underline words in the text and use the "Notes" column to make comments or jot down any questions you have. You may also want to note any unfamiliar vocabulary words here.

You will also see sample student annotations to go along with the Skill lesson for that text.

 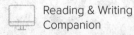 Reading & Writing Companion

3 First Read

During your first reading of each selection, you should just try to get a general idea of the content and message of the reading. Don't worry if there are parts you don't understand or words that are unfamiliar to you. You'll have an opportunity later to dive deeper into the text.

4 Think Questions

These questions will ask you to start thinking critically about the text, asking specific questions about its purpose, and making connections to your prior knowledge and reading experiences. To answer these questions, you should go back to the text and draw upon specific evidence to support your responses. You will also begin to explore some of the more challenging vocabulary words in the selection.

5 Skills

Each Skill includes two parts: Checklist and Your Turn. In the Checklist, you will learn the process for analyzing the text. The model student annotations in the text provide examples of how you might make your own notes following the instructions in the Checklist. In the Your Turn, you will use those same instructions to practice the skill.

---

3 First Read

Read "Are the New 'Golden Age' TV Shows the New Novels?" After you read, complete the Think Questions below.

4 THINK QUESTIONS

1. What does Kirsch say about how TV has changed recently? What is the "new genre" he mentions? Use evidence from the text to support your answer.

2. Why do people often compare "good" TV to the writing of Charles Dickens? What does Kirsch say about Dickens's writing that welcomes this comparison? Use evidence from the text to support your answer.

3. What are the reasons Hamid gives for watching more television than in the past? Use evidence from the text to support your answer.

4. What is the meaning of the word **capacious** as it is used in the text? Write your best definition here, along with a brief explanation of how you inferred its meaning through context.

5. Read the following dictionary entry:

idiom
id•i•om /ˈidēəm/ noun

1. a group of words, that when used together, have an unclear meaning when read literally
2. a form of expression natural to a language, person, or group of people
3. the dialect of a people or part of a country
4. a characteristic mode of expression in music, literature or art

Which definition most closely matches the meaning of idiom as it is used in paragraph 4? Write the correct definition of idiom here and explain how you figured out its meaning.

---

5 Skill: Informational Text Elements

Use the Checklist to analyze Informational Text Elements in "Are the New 'Golden Age' TV Shows the New Novels?" Refer to the sample student annotations about Informational Text Elements in the text.

••• CHECKLIST FOR INFORMATIONAL TEXT ELEMENTS

In order to identify characteristics and structural elements of informational texts, note the following:

✓ key details in the text that provide information about individuals, events, and ideas

✓ interactions between specific individuals, ideas, or events

✓ important developments over the course of the text

✓ transition words and phrases that signal interactions between individuals, events, and ideas, such as *because, as a consequence,* or *as a result*

✓ similarities and differences of types of information in a text

To analyze a complex set of ideas or sequence of events and explain how specific

✓ individuals, ideas, or events interact and develop over the course of the text, consider the following questions:

✓ How does the author present the information as a sequence of events?

✓ How does the order in which ideas or events are presented affect the connections between them?

✓ How do specific individuals, ideas, or events interact and develop over the course of the text?

✓ What other features, if any, help readers to analyze the events, ideas, or individuals in the text?

⟳ YOUR TURN

1. What does the author's use of the transition phrase "for instance" tell the reader?

   ○ A. that the sentence includes an example to support the idea in the sentence before it
   ○ B. that the sentence includes an example to support the idea in the sentence after it
   ○ C. that the author's main point in the paragraph is explained in the sentence.
   ○ D. that the second half of the paragraph discusses a new topic

2. Why does the author compare Gilbert Osmond to Tony Soprano in paragraph 5?

   ○ A. to conclude that Soprano is a more likeable character than Osmond
   ○ B. to show a counterexample to his thesis that he then refutes
   ○ C. to give clear and concrete evidence to support his thesis
   ○ D. to refer to a character in a novel that all Americans have read

---

Close Read & Skills Focus

6

After you have completed the First Read, you will be asked to go back and read the text more closely and critically. Before you begin your Close Read, you should read through the Skills Focus to get an idea of the concepts you will want to focus on during your second reading. You should work through the Skills Focus by making annotations, highlighting important concepts, and writing notes or questions in the "Notes" column. Depending on instructions from your teacher, you may need to respond online or use a separate piece of paper to start expanding on your thoughts and ideas.

Write

7

Your study of each selection will end with a writing assignment. For this assignment, you should use your notes, annotations, personal ideas, and answers to both the Think and Skills Focus questions. Be sure to read the prompt carefully and address each part of it in your writing.

English Language Learner

8

The English Language Learner texts focus on improving language proficiency. You will practice learning strategies and skills in individual and group activities to become better readers, writers, and speakers.

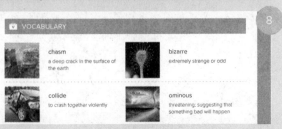

Extended Writing Project and Grammar

This is your opportunity to use genre characteristics and craft to compose meaningful, longer written works exploring the theme of each unit. You will draw information from your readings, research, and own life experiences to complete the assignment.

1 Writing Project

After you have read all of the unit text selections, you will move on to a writing project. Each project will guide you through the process of writing your essay. Student models will provide guidance and help you organize your thoughts. One unit ends with an **Extended Oral Project** which will give you an opportunity to develop your oral language and communication skills.

2 Writing Process Steps

There are four steps in the writing process: Plan, Draft, Revise, and Edit and Publish. During each step, you will form and shape your writing project, and each lesson's peer review will give you the chance to receive feedback from your peers and teacher.

3 Writing Skills

Each Skill lesson focuses on a specific strategy or technique that you will use during your writing project. Each lesson presents a process for applying the skill to your own work and gives you the opportunity to practice it to improve your writing.

UNIT 4

Sculpting Reality

What is the power of story?

Genre Focus: **POETRY**

Texts

 Paired Readings

1   Literary Focus: Romanticism

6   Ozymandias
POETRY *Percy Bysshe Shelley*

12   Facing It
POETRY *Yusef Komunyakaa*

15   Ode on a Grecian Urn
POETRY *John Keats*

24   Lines Composed a Few Miles Above Tintern Abbey
POETRY *William Wordsworth*

37   Stung
POETRY *Heid E. Erdrich*

39   Catalog of Unabashed Gratitude
POETRY *Ross Gay*

47   Literary Focus: Victorianism

53   The Cry of the Children
POETRY *Elizabeth Barrett Browning*

59   A Tale of Two Cities
FICTION *Charles Dickens*

63   Jane Eyre
FICTION *Charlotte Brontë*

67   Jabberwocky Baby
INFORMATIONAL TEXT *Wanda Coleman*

71   Dear Mama
POETRY *Wanda Coleman*

77   Freedom
ARGUMENTATIVE TEXT *Ursula K. Le Guin*

80   Why I Write
INFORMATIONAL TEXT *Joan Didion*

Reading & Writing Companion

Extended Writing Project and Grammar

98 | **Plan**

Planning Research
Evaluating Sources
Research and Notetaking

116 | **Draft**

Critiquing Research
Paraphrasing
Sources and Citations
Print and Graphic Features

130 | **Revise**

Using a Style Guide
Grammar: Contested Usage
Grammar: Hyphens

139 | **Edit and Publish**

English Language Learner Resources

141 | **A Golden Coin**
POETRY

151 | **A Modern Man**
INFORMATIONAL TEXT

Unit 4: Sculpting Reality

What is the power of the story?

CHARLOTTE BRONTË

When she was a twenty-year-old schoolteacher, Charlotte Brontë (1816–1855) self-financed the publication of a volume of poems she and her two younger sisters had written, using pseudonyms to disguise their gender. Although only two copies of the book sold, Brontë was not dismayed. She refused to let publishers ignore her. Her persistence paid off when a year later her novel *Jane Eyre* was published and became a runaway success.

ELIZABETH BARRETT BROWNING

The most esteemed female poet of the English-speaking world during the 19th century, Elizabeth Barrett Browning (1806–1861) spent her childhood engrossed in literature. Before she was a teenager, Browning had read the works of Shakespeare, Homer, and Milton—as well as the Old Testament in its original Hebrew. Her voracious appetite for words evolved into a career as a poet. Browning's works incorporated passionate admonishments of the social injustices of her time, including the American slave trade, British child labor, and women's oppression.

WANDA COLEMAN

Known as "the L.A. Blueswoman," Wanda Coleman (1946–2013) called Southern California home for her whole life. She was pleased to be described as uncompromising by literary critics, and her poetry often explored African American identity in the context of racism and economic hardship. Coleman's first poems were printed in a local newspaper when she was just thirteen years old. In addition to other poetry, she went on to publish essays, screenplays, and fiction for the rest of her life.

CHARLES DICKENS

Widely considered the greatest novelist of the Victorian era, Charles Dickens (1812–1870) was forced to leave school at the age of twelve and sent to work in a London factory after his father was sent to debtor's prison. This early experience led Dickens to take an interest in the lives of working-class people, a theme which he explored throughout his fiction. Dickens's novels—many of them serialized in popular magazines—were immensely popular and appealed to people from all walks of life, from factory workers to Queen Victoria herself.

JOAN DIDION

For California-born journalist and author Joan Didion (b. 1934), writing is synonymous with experience. She wrote in *The White Album* (1979), "We tell ourselves stories in order to live." Didion has reported on and written about a wide range of subjects, from the evolving American cultural landscape to personal narratives about the deaths of her husband and daughter. In 2015, Didion appeared in an advertisement for the French fashion label Céline, demonstrating her enduring status as a style icon.

HEID E. ERDRICH

A member of the Turtle Mountain Band of the Ojibwe tribe, Heid E. Erdrich (b. 1963) was raised in North Dakota by an Ojibwe mother and German American father who taught at the nearby Bureau of Indian Affairs boarding school. The author of several poetry collections, she explores themes of history, biology, motherhood, and spirituality in her writing. Erdrich co-edited the anthology *Sister Nations: Native American Women on Community*, a collection of fiction, prose, and poetry that celebrates the rich and diverse writing of contemporary Native American women.

ROSS GAY

American author Ross Gay (b. 1974) grew up outside Philadelphia and played college football before becoming a renowned poet and professor. He currently writes and teaches in Indiana, where he also tends to the Bloomington Community Orchard. Gay helped start the publicly-owned orchard in 2010, which is maintained by volunteers and shares its harvest with the community. In his poetry, Gay strives to explore and create compassion.

URSULA K. LE GUIN

American author Ursula K. Le Guin (1929–2018) published children's books, short story collections, poetry, screenplays, essays, and novels in her lifetime. Early in her career, she faced years of rejection, and first found success in the genres of fantasy and science fiction. "We read books to find out who we are," wrote Le Guin in *The Language of the Night* (1979). Her most popular novels exhibited how the genre of science fiction could reflect real issues of human nature and the environment.

JOHN KEATS

When John Keats (1795–1821) abandoned his training as an apothecary and surgeon to become a poet, it was not at the encouragement of the literary community. In fact, Keats, who after his lifetime would be considered among the most beloved English poets, was first received by critics as "unintelligible." Keats is best known for a series of odes, and he only wrote poetry seriously for about six years before succumbing to tuberculosis. His friend Percy Bysshe Shelley wrote the epic poem *Adonais* (1821) as an elegy for Keats in the days after his death.

YUSEF KOMUNYAKAA

Yusef Komunyakaa (b. 1947) spent his youth in Bogalusa, Louisiana, daydreaming of the world outside his rural town and was often found listening to his mother's waist-high wooden radio. He revered jazz and blues music especially and mentions the music of Louis Armstrong, Otis Redding, Thelonious Monk, and others among his sixteen collections of poetry. He served in the U.S. Army during the Vietnam War and currently lives and works in New York.

PERCY BYSSHE SHELLEY

English poet Percy Bysshe Shelley (1792–1822) was a literary icon of the Romantic era, which emphasized the importance of the imagination. He received an upper-class education and traveled throughout Europe as a young man. In addition to writing poetry and plays, Shelley also wrote political pamphlets, some of which he distributed with hot air balloons. He was married to Mary Shelley, the author of the novel *Frankenstein* (1818). Just before his thirtieth birthday, the poet drowned off the coast of Italy while sailing.

WILLIAM WORDSWORTH

William Wordsworth (1770–1850) published *Lyrical Ballads* with Samuel Taylor Coleridge in 1798, introducing Romanticism to English poetry with poems like Wordsworth's "Lines Composed a Few Miles above Tintern Abbey" and Coleridge's "The Rime of the Ancient Mariner." Wordsworth's love for the natural world was nurtured in his youth when he lived in a house along the River Derwent in Northern England. The exploration of human connection to nature imbued his writings throughout his lifetime.

Introduction

This informational text offers historical and cultural background about the society that gave rise to Romanticism. Romantic poets like William Wordsworth, Lord Byron, and John Keats were rejecting ideals of the Enlightenment that emphasized science, order, and modernization, turning instead to the freedom of nature. During the Romantic period, poets wrote of the importance of deep reflection and connection to the natural world. They were daunted by a society in which the Industrial Revolution had engendered deep inequality and poor health. The antidote, Romantic poets proclaimed, was nature.

"They believed the peacefulness and untouched beauty of the natural world enriched the soul."

Copyright © BookheadEd Learning, LLC

1 Think of all the technology you use today compared with what your parents had. You can watch movies on a screen that fits in your pocket. You can buy almost any product or service without having to leave your home. You can summon a virtual assistant with a word or phrase. There are so many things you are able to do that your parents could not when they were your age. New technology also creates new problems, however, such as cyberbullying, catfishing, and internet addiction. Some people may even question if all this technology is good for us. This is not the first time people have felt this way. The literary period known as **Romanticism** was born from concerns about modernization, and the movement flourished in the first half of the nineteenth century.

A Time of Upheaval

2 The start of the Romantic movement can be traced to the 1798 publication of William Wordsworth's collection of poetry, *Lyrical Ballads*, which also includes poems by Samuel Taylor Coleridge. Wordsworth, Coleridge, and other early writers in the movement, such as William Blake, are considered part of the first generation of Romantics. These poets were writing at a time when society was being transformed by two major events: the Industrial Revolution and the Enlightenment. The Industrial Revolution was a transition from an economy based on farming and handmade goods to one based on manufacturing. This change was possible thanks to inventions like steam engines and weaving machines. These developments tended to move people away from nature. People began to leave the countryside and come to the cities, which quickly became overcrowded and polluted. A class of ultra-wealthy industrialists rose to power, while factory workers lived and labored in poor, unsafe, and unhealthful conditions. The Romantic poet Lord Byron, in his narrative poem *The Corsair*, questioned whether the Industrial Revolution really represented progress:

3 Such hath it been—shall be—beneath the sun
The many still must labor for the one.

4 While the Industrial Revolution changed how people lived and worked, the Enlightenment changed how they thought. The Enlightenment was an

NOTES

Bridal Procession on the Hardangerfjord, by
Adolph Tidemand and Hans Gude, 1848

intellectual movement that championed the power of **reason.** People felt empowered to overturn old social structures and showed skepticism towards religion. They began to replace monarchies with democracies. They believed science and civilization could conquer nature.

5 The Industrial Revolution and the Enlightenment brought many benefits to society, but they also brought problems. Some people worried that the growing gap between humans and the natural world could be harmful. They felt that Enlightenment thinking focused on cold logic and materialism, which they worried would result in the neglect of human emotions and spirit. From these concerns sprang the Romantic movement in arts and letters.

Nature vs. Science

6 Romanticism values emotions over reason, individualism over **conformity,** and freedom over order. They believed the peacefulness and untouched beauty of the natural world enriched the soul. Not surprisingly, Romanticism contributed to the formation of the environmentalist movement. Although modern environmentalism is connected to fields of science like **ecology** and biology, the Romantics were generally opposed to science, which was seen as an attempt to impose rules and order upon the natural world. Unlike the organized gardens championed by Enlightenment thinkers, Romantics tended to believe that true enlightenment could be found in the wilderness; "civilizing" nature would corrupt it just as civilization can corrupt humanity. As Romantic poet William Wordsworth wrote in "The Tables Turned":

7   Our meddling intellect
    Mis-shapes the beauteous forms of things;
    —We murder to dissect.

8 Distrust toward science can also be seen in another work by a famous Romantic writer, Mary Wollstonecraft Shelley's *Frankenstein,* which introduced the character of the "mad scientist" and explored themes of taking science too far.

Copyright © BookheadEd Learning, LLC

NOTES

The Poetic Quest

9 Romanticism prized creativity, and so followers made great contributions to various forms of art. Poetry was particularly esteemed. Wordsworth called poetry a "spontaneous overflow of powerful feelings" and considered it "the language really used" by people. Inspired by the likes of Wordsworth, a younger "second generation" of Romantic poets saw it as their responsibility to guide people in a search for truth and beauty. Percy Bysshe Shelley, husband of Mary Wollstonecraft Shelley, claimed "poets are the unacknowledged legislators of the World." Prominent Romantic poets wrote poems that can be interpreted as allegories for the quest to guide other Romantics. John Keats's poetry is one example of how imagination can allow one to search for beauty and truth without leaving home.

John Keats, a British poet, one of the most important writers of Romanticism

10 Major Concepts

- **The Preeminence of Nature—**As the Industrial Revolution began to transform Britain into a nation of cities and factories, Romantics sought inspiration in the beauty of the natural world, the lives of ordinary workers, and the innocence of childhood. This first generation of Romantic poets included William Wordsworth, William Blake, and Samuel Taylor Coleridge.

- **The Quest for Truth and Beauty—**A second generation of English Romantics inherited many of the enthusiasms and value of their predecessors. During their tragically brief lives, Romantic poets such as Lord Byron, Percy Bysshe Shelley, and John Keats each pursued the ideals of truth and beauty.

Style and Form

11 English Romantic Poetry

- Although Romantics emphasized emotion and the freedom of the human spirit, they still wrote poetry in a structured poetic form to create meaning.

- Nature was an important feature of Romantic poetry and a source of inspiration.

NOTES

- Romantic poetry involved **contemplation** and reflection on the part of the speaker.

- Romantic poets often allude to the art, literature, and culture of the ancient Greeks. Latin classics were a part of the formal education of most Romantics, and many prominent Romantics, such as Samuel Taylor Coleridge, John Keats, and Percy Shelley all wrote in or translated works from the original Greek.

12 Romanticism can be embodied in the idiom "stop and smell the roses." Modern life can be hectic. Honking traffic and ringing smartphones can make a person feel stressed. Many people benefit from putting aside part of the day for self-reflection and enjoying the outdoors. Romanticism remains popular not only because of the sheer volume of the movement's contributions to art but also because people still need to be reminded not to neglect their emotional well-being. What aspects of modern life do you think Romantics would approve or disapprove of?

Reading & Writing Companion

Literary Focus

Read "Literary Focus: Romanticism." After you read, complete the Think Questions below.

 THINK QUESTIONS

1. Why were followers of Romanticism unhappy about the Industrial Revolution and the Enlightenment?

2. What might William Wordsworth have meant when he wrote "Our meddling intellect / Mis-shapes the beauteous forms of things; / — We murder to dissect"?

3. How is the Romantic poets' interest in beauty related to other ideas of Romanticism?

4. Use context clues to determine the meaning of the word **conformity**. Write your best definition here, along with the words and phrases that were most helpful in determining the word's meaning. Then, check a dictionary to confirm your understanding.

5. The word **ecology** likely stems from the Greek *oikos*, meaning "house or habitation," and *logos*, meaning "word or account." With this information in mind, write your best definition of the word **ecology** as it used in this text. Cite any words or phrases that were particularly helpful in coming to your conclusion.

Ozymandias

POETRY
Percy Bysshe Shelley
1818

Introduction

Percy Bysshe Shelley (1792–1822) was known for his radical ideas and unconventional lifestyle. Like *Frankenstein*, which was written by his second wife, Mary Shelley, the poem "Ozymandias" was composed in response to a challenge. Shelley and his friend, poet Horace Smith, submitted poems to the *The Examiner* on the occasion of the statue of Pharaoh Rameses II being transported from Egypt to London. Shelley's 14-line sonnet appeared in the paper first in January of 1818. The imaginative poet invented a traveler and a sculptor's inscription, evoking the ancient relic's ruin as a metaphor for the fall of dynasties and the limitations of tyrants.

"Look on my works, ye Mighty, and despair!"

1   I met a traveller from an antique land
2   Who said: 'Two vast and trunkless legs of stone
3   Stand in the desert. Near them, on the sand,
4   Half sunk, a shattered **visage** lies, whose frown,
5   And wrinkled lip, and sneer of cold command,
6   Tell that its sculptor well those passions read
7   Which yet survive, stamped on these lifeless things,
8   The hand that **mocked** them and the heart that fed.
9   And on the **pedestal** these words appear—
10   "My name is Ozymandias, king of kings:
11   Look on my works, ye Mighty, and **despair**!"
12   Nothing beside remains. Round the decay
13   Of that **colossal** wreck, boundless and bare
14   The lone and level sands stretch far away.

Statue of Ramesses II. Egyptian civilisation, New Kingdom, Dynasty XIX. Aswan, Nubian Museum

Shelley, Percy Bysshe. "Ozymandias." The Examiner, 1 Feb. 1818, pp. 73.

NOTES

Skill:
Media

How ideas remain relevant from one medium to another, can be illustrated by a modern doctor quoting "Ozymandias" during surgery. In "A Strange Relativity: Altered Time for Surgeon-Turned Patient" Dr. Paul Kalanithi expresses a desire to accomplish something in the time he has left.

This reminds me of how the once colossal accomplishment in "Ozymandias" is now a ruin.

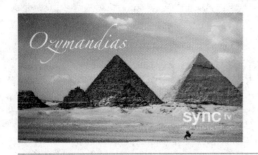

First Read

Read "Ozymandias." After you read, complete the Think Questions below.

 THINK QUESTIONS

1. How does the traveler in the poem describe the statue and the area that surrounds it? Cite specific details from the text to support your response.

2. In the inscription on the pedestal, what does the term *works* refer to? Use specific details from the text to support your answer.

3. In the video "A Strange Relativity: Altered Time for Surgeon-Turned-Patient," Paul Kalanithi explains that "clocks are now kind of irrelevant to me." Do you think the speaker of "Ozymandias" would agree with this opinion about time? Use evidence from the poem to support your response.

4. Use context to determine the meaning of the word **pedestal** as it is used in line 9 of the poem "Ozymandias." Write your definition of *pedestal* here and tell how you determined its meaning. Then write a synonym for this term. Check your inferred meaning of *pedestal* in a dictionary. Consult a print or digital dictionary, or a thesaurus to verify the synonym you wrote.

5. Use context to determine the meaning of the word **colossal** as it is used in line 13 of the poem "Ozymandias." Check the etymology and part of speech of the word in a general or specialized dictionary, or in another reference. Then write the definition of *colossal* here and explain how it is derived from the Greek.

Reading & Writing Companion

Skill:
Media

Use the Checklist to analyze Media in "Ozymandias." Refer to the sample student annotations about Media in the text.

••• CHECKLIST FOR MEDIA

In order to identify multiple interpretations of a story, drama, or poem, do the following:

- ✓ note the similarities and differences in different media, such as the live production of a play or a recorded novel or poetry

- ✓ evaluate how each version interprets the source text

- ✓ consider how, within the same medium, a story can have multiple interpretations if told by writers from different time periods and cultures

- ✓ consider how stories told in the same medium will likely reflect the specific objectives as well as the respective ideas, concerns, and values of each writer

To analyze multiple interpretations of a story, drama, or poem, evaluating how each version interprets the source text, consider the following questions:

- ✓ What medium is being used, and how does it affect the interpretation of the source text?

- ✓ What are the main similarities and differences between the two (or more) versions?

- ✓ If each version is from a different time period and/or culture, what does each version reveal about the author's objectives and the time period and culture in which it was written?

Please note that excerpts and passages in the StudySync® library and this workbook are intended as touchstones to generate interest in an author's work. The excerpts and passages do not substitute for the reading of entire texts, and StudySync® strongly recommends that students seek out and purchase the whole literary or informational work in order to experience it as the author intended. Links to online resellers are available in our digital library. In addition, complete works may be ordered through an authorized reseller by filling out and returning to StudySync® the order form enclosed in this workbook.

Reading & Writing Companion   **9**

Skill:
Media

Reread lines 9–14 of "Ozymandias" and watch the StudySyncTV episode. Then, using the Checklist on the previous page, answer the multiple-choice questions below.

⟳ YOUR TURN

1. In the clip, Dr. Kalanithi describes his relationship with time. How do his words reflect the theme shown in these lines of "Ozymandias"?

   ○ A. Even a doctor, someone in a position of power, or on a "pedestal," can be struck down by illness, much like the rulers of ancient Egypt.

   ○ B. Medical training, like the "king of kings," wants to show power over the future, but time extends beyond all of us.

   ○ C. Cancer, like the decay mentioned in the poem, cause "despair" and a "colossal wreck" for all of its victims.

   ○ D. Being a surgeon, like "the colossal wreck," often results in financial and personal stress, causing pain over time.

2. What is the most likely reason the video included scenes from Dr. Kalanithi and his family enjoying a Thanksgiving meal?

   ○ A. The video is a tribute to Dr. Kalanithi's family and friends, and the memories they share.

   ○ B. The video was made to remind Dr. Kalanithi's family and friends to live each day to the fullest.

   ○ C. The video evokes the idea of gratitude for the time we have on earth, even if that time is short.

   ○ D. The video uses the scenes to underscore one of the themes of the importance of family.

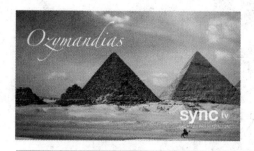

Close Read

Reread "Ozymandias." As you reread, complete the Skills Focus questions below. Then use your answers and annotations from the questions to help you complete the Write activity.

◎ SKILLS FOCUS

1. Identify a detail that contributes to an overall theme in the poem and write a sentence that explains why you chose it.

2. All sonnets contain a volta, which means "turn" in Italian. More specifically, a volta is a turning point in which there is a shift in language, style, meaning or tone. Highlight the volta in "Ozymandias" and explain how it represents a turning point.

3. The words on the pedestal of Ozymandias' statue are "My name is Ozymandias, king of kings: / Look on my works, ye Mighty, and despair!" How does the video of Dr. Kalanithi influence or change your reading of these words?

4. Most of this sonnet repeats the story told by "a traveller." What is the power of this story "from an antique land?" Why is the narrator of the poem repeating what he heard the traveller say?

✏ WRITE

LITERARY ANALYSIS: The scholar and literary critic Donald H. Reiman has stated that Shelley "dedicated his efforts to the destruction of tyranny in all its forms." In the video "A Strange Relativity," Dr. Paul Kalanithi invokes "Ozymandias" while reflecting on his new relationship with time, which he describes as "peculiar and free." Write a short essay indicating whether you find evidence of a philosophy of destroying the tyranny of time in "Ozymandias." How accurate is the interpretation put forth in the video? Remember to use textual evidence to support your claim.

Please note that excerpts and passages in the StudySync® library and this workbook are intended as touchstones to generate interest in an author's work. The excerpts and passages do not substitute for the reading of entire texts, and StudySync® strongly recommends that students seek out and purchase the whole literary or informational work in order to experience it as the author intended. Links to online resellers are available in our digital library. In addition, complete works may be ordered through an authorized reseller by filling out and returning to StudySync® the order form enclosed in this workbook.

Reading & Writing
Companion

11

Facing It

POETRY

Yusef Komunyakaa

1988

Introduction

The poetry of Yusef Komunyakaa (b. 1947) sheds light on some of the deepest and darkest elements of the human experience. He draws on his own background, exploring the intersection between African American culture and war. In his collection of poetry *Dien Cai Dau* (Vietnamese for "crazy"), Komunyakaa writes of his experience as a correspondent and editor during the Vietnam War (1955–1975) in a conversational style. "Facing It," one of the poems included in this collection, shows Komunyakaa reflecting on his first visit to the Vietnam Veterans Memorial.

"I go down the 58,022 names, / half-expecting to find / my own in letters like smoke."

1 My black face fades,
2 hiding inside the black granite.
3 I said I wouldn't
4 dammit: No tears.
5 I'm stone. I'm flesh.
6 My clouded **reflection** eyes me
7 like a bird of prey, the **profile** of night
8 slanted against morning. I turn
9 this way—the stone lets me go.
10 I turn that way—I'm inside
11 the Vietnam Veterans **Memorial**
12 again, **depending** on the light
13 to make a difference.
14 I go down the 58,022 names,
15 half-expecting to find
16 my own in letters like smoke.
17 I touch the name Andrew Johnson;
18 I see the booby trap's white flash.
19 Names shimmer on a woman's blouse
20 but when she walks away
21 the names stay on the wall.
22 Brushstrokes flash, a red bird's
23 wings cutting across my stare.
24 The sky. A plane in the sky.
25 A white vet's **image** floats
26 closer to me, then his pale eyes
27 look through mine. I'm a window.

Please note that excerpts and passages in the StudySync® library and this workbook are intended as touchstones to generate interest in an author's work. The excerpts and passages do not substitute for the reading of entire texts, and StudySync® strongly recommends that students seek out and purchase the whole literary or informational work in order to experience it as the author intended. Links to online resellers are available in our digital library. In addition, complete works may be ordered through an authorized reseller by filling out and returning to StudySync® the order form enclosed in this workbook.

Reading & Writing Companion **13**

28 He's lost his right arm
29 inside the stone. In the black mirror
30 a woman's trying to erase names:
31 No, she's brushing a boy's hair.

"Facing It" from Pleasure Dome: New and Collected Poems © 2001 by Yusef Komunyakaa. Published by Wesleyan University Press. Used by permission.

✏ WRITE

POETRY: In the poem "Facing It," the speaker describes his experience at the Vietnam Veterans Memorial. Write a poem that expresses your thoughts and feelings as you imagine yourself at the site of a memorial that you have personally visited or that you have researched.

Ode on a Grecian Urn

POETRY
John Keats
1820

Introduction

What is the relationship between art and life, between beauty and truth? The Romantic poet John Keats (1795–1821) only lived to be 25 years old, having grown up in England and dying from tuberculosis in a bedroom that overlooked the Piazza di Spagna in Rome. "Ode on a Grecian Urn" was written only a year before his death, and like much of Keats's work it examines the relationships between life, death, beauty, and truth with depth and lyrical insight.

"More happy love! more happy, happy love!"

NOTES

Skill: Poetic Elements and Structure

In the tradition of odes, the speaker of "Ode on a Grecian Urn" uses formal language to address the urn directly. In contrast, the speaker of the contemporary elegy "Facing It" expresses the rawness of his emotions through the use of vernacular language.

Skill: Figurative Literature

Keats personifies the urn by calling it a "sylvan historian." In "Facing It", Yusef Komunyakaa says his face is "hiding" inside the stone of the wall, which is also personification. It's as if he is a part of the wall even as he stands looking at it.

1 Thou still unravish'd bride of quietness,
2 Thou **foster**-child of silence and slow time,
3 **Sylvan** historian, who canst thus express
4 A flowery tale more sweetly than our rhyme:
5 What leaf-fring'd legend haunts about thy shape
6 Of deities or mortals, or of both,
7 In Tempe[1] or the dales of Arcady?[2]
8 What men or gods are these? What maidens loth?
9 What mad pursuit? What struggle to escape?
10 What pipes and timbrels? What wild ecstasy?

11 Heard melodies are sweet, but those unheard
12 Are sweeter; therefore, ye soft pipes, play on;
13 Not to the sensual ear, but, more endear'd,
14 Pipe to the spirit ditties of no tone:
15 Fair youth, beneath the trees, thou canst not leave
16 Thy song, nor ever can those trees be bare;
17 Bold Lover, never, never canst thou kiss,
18 Though winning near the goal—yet, do not grieve;
19 She cannot fade, though thou hast not thy bliss,
20 For ever wilt thou love, and she be fair!

21 Ah, happy, happy boughs! that cannot shed
22 Your leaves, nor ever bid the Spring adieu;
23 And, happy melodist, unwearied,
24 For ever piping songs for ever new;
25 More happy love! more happy, happy love!
26 For ever warm and still to be enjoy'd,
27 For ever panting, and for ever young;
28 All breathing human passion far above,

Ancient Greek urn

---

1. **Tempe** a beautiful valley in Arcadia
2. **Arcady** Arcadia, a mountainous region in Greece, traditionally considered an ideal rustic landscape

29   That leaves a heart high-sorrowful and cloy'd,

30   A burning forehead, and a parching tongue.

31   Who are these coming to the sacrifice?

32   To what green altar, O mysterious priest,

33   Lead'st thou that heifer lowing at the skies,

34   And all her silken flanks with garlands drest?

35   What little town by river or sea shore,

36   Or mountain-built with peaceful citadel,

37   Is emptied of this folk, this pious morn?

38   And, little town, thy streets for evermore

39   Will silent be; and not a soul to tell

40   Why thou art **desolate**, can e'er return.

41   O Attic shape![3] Fair attitude! with brede

42   Of marble men and maidens overwrought,

43   With forest branches and the trodden weed;

44   Thou, silent form, dost tease us out of thought

45   As doth eternity: Cold **Pastoral**!

46   When old age shall this **generation** waste,

47   Thou shalt remain, in midst of other woe

48   Than ours, a friend to man, to whom thou say'st,

49   "Beauty is truth, truth beauty,"—that is all

50   Ye know on earth, and all ye need to know.

---

3. **Attic shape** in the simple, graceful style characteristic of Attica, the region in Greece where Athens was located

First Read

Read "Ode on a Grecian Urn." After you read, complete the Think Questions below.

THINK QUESTIONS

1. In the first stanza of the poem, what is it that can express "A flowery tale more sweetly than our rhyme"?

2. In the second stanza, Keats writes of the "Bold Lover" who can never kiss his beloved. Why, according to the poem, should he not grieve?

3. In what sense is the urn "a friend to man"? Explain what Keats means by this phrase, using textual evidence from the poem to support your response.

4. Use context clues to determine the meaning of the word **sylvan** as it is used in stanza 1. Write your definition of *sylvan* here and explain which clues helped you determine the word's meaning.

5. Read the following dictionary entry:

    des•o•late /ˈde-sə-lət, ˈde-zə-/ *adjective*
    Adjective

    1. lacking the items that make people feel welcome in a place
    2. very lonely and sad
    3. (of a place) deserted and bleak

    Which of these definitions most closely matches the meaning of **desolate** as it is used in stanza 4? Write the correct definition of *desolate* here and explain which clues helped you figure it out.

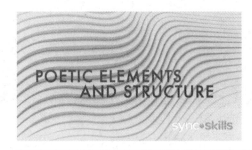

Skill:
Poetic Elements and Structure

Use the Checklist to analyze Poetic Elements and Structure in "Ode on a Grecian Urn." Refer to the sample student annotations about Poetic Elements and Structure in the text.

••• CHECKLIST FOR POETIC ELEMENTS AND STRUCTURE

In order to analyze a poet's choices concerning how to structure specific parts of a poem, note the following:

✓ the form and overall structure of the poem

✓ the rhyme, rhythm, and meter, if present

✓ lines and stanzas in the poem that suggest its meanings and aesthetic impact

✓ how the poet began or ended the poem

✓ if the poet provided a comedic or tragic resolution

✓ poetic terminology, such as the following:

- **ode:** a type of lyric poem that is serious with an elevated tone and style that usually celebrates a person, a quality, or an object, or expresses a private meditation
- **apostrophe:** a figure of speech in which an idea, personified object, or absent person is directly addressed (Nearly all odes include an apostrophe.)
- **elegy:** a poem that laments a death or some other great loss

To analyze how an author's choices concerning how to structure specific parts of a poem contribute to its overall structure and meaning as well as its aesthetic impact, consider the following questions:

✓ How does the poet structure the poem? What is the structure of specific parts?

✓ How do the poet's choices contribute to the poem's overall structure, meaning, and aesthetic impact?

✓ How does the poem reflect a specific literary time period and culture?

✓ How is this poem different from the poetry of other literary time periods and cultures?

Skill:
Poetic Elements and Structure

Reread lines 1–10 of "Ode on a Grecian Urn" and lines 1–16 of "Facing It." Then, using the Checklist on the previous page, answer the multiple-choice questions below.

⟳ YOUR TURN

1. Based on the excerpts from "Ode on a Grecian Urn" and "Facing It," a reader can assume that over time, there has been a trend for poetry to become—

   ○ A. less rigid in structure.
   ○ B. more consistent in rhyme scheme.
   ○ C. less like an elegy.
   ○ D. more likely to use apostrophe.

2. How does the rhyme scheme in "Ode on a Grecian Urn" contribute to its meaning?

   ○ A. The consistent repetition of sounds moves the reader through the speaker's positive contemplations.
   ○ B. The use of a traditional structure makes the speaker seem less excited about the urn.
   ○ C. The internal rhyming sounds help the reader connect the speaker's flowing contemplations.
   ○ D. The use of rhyming couplets highlights how the speaker is singing the urn's praises.

3. Compare the rhyme scheme in "Facing It" to that of "Ode on a Grecian Urn." How is the rhyme scheme different, and how does it contribute to the meaning of the poem?

   ○ A. The absence of a rhyme scheme in "Facing It" makes the poem flow more naturally and feel more somber, which reflects how war makes the speaker feel.
   ○ B. The absence of a rhyme scheme in "Facing It" means the poem's language is often harder to understand, which reflects how the speaker feels about war.
   ○ C. The absence of a rhyme scheme in "Facing It" puts all of the emphasis on the visual aspects of the poem, which parallels how the speaker interacts with the wall.
   ○ D. The absence of a rhyme scheme in "Facing It" means punctuation and line spacing stop the reader at particular points, which mimics how the speaker interacts with the wall.

Skill:
Figurative Language

Use the Checklist to analyze Figurative Language in "Ode on a Grecian Urn." Refer to the sample student annotations about Figurative Language in the text.

••• CHECKLIST FOR FIGURATIVE LANGUAGE

In order to determine the meaning of figurative language in context, note the following:

✓ words that mean one thing literally and suggest something else

✓ similes, metaphors, or personification

✓ figures of speech, including

- paradoxes, or a seemingly contradictory statement that when further investigated or explained proves to be true, such as

  > a character described as "a wise fool"

  > a character stating, "I must be cruel to be kind"

- hyperbole, or exaggerated statements not meant to be taken literally, such as

  > a child saying, "I'll be doing this homework until I'm 100!"

  > a claim such as, "I'm so hungry I could eat a horse!"

In order to interpret figurative language in context and analyze its role in the text, consider the following questions:

✓ Where is there figurative language in the text and what seems to be the purpose of the author's use of it?

✓ Why does the author use a figure of speech rather than literal language?

✓ What impact does exaggeration or hyperbole have on your understanding of the text?

✓ Where are there examples of paradoxes and how do they affect the meaning in the text?

✓ Which phrases contain references that seem contradictory?

✓ Where are contradictory words and phrases used to enhance the reader's understanding of the character, object, or idea?

✓ How does the figurative language develop the message or theme of the literary work?

Skill:
Figurative Language

Reread lines 41–50 of "Ode on a Grecian Urn" and lines 14–23 of "Facing It." Then, using the Checklist on the previous page, answer the multiple-choice questions below.

⟳ YOUR TURN

1. Which phrase is a simile?

   ○ A. "Thou, silent form"
   ○ B. "Beauty is truth"
   ○ C. "Brushstrokes flash"
   ○ D. "letters like smoke"

2. The phrase "a friend to man" in line 48 of "Ode on a Grecian Urn" can best be described as an example of—

   ○ A. personification.
   ○ B. paradox.
   ○ C. hyperbole.
   ○ D. simile.

3. Which statement best explains what the phrase "a friend to man" means in line 48 of "Ode on a Grecian Urn"?

   ○ A. The urn is "a friend to man" because it teaches people that nature is a source of timeless beauty.
   ○ B. The urn is "a friend to man" because it teaches people that there is beauty in truth and truth in beauty.
   ○ C. The scenes depicted on the urn are "a friend to man" because they stop us from forgetting important historical moments.
   ○ D. The scenes depicted on the urn are "a friend to man" because they show us that there is value in telling stories of the past.

Close Read

Reread "Ode on a Grecian Urn." As you reread, complete the Skills Focus questions below. Then use your answers and annotations from the questions to help you complete the Write activity.

◎ SKILLS FOCUS

1. Identify figurative language that the poet uses to describe the urn in the first stanza. What does this example of figurative language reveal about the speaker's view of the urn?

2. Notice all the question marks and the repetition of the word *What* in the first stanza. What is the effect of the poet's choice to structure the stanza this way? What does this structure suggest about the urn?

3. Highlight a section of the second stanza of "Ode on a Grecian Urn" that describes the difference between heard and unheard music. Explain how this distinction helps develop the poem's theme.

4. Identify a section of the fifth stanza that focuses on the passage of time and explain how this section reflects the poem's theme.

5. In "Ode on a Grecian Urn," the speaker views three different stories on an urn, and each has a different emotional impact. What is the power of these stories over the speaker? Support your answer with textual evidence.

✏ WRITE

LITERARY ANALYSIS: "Ode on a Grecian Urn" is a famous ode devoted to an ancient Greek urn. "Facing It" is an elegy written by a contemporary American poet about a visit to the Vietnam Veterans Memorial. Write an essay that analyzes how these texts use figurative language as well as poetic elements and structure to express ideas about art, culture, and society. Support your analysis with textual evidence from "Ode on a Grecian Urn."

Please note that excerpts and passages in the StudySync® library and this workbook are intended as touchstones to generate interest in an author's work. The excerpts and passages do not substitute for the reading of entire texts, and StudySync® strongly recommends that students seek out and purchase the whole literary or informational work in order to experience it as the author intended. Links to online resellers are available in our digital library. In addition, complete works may be ordered through an authorized reseller by filling out and returning to StudySync® the order form enclosed in this workbook.

Reading & Writing Companion   **23**

Lines Composed a Few Miles Above Tintern Abbey

On Revisiting the Banks of the Wye during a Tour, July 13, 1798

POETRY

William Wordsworth

1798

Introduction

William Wordsworth (1770–1850) gave "Lines Composed a Few Miles above Tintern Abbey, On Revisiting the Banks of the Wye during a Tour, July 13, 1798" one of literature's most specific titles, recalling his thoughts at a particular place that left a deep impression on him, by the Wye River near Wales. It was a place of peace in a life sometimes troubled by tragedy: the early death of both parents, the loss of two young children, and his separation from his beloved sister, to whom the poem is addressed. Meditating on the natural world around Tintern Abbey, Wordsworth also explores the way nature can soothe the soul in a world growing ever busier and less peaceful.

O sylvan Wye! thou wanderer thro' the woods, How often has my spirit turned to thee!

Artist David Cox the elder, Walter de Clare, 'Tintern Abbey,' circa 1840.

1 Five years have past; five summers, with the length
2 Of five long winters! and again I hear
3 These waters, rolling from their mountain-springs
4 With a soft inland murmur.— Once again
5 Do I behold these steep and lofty cliffs,
6 That on a wild secluded scene impress
7 Thoughts of more deep seclusion; and connect
8 The landscape with the quiet of the sky.
9 The day is come when I again **repose**
10 Here, under this dark sycamore, and view
11 These plots of cottage-ground, these orchard-tufts,
12 Which at this season, with their unripe fruits,
13 Are clad in one green hue, and lose themselves
14 'Mid groves and copses. Once again I see
15 These hedge-rows, hardly hedge-rows, little lines
16 Of sportive wood run wild: these pastoral farms,
17 Green to the very door; and wreaths of smoke
18 Sent up, in silence, from among the trees!
19 With some uncertain notice, as might seem
20 Of vagrant dwellers in the houseless woods,
21 Or of some Hermit's cave, where by his fire
22 The Hermit sits alone.

23   These beauteous forms,
24 Through a long absence, have not been to me
25 As is a landscape to a blind man's eye:
26 But oft, in lonely rooms, and 'mid the din
27 Of towns and cities, I have owed to them,
28 In hours of weariness, sensations sweet,

NOTES

 Skill: Figurative Language

The speaker repeats "length" and "long" to make a hyperbole about how difficult it has been to be away from this place.

"Soft inland murmur" is a sensory metaphor suggesting that the sounds of nature are calling to the speaker.

Copyright © BookheadEd Learning, LLC

29 Felt in the blood, and felt along the heart;
30 And passing even into my purer mind
31 With **tranquil** restoration:—feelings too
32 Of unremembered pleasure: such, perhaps,
33 As have no slight or trivial influence
34 On that best portion of a good man's life,
35 His little, nameless, unremembered, acts
36 Of kindness and of love. Nor less, I trust,
37 To them I may have owed another gift,
38 Of aspect more sublime; that blessed mood,
39 In which the burthen of the mystery,
40 In which the heavy and the weary weight
41 Of all this unintelligible world,
42 Is lightened:—that serene and blessed mood,
43 In which the affections gently lead us on,—
44 Until, the breath of this corporeal frame
45 And even the motion of our human blood
46 Almost suspended, we are laid asleep
47 In body, and become a living soul:
48 While with an eye made quiet by the power
49 Of harmony, and the deep power of joy,
50 We see into the life of things.

51   If this
52 Be but a vain belief, yet, oh! how oft—
53 In darkness and amid the many shapes
54 Of joyless daylight; when the fretful stir
55 Unprofitable, and the fever of the world,
56 Have hung upon the beatings of my heart—
57 How oft, in spirit, have I turned to thee,
58 O **sylvan**[1] Wye![2] thou wanderer thro' the woods,
59 How often has my spirit turned to thee!

60 And now, with gleams of half-extinguished thought,
61 With many recognitions dim and faint,
62 And somewhat of a sad perplexity,
63 The picture of the mind revives again:
64 While here I stand, not only with the sense
65 Of present pleasure, but with pleasing thoughts
66 That in this moment there is life and food
67 For future years. And so I dare to hope,
68 Though changed, no doubt, from what I was when first

Skill:
Context Clues

Burthen is preceded by the article "the" and followed by the preposition "of," so it is probably a noun.

The repetition of "in which" suggests that "burthen of the mystery" is related to "the heavy and the weary weight."

---

1. **sylvan** related to woods or forest
2. **Wye** the river along whose banks William Wordsworth walked during his visit

69 I came among these hills; when like a roe
70 I bounded o'er the mountains, by the sides
71 Of the deep rivers, and the lonely streams,
72 Wherever nature led: more like a man
73 Flying from something that he dreads, than one
74 Who sought the thing he loved. For nature then
75 (The coarser pleasures of my boyish days
76 And their glad animal movements all gone by)
77 To me was all in all.—I cannot paint
78 What then I was. The sounding **cataract**[3]
79 Haunted me like a passion: the tall rock,
80 The mountain, and the deep and gloomy wood,
81 Their colours and their forms, were then to me
82 An appetite; a feeling and a love,
83 That had no need of a remoter charm,
84 By thought supplied, not any interest
85 Unborrowed from the eye.—That time is past,
86 And all its aching joys are now no more,
87 And all its dizzy raptures. Not for this
88 **Faint**[4] I, nor mourn nor murmur; other gifts
89 Have followed; for such loss, I would believe,
90 Abundant recompense. For I have learned
91 To look on nature, not as in the hour
92 Of thoughtless youth; but hearing oftentimes
93 The still sad music of humanity,
94 Nor harsh nor grating, though of ample power
95 To chasten and **subdue**.—And I have felt
96 A presence that disturbs me with the joy
97 Of elevated thoughts; a sense sublime
98 Of something far more deeply interfused,
99 Whose dwelling is the light of setting suns,
100 And the round ocean and the living air,
101 And the blue sky, and in the mind of man:
102 A motion and a spirit, that impels
103 All thinking things, all objects of all thought,
104 And rolls through all things. Therefore am I still
105 A lover of the meadows and the woods
106 And mountains; and of all that we behold
107 From this green earth; of all the mighty world
108 Of eye, and ear,—both what they half create,
109 And what perceive; well pleased to recognise
110 In nature and the language of the sense

 Skill: Figurative Language

The speaker uses contradictory language, describing a positive feeling, "joy" as something "that disturbs." Wordsworth uses a paradox to illustrate the intense impact that nature has on him.

---

3. **cataract** a waterfall
4. **faint** to lose heart; to become depressed

NOTES

111 The anchor of my purest thoughts, the nurse,
112 The guide, the guardian of my heart, and soul
113 Of all my moral being.

114   Nor perchance,
115 If I were not thus taught, should I the more
116 Suffer my genial spirits to decay:
117 For thou art with me here upon the banks
118 Of this fair river; thou my dearest Friend,
119 My dear, dear Friend; and in thy voice I catch
120 The language of my former heart, and read
121 My former pleasures in the shooting lights
122 Of thy wild eyes. Oh! yet a little while
123 May I behold in thee what I was once,
124 My dear, dear Sister! and this prayer I make,
125 Knowing that Nature never did betray,
126 The heart that loved her; 'tis her privilege,
127 Through all the years of this our life, to lead
128 From joy to joy: for she can so inform
129 The mind that is within us, so impress
130 With quietness and beauty, and so feed
131 With lofty thoughts, that neither evil tongues,
132 Rash judgments, nor the sneers of selfish men,
133 Nor greetings where no kindness is, nor all
134 The dreary intercourse of daily life,
135 Shall e'er prevail against us, or disturb
136 Our cheerful faith, that all which we behold
137 Is full of blessings. Therefore let the moon
138 Shine on thee in thy solitary walk;
139 And let the misty mountain-winds be free
140 To blow against thee: and, in after years,
141 When these wild ecstasies shall be matured
142 Into a sober pleasure; when thy mind
143 Shall be a mansion for all lovely forms,
144 Thy memory be as a dwelling-place
145 For all sweet sounds and harmonies; oh! Then,
146 If solitude, or fear, or pain, or grief,
147 Should be thy portion, with what healing thoughts
148 Of tender joy wilt thou remember me,
149 And these my exhortations! Nor, perchance—
150 If I should be where I no more can hear
151 Thy voice, nor catch from thy wild eyes these gleams
152 Of past existence—wilt thou then forget
153 That on the banks of this delightful stream
154 We stood together; and that I, so long

155 A worshipper of Nature, hither came
156 Unwearied in that service: rather say
157 With warmer love—oh! with far deeper zeal
158 Of holier love. Nor wilt thou then forget,
159 That after many wanderings, many years
160 Of absence, these steep woods and lofty cliffs,
161 And this green pastoral landscape, were to me
162 More dear, both for themselves and for thy sake!

First Read

Read "Lines Composed a Few Miles Above Tintern Abbey, On Revisiting the Banks of the Wye during a Tour. July 13, 1798." After you read, complete the Think Questions below.

☁ THINK QUESTIONS

1. What is the effect of the opening eight lines of the poem in light of the poem's title? In what way do these lines clarify the author's relationship to the countryside around Tintern Abbey? Explain using textual evidence to support your answer.

2. Based on the second stanza, did the speaker in the poem forget the countryside around Tintern Abbey when he was away from it? Explain, using textual evidence to support your answer.

3. In the third stanza, the author mentions "the fretful stir / Unprofitable, and the fever of the world." What is he referring to with these words? Cite any other relevant quotes or passages from the poem in your answer.

4. In describing the beauties of nature in the fourth stanza, the author mentions "deep rivers and lonely streams" as well as the "sounding cataract." Using context clues, define *cataract*. Write your definition here, and explain how you inferred it.

5. Use context clues to determine the definition of **subdue** as it is used in the poem. Write your definition of *subdue* here, and explain how you inferred it.

Copyright © BookheadEd Learning, LLC

Skill:
Context Clues

Use the Checklist to analyze Context Clues in "Lines Composed a Few Miles Above Tintern Abbey, On Revisiting the Banks of the Wye during a Tour. July 13, 1798." Refer to the sample student annotations about Context Clues in the text.

••• CHECKLIST FOR CONTEXT CLUES

In order to use context as a clue to the meaning of a word or phrase, note the following:

- ✓ clues about the word's part of speech
- ✓ clues in the surrounding text about the word's meaning
- ✓ words with similar denotations that seem to differ slightly in meaning
- ✓ signal words that cue a type of context clue, such as:
  - *comparably*, *related to*, or *similarly* to signal a comparison context clue
  - *on the other hand*, *however*, or *in contrast* to signal a contrast context clue
  - *by reason of*, *because*, or *as a result* to signal a cause-and-effect context clue

To determine the meaning of a word or phrase as they are used in a text, consider the following questions:

- ✓ What is the meaning of the overall sentence, paragraph, or text?
- ✓ How does the position of the word in the sentence help me define it?
- ✓ How does the word function in the sentence? What clues help identify the word's part of speech?
- ✓ What clues in the text suggest the word's definition?
- ✓ What do I think the word means?

To verify the preliminary determination of the meaning of the word or phrase based on context, consider the following questions:

- ✓ Does the definition I inferred make sense within the context of the sentence?
- ✓ Which of the dictionary's definitions makes sense within the context of the sentence?

Skill:
Context Clues

Reread lines 115–138 of "Lines Composed a Few Miles Above Tintern Abbey, On Revisiting the Banks of the Wye during a Tour. July 13, 1798." Then, using the Checklist on the previous page, answer the multiple-choice questions below.

↻ YOUR TURN

1. What clues could you use to accurately determine the part of speech of the word *former*?

   ○ A. *Former* is used twice to modify the verbs that the speaker uses such as catch and read. It must be an adverb.

   ○ B. *Former* is used twice following the pronoun my, suggesting that the speaker possesses it. It must be a noun.

   ○ C. *Former* is used twice, once to describe heart and once to describe pleasure. It must be an adjective.

   ○ D. *Former* is used twice following the pronoun my and to describe wild eyes. It must be an adjective.

2. This question has two parts. First, answer Part A. Then, answer Part B.

   Part A: Based on context clues in the poem, what is most likely the meaning of the word *former*?

   ○ A. Something that is now destroyed or has changed form

   ○ B. A person that forms, or makes, something

   ○ C. Something that in the past used to have a particular role

   ○ D. A frame or core around which an electrical coil can be wound

   Part B: Which line from the poem BEST supports the answer to Part A?

   ○ A. "Of this fair river; thou my dearest Friend,"

   ○ B. "My dear, dear Friend; and in thy voice I catch"

   ○ C. "Of thy wild eyes. Oh! yet a little while"

   ○ D. "May I behold in thee what I was once,"

Skill:
Figurative Language

Use the Checklist to analyze Figurative Language in "Lines Composed a Few Miles Above Tintern Abbey, On Revisiting the Banks of the Wye during a Tour. July 13, 1798." Refer to the sample student annotations about Figurative Language in the text.

••• CHECKLIST FOR FIGURATIVE LANGUAGE

In order to determine the meaning of a figure of speech in context, note the following:

- ✓ words that mean one thing literally and suggest something else

- ✓ similes, metaphors, or personification

- ✓ figures of speech, including

  - paradoxes, or a seemingly contradictory statement that when further investigated or explained proves to be true, such as:

    > a character described as "a wise fool"

    > a character stating "I must be cruel to be kind"

  - hyperbole, or exaggerated statements not meant to be taken literally, such as:

    > a child saying " I'll be doing this homework until I'm 100!"

    > a claim such as, "I'm so hungry I could eat a horse!"

  - sensory metaphors, or comparisons that emphasize the senses such as:

    > A character being compared to a light "When she walked in, she lit up the entire room."

    > A place described using language related to taste "The visit to the restaurant was bittersweet."

In order to interpret a figure of speech in context and analyze its role in the text, consider the following questions:

- ✓ Where is there a figure of speech or figurative language in the text and what seems to be the purpose of it?

- ✓ What impact does exaggeration or hyperbole have on your understanding of the text?

- ✓ How does the figurative language develop the message or theme?

Skill:
Figurative Language

Reread lines 64–95 of "Lines Composed a Few Miles Above Tintern Abbey, On Revisiting the Banks of the Wye during a Tour. July 13, 1798." Then, using the Checklist on the previous page, answer the multiple-choice questions below.

YOUR TURN

1. The author uses references to animals in phrases such as "like a roe," "bounded o'er the mountains," and "glad animal movements" to—

   ○ A. suggest that the speaker used to enjoy watching the movements of the animals in their natural environment, and that he continues to enjoy it during this second visit.

   ○ B. convey that in his youth, the speaker experienced nature in the way an animal lives in the natural world, with feeling and instinct rather than intellectual thought.

   ○ C. express a negative tone about the behaviors of boyhood, which can be immature and superficial compared to the way the speaker is now approaching nature.

   ○ D. help readers understand that the speaker, now more mature, wishes he still had the ability to live comfortably in nature, as animals do.

2. The speaker says that he now has "other gifts." His use of the phrases "hearing oftentimes / The still sad music of humanity, / Nor harsh nor grating . . ." is an effective description of one of these gifts because it—

   ○ A. suggests in a positive way that although the speaker has matured, he still has the views of nature he held as a youth.

   ○ B. emphasizes the viewpoint that humanity, like nature, is at times cruel and disagreeable but yet should be viewed as a gift.

   ○ C. conveys that the speaker believes that a sense of harmony between nature and humanity is impossible.

   ○ D. shows that the speaker has gained a deeper appreciation of nature, one in which he recognizes a connection between nature and one's spiritual life.

3. Identify the paradox from the statements below.

◯ A. "And all its aching joys are now no more,"

◯ B. "Wherever nature led: more like a man"

◯ C. "Have followed; for such loss, I would believe"

◯ D. "An appetite; a feeling and a love"

Please note that excerpts and passages in the StudySync® library and this workbook are intended as touchstones to generate interest in an author's work. The excerpts and passages do not substitute for the reading of entire texts, and StudySync® strongly recommends that students seek out and purchase the whole literary or informational work in order to experience it as the author intended. Links to online resellers are available in our digital library. In addition, complete works may be ordered through an authorized reseller by filling out and returning to StudySync® the order form enclosed in this workbook.

Reading & Writing
Companion

35

Close Read

Reread "Lines Composed a Few Miles Above Tintern Abbey, On Revisiting the Banks of the Wye during a Tour. July 13, 1798." As you reread, complete the Skills Focus questions below. Then use your answers and annotations from the questions to help you complete the Write activity.

◎ SKILLS FOCUS

1. Find an example of imagery that reflects the thoughts and feelings of the speaker. Use context clues to determine the nuanced meaning of the image.

2. Choose a passage that helps you visualize the landscape. Explain how the descriptions and sensory metaphors deepen your understanding of the message of the poem.

3. Locate an example of figurative language, such as hyperbole, paradox, metaphor, or simile in the poem. Explain how it contributes to the overall meaning of the poem.

4. Throughout the poem, the speaker experiences nature while also remembering his youth. What effect do the memories of younger days have on the poem? What is the power of this story over the speaker's current experience?

✏ WRITE

LITERARY ANALYSIS: The essence of Romantic poetry is the precise choice of language that invokes the emotional response of the individual in relation to nature. Wordsworth revolutionized the literary form by exploiting the power of words to reveal the emotional depth of everyday experiences. Write an essay in which you analyze and evaluate Wordsworth's use of figurative language to contribute to the poem's message and emotional effect. Use context clues to analyze language and ideas that might be challenging.

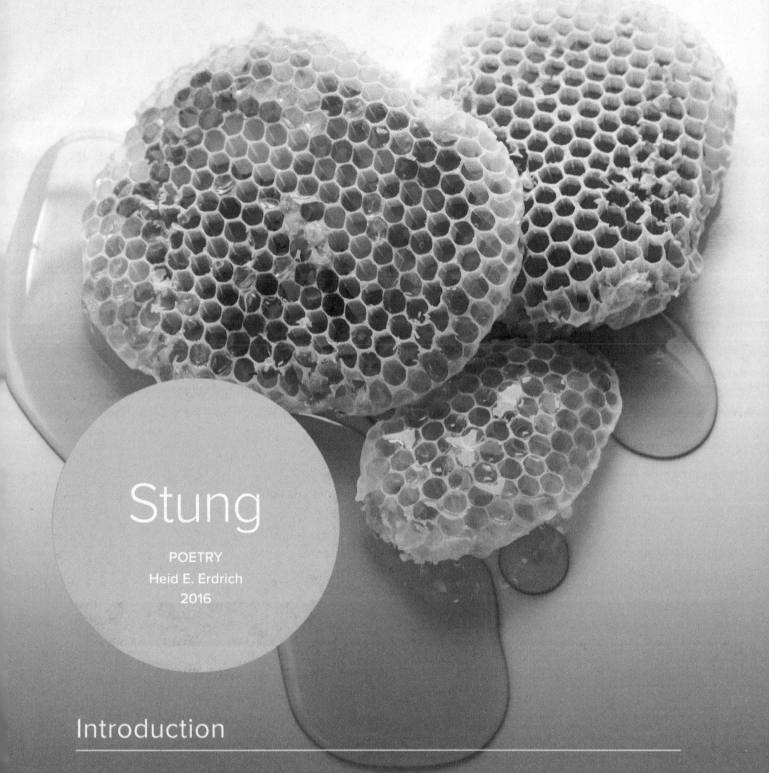

Stung

POETRY
Heid E. Erdrich
2016

Introduction

Heid E. Erdrich (b. 1963) is a Native American poet from the Ojibwe Nation. Aside from penning five full-length collections of poetry, Erdrich teaches for the MFA program at Augsburg College. In "Stung," Erdrich's speaker details an unexpected encounter with a bee.

In the cold, she hardly had her wits to buzz.

Copyright © BookheadEd Learning, LLC

1 She couldn't help but sting my finger,
2 clinging a moment before I flung her
3 to the ground. Her gold is true, not the trick
4 evening light plays on my roses.
5 She curls into herself, stinger twitching,
6 **gilt** wings folded. Her whole life just a few weeks,
7 and my pain **subsided** in a moment.
8 In the cold, she hardly had her wits to buzz.
9 No warning from either of us:
10 she sleeping in the richness of those petals,
11 then the hand, my hand, cupping the bloom
12 in devastating force, crushing the petals for the scent.
13 And she **mortally** threatened, wholly unaware
14 that I do this daily, alone with the gold last light,
15 in what seems to me an act of love.

From *The Mother's Tongue*, 2005. Used by permission of Heid Erdrich.

✎ WRITE

POETRY: Write a poem about your own encounter with a bee or another animal. Include details that make clear the kind of encounter it was: frightening, awe-inspiring, or comical, for example. You can model your poem after Erdrich's, writing 15 lines of free verse. And like her, you can include lines from the perspective of the animal. After your first draft, evaluate your details to make sure they are well-chosen, and replace words that are too general.

Catalog of Unabashed Gratitude

POETRY
Ross Gay
2015

Introduction

Written by poet Ross Gay (b. 1974), "Catalog of Unabashed Gratitude" is a tribute to both the marvelous and the mundane in modern life. Central to the poem is a community orchard in Bloomington, Indiana, a one-acre piece of land that is holds importance to Gay—he helped build it and now serves on the board of its non-profit organization. "Catalog of Unabashed Gratitude" was published in a 2015 poetry collection of the same title. The book was a finalist for the 2015 National Book Award for Poetry and winner of the 2016 National Book Critics Circle Award for Poetry. Gay, a professor of English, currently teaches at Indiana University.

"Friends, will you bear with me today, for I have awakened"

Copyright © BookheadEd Learning, LLC

1   Friends, will you bear with me today,

2   for I have awakened

3   from a dream in which a robin

4   made with its shabby wings a kind of veil

5   behind which it shimmied and stomped something from the south

6   of Spain, its breast aflare,

7   looking me dead in the eye

8   from the branch that grew into my window,

9   coochie-cooing my chin,

10   the bird shuffling its little talons left, then right,

11   while the leaves bristled

12   against the plaster wall, two of them drifting

13   onto my blanket while the bird

14   opened and closed its wings like a matador

15   giving up on murder,

16   jutting its beak, turning a circle,

17   and flashing, again,

18   the ruddy bombast of its breast

19   by which I knew upon waking

20   it was telling me

21   in no **uncertain** terms

22   to bellow forth the tubas and sousaphones,

23   the whole rusty brass band of gratitude

24   not quite dormant in my belly—

25   it said so in a human voice,

26   "Bellow forth"—

27   and who among us could ignore such odd

28   and **precise** counsel?

29   Hear ye! hear ye! I am here

30   to holler that I have hauled tons—by which I don't mean lots,

31   I mean *tons* — of cowshit

32   and stood ankle deep in swales of maggots

33   swirling the spent beer grains

34   the brewery man was good enough to dump off

35 holding his nose, for they smell very bad,

36 but make the compost writhe giddy and lick its lips,

37 twirling dung with my pitchfork

38 again and again

39 with hundreds and hundreds of other people,

40 we dreamt an orchard this way,

41 furrowing our brows,

42 and hauling our wheelbarrows,

43 and sweating through our shirts,

44 and two years later there was a party

45 at which trees were sunk into the well-fed earth,

46 one of which, a liberty apple, after being watered in

47 was tamped by a baby barefoot

48 with a bow hanging in her hair

49 biting her lip in her joyous work

50 and friends this is the realest place I know,

51 it makes me squirm like a worm I am so grateful,

52 you could ride your bike there

53 or roller skate or catch the bus

54 there is a fence and a gate twisted by hand,

55 there is a fig tree taller than you in Indiana,

56 it will make you gasp.

57 It might make you want to stay alive even, thank you;

58 and thank you

59 for not taking my pal when the engine

60 of his mind dragged him

61 to swig fistfuls of Xanax and a bottle or two of booze,

62 and thank you for taking my father

63 a few years after his own father went down thank you

64 mercy, mercy, thank you

65 for not smoking meth with your mother

66 oh thank you thank you

67 for leaving and for coming back,

68 and thank you for what inside my friends'

69 love bursts like a throng of roadside goldenrod

70 gleaming into the world,

71 likely hauling a shovel with her

72 like one named Aralee ought,

73 with hands big as a horse's,

74 and who, like one named Aralee ought,

75 will laugh time to time til the juice

76 runs from her nose; oh

77 thank you

78 for the way a small thing's wail makes

Please note that excerpts and passages in the StudySync® library and this workbook are intended as touchstones to generate interest in an author's work. The excerpts and passages do not substitute for the reading of entire texts, and StudySync® strongly recommends that students seek out and purchase the whole literary or informational work in order to experience it as the author intended. Links to online resellers are available in our digital library. In addition, complete works may be ordered through an authorized reseller by filling out and returning to StudySync® the order form enclosed in this workbook.

Reading & Writing Companion   41

79   the milk or what once was milk

80   in us gather into horses

81   huckle-buckling across a field;

82   and thank you, friends, when last spring

83   the hyacinth bells rang

84   and the crocuses flaunted

85   their upturned skirts, and a quiet roved

86   the beehive which when I entered

87   were snugged two or three dead

88   fist-sized clutches of bees between the frames,

89   almost clinging to one another,

90   this one's tiny head pushed

91   into another's tiny wing,

92   one's forelegs resting on another's face,

93   the translucent paper of their wings fluttering

94   beneath my breath and when

95   a few dropped to the frames beneath:

96   honey; and after falling down to cry,

97   everything's glacial shine.

98   And thank *you*, too. And thanks

99   for the corduroy couch I have put you on.

100   Put your feet up. Here's a light blanket,

101   a pillow, dear one,

102   for I can feel this is going to be long.

103   I can't stop

104   my gratitude, which includes, dear reader,

105   you, for staying here with me,

106   for moving your lips just so as I speak.

107   Here is a cup of tea. I have spooned honey into it.

108   And thank you the tiny bee's shadow

109   **perusing** these words as I write them.

110   And the way my love talks quietly

111   when in the hive,

112   so quietly, in fact, you cannot hear her

113   but only notice barely her lips moving

114   in conversation. Thank you what does not scare her

115   in me, but makes her reach my way. Thank you the love

116   she is which hurts sometimes. And the time

117   she misremembered elephants

118   in one of my poems which, oh, here

119   they come, garlanded with morning glory and wisteria

120   blooms, trombones all the way down to the river.

121   Thank you the quiet

122   in which the river bends around the elephant's

123   solemn trunk, polishing stones, floating

124   on its gentle back

125   the flock of geese flying overhead.

126   And to the quick and gentle flocking

127   of men to the old lady falling down

128   on the corner of Fairmount and 18th, holding patiently

129   with the softest parts of their hands

130   her cane and purple hat,

131   gathering for her the contents of her purse

132   and touching her shoulder and elbow;

133   thank you the cockeyed court

134   on which in a half-court 3 vs. 3[1] we oldheads

135   made of some runny-nosed kids

136   a shambles, and the 61-year-old

137   after flipping a reverse lay-up off a back door cut

138   from my no-look pass to seal the game

139   ripped off his shirt and threw punches at the gods

140   and hollered at the kids to admire the pacemaker's scar

141   grinning across his chest; thank you

142   the glad accordion's wheeze

143   in the chest; thank you the bagpipes.

144   And you, again, you, for the true kindness

145   it has been for you to remain awake

146   with me like this, nodding time to time

147   and making that noise which I take to mean

148   *yes*, or, *I understand*, or, *please go on*

149   *but not too long*, or, *why are you spitting*

150   *so much*, or, *easy Tiger*

151   *hands to yourself*. I am excitable.

152   I am sorry. I am grateful.

153   I just want us to be friends now, forever.

154   Take this bowl of blackberries from the garden.

155   The sun has made them warm.

156   I picked them just for you. I promise

157   I will try to stay on my side of the couch.

158   And thank you the baggie of dreadlocks I found in a drawer

159   while washing and folding the clothes of our murdered friend;

1. **half-court 3 vs. 3** an informal way of playing basketball where each team has three players and they only use half the court

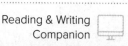

160 the photo in which his arm slung
161 around the sign to "the trail of silences"; thank you
162 the way before he died he held
163 his hands open to us; for coming back
164 in a waft of incense or in the shape of a boy
165 in another city looking
166 from between his mother's legs,
167 or disappearing into the stacks after brushing by;
168 for moseying back in dreams where,
169 seeing us lost and scared
170 he put his hand on our shoulders
171 and pointed us to the temple across town;

172 and thank you to the man all night long
173 hosing a mist on his early-bloomed
174 peach tree so that the hard frost
175 not waste the crop, the ice
176 in his beard and the ghosts
177 lifting from him when the warming sun
178 told him *sleep now*; thank you
179 the ancestor who loved you
180 before she knew you
181 by smuggling seeds into her braid for the long
182 journey, who loved you
183 before he knew you by putting
184 a walnut tree in the ground, who loved you
185 before she knew you by not slaughtering
186 the land; thank you
187 who did not bulldoze the ancient grove
188 of dates and olives,
189 who sailed his keys into the ocean
190 and walked softly home; who did not fire, who did not
191 plunge the head into the toilet, who said *stop,*
192 *don't do that*; who lifted some broken
193 someone up; who volunteered
194 the way a plant birthed of the reseeding plant
195 is called a *volunteer*, like the plum tree
196 that marched beside the raised bed
197 in my garden, like the arugula that marched
198 itself between the blueberries,
199 nary[2] a bayonet, nary an army, nary a nation,
200 which usage of the word volunteer
201 familiar to gardeners the wide world

2. **nary** an alternate way to say "not," usually suggesting "not a single one" of what it describes

202   made my pal shout "Oh!" and dance
203   and plunge his knuckles
204   into the **lush** soil before gobbling two strawberries
205   and digging a song from his guitar
206   made of wood from a tree someone planted, thank you;

207   thank you zinnia, and gooseberry, rudbeckia
208   and pawpaw, Ashmead's kernel, cockscomb
209   and scarlet runner, feverfew and lemonbalm;
210   thank you knitbone and sweetgrass and sunchoke
211   and false indigo whose petals stammered apart
212   by bumblebees good lord please give me a minute . . .
213   and moonglow and catkin and crookneck
214   and painted tongue and seedpod and johnny jump-up;
215   thank you what in us rackets glad
216   what gladrackets us;

217   and thank you, too, this knuckleheaded heart, this pelican heart,
218   this gap-toothed heart flinging open its gaudy maw
219   to the sky, oh clumsy,
220   oh giddy, oh dumbstruck,
221   oh rickshaw, oh goat twisting
222   its head at me from my peach tree's highest branch,
223   balanced impossibly gobbling the last fruit,
224   its tongue working like an engine,
225   a lone sweet drop tumbling by some miracle
226   into my mouth like the smell of someone I've loved;
227   heart like an elephant screaming
228   at the bones of its dead;
229   heart like the lady on the bus
230   dressed head to toe in gold, the sun
231   shivering her shiny boots, singing
232   Erykah Badu to herself
233   leaning her head against the window;

234   and thank you the way my father one time came back in a dream
235   by plucking the two cables beneath my chin
236   like a bass fiddle's strings
237   and played me until I woke singing,
238   no kidding, singing, smiling,
239   *thank you, thank you,*
240   stumbling into the garden where
241   the Juneberry's flowers had burst open
242   like the bells of French horns, the lily
243   my mother and I planted oozed into the air,

Please note that excerpts and passages in the StudySync® library and this workbook are intended as touchstones to generate interest in an author's work. The excerpts and passages do not substitute for the reading of entire texts, and StudySync® strongly recommends that students seek out and purchase the whole literary or informational work in order to experience it as the author intended. Links to online resellers are available in our digital library. In addition, complete works may be ordered through an authorized reseller by filling out and returning to StudySync® the order form enclosed in this workbook.

Reading & Writing Companion   45

244 the bazillion ants **labored** in their earthen workshops
245 below, the collard greens waved in the wind
246 like the sails of ships, and the wasps
247 swam in the mint bloom's viscous swill;

248 and you, again you, for hanging tight, dear friend.
249 I know I can be long-winded sometimes.
250 I want so badly to rub the sponge of gratitude
251 over every last thing, including you, which, yes, awkward,
252 the suds in your ear and armpit, the little sparkling gems
253 slipping into your eye. Soon it will be over,

254 which is precisely what the child in my dream said,
255 holding my hand, pointing at the roiling sea and the sky
256 hurtling our way like so many buffalo,
257 who said *it's much worse than we think,*
258 *and sooner*; to whom I said
259 *no duh child in my dreams*, what do you think
260 this singing and shuddering is,
261 what this screaming and reaching and dancing
262 and crying is, other than loving
263 what every second goes away?
264 Goodbye, I mean to say.
265 And thank you. Every day.

"Catalog of Unabashed Gratitude" from *Catalog of Unabashed Gratitude*, by Ross Gay, © 2015. All rights are controlled by the University of Pittsburgh Press, Pittsburgh, PA. Used by permission of the University of Pittsburgh Press.

✎ WRITE

PERSONAL RESPONSE: Write a personal response in which you examine the speaker's argument and state whether you agree or disagree with his message about gratitude. Remember to cite relevant textual evidence and include original commentary to support your response.

LITERARY FOCUS:
Victorianism

Introduction

This informational text offers historical and cultural background information about the Victorian era and how it influenced the literature of the time. Many writers sought to respond to and portray both the progress and inequities that existed in a society increasingly dominated by new inventions and structures. While inventions like the electric telegraph and canned food revolutionized communication and the manufacturing business, this new urban landscape was one of bleak and inhumane conditions for those attempting to survive in the lower classes of society. Victorian literature was marked by realism, a commitment by writers to portray both the good and the bad that existed in a world marked by modernization.

"Amidst all the progress, some people were being left behind."

1   If you've ever attended a comic-book convention or even seen pictures of one, you may have noticed a particular type of cosplayer. They'll wear top hats, vests, and goggles, often decorated with clockwork gears. These people are taking part in steampunk subculture. They enjoy fashion, artwork, and media set in a fictionalized, sci-fi version of the nineteenth century. Much of the steampunk aesthetic borrows directly from the culture and ideals of nineteenth century England. This time period is called the Victorian Age and, as any steampunk fan will attest, it continues to fascinate people today.

The Victorian Age

A portrait of Queen Victoria of Great Britain (1819–1901). Queen Victoria was one of the most famous British monarchs, reigning from 1837 to 1901, a period which established Great Britain as one of the world's leading powers.

2   The Victorian Age, like other periods in British history, derives its name from the monarch of the time, Queen Victoria. During her reign, from 1837 to 1901, the British empire expanded to cover over one-fifth of the earth. Almost one in four people were subjects of Queen Victoria. Much of this was made possible by the first Industrial Revolution. Steam-powered locomotives and ships made it possible for merchants and military to travel all over the world, even to the Arctic and Antarctic. The rise of factories created a need for raw materials to import and customers to buy the exported manufactured goods. Factories also created a demand for workers, and cities swelled as people left the countryside to seek work.

Copyright © BookheadEd Learning, LLC

3   Cities were not only growing in population and land area, they were becoming taller as well. As techniques for producing cast iron improved, iron-framed buildings began to replace wooden and brick structures. This stronger building material, as well as steam-powered elevators, allowed taller buildings to be erected. Communication also improved during this time. The electric telegraph was invented in 1837 and quickly spread through the British empire. Even continents were linked with **transoceanic** cables. In 1876, the next great step in communication revolutionized the way people spoke to each other: the telephone. By the end of Victoria's reign, radio was being developed. Other Victorian developments included photography, vaccination, and canned food.

4   Not everything was progress and comfort, however. For most, city life was unpleasant. Until unions began to form, most workers were severely underpaid and overworked. Men, women, and even very young children were made to work in dangerous conditions, like deep mine shafts or buildings with little-to-no fire safety measures. Scientists like Louis Pasteur would not develop germ theory, the understanding that many diseases are caused by microorganisms until the 1860s. His process of pasteurization made food safer, but it still took time for people to understand the importance of good hygiene and sanitation. In the crowded, dirty conditions of major cities like London, epidemics of diseases like scarlet fever, cholera, and tuberculosis (consumption) were tragically common. Nor did people realize the effects of burning coal or dumping chemicals into rivers. Emissions from coal burning plants are now known to be linked to early death and other adverse health effects in the Victorian era. Society was rushing to reap the benefits of new technology, but people were slower to adapt to the risks and dangers technology brought with it.

The Age of the Novel

5   In the Victorian era, novels reigned supreme. Novels were already common during the Romantic period, but Romantics viewed them as **inferior** to poetry. Indeed, most novels were written by women, who were also treated as lesser. While Romantics styled themselves as elites, changes in the Victorian Age made literature more available to everyone. A growing middle class and education reforms ensured more people were literate. New technology made it cheaper to produce books, newspapers, and magazines. People who couldn't afford even those were still able to read, thanks to the 1850 Public Libraries Act, which allowed libraries to stop charging **subscriptions** and loan books for free. Reading was now a hobby for the common person, and novels became the common genre, as they often emphasize enjoyability over artistry. Writing was no longer a leisure activity for the wealthy: it was a booming business, and more people were writing than ever before.

6   Literary magazines were profitable and gave authors a large audience. Many writers therefore tailored their work to be suitable for publishing in **periodicals**. As a result, the serial novel became a popular trend during the Victorian Age.

NOTES

Just as a TV series differs from a movie by telling a story over the course of many episodes, a serial novel is released a chapter at a time instead of all at once. Some authors, including Charles Dickens, would not even have a complete story planned when they began publishing chapters. Instead, they would use the reactions of their readers to decide how to shape the rest of the story.

Dickens' Dream. British writer Charles Dickens sleeping on a chair and dreaming about the characters of his novels.

Subgenres: Social-Problem and Regionalist Novels

7 Although the Industrial Revolution caused problems like poverty and poor living conditions, it also brought solutions. Increased literacy and improved printing technology made it possible to reach and inform far more people than ever before of the social problems that plagued the Victorian Age. Social-problem, or "Condition-of-England," novels became a common subgenre. Works of realistic fiction such as Dickens's *Hard Times* and *Oliver Twist* revealed the poverty and exploitation of London's lower classes. Dickens also drew attention to the corruption in the legal system with his novel *Bleak House.* And poet Elizabeth Barrett Browning's 1857 *Aurora Leigh* was a groundbreaking critique of Victorian views toward women.

8 Another subgenre that found great success in the Victorian Age was the regionalist novel. Like the Romantics, many nineteenth-century people wanted an escape from city life, so novels focusing on the people and landscape of the countryside appealed to a wide audience. While Romanticism idealized nature and pastoral regions, Victorian regionalist writing tended to be more realistic. Regionalist novels were usually set in real locations and often referred to natural or physical landmarks. The character of the people was included as well, through the use of local dialect, unique political or social values, and **parodies** of local residents. Emily Brontë's *Wuthering Heights* was notable for its brutal depiction of life on the Yorkshire moors in Northern England. Brontë's sister, Charlotte Brontë, wrote *Jane Eyre*, which features a woman in conflict due to social issues common in Yorkshire.

9 **Major Concepts**
• **The Rise of Realism**—The literary movement of realism gained prominence in the late nineteenth and early twentieth centuries. Realism seeks to

portray life as it is really lived, good and bad. Realistic fiction often focuses on middle- and working-class conditions and characters. Social reform is a frequent goal of realistic writing.

- **Victorian Social Classes**—Through literature, writers depicted the condition of England in a socially realistic way. They examined the different social classes, from the very rich to the growing middle class to the poorest peasants. Victorian stories spoke out on behalf of the poor and helpless and also recounted stories about social progress and lifting oneself up to the middle class.

Style and Form

10 **Victorian Novels**

- Many Victorian novelists used realism to portray practical problems and convey stories that had a moral message for their readers.

- Condition-of-England novels were common. Victorian literature often depicted contemporary life and often provided criticism of social problems caused by industrialism.

- Victorian novels often reflected values of the period such as social propriety, modesty, and Christian morality. The protagonists of Victorian novels lead difficult lives but often succeed in the end through hard work, perseverance, love, and luck.

- Because many were originally published in serial format, Victorian novels can be long and sprawling. They usually contain frequent cliffhangers that writers used to keep their readers interested and wanting to read the next installment.

11 **Victorian Poetry**

- Far less idealistic about nature than the Romantics, Victorian poets were more concerned with the realities of life, including the suffering caused by industry and technological **advancement**.

- Victorian poetry contemplated questions of morality and emphasized ideals such as truth, justice, and love.

- Notable features of Victorian poetry include sensory elements and imagery as well as sentimentality to convey experiences and struggles of religion, science, nature, and romance.

12 The Victorian Age was a time of rapid changes in society. Social hierarchies, technology, the roles of women, and many other aspects of life were undergoing transformations. Amidst all the progress, some people were being left behind. During this period people sought to find a balance and decide which parts of the past should be held onto and which should be relinquished for the future. Anyone who is dealing with transition can find something relatable in Victorian literature. How is the modern world similar to the Victorian era?

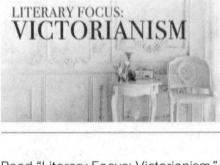

LITERARY FOCUS:
VICTORIANISM

Literary Focus

Read "Literary Focus: Victorianism." After you read, complete the Think Questions below.

☁ THINK QUESTIONS

1. What were some benefits and problems of the Industrial Revolution? Cite evidence from the text to support your response.

2. Why did novels become so popular during the Victorian Age? Explain, citing evidence from the text to support your response.

3. What were the goals of Victorian writers? How did they differ from those of the Romantics? Cite evidence from the text to support your explanations.

4. The word **transoceanic** uses the Latin prefix *trans-*, meaning "across." With this information in mind, write your best definition of the word **transoceanic** as it is used in this text. Cite any words or phrases that were particularly helpful in coming to your conclusion.

5. Use context clues to determine the meaning of the word **periodicals**. Write your best definition here, along with the words and phrases that were most helpful in determining the word's meaning. Then, check a dictionary to confirm your understanding.

The Cry of the Children

POETRY
Elizabeth Barrett Browning
1843

Introduction

Elizabeth Barrett Browning (1806–1861), was a popular and celebrated British poet of the Victorian era. She spent much of her life indoors, isolated from the outside world due to her chronic poor health and weak lungs. Following a prolonged and romantic exchange of letters, she married Victorian poet Robert Browning in 1845. She is perhaps best known for her poem "How Do I Love Thee?" from her collection titled *Sonnets from the Portuguese*. However, she was passionately moved by the suffering of others and addressed these darker thoughts and concerns in her poetry as well. "The Cry of the Children" exposes the grueling and unethical working conditions many children were forced to endure in industrialized England. Browning first published "The Cry of the Children" in 1843. Shortly thereafter, Parliament enacted massive and much-needed reforms to child labor laws.

". . . how long, O cruel nation,
Will you stand, to move the world,
on a child's heart,—"

NOTES

1 *"Pheu pheu, ti prosderkesthe m ommasin, tekna;"*
2 *[[Alas, alas, why do you gaze at me with your eyes, my children.]]—Medea.*
3 Do ye hear the children weeping, O my brothers,
4 Ere the sorrow comes with years?
5 They are leaning their young heads against their mothers,—
6 And that cannot stop their tears.
7 The young lambs are bleating[1] in the meadows;
8 The young birds are chirping in the nest;
9 The young fawns are playing with the shadows;
10 The young flowers are blowing toward the west—
11 But the young, young children, O my brothers,
12 They are weeping bitterly!
13 They are weeping in the playtime of the others,
14 In the country of the free.

15 Do you question the young children in the sorrow,
16 Why their tears are falling so?
17 The old man may weep for his to-morrow
18 Which is lost in Long Ago—
19 The old tree is leafless in the forest—
20 The old year is ending in the frost—
21 The old wound, if stricken, is the sorest—
22 The old hope is hardest to be lost:
23 But the young, young children, O my brothers,
24 Do you ask them why they stand
25 Weeping sore before the bosoms of their mothers,
26 In our happy Fatherland?

Illustration from *The Life and Adventures of Michael Armstrong, the Factory Boy*, by Frances Trollope, Auguste Hervieu [illustrator], 1876

---

1. **bleating** the sound of a sheep or goat crying out

27 They look up with their pale and sunken faces,
28 And their looks are sad to see,
29 For the man's grief **abhorrent,** draws and presses
30 Down the cheeks of infancy—
31 "Your old earth," they say, "is very dreary;"
32 "Our young feet," they say, "are very weak!"
33 Few paces have we taken, yet are weary—
34 Our grave-rest is very far to seek!
35 Ask the old why they weep, and not the children,
36 For the outside earth is cold—
37 And we young ones stand without, in our bewildering,
38 And the graves are for the old!"

39 "True," say the children, "it may happen
40 That we die before our time!
41 Little Alice died last year her grave is shapen
42 Like a snowball, in the rime.
43 We looked into the pit prepared to take her—
44 Was no room for any work in the close clay:
45 From the sleep wherein she lieth none will wake her,
46 Crying, 'Get up, little Alice! it is day.'
47 If you listen by that grave, in sun and shower,
48 With your ear down, little Alice never cries;
49 Could we see her face, be sure we should not know her,
50 For the smile has time for growing in her eyes ,—
51 And merry go her moments, **lulled** and stilled in
52 The shroud, by the kirk-chime!
53 It is good when it happens," say the children,
54 "That we die before our time!"

55 Alas, the wretched children! they are seeking
56 Death in life, as best to have!
57 They are binding up their hearts away from breaking,
58 With a **cerement** from the grave.
59 Go out, children, from the mine and from the city—
60 Sing out, children, as the little thrushes[2] do—
61 Pluck you handfuls of the meadow-cowslips[3] pretty
62 Laugh aloud, to feel your fingers let them through!
63 But they answer, "Are your cowslips of the meadows
64 Like our weeds anear the mine?
65 Leave us quiet in the dark of the coal-shadows,
66 From your pleasures fair and fine!

2. **thrush** a common songbird
3. **cowslips** a wild plant with small yellow flowers

67 "For oh," say the children, "we are weary,

68 And we cannot run or leap—

69 If we cared for any meadows, it were merely

70 To drop down in them and sleep.

71 Our knees tremble sorely in the stooping—

72 We fall upon our faces, trying to go;

73 And, underneath our heavy eyelids drooping,

74 The reddest flower would look as pale as snow.

75 For, all day, we drag our burden tiring,

76 Through the coal-dark, underground—

77 Or, all day, we drive the wheels of iron

78 In the factories, round and round.

79 "For all day, the wheels are droning, turning,—

80 Their wind comes in our faces,—

81 Till our hearts turn,—our heads, with pulses burning,

82 And the walls turn in their places

83 Turns the sky in the high window blank and reeling—

84 Turns the long light that droppeth down the wall,—

85 Turn the black flies that crawl along the ceiling—

86 All are turning, all the day, and we with all!—

87 And all day, the iron wheels are droning;

88 And sometimes we could pray,

89 'O ye wheels,' (breaking out in a mad moaning)

90 'Stop! be silent for to-day!' "

91 Ay! be silent! Let them hear each other breathing

92 For a moment, mouth to mouth—

93 Let them touch each other's hands, in a fresh wreathing

94 Of their tender human youth!

95 Let them feel that this cold metallic motion

96 Is not all the life God fashions or **reveals**—

97 Let them prove their inward souls against the notion

98 That they live in you, or under you, O wheels!—

99 Still, all day, the iron wheels go onward,

100 As if Fate in each were stark;

101 And the children's souls, which God is calling sunward,

102 Spin on blindly in the dark.

103 Now tell the poor young children, O my brothers,

104 To look up to Him and pray—

105 So the blessed One, who blesseth all the others,

106 Will bless them another day.

107 They answer, "Who is God that He should hear us,

108 While the rushing of the iron wheels is stirred?

109 When we sob aloud, the human creatures near us
110 Pass by, hearing not, or answer not a word!
111 And we hear not (for the wheels in their **resounding**)
112 Strangers speaking at the door:
113 Is it likely God, with angels singing round Him,
114 Hears our weeping any more?

115 "Two words, indeed, of praying we remember;
116 And at midnight's hour of harm,—
117 'Our Father,' looking upward in the chamber,
118 We say softly for a charm.
119 We know no other words, except 'Our Father,'
120 And we think that, in some pause of angels' song,
121 God may pluck them with the silence sweet to gather,
122 And hold both within His right hand which is strong.
123 'Our Father!' If He heard us, He would surely
124 (For they call Him good and mild)
125 Answer, smiling down the steep world very purely,
126 'Come and rest with me, my child.'

127 "But, no!" say the children, weeping faster,
128 "He is speechless as a stone;
129 And they tell us, of His image is the master
130 Who commands us to work on."
131 "Go to!" say the children,—"up in Heaven,
132 Dark, wheel-like, turning clouds are all we find!
133 Do not mock us; grief has made us unbelieving—
134 We look up for God, but tears have made us blind."
135 Do ye hear the children weeping and disproving,
136 O my brothers, what ye preach?
137 For God's possible is taught by His world's loving—
138 And the children doubt of each.

139 And well may the children weep before you;
140 They are weary ere they run;
141 They have never seen the sunshine, nor the glory
142 Which is brighter than the sun:
143 They know the grief of man, without its wisdom;
144 They sink in the despair, without its calm—
145 Are slaves, without the liberty in Christdom,—
146 Are martyrs, by the pang without the palm,—
147 Are worn, as if with age, yet unretrievingly
148 No dear remembrance keep,—
149 Are orphans of the earthly love and heavenly:
150 Let them weep! let them weep!

151 They look up, with their pale and sunken faces,
152 And their look is dread to see,
153 For they think you see their angels in their places,
154 With eyes meant for Deity[4];—
155 "How long," they say, "how long, O cruel nation,
156 Will you stand, to move the world, on a child's heart,—
157 Stifle down with a mailed heel its **palpitation**,
158 And tread onward to your throne amid the mart?[5]
159 Our blood splashes upward, O our tyrants,
160 And your purple shews your path;
161 But the child's sob curseth deeper in the silence
162 Than the strong man in his wrath!"

4. **Deity** a god, goddess, or divine being
5. **mart** a marketplace

✏ WRITE

POETRY: This is a protest poem written to call attention to the terrible conditions endured by children who worked in British coal mines in the nineteenth century—conditions that endangered their souls as well as their health. Think about a cruel situation you would like to end. Perhaps you can find information about modern-day child labor or envision a way to help homeless students succeed in school. Write a poem, as Elizabeth Barrett Browning did, to raise awareness of the issue and persuade the reader that the situation should not be tolerated. Be sure to describe the situation as you see it, using figurative language to stir the sympathies of your readers and persuade them to take action.

A Tale of Two Cities

FICTION
Charles Dickens
1860

Introduction

A Tale of Two Cities is an 1859 novel by Charles Dickens (1812–1870), one of the greatest and most popular writers of the Victorian era. Mixing fact and fiction, the story is set during the French Revolution near the end of the 18th century. Through this period of crisis and contradiction are intertwined human tales of suffering, justice, and courageous sacrifice. The novel opens with a rhythmic recitation of contrasts and similarities between the two titular settings, London and Paris.

"It was the best of times, it was the worst of times . . ."

Chapter I
The Period

1. It was the best of times, it was the worst of times, it was the age of wisdom, it was the age of foolishness, it was the epoch of belief, it was the epoch of incredulity, it was the season of Light, it was the season of Darkness, it was the spring of hope, it was the winter of despair, we had everything before us, we had nothing before us, we were all going direct to Heaven, we were all going direct the other way—in short, the period was so far like the present period, that some of its noisiest **authorities** insisted on its being received, for good or for evil, in the superlative degree of comparison only.

Charles Dickens

2. There were a king with a large jaw and a queen with a plain face, on the throne of England; there were a king with a large jaw and a queen with a fair face, on the throne of France. In both countries it was clearer than crystal to the lords of the State preserves of loaves and fishes[1], that things in general were settled for ever.

3. It was the year of Our Lord one thousand seven hundred and seventy-five. Spiritual revelations were conceded to England at that favoured period, as at this. Mrs. Southcott[2] had recently attained her five-and-twentieth blessed birthday, of whom a prophetic private in the Life Guards had heralded the sublime appearance by announcing that arrangements were made for the swallowing up of London and Westminster. Even the Cock-lane ghost[3] had

---

1. **the lords of the State preserves of loaves and fishes** the aristocrats who manage the royal food supply
2. **Mrs. Southcott** Joanna Southcott, a woman who claimed to be a religious prophet
3. **Cock-lane Ghost** a reference to a purported haunting in a house on Cock Lane in London that attracted mass public attention

been laid only a round dozen of years, after rapping out its messages, as the spirits of this very year last past (supernaturally deficient in originality) rapped out theirs. Mere messages in the earthly order of events had lately come to the English Crown and People, from a congress of British subjects in America: which, strange to relate, have proved more important to the human race than any communications yet received through any of the chickens of the Cock-lane brood.

4 France, less favoured on the whole as to matters spiritual than her sister of the shield and trident, rolled with **exceeding** smoothness down hill, making paper money and spending it. Under the guidance of her Christian pastors, she entertained herself, besides, with such humane achievements as sentencing a youth to have his hands cut off, his tongue torn out with pincers, and his body burned alive, because he had not kneeled down in the rain to do honour to a dirty procession of monks which passed within his view, at a distance of some fifty or sixty yards. It is likely enough that, rooted in the woods of France and Norway, there were growing trees, when that sufferer was put to death, already marked by the Woodman, Fate, to come down and be sawn into boards, to make a certain movable framework with a sack and a knife in it[4], terrible in history. It is likely enough that in the rough outhouses of some tillers of the heavy lands **adjacent** to Paris, there were sheltered from the weather that very day, rude carts, bespattered with **rustic** mire, snuffed about by pigs, and roosted in by poultry, which the Farmer, Death, had already set apart to be his tumbrils[5] of the Revolution. But that Woodman and that Farmer, though they work unceasingly, work silently, and no one heard them as they went about with muffled tread: the rather, forasmuch as to entertain any suspicion that they were awake, was to be atheistical and traitorous.

5 In England, there was scarcely an amount of order and protection to justify much national boasting. Daring burglaries by armed men, and highway robberies, took place in the capital itself every night; families were publicly cautioned not to go out of town without removing their furniture to upholsterers' warehouses for security; the highwayman in the dark was a City tradesman in the light, and, being recognised and challenged by his fellow-tradesman whom he stopped in his character of "the Captain," gallantly shot him through the head and rode away; the mall was waylaid by seven robbers, and the guard shot three dead, and then got shot dead himself by the other four, "in consequence of the failure of his ammunition:" after which the mall was robbed in peace; that magnificent potentate, the Lord Mayor of London, was made to stand and deliver on Turnham Green, by one highwayman, who despoiled the illustrious creature in sight of all his retinue[6]; prisoners in

4. **a certain movable framework with a sack and a knife in it** the guillotine
5. **tumbrils** the type of cart used during the French Revolution to take prisoners to the guillotine
6. **retinue** a group of followers or supporters; an entourage

NOTES

London gaols fought battles with their turnkeys[7], and the majesty of the law fired blunderbusses in among them, loaded with rounds of shot and ball; thieves snipped off diamond crosses from the necks of noble lords at Court drawing-rooms; musketeers went into St. Giles's, to search for contraband goods, and the mob fired on the musketeers, and the musketeers fired on the mob, and nobody thought any of these occurrences much out of the common way. In the midst of them, the hangman, ever busy and ever worse than useless, was in constant **requisition**; now, stringing up long rows of miscellaneous criminals; now, hanging a housebreaker on Saturday who had been taken on Tuesday; now, burning people in the hand at Newgate by the dozen, and now burning pamphlets at the door of Westminster Hall; to-day, taking the life of an atrocious murderer, and to-morrow of a wretched pilferer who had robbed a farmer's boy of sixpence.

6   All these things, and a thousand like them, came to pass in and close upon the dear old year one thousand seven hundred and seventy-five. Environed by them, while the Woodman and the Farmer worked unheeded, those two of the large jaws[8], and those other two of the plain and the fair faces[9], trod with stir enough, and carried their divine rights with a high hand. Thus did the year one thousand seven hundred and seventy-five conduct their Greatnesses, and myriads of small creatures—the creatures of this chronicle among the rest—along the roads that lay before them.

---

7. **turnkey** a guard
8. **those two of the large jaws** the kings of England and France
9. **those other two of the plain and the fair faces** the queens of England and France

---

✎ WRITE

LITERARY ANALYSIS: Charles Dickens's novel *A Tale of Two Cities* explores many different dualities in ideas, settings, and characters. Write a response in which you describe the dualities and contrasts presented in Chapter 1. Make sure to support your response with textual evidence.

Jane Eyre

FICTION
Charlotte Brontë
1847

Introduction

Charlotte Brontë (1816–1855) is one of the best-known English novelists of the 19th century. Many of her works, including *Jane Eyre*, were published under the pseudonym Currer Bell in order to disguise her sex, as female authors were not commonly accepted in England during this time period. In *Jane Eyre*, the novel's protagonist, Jane, grows up as an orphan and regularly feels like an outcast. Eventually, she takes a job caring for a young girl, Adèle, at Thornfield Hall. In this excerpt from the novel, Jane has recently arrived at Thornfield Hall and begun her new job. She describes her feelings toward Adèle, the work, and her larger desires for life.

"... they must have action; and they will make it if they cannot find it."

1   The promise of a smooth career, which my first calm introduction to Thornfield Hall seemed to pledge, was not belied on a longer acquaintance with the place and its inmates. Mrs. Fairfax turned out to be what she appeared, a **placid**-tempered, kind-natured woman, of competent education and average intelligence. My pupil was a lively child, who had been spoilt and indulged, and therefore was sometimes wayward; but as she was committed entirely to my care, and no injudicious interference from any quarter ever thwarted my plans for her improvement, she soon forgot her little freaks, and became obedient and teachable. She had no great talents, no marked traits of character, no peculiar development of feeling or taste which raised her one inch above the ordinary level of childhood; but neither had she any deficiency or vice which sunk her below it. She made reasonable progress, entertained for me a **vivacious**, though perhaps not very profound, affection; and by her simplicity, gay prattle[1], and efforts to please, inspired me, in return, with a degree of attachment sufficient to make us both content in each other's society.

Illustration of Charlotte Bronte

2   This, *par parenthèse*[2], will be thought cool language by persons who entertain solemn doctrines about the angelic nature of children, and the duty of those charged with their education to conceive for them an idolatrous devotion: but I am not writing to flatter parental egotism, to echo cant[3], or prop up humbug[4]; I am merely telling the truth. I felt a **conscientious** solicitude for Adèle's welfare and progress, and a quiet liking for her little self: just as I cherished towards Mrs. Fairfax a thankfulness for her kindness, and a pleasure in her

---

1. **gay prattle** pleasant and empty conversation
2. **par parenthèse** incidentally
3. **echo cant** a monotonous, rhythmic chant that has two "sides" calling in tandem
4. **prop up humbug** to support deceptive or false speech or action

society proportionate to the tranquil regard she had for me, and the moderation of her mind and character.

3   Anybody may blame me who likes, when I add further, that, now and then, when I took a walk by myself in the grounds; when I went down to the gates and looked through them along the road; or when, while Adèle played with her nurse, and Mrs. Fairfax made jellies in the storeroom, I climbed the three staircases, raised the trap-door of the attic, and having reached the leads, looked out afar over sequestered field and hill, and along dim sky-line—that then I longed for a power of vision which might overpass that limit; which might reach the busy world, towns, regions full of life I had heard of but never seen—that then I desired more of practical experience than I possessed; more of intercourse with my kind, of acquaintance with variety of character, than was here within my reach. I valued what was good in Mrs. Fairfax, and what was good in Adèle; but I believed in the existence of other and more vivid kinds of goodness, and what I believed in I wished to behold.

4   Who blames me? Many, no doubt; and I shall be called discontented. I could not help it: the restlessness was in my nature; it **agitated** me to pain sometimes. Then my sole relief was to walk along the corridor of the third storey, backwards and forwards, safe in the silence and solitude of the spot, and allow my mind's eye to dwell on whatever bright visions rose before it—and, certainly, they were many and glowing; to let my heart be heaved by the exultant movement, which, while it swelled it in trouble, expanded it with life; and, best of all, to open my inward ear to a tale that was never ended—a tale my imagination created, and narrated continuously; quickened with all of incident, life, fire, feeling, that I desired and had not in my actual existence.

5   It is in vain to say human beings ought to be satisfied with tranquillity: they must have action; and they will make it if they cannot find it. Millions are condemned to a stiller doom than mine, and millions are in silent revolt against their lot. Nobody knows how many rebellions besides political rebellions ferment in the masses of life which people earth. Women are supposed to be very calm generally: but women feel just as men feel; they need exercise for their faculties, and a field for their efforts, as much as their brothers do; they suffer from too rigid a restraint, too absolute a **stagnation**, precisely as men would suffer; and it is narrow-minded in their more privileged fellow-creatures to say that they ought to confine themselves to making puddings and knitting stockings, to playing on the piano and embroidering bags. It is thoughtless to condemn them, or laugh at them, if they seek to do more or learn more than custom has pronounced necessary for their sex.

Please note that excerpts and passages in the StudySync® library and this workbook are intended as touchstones to generate interest in an author's work. The excerpts and passages do not substitute for the reading of entire texts, and StudySync® strongly recommends that students seek out and purchase the whole literary or informational work in order to experience it as the author intended. Links to online resellers are available in our digital library. In addition, complete works may be ordered through an authorized reseller by filling out and returning to StudySync® the order form enclosed in this workbook.

Reading & Writing Companion   65

WRITE

ARGUMENTATIVE: In this excerpt, Jane mentions many positive and negative aspects of her current situation at Thornfield Hall. Considering the evidence, is Jane content with her current situation? Using textual evidence to support your claim, write a response of at least 300 words arguing whether or not Jane is happy at Thornfield Hall.

Jabberwocky Baby

INFORMATIONAL TEXT
Wanda Coleman
2005

Introduction

Wanda Coleman (1946–2013) was a nationally renowned poet who frequently wrote about the complexities of growing up and living as a black woman in the city of Los Angeles. "Jabberwocky Baby" is from Coleman's *The Riot Inside Me*, a collection of writings on art, politics, race, and class—and on the practice of writing itself. Here, she investigates the alienation she endured as a book-loving African American child growing up in 1950s and 60s, and how the topsy-turvy surreality of Lewis Carroll's works reflected her own adolescence and came to have a profound effect on her poetry.

"My reading appetite had no limits."

NOTES

1   The stultifying intellectual loneliness of my 1950s and '60s upbringing was dictated by my looks—dark skin and unconkable kinky hair. Boys gawked at me, and girls tittered behind my back. Black teachers shook their heads in pity, and White teachers stared in amusement or in wonder. I found this **rejection** unbearable and, encouraged by my parents to read, sought an escape in books, which were usually hard to come by. There were no colored-owned bookstores in our neighborhood. The libraries discouraged Negro readers.

2   My reading appetite had no limits. At six or seven I was slogging through Papa's **dull** issues of *National Geographic* and Mama's tepid copies of *Reader's Digest* and her favorite murder mysteries. At age ten I consumed the household copy of the complete works of Shakespeare, and while the violence was striking—and *Hamlet* engrossing, particularly Ophelia—I was too immature to fully appreciate The Bard until frequent rereadings during my mid-teens. In high school I would read Plato's *Dialogues*, Aristotle's *Metaphysics*, Machiavelli's *The Prince*, and Alexander Pope, and my teachers would complain to my parents that I was reading the wrong kind of literature, that my "little learning" was "a dangerous thing."

3   One Christmas, around age ten, I received Johanna Spyri's *Heidi* as a well-intended gift. I had long exhausted our teensy library, including my father's collections of *Knight*, *Esquire*, and *Playboy* (kept in the garage), and had begun sneaking through my mother's dresser drawers to scarf on unexpurgated Henry Miller. But between my raids on the adults-only stuff, there were only the Sunday funnies (*Brenda Starr*), comic books (*Archie, Little Lulu*), and *Heidi*, reread in desperation until I could quote chunks of the text, **mentally** squeezing it for what I imagined to be hidden underneath. One early-spring day, my adult first-cousin Rubyline came by the house with a nourishing belated Christmas gift: an illustrated one-volume edition of *Alice's Adventures in Wonderland* and *Through the Looking-Glass*. (Later, on my twelfth birthday, she would also give me my first *Roget's*, which I still use.)

4   In love with poetry since kindergarten, my "uffish" vows were startlingly renewed with *Alice*. Saved, I promptly retired *Heidi* and steeped myself in

Alice to an iambic spazz. "Jabberwocky" is one of only about a dozen poems I've ever loved enough to memorize (among the others are Poe's "Raven," Service's "Cremation of Sam McGee," Byron's "Prisoner of Chillon," Coleridge's "Rime of the Ancient Mariner," Henley's "Invictus," and E.A. Robinson's "Richard Cory").

5   Lewis Carroll's influence on my poetry is easily **discerned**. I occasionally allude to characters from *Alice* (the White Rabbit, the Cheshire Cat, and my favorite, the Red Queen), dot poems with references to his memorable lines and phrases, and have even written a poem in homage ("Black Alice Laments," in *Mercurochrome*). In one of my poetic fugues, I imagine my own mad tea party, to which I invite deceased surrealist writers and artists whom I admire ("The Ron Narrative Reconstructions," in *Bathwater Wine*).

6   Many have referred to Carroll's rhymes as nonsense, but in my childhood world—Los Angeles in the '50s—they made perfect sense. It was a city where up was down and down was up. Black adults were always scrounging for money, regardless of how good or how bad they were. White people laughed at things that were not funny. Distances were deceptive and maps untrustworthy. My parents were constantly getting lost and were frightened of asking the police or fireman for assistance, those same authorities White teachers said were friendly and there to protect and serve us. Smiling White adults were instantly and incomprehensibly nasty to us the moment our parents were not around. Waiters, waitresses, and drive-in car hops were hostile, always got our orders wrong, served our food cold, or made us wait until they had attended to everyone else beforehand. Store clerks refused to take our money unless we asked for the correct amount first. White doctors and nurses would never touch us with their bare hands, and seldom with gloves on. White ministers smiled while calling us heathens and pickaninnies. Black and Mexican children were **chastised** or ignored for behavior that earned White children recognition and praise. All White people lied. Nothing was what it seemed. We were free citizens, yet there were places in the city that we could not visit after sundown.

7   The daily upheavals in my reality made the Looking-Glass world seem not only logical but somewhere I wished I could go for vacation.

From *The Riot Inside Me* by Wanda Coleman. Copyright © Wanda Coleman, 2005.

WRITE

PERSONAL RESPONSE: Write a short personal response about a poem or any other work of art that is meaningful to you. Choose details about this work of art carefully so that they point to key ideas that you absorbed. What impact did the work have on you? Consider if there was a line that sounded so true, it would not leave your head.

Dear Mama

POETRY
Wanda Coleman
1987

Introduction

Wanda Coleman (1946–2013) was recognized as the unofficial poet laureate of Los Angeles, and was once nominated for state poet laureate of California. Her artistic interests spanned many genres of literature as well as performance art. Coleman was known for writing in colloquial English and from the perspectives of those who are often ignored and oppressed: the poor, women of color, and the underclass. In this poem, "Dear Mama," the speaker marvels at her changing relationship with her mother, and deals with the daunting realization of what mortality means for both mother and child.

"The thought stark and irrevocable / of being here without you / shakes me."

NOTES

1 when did we become friends?
2 it happened so gradual i didn't notice
3 maybe i had to get my run out first
4 take a big bite of the honky world and choke on it
5 maybe that's what has to happen with some uppity youngsters
6 if it happens at all

7 and now
8 the thought **stark** and **irrevocable**
9 of being here without you
10 shakes me

11 beyond love, fear, regret or anger
12 into that **realm** children go
13 who want to care for/protect their parents
14 as if they could
15 and sometimes the lucky ones do

16 into the realm of making every moment
17 important
18 laughing as though laughter wards off death
19 each word given
20 received like **spanish eight**

21 treasure to bury within
22 against that shadow day
23 when it will be the only coin i possess
24 with which to buy peace of mind

___

From *Heavy Daughter Blues* by Wanda Coleman. Copyright © Wanda Coleman, 1991.

Skill: Language, Style, and Audience

The poet uses unusual syntax—placing the adjectives stark *and* irrevocable *after the noun they modify* (thought)*—perhaps as a way of slowing the reader down to allow them to absorb the seriousness of the situation.*

First Read

Read "Dear Mama." After you read, complete the Think Questions below.

☁ THINK QUESTIONS

1. Why will the speaker eventually need "to buy peace of mind"? Explain, citing textual evidence to support your response.

2. How does the speaker's relationship with her mother change over the course of her life? Be specific, and be sure to cite textual evidence in order to back up your assertions.

3. Explain how the author uses simile and metaphor in the last two stanzas of the poem. Cite lines from the text that help support your explanation.

4. Use context clues to determine the meaning of **irrevocable** as it is used in "Dear Mama." Write your definition of *irrevocable* here, along with the words or phrases that helped you determine its meaning. Then check a print or an online dictionary to confirm your understanding.

5. The word **realm** stems from the Latin word *regimen*, meaning control. With this information in mind, explain how that meaning connects to how you think the word is used in this poem. Write your explanation and definition of *realm* here, along with any words or phrases that helped you come to your conclusions.

Please note that excerpts and passages in the StudySync® library and this workbook are intended as touchstones to generate interest in an author's work. The excerpts and passages do not substitute for the reading of entire texts, and StudySync® strongly recommends that students seek out and purchase the whole literary or informational work in order to experience it as the author intended. Links to online resellers are available in our digital library. In addition, complete works may be ordered through an authorized reseller by filling out and returning to StudySync® the order form enclosed in this workbook.

Reading & Writing Companion   **73**

Skill: Language, Style, and Audience

Use the Checklist to analyze Language, Style, and Audience in "Dear Mama." Refer to the sample student annotations about Language, Style, and Audience in the text.

••• CHECKLIST FOR LANGUAGE, STYLE, AND AUDIENCE

In order to determine an author's style and possible intended audience, do the following:

✓ identify and define any unfamiliar words or phrases that have multiple meanings

✓ identify any particularly unusual, difficult, or effective syntax

✓ identify language that is particularly fresh, engaging, or beautiful

✓ analyze the surrounding words and phrases as well as the context in which the specific words are being used

✓ note the audience—both intended and unintended—and possible reactions to the author's word choice and style

✓ examine your reaction to the author's word choice and how the author's choice affected your reaction

To analyze the impact of a specific word choice on meaning including words with multiple meanings or language that is particularly fresh, engaging, or beautiful, consider the following questions:

✓ How does the author's use of fresh, engaging, or beautiful language enhance or change what is being described? How would a specific phrase or sentence sound different or shift in meaning if a synonym were used?

✓ How does the rhyme scheme, meter, and other poetic language affect the meaning?

✓ How does word choice, including different possible meanings from other countries, help determine meaning?

✓ How would the text be different with other words or different syntax? How does the author's use of varied syntax influence the meaning of the text?

Skill: Language, Style, and Audience

Reread lines 16–24 of "Dear Mama." Then, using the Checklist on the previous page, answer the multiple-choice questions below.

♻ YOUR TURN

1. This question has two parts. First, answer Part A. Then, answer Part B.

   Part A: What does the speaker compare to "spanish eight" in these lines?

   ○ A. death
   ○ B. protection
   ○ C. conversation
   ○ D. inner peace

   Part B: The poet uses this figurative language to—

   ○ A. suggest that inner peace, like treasure, is hard to find.
   ○ B. show how much the speaker values time with her mother.
   ○ C. stress that money cannot buy happiness in times of grief.
   ○ D. hint that the speaker is interested in money she will inherit.

2. A verb is missing from lines 19–20. Which of these sentences, with alternative syntax, best retains a probable intended meaning of the sentence?

   ○ A. "Each word is given and received like spanish eight."
   ○ B. "Each word given is received like spanish eight."
   ○ C. "Each word must be received like spanish eight."
   ○ D. Both A and B can be probable intended meanings.

Close Read

Reread "Dear Mama." As you reread, complete the Skills Focus questions below. Then use your answers and annotations from the questions to help you complete the Write activity.

◎ SKILLS FOCUS

1. The poet uses informal language in the first stanza before switching to more elevated language in the second stanza. Identify an example of elevated language in the second stanza. Then evaluate the effect of this shift in style.

2. Highlight details in the poem that help reveal the poem's theme and explain how these details relate to the poem's theme.

3. A lyric poem is a short poetic form meant to express a state of mind, a thought process, or a particular feeling of a speaker. Identify a detail that shows the speaker's emotion, and explain why this poem is characteristic of lyric poetry.

4. "Dear Mama" and "Jabberwocky Baby" discuss the power stories and memories have in our relationships with families. Using textual evidence from the last two stanzas of "Dear Mama," explain how the speaker imagines she will use memories of her mother.

✏ WRITE

CORRESPONDENCE: Using Coleman's poem as a model, write a letter (in prose or poetry) to someone important to you and include enough details for the reader to understand why this person is important in your life. Title the letter "Dear ____" and begin the body with a question, as Coleman does with "when did we become friends?" Answer the question in your letter and use figurative language to express the unique relationship you have with the person you are writing to.

Copyright © Bookhead Ed Learning, LLC

Freedom

ARGUMENTATIVE TEXT
Ursula K. Le Guin
2014

Introduction

Ursula K. Le Guin (1929–2018) was an American author who wrote science fiction and fantasy novels. She has been described as one of America's greatest science fiction writers and a great influence to many others. Some of Le Guin's best known works include *The Left Hand of Darkness* and *The Dispossessed*. Her science fiction novels and short stories often deal with themes related to anthropology, the environment, gender, and religion. This speech was given as an acceptance of the 2014 National Book Foundation Medal for Distinguished Contribution to American Letters award, which Le Guin received when she was 84 years old.

"Resistance and change often begin in art. Very often in our art, the art of words."

NOTES

1   To the givers of this beautiful reward, my thanks, from the heart. My family, my agents, my editors, know that my being here is their doing as well as my own, and that the beautiful reward is theirs as much as mine. And I rejoice in accepting it for, and sharing it with, all the writers who've been excluded from literature for so long—my fellow authors of fantasy and science fiction, writers of the imagination, who for fifty years have watched the beautiful rewards go to the so-called realists.

2   Hard times are coming, when we'll be wanting the voices of writers who can see alternatives to how we live now, can see through our fear-stricken society and its obsessive technologies to other ways of being, and even imagine real grounds for hope. We'll need writers who can remember freedom—poets, visionaries—realists of a larger reality.

3   Right now, we need writers who know the difference between production of a market **commodity** and the practice of an art. Developing written material to suit sales strategies in order to maximise corporate profit and advertising revenue is not the same thing as responsible book publishing or authorship.

4   Yet I see sales departments given control over editorial. I see my own publishers, in a silly panic of **ignorance** and greed, charging public libraries for an e-book six or seven times more than they charge customers. We just saw a profiteer try to punish a publisher for **disobedience**, and writers threatened by corporate fatwa. And I see a lot of us, the producers, who write the books and make the books, accepting this—letting commodity profiteers sell us like deodorant, and tell us what to publish, what to write.

5   Books aren't just commodities; the profit **motive** is often in conflict with the aims of art. We live in capitalism, its power seems inescapable—but then, so did the divine right of kings. Any human power can be resisted and changed by human beings. Resistance and change often begin in art. Very often in our art, the art of words.

6   I've had a long career as a writer, and a good one, in good company. Here at the end of it, I don't want to watch American literature get sold down the river. We who live by writing and publishing want and should demand our fair share of the **proceeds**; but the name of our beautiful reward isn't profit. Its name is freedom. Thank you.

Copyright © 2016 by Ursula K. Le Guin. First appeared in *Words Are My Matter* published by Small Beer Press. Reprinted by permission of Curtis Brown, Ltd.

 WRITE

DISCUSSION: In her acceptance speech, Ursula K. Le Guin argues passionately against the profit motive in book publishing. Think about the effects of the profit motive on society. Do you think its effects are good, bad, or neutral overall? What are the positive aspects of the profit motive and what are the negative aspects? What can be done to prevent those pursuing profit from exploiting other members of society? To prepare for the discussion, use the graphic organizer to write down your ideas about these questions. After your discussion, you will write a reflection.

Please note that excerpts and passages in the StudySync® library and this workbook are intended as touchstones to generate interest in an author's work. The excerpts and passages do not substitute for the reading of entire texts, and StudySync® strongly recommends that students seek out and purchase the whole literary or informational work in order to experience it as the author intended. Links to online resellers are available in our digital library. In addition, complete works may be ordered through an authorized reseller by filling out and returning to StudySync® the order form enclosed in this workbook.

Reading & Writing
Companion

79

Why I Write

INFORMATIONAL TEXT

Joan Didion

1976

Introduction

Joan Didion (b. 1934) is an American novelist, journalist, playwright, and essayist who was a finalist for the Pulitzer Prize in 2005 for her memoir, *The Year of Magical Thinking*. Didion's literary heroes include Ernest Hemingway, Henry James, and George Eliot. Her writing is known for its focus on sentence structure and the influence of media. Didion was born in California, attended UC Berkeley, and currently lives in New York City. The essay "Why I Write" was first published in the *New York Times Book Review* in 1976.

Like many writers I have only this one "subject," this one "area": the act of writing.

1 Of course I stole the title from this talk, from George Orwell. One reason I stole it was that I like the sound of the words: Why I Write. There you have three short **unambiguous** words that share a sound, and the sound they share is this:

2 *I*

3 *I*

4 *I*

5 In many ways writing is the act of saying *I*, of **imposing** oneself upon other people, of saying *listen to me, see it my way, change your mind*. It's an aggressive, even a hostile act. You can disguise its aggressiveness all you want with veils of subordinate clauses and qualifiers and tentative subjunctives, with ellipses and evasions—with the whole manner of intimating rather than claiming, of alluding rather than stating—but there's no getting around the fact that setting words on paper is the tactic of a secret bully, an invasion, an imposition of the writer's sensibility on the readers' most private space.

6 I stole the title not only because the words sounded right but because they seemed to sum up, in a no-nonsense way, all I have to tell you. Like many writers I have only this one "subject," this one "area": the act of writing. I can bring you no reports from any other front. I may have other interests: I am "interested," for example, in marine biology, but I don't flatter myself that you would come out to hear me talk about it. I am not a scholar. I am not in the least an intellectual, which is not to say that when I hear the word "intellectual" I reach for my gun, but only to say that I do not think in **abstracts**. During the years when I was an undergraduate at Berkeley, I tried, with a kind of hopeless late-adolescent energy, to buy some temporary visa into the world of ideas, to forge for myself a mind that could deal with the abstract.

7 In short I tried to think. I failed. My attention veered inexorably back to the specific, to the tangible, to what was generally considered, by everyone I knew then and for that matter have known since, the peripheral. I would try to

Skill:
Summarizing

Didion continues to explain the essay title's significance by clarifying that she's explaining what she knows best— writing—by using only her personal knowledge, rather than abstract ideas about the nature of writing.

NOTES

contemplate the Hegelian dialectic and would find myself concentrating instead on a flowering pear tree outside my window and the particular way the petals fell on my floor. I would try to read linguistic theory and would find myself wondering instead if the lights were on in the bevatron[1] up the hill. When I say that I was wondering if the lights were on in the bevatron you might immediately suspect, if you deal in ideas at all, that I was registering the bevatron as a political symbol, thinking in shorthand about the military-industrial complex and its role in the university community, but you would be wrong. I was only wondering if the lights were on in the bevatron, and how they looked. A physical fact.

8   I had trouble graduating from Berkeley, not because of this inability to deal with ideas—I was majoring in English, and I could locate the house-and-garden imagery in *The Portrait of a Lady* as well as the next person, "imagery" being by definition the kind of specific that got my attention—but simply because I had neglected to take a course in Milton. For reasons which now sound baroque I needed a degree by the end of that summer, and the English department finally agreed, if I would come down from Sacramento every Friday and talk about the cosmology of *Paradise Lost*, to certify me proficient in Milton. I did this. Some Fridays I took the Greyhound bus, other Fridays I caught the Southern Pacific's City of San Francisco on the last leg of its transcontinental trip. I can no longer tell you whether Milton put the sun or the earth at the center of his universe in *Paradise Lost*, the central question of at least one century and a topic about which I wrote 10,000 words that summer, but I can still recall the exact **rancidity** of the butter in the City of San Francisco's dining car, and the way the tinted windows on the Greyhound bus cast the oil refineries around Carquinez Straits into a grayed and obscurely sinister light. In short my attention was always on the periphery, on what I could see and taste and touch, on the butter, and the Greyhound bus. During those years I was traveling on what I knew to be a very shaky passport, forged papers: I knew that I was no legitimate resident in any world of ideas. I knew I couldn't think. All I knew then was what I couldn't do. All I knew was what I wasn't, and it took me some years to discover what I was.

9   Which was a writer.

10   By which I mean not a "good" writer or a "bad" writer but simply a writer, a person whose most absorbed and passionate hours are spent arranging words on pieces of paper. Had my credentials been in order I would never have become a writer. Had I been blessed with even limited access to my own mind there would have been no reason to write. I write entirely to find out what I'm thinking, what I'm looking at, what I see and what it means. What I want and what I fear. Why did the oil refineries around Carquinez Straits

---

1. **bevatron** a particle accelerator that accelerates protons up to several billion electron volts

---

Skill: Author's Purpose and Point of View

Didion's purpose is to explain why she writes, but her point of view about her own profession is odd: she writes to "find out" what she thinks. To help the reader understand this, she uses specific questions about what interests her.

seem sinister to me in the summer of 1956? Why have the night lights in the bevatron burned in my mind for twenty years? *What is going on in these pictures in my mind?*

11 When I talk about pictures in my mind I am talking, quite specifically, about images that shimmer around the edges. There used to be an illustration in every elementary psychology book showing a cat drawn by a patient in varying stages of schizophrenia. This cat had a shimmer around it. You could see the molecular structure breaking down at the very edges of the cat: the cat became the background and the background the cat, everything interacting, exchanging ions. People on hallucinogens describe the same perception of objects. I'm not a schizophrenic, nor do I take hallucinogens, but certain images do shimmer for me. Look hard enough, and you can't miss the shimmer. It's there. You can't think too much about these pictures that shimmer. You just lie low and let them develop. You stay quiet. You don't talk to many people and you keep your nervous system from shorting out and you try to locate the cat in the shimmer, the grammar in the picture.

12 Just as I meant "shimmer" literally I mean "grammar" literally. Grammar is a piano I play by ear, since I seem to have been out of school the year the rules were mentioned. All I know about grammar is its infinite power. To shift the structure of a sentence alters the meaning of that sentence, as definitely and inflexibly as the position of a camera alters the meaning of the object photographed. Many people know about camera angles now, but not so many know about sentences. The arrangement of the words matters, and the arrangement you want can be found in the picture in your mind. The picture dictates the arrangement. The picture dictates whether this will be a sentence with or without clauses, a sentence that ends hard or a dying-fall sentence, long or short, active or passive. The picture tells you how to arrange the words and the arrangement of the words tells you, or tells me, what's going on in the picture. *Nota bene*[2]:

> **Skill: Figurative Language**
>
> *Didion uses a simile here to highlight the power of how sentences are constructed. She compares sentence structure to a camera, which seems to imply that a writer is like a photographer.*

13 It tells you.

14 You don't tell it.

15 Let me show you what I mean by pictures in the mind. I began *Play It as It Lays* just as I have begun each of my novels, with no notion of "character" or "plot" or even "incident." I had only two pictures in my mind, more about which later, and a technical intention, which was to write a novel so elliptical and fast that it would be over before you noticed it, a novel so fast that it would scarcely exist on the page at all. About the pictures: the first was of white space. Empty space. This was clearly the picture that dictated the

---

2. **nota bene** "observe carefully," a Latin phrase used to draw attention to what is written next

narrative intention of the book—a book in which anything that happened would happen off the page, a "white" book to which the reader would have to bring his or her own bad dreams—and yet this picture told me no "story," suggested no situation. The second picture did. This second picture was of something actually witnessed. A young woman with long hair and a short white halter dress walks through the casino at the Riviera in Las Vegas at one in the morning. She crosses the casino alone and picks up a house telephone. I watch her because I have heard her paged, and recognize her name: she is a minor actress I see around Los Angeles from time to time, in places like Jax and once in a gynecologist's office in the Beverly Hills Clinic, but have never met. I know nothing about her. Who is paging her? Why is she here to be paged? How exactly did she come to this? It was precisely this moment in Las Vegas that made *Play It as It Lays* begin to tell itself to me, but the moment appears in the novel only **obliquely**, in a chapter which begins:

16 "Maria made a list of things she would never do. She would never: walk through the Sands or Caesar's alone after midnight. She would never: ball at a party, do S-M unless she wanted to, borrow furs from Abe Lipsey, deal. She would never: carry a Yorkshire in Beverly Hills."

17 That is the beginning of the chapter and that is also the end of the chapter, which may suggest what I meant by "white space."

18 I recall having a number of pictures in my mind when I began the novel I just finished, *A Book of Common Prayer*. As a matter of fact one of these pictures was of that bevatron I mentioned, although I would be hard put to tell you a story in which nuclear energy figured. Another was a newspaper photograph of a hijacked 707 burning on the desert in the Middle East. Another was the night view from a room in which I once spent a week with paratyphoid, a hotel room on the Colombian coast. My husband and I seemed to be on the Colombian coast representing the United States of America at a film festival (I recall invoking the name "Jack Valenti" a lot, as if its reiteration could make me well), and it was a bad place to have fever, not only because my indisposition offended our hosts but because every night in this hotel the generator failed. The lights went out. The elevator stopped. My husband would go to the event of the evening and make excuses for me and I would stay alone in this hotel room, in the dark. I remember standing at the window trying to call Bogota (the telephone seemed to work on the same principle as the generator) and watching the night wind come up and wondering what I was doing eleven degrees off the equator with a fever of 103. The view from that window definitely figures in *A Book of Common Prayer*, as does the burning 707, and yet none of these pictures told me the story I needed.

19 The picture that did, the picture that shimmered and made these other images **coalesce**, was the Panama airport at 6 A.M. I was in this airport only once, on

Copyright © BookheadEd Learning, LLC

a plane to Bogota that stopped for an hour to refuel, but the way it looked that morning remained superimposed on everything I saw until the day I finished *A Book of Common Prayer*. I lived in that airport for several years. I can still feel the hot air when I step off the plane, can see the heat already rising off the tarmac at 6 A.M. I can feel my skirt damp and wrinkled on my legs. I can feel the asphalt stick to my sandals. I remember the big tail of a Pan American plane floating motionless down at the end of the tarmac. I remember the sound of a slot machine in the waiting room. I could tell you that I remember a particular woman in the airport, an American woman, a *norteamericana*, a thin *norteamericana* about 40 who wore a big square emerald in lieu of a wedding ring, but there was no such woman there.

20 I put this woman in the airport later. I made this woman up, just as I later made up a country to put the airport in, and a family to run the country. This woman in the airport is neither catching a plane nor meeting one. She is ordering tea in the airport coffee shop. In fact she is not simply "ordering" tea but insisting that the water be boiled, in front of her, for twenty minutes. Why is this woman in this airport? Why is she going nowhere, where has she been? Where did she get that big emerald? What derangement, or disassociation, makes her believe that her will to see the water boiled can possibly prevail?

21 "She had been going to one airport or another for four months, one could see it, looking at the visas on her passport. All those airports where Charlotte Douglas's passport had been stamped would have looked alike. Sometimes the sign on the tower would say "Bienvenidos" and sometimes the sign on the tower would say "Bienvenue," some places were wet and hot and others dry and hot, but at each of these airports the pastel concrete walls would rust and stain and the swamp off the runway would be littered with the fuselages of cannibalized Fairchild F-227's and the water would need boiling.

22 "I knew why Charlotte went to the airport even if Victor did not.

23 "I knew about airports."

24 These lines appear about halfway through *A Book of Common Prayer*, but I wrote them during the second week I worked on the book, long before I had any idea where Charlotte Douglas had been or why she went to airports. Until I wrote these lines I had no character called "Victor" in mind: the necessity for mentioning a name, and the name "Victor," occurred to me as I wrote the sentence. *I knew why Charlotte went to the airport* sounded incomplete. *I knew why Charlotte went to the airport even if Victor did not* carried a little more narrative drive. Most important of all, until I wrote these lines I did not know who "I" was, who was telling the story. I had intended until that moment that the "I" be no more than the voice of the author, a nineteenth-century omniscient narrator. But there it was:

25   "I knew why Charlotte went to the airport even if Victor did not.

26   "I knew about airports."

27   This "I" was the voice of no author in my house. This "I" was someone who not only knew why Charlotte went to the airport but also knew someone called "Victor." Who was Victor? Who was this narrator? Why was this narrator telling me this story? Let me tell you one thing about why writers write: had I known the answer to any of these questions I would never have needed to write a novel.

"Why I Write" by Joan Didion.
Copyright © 1976 by Joan Didion.
Originally Published in THE NEW YORK TIMES BOOK REVIEW.
Reprinted by permission of the author.

First Read

Read "Why I Write." After you read, complete the Think Questions below.

☁ THINK QUESTIONS

1. What reason does Didion give for "stealing" the title of her essay? Use textual evidence to support your answer.

2. How does Didion describe her experience as an English major at UC Berkeley? Use textual evidence to support your answer.

3. Explain what Didion means when she writes "Grammar is a piano I play by ear." Be specific, quoting details or passages from the text.

4. Read the following dictionary entry:

   abstract
   ab•stract /ab'strakt,'ab,strakt/

   noun

   1. a summary of the contents of a book, article, or study
   2. a theoretical concern or consideration about something

   verb

   3. to isolate or remove

   adjective

   4. existing in thought or concept but not physical or tangible

   Which definition most closely matches the meaning of **abstract** as it is used in the text? Write the best definition of *abstract* in your own words, along with a brief explanation of how you figured it out.

5. What is the meaning of the word **coalesce** as it is used in paragraph 20? Write your best definition of *coalesce* here, along with a brief explanation of how you figured out its meaning.

Skill:
Summarizing

Use the Checklist to analyze Summarizing in "Why I Write." Refer to the sample student annotations about Summarizing in the text.

••• CHECKLIST FOR SUMMARIZING

In order to determine how to write an objective summary of a text, note the following:

✓ answers to the basic questions *who, what, where, when, why,* and *how*

✓ in literature or nonfiction, note how two or more themes or central ideas are developed over the course of the text, and how they interact and build on one another to produce a complex account

✓ stay objective, and do not add your own personal thoughts, judgments, or opinions to the summary

To provide an objective summary of a text, consider the following questions:

✓ What are the answers to basic *who, what, where, when, why,* and *how* questions in literature and works of nonfiction?

✓ Does my summary include how two or more themes or central ideas are developed over the course of the text, and how they interact and build on one another in my summary?

✓ Is my summary objective, or have I added my own thoughts, judgments, and personal opinions?

Skill:
Summarizing

Reread paragraph 15 of "Why I Write." Then, using the Checklist on the previous page, answer the multiple-choice questions below.

⟳ YOUR TURN

1. The following sentence is a student's summary of this paragraph: "Didion starts writing a novel without planning any of the characters or plot events." How does this summary need to be improved?

   ○ A. The summary needs to include the important points about the images Didion had in mind and their role in her creation of *Play It as It Lays*.

   ○ B. The summary needs to include details about the minor actress that Didion used as inspiration for her main character in *Play It as It Lays*.

   ○ C. The summary needs to explain the role of white space in Didion's conception of the novel *Play It as It Lays*.

   ○ D. The summary needs to explain why Didion wanted the action to take place off the page in the novel *Play It as It Lays*.

2. If you were to write a summary of this essay, what two central ideas do you notice in this paragraph that are repeated from the beginning of the essay?

   ○ A. Didion always starts her writing process without having in mind who her characters will be or what events will be in plot.

   ○ B. Didion uses her personal experience to discuss the writing process and is interested in specifics rather than the abstract.

   ○ C. Didion writes elliptical novels that move quickly and uses personal experiences as inspiration.

   ○ D. Didion wants readers to use their own experiences to understand the point of her novels.

Please note that excerpts and passages in the StudySync® library and this workbook are intended as touchstones to generate interest in an author's work. The excerpts and passages do not substitute for the reading of entire texts, and StudySync® strongly recommends that students seek out and purchase the whole literary or informational work in order to experience it as the author intended. Links to online resellers are available in our digital library. In addition, complete works may be ordered through an authorized reseller by filling out and returning to StudySync® the order form enclosed in this workbook.

Reading & Writing Companion   **89**

3. Which statement does not present any bias in its summary of paragraph 15?

- ○ A. Didion begins writing a novel by first thinking of the narrative intention; *Play It as It Lays* is intended to be elliptical and fast, and it focuses on the uneventful moment of a woman in a casino being paged.

- ○ B. Didion describes her writing process by explaining how she came up with the strange idea for *Play It as It Lays*; she watched a woman being paged in a casino and wanted to know more details about the woman's life.

- ○ C. Didion has an interesting writing process because she does not plan the characters and plot; in *Play It as It Lays*, for example, she started the novel with only an image of white space and of a woman she saw being paged in a casino in her mind.

- ○ D. Didion begins writing a novel because of images in her mind, instead of planning the characters and plot; she began *Play It as It Lays*, for example, with the images in her mind of white space and a woman she saw being paged in a casino.

Skill: Author's Purpose and Point of View

Use the Checklist to analyze Author's Purpose and Point of View in "Why I Write." Refer to the sample student annotations about Author's Purpose and Point of View in the text.

••• CHECKLIST FOR AUTHOR'S PURPOSE AND POINT OF VIEW

In order to identify author's purpose and point of view, note the following:

✓ whether the writer is attempting to establish trust by citing his or her experience or education

✓ whether the evidence the author provides is convincing and that the argument or position is logical

✓ what words and phrases the author uses to appeal to the emotions

✓ the author's use of rhetoric, or the art of speaking and writing persuasively, such as the use of repetition to drive home a point as well as allusion and alliteration

✓ the author's use of rhetoric to contribute to the power, persuasiveness, or beauty of the text

To determine the author's purpose and point of view, consider the following questions:

✓ How does the author try to convince me that he or she has something valid and important for me to read?

✓ What words or phrases express emotion or invite an emotional response? How or why are they effective or ineffective?

✓ What words and phrases contribute to the power, persuasiveness, or beauty of the text? Is the author's use of rhetoric successful? Why or why not?

Please note that excerpts and passages in the StudySync® library and this workbook are intended as touchstones to generate interest in an author's work. The excerpts and passages do not substitute for the reading of entire texts, and StudySync® strongly recommends that students seek out and purchase the whole literary or informational work in order to experience it as the author intended. Links to online resellers are available in our digital library. In addition, complete works may be ordered through an authorized reseller by filling out and returning to StudySync® the order form enclosed in this workbook.

Reading & Writing
Companion

91

Skill: Author's Purpose and Point of View

Reread paragraphs 22–27 of "Why I Write." Then, using the Checklist on the previous page, answer the multiple-choice questions below.

↻ YOUR TURN

1. This question has two parts. First, answer Part A. Then, answer Part B.

    Part A: Which statement best explains the stance Didion is expressing about her motivations for writing?

    ○ A. Didion writes because she wants to learn the answers to questions.

    ○ B. Didion writes to explain her knowledge in subjects important to her.

    ○ C. Didion writes to experiment with new forms of narrative point of view.

    ○ D. Didion writes because she has specific characters that she wants to describe.

    Part B: Which evidence best supports your answer to Part A?

    ○ A. "'I knew about airports.'" (paragraph 23)

    ○ B. "*I knew why Charlotte went to the airport* sounded incomplete." (paragraph 24)

    ○ C. "... that the 'I' be no more than the voice of the author, a nineteenth-century omniscient narrator." (paragraph 24)

    ○ D. "... had I known the answer to any of these questions I would never have needed to write a novel." (paragraph 27)

2. How does Didion establish trust with her audience in these paragraphs?

    ○ A. Didion tells the reader that she knows a lot about airports in an important part of her novel *A Book of Common Prayer*.

    ○ B. Didion uses examples from her own writing process to make a claim about writers more generally.

    ○ C. Didion explains how she comes up with her characters so that the reader can better relate to them.

    ○ D. Didion describes how she planned her novel *A Book of Common Prayer* to show how all writers write.

3. Why does Didion focus on the word "I" in paragraph 27?

   ○ A. Didion uses the word to highlight that her writing is based exclusively on her personal experiences.

   ○ B. Didion likes using the word because she believes it creates a useful distance between herself and her audience.

   ○ C. Didion repeats the word throughout the essay as a way to illustrate the detailed planning that goes into her novels.

   ○ D. Didion repeats the word throughout the essay to remind her audience of the argument she introduced at the beginning.

Skill:
Figurative Language

Use the Checklist to analyze Figurative Language in "Why I Write." Refer to the sample student annotations about Figurative Language in the text.

••• CHECKLIST FOR FIGURATIVE LANGUAGE

In order to determine the meaning of figurative language in context, note the following:

✓ words that mean one thing literally and suggest something else

✓ similes, metaphors, or personification

✓ figures of speech, including

- paradoxes, or a seemingly contradictory statement that when further investigated or explained proves to be true, such as

    > a character described as "a wise fool"

    > a character stating, "I must be cruel to be kind"

- hyperbole, or exaggerated statements not meant to be taken literally, such as

    > a child saying, "I'll be doing this homework until I'm 100!"

    > a claim such as, "I'm so hungry I could eat a horse!"

In order to interpret figurative language in context and analyze its role in the text, consider the following questions:

✓ Where is there figurative language in the text and what seems to be the purpose of the author's use of it?

✓ Why does the author use a figure of speech rather than literal language?

✓ What impact does exaggeration or hyperbole have on your understanding of the text?

✓ Where are there examples of paradoxes and how do they affect the meaning in the text?

✓ Which phrases contain references that seem contradictory?

✓ Where are contradictory words and phrases used to enhance the reader's understanding of the character, object, or idea?

✓ How does the figurative language develop the message or theme of the literary work?

Skill:
Figurative Language

Reread paragraph 12 of "Why I Write." Then, using the Checklist on the previous page, answer the multiple-choice questions below.

⟳ YOUR TURN

1. This question has two parts. First, answer Part A. Then, answer Part B.

   Part A: Which type of figurative language does Didion use in this section of the text?

   ○ A. simile

   ○ B. paradox

   ○ C. onomatopoeia

   ○ D. personification

   Part B: Why does Didion use this type of figurative language?

   ○ A. Didion uses contradictions when describing sentences to highlight the strangeness of language.

   ○ B. Didion gives human qualities to the picture to make it seem the picture writes instead of her.

   ○ C. Didion compares camera angles to novels to highlight the control an author has.

   ○ D. Didion uses words that imitate sounds to give a musical quality to her writing.

Please note that excerpts and passages in the StudySync® library and this workbook are intended as touchstones to generate interest in an author's work. The excerpts and passages do not substitute for the reading of entire texts, and StudySync® strongly recommends that students seek out and purchase the whole literary or informational work in order to experience it as the author intended. Links to online resellers are available in our digital library. In addition, complete works may be ordered through an authorized reseller by filling out and returning to StudySync® the order form enclosed in this workbook.

Reading & Writing
Companion

95

Close Read

Reread "Why I Write." As you reread, complete the Skills Focus questions below. Then use your answers and annotations from the questions to help you complete the Write activity.

◎ SKILLS FOCUS

1. Identify details that show Didion's view of writing. Explain how these details support the author's purpose and point of view.

2. Reread paragraph 16, in which Didion describes an experience that inspired her writing. How does Didion use figurative language in this paragraph to help her audience understand why she found this experience inspiring?

3. Reread the introduction and conclusion. What key information and central ideas do these paragraphs contain that would be useful when summarizing this essay?

4. In "Freedom," author Ursula K. Le Guin warns that greed may have a negative impact on creativity in the publishing industry. Le Guin writes, "Right now, we need writers who know the difference between production of a market commodity and the practice of an art." Identify textual evidence in "Why I Write" that supports the idea that writing can be "the practice of an art." Write a sentence that compares the writers' ideas.

5. In "Why I Write," Joan Didion explains what motivates her to write, and how this purpose influences her process. What is the power of a story over Didion, as an author? Support your answer with textual evidence.

✎ WRITE

EXPLANATORY ESSAY: Write a short paper analyzing what you learn about Joan Didion's writing style and point of view from this essay. Why does she write? What does she believe about herself? Her statements are not always simple or obvious, so you will have to look closely at how Didion's content and style, particularly her use of figurative language, interact to develop her point of view. Pay special attention to the last sentence, which seems to achieve the purpose of asserting why she writes. Be sure to explain your understanding of this sentence in your analysis. Use textual evidence from the essay to support your points.

Extended
Writing
Project and
Grammar

EXTENDED
WRITING
PROJECT
RESEARCH WRITING

Research Writing Process: Plan

PLAN	DRAFT	REVISE	EDIT AND PUBLISH

As the Industrial Revolution transformed Britain in the 18th and 19th centuries, the English Romantic poets sought inspiration in the beauty of the natural world. Romanticism's passionate defense of and nostalgia for nature have continued to this day, represented in environmental movements.

WRITING PROMPT

How can we better value nature through our daily behaviors?

Think of a daily behavior that the average person may not know is damaging to nature. For example, people may not think about reducing their use of plastic bags when cleaning up after their dogs or may not consider the consequences of constantly upgrading their phones and other technology. Research your topic, and structure your essay to be clear, informative, and convincing. Then, write an informative research essay, using both informative text structures and source materials to support your claim and make your informative essay convincing. Be sure to include the following elements:

- an introduction that clearly expresses your thesis on a topic related to daily behaviors and their impact on nature
- a clear thesis statement that informs and engages the reader
- a clear and logical informative text structure
- a formal style with an appropriate register and purposeful vocabulary, tone, and voice
- a conclusion that wraps up your ideas
- a works cited page

Writing to Sources

As you gather ideas and information from sources, be sure to:

- use evidence from multiple sources, and
- avoid overly relying on one source.

Copyright © BookheadEd Learning, LLC

Introduction to Informative Research Writing

Informative research writing examines a researchable topic and presents information supported by evidence from a variety of reliable sources. The characteristics of informative research writing include:

- a clear thesis statement that presents a claim about your topic

- supporting details from a variety of sources

- a text structure that organizes ideas in a clear, impactful, and convincing manner

- a conclusion that rephrases the thesis

- in-text citations and a works cited page

As you continue with this Extended Writing Project, you'll receive more instruction and practice in crafting each of the characteristics of informative research writing to create your own research paper.

Please note that excerpts and passages in the StudySync® library and this workbook are intended as touchstones to generate interest in an author's work. The excerpts and passages do not substitute for the reading of entire texts, and StudySync® strongly recommends that students seek out and purchase the whole literary or informational work in order to experience it as the author intended. Links to online resellers are available in our digital library. In addition, complete works may be ordered through an authorized reseller by filling out and returning to StudySync® the order form enclosed in this workbook.

Reading & Writing Companion   99

Before you get started, read this informative research essay that one student, Rishal, wrote in response to the writing prompt. As you read the Model, highlight and annotate the features of informative research writing that Rishal included in his essay.

 NOTES

☰ STUDENT MODEL

Nurture Nature

A Damaging Relationship

1   Did you know that it takes on average 66 days to establish a habit? Yet, in today's fast-paced world, many people do not stop and think about how their daily habits impact the environment around them. Although nature isn't always a consideration when going through our daily routine, even the smallest decisions and behaviors can have a lasting impact on the environment, either positively or negatively. Humans did not always have such a damaging relationship with the environment. The great civilizations of the past, such as ancient Greece, celebrated nature instead of trying to dominate it. Things started to change during the Industrial Revolution. Nonetheless, during the 1800s, Romantic writers praised nature and were skeptical of industrial development. Two-hundred years later, the environment is rarely something we think about while going through our daily lives. With more and more damage being done to the environment, we need to take action to reduce the harmful daily burdens we place on the environment due to our behaviors, habits, and choices.

An Unexpected Truth

2   One of the daily behaviors that is unexpectedly damaging to the environment is recycling. This common, well-meaning habit isn't as good for the environment as people tend to think. When people think about how to reduce the amount of trash in their community, they usually think mainly of recycling.

NOTES

28% OF AMERICANS LIVE IN AREAS SEEN TO **STRONGLY ENCOURAGE** RECYCLING

% OF US ADULTS WHO SAY PEOPLE IN THEIR LOCAL COMMUNITY _____ RECYCLING AND RE-USE.

STRONGLY ENCOURAGE	ENCOURAGE BUT ARE NOT OVERLY CONCERNED	DO NOT ENCOURAGE
28%	48%	22%

NOTE: RESPONDENTS WHO DID NOT GIVE AN ANSWER ARE NOT SHOWN. SOURCE: SURVEY CONDUCTED MAY 10-JUNE 6 2016 PEW RESEARCH CENTER

"The Politics of Climate," Pew Research Center, Washington, D.C. October 4, 2016. http://www.pewresearch.org/fact-tank/2016/10/07/perceptions-and-realities-of-recycling-vary-widely-from-place-to-place/

As this graph demonstrates, almost 80% of U.S. communities encourage recycling, according to data collected by the Pew Research Center. Many cities and towns have recycling containers in public places, and some even provide them individually to homes and office buildings. Recently, however, recycling has become a less helpful option for improving the environment.

A New Challenge

3   Americans recycle nearly 70 million tons of material per year (Albeck-Ripka). Previously, most of this material went to China for processing. This was because China is the largest processor of recycled materials in the world. All that changed in 2018. China announced that it would temporarily stop accepting recycled material from other countries. China produced enough recyclable material within its own borders to meet its needs. It threatened to make the changes permanent.

4   What this meant was that the United States suddenly had to figure out what to do with tons and tons of materials collected for recycling. There are too few factories in our country to process such a large quantity of recyclables. Other nations such as Indonesia and Vietnam have such factories, but they can handle only a fraction of the amount that China used to process. The Los Angeles Times Editorial Board said of the situation in California: "Bales of mixed paper (cereal boxes, junk mail and the like) and plastics are piling up in warehouses up and down the state." Some communities have even started depositing their recyclables in landfills.

An Inefficient Process

5   As the NBC News footage of a recycling plant shows (watch the news footage in the Plan lesson on the StudySync site), recycling even a fraction of these 70 million tons is not a clean and easy process. In these ten seconds of video, we hear considerable sound pollution and see piles of waste being moved around by machinery and clouds of exhaust pouring out of a factory in Seattle, Washington. This short glimpse into the process gives us a sense of how wasteful even recycling can be.

A Simple Solution

6   Yet, what are we to do with our trash if recycling is no longer the best answer?

7   The answer is simple: We must produce less trash.

8   Where do we start?

9   When looking where to start trash reduction programs, we need look no further than plastic. Many people do not even bother recycling plastics and other trash and just throw them in the garbage. The garbage is taken to landfills. While landfills may seem like a viable solution, some parts of the United States are running out of space for landfills. For example, the Northeast has to pay neighboring states to accept its trash because the region no longer has adequate space to manage its own landfills (Lakeshore Recycling Services).

10   Plastic trash takes the longest to biodegrade, or break down. For example, a plastic shopping bag takes at least ten years to break down. A plastic soft drink bottle takes about 450 years to biodegrade (New Hampshire Department of Environmental Services). When people don't throw plastic waste into a recycle bin or even a garbage can, nature can be seriously harmed. For instance, fish mistake the plastic for food and die after eating it. Huge sections of the Pacific Ocean are covered with plastic trash that has drifted out to sea and been collected together by currents. This, in combination with climate change, has created huge "dead zones" where there is little life near the ocean's surface. All of the marine life near the surface suffers from a lack of oxygen. The plastic also blocks out sunlight, interfering with photosynthesis in tiny plants called phytoplankton. These plants form the base of the oceanic food chain.

11 Another problem with plastic is that it does not recycle well. Most plastics can be recycled into lower-quality material that is only useful for cheap products like synthetic fabric and bumper stickers (Somerville). In addition, factories that recycle plastics require a great deal of energy, often generating greenhouse gases and other pollution. Although we should continue to recycle as much paper as we have factory space for, recycling plastic is much less efficient.

A Growing Community

12 Some people have already started working on the problem. As the graph below shows, approximately 75% of U.S. adults are concerned for the environment, and 20% consistently take action as a result of that concern. This is a community that must keep growing, and effective strategies for trash reduction are already emerging.

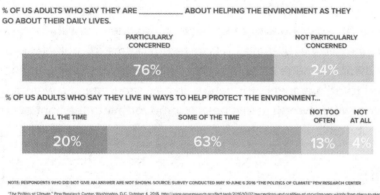

MOST AMERICANS REPORT CONCERN FOR THE ENVIRONMENT; ONE-IN-FIVE TRY TO ACT ON THAT CONCERN ALL THE TIME

% OF US ADULTS WHO SAY THEY ARE _____ ABOUT HELPING THE ENVIRONMENT AS THEY GO ABOUT THEIR DAILY LIVES.

PARTICULARLY CONCERNED	NOT PARTICULARLY CONCERNED
76%	24%

% OF US ADULTS WHO SAY THEY LIVE IN WAYS TO HELP PROTECT THE ENVIRONMENT...

ALL THE TIME	SOME OF THE TIME	NOT TOO OFTEN	NOT AT ALL
20%	63%	13%	4%

NOTE: RESPONDENTS WHO DID NOT GIVE AN ANSWER ARE NOT SHOWN. SOURCE: SURVEY CONDUCTED MAY 10-JUNE 6 2016 "THE POLITICS OF CLIMATE" PEW RESEARCH CENTER

"The Politics of Climate." Pew Research Center, Washington, D.C. October 4, 2016. http://www.pewresearch.org/fact-tank/2016/10/07/perceptions-and-realities-of-recycling-vary-widely-from-place-to-place/

13 One of the most effective strategies is banning stores from giving out plastic shopping bags. In Kenya, a ban on plastic bags has resulted in cleaner waterways and a less contaminated food supply chain (Watts). After the state of California banned plastic shopping bags, there was a drop in the amount of litter on beaches. Manufacturers of plastic shopping bags have lobbied heavily against these laws. Another campaign against plastic involves plastic straws. Seattle has banned plastic straws and plastic utensils in restaurants. "Plastic pollution is surpassing crisis levels in the world's oceans, and I'm proud Seattle is leading the way and setting an example for the

nation by enacting a plastic straw ban," Seattle Public Utilities General Manager Mami Hara said (CBS News). The city was inspired by a similar ban in Great Britain. India has announced it will institute the same type of ban in several years. Each community that takes action against plastic waste inspires other communities to do the same.

A Huge Difference

14 We can make a huge difference if we all change our daily routines. Individuals can take easy and immediate action and make better decisions when it comes to their impact on nature, especially when it comes to recycling. For example, when you order carry-out, ask that no plastic utensils or straws be included.

15 Staying informed will help you adjust your daily routines to respond to new facts and discoveries in the field. By sharing your research and the strategies you've implemented, you can support your friends and family members in understanding the problem and help them value nature in a more sustainable, beneficial manner.

16 Nature needs to be nurtured. Nature provides us with food, water, and the air we breathe. Yet, in return, some of our choices and behaviors damage it. Nature should be a source of inspiration. We need to be advocates for nature, just as the Romantic writers were. William Wordsworth said it best: "Come forth into the light of things; let nature be your teacher."

Works Cited

Albeck-Ripka, Livia. "Your Recycling Gets Recycled, Right? Maybe, or Maybe Not." *The New York Times,* 29 May 2018, www.nytimes. com/2018/05/29/climate/ Recycling-landfills-plastic-papers.html. Accessed 20 Oct. 2018.

Anderson, Monica. "For Earth Day, Here's How Americans View Environmental Issues." *Pew Research Center,* 20 Apr. 2017, http:// www.pewresearch.org/fact-tank/2017/04/20/for-earth-day-heres-how-americans-view-environmental-issues/. Accessed 31 Dec. 2018.

CBS News. "Seattle Becomes First U.S. City to Ban Plastic Utensils and Straws." *CBS News*, 2 Jul. 2018, www.cbsnews.com/news/ seattle-becomes-first-u-s-city-to-ban-plastic-utensils-and-straws/. Accessed 20 Oct. 2018.

Dean, Signe. "Here's How Long It Really Takes to Break a Habit, According to Science." *Science Alert,* 9 Jun. 2018, www. sciencealert.com/how-long-it-takes-to-break-a-habit-according-to-science. Accessed 21 Nov. 2018.

Desilver, Drew. "Perceptions and Realities of Recycling Vary Widely From Place to Place." *Pew Research Center*, 7 Oct. 2016, http:// www.pewresearch.org/fact-tank/2016/10/07/perceptions-and-realities-of-recycling-vary-widely-from-place-to-place/ft16-10-05recyclingencouraged/. Accessed 31 Dec. 2018.

Lakeshore Recycling Services. "Roundup of Successful Waste Reduction Campaigns by Cities." *Lakeshore Recycling Services*, 25 Apr. 2018. www.lrsrecycles.com/ roundup-successful-waste-reduction-campaigns-cities/. Accessed 31 Dec. 2018.

Los Angeles Times Editorial Board. "California Has a Recycling Crisis." *The Los Angeles Times,* 26 May 2018, www.latimes.com/opinion/ editorials/la-ed-recycling-crisis-20180526-story.html. Accessed 20 Oct. 2018.

NBC News X Press. "Recycling Center." *NBC News X Press*, 25 Jun. 2018. https://www.nbcnewsarchivesxpress.com/contentdetails/1937321. Accessed 23 Nov. 2018.

New Hampshire Department of Environmental Services. "Approximate Time It Takes Garbage to Decompose in Its Environment." New Hampshire Department of Environmental Services, 23 Mar. 2017, www.des.nh.gov/organization/ divisions/water/wmb/coastal/trash/documents/marinedebris.pdf. Accessed 7 Jan. 2019.

Scientific American. "'Dead' Sea of Plastic Bottles." *Scientific American*, www.scientificamerican.com/article/dead-sea-of-plastic-bottles/. Accessed 2 Oct. 2018.

Somerville, Madeleine. "Yes, You Recycle. But Until You Start Reducing, You're Still Killing the Planet." *The Guardian*, 19 May 2016, www.theguardian.com/lifeandstyle/ 2016/jan/19/eco-friendly-living-sustainability-recycling-reducing-saving-the-planet. Accessed 20 Oct. 2018.

Watts, Jonathan. "Eight Months On, Is the World's Most Drastic Plastic Bag Ban Working?" *The Guardian*, 25 Apr. 2018, https://www.theguardian.com/world/2018/apr/25/nairobi-clean-up-highs-lows-kenyas-plastic-bag-ban. Accessed 20 Oct. 2018.

✎ WRITE

When writing, it is important to consider your audience and purpose so you can write appropriately for them. Reread the prompt to determine your purpose for writing.

To begin, review the questions below and then select a strategy, such as brainstorming, journaling, reading, or discussing, to generate ideas.

- **Topic:** What topic about the human impact on nature do you find most interesting?
- **Purpose:** What is your reason for writing? What message do you want to express?
- **Audience:** Who is your audience? How will knowing your audience help you write a better essay?
- **Questions:** What do you want to learn about your topic? What questions do you want to research?

Response Instructions

Use the questions in the bulleted list to write a one-paragraph research summary. Your summary should include possible research questions based on the prompt.

This is your first step in writing an informative research essay. As you progress through this Extended Writing Project, you will develop a research plan and will have opportunities to critique your research plan at each step of the writing process. If necessary, you will be able to implement changes. For example, as you begin reviewing sources, you may find that your major research question is too broad. If so, you can modify your major research question and then refocus and revise your research plan as needed.

Please note that excerpts and passages in the StudySync® library and this workbook are intended as touchstones to generate interest in an author's work. The excerpts and passages do not substitute for the reading of entire texts, and StudySync® strongly recommends that students seek out and purchase the whole literary or informational work in order to experience it as the author intended. Links to online resellers are available in our digital library. In addition, complete works may be ordered through an authorized reseller by filling out and returning to StudySync® the order form enclosed in this workbook.

Reading & Writing Companion **107**

Skill:
Planning Research

In order to conduct a short or more sustained research project to answer a question or solve a problem, do the following:

- select a topic or problem to research

- think about what you want to find out and what kind of research can contribute to the project

- start to formulate your major research question by asking open-ended questions that begin "How. . .?" and "Why. . .?" and then choose a question that you are interested in exploring

- synthesize multiple sources on the subject to look at information from different points of view, while demonstrating understanding of the subject under investigation

In order to conduct a short or more sustained research project to answer a question or solve a problem, consider the following questions:

- Does my major research question allow me to explore a new issue, an important problem worth solving, or a fresh perspective on a topic?

- Can I research my question within my given time frame and with the resources available to me?

- Have I synthesized multiple sources on the question or problem, looking for different points of view?

- Have I demonstrated understanding of the subject under investigation in my research project?

⟳ YOUR TURN

Read the research questions below. Then, complete the chart by sorting the questions into the correct category. Write the corresponding letter for each question in the appropriate column.

	Research Questions
A	Why do people choose to spend time outdoors?
B	Why did the bald eagle become an endangered species?
C	How does pollution lead to microplastics in the ocean or carcinogens in the air?
D	What are major pollutants in the world today?
E	How has America treated wild animals throughout its history?
F	How does pollution affect air and water quality in the U.S.?
G	Does hiking make people live longer?
H	How are endangered species currently being protected in the U.S.? What can be improved?
I	How does spending time outdoors or in nature affect people's health and mood?

Topic	Too Narrow	Appropriate	Too Broad
Endangered Species			
Pollution			
Spending Time Outdoors			

YOUR TURN

Develop a research question for formal research. Then, write a short plan for how you will go about doing research for your essay.

Process	Plan
Research Question	
Step 1	
Step 2	
Step 3	
Step 4	

Skill:
Evaluating Sources

••• CHECKLIST FOR EVALUATING SOURCES

Once you gather your sources, identify the following:

- where information seems inaccurate, biased, or outdated

- where information strongly relates to your task, purpose, and audience

- where information helps you make an informed decision or solve a problem

In order to conduct advanced searches to gather relevant, credible, and accurate print and digital sources, use the following questions as a guide:

- Are there specific terms or phrases that I can use to adjust my search?

- Can I use *and*, *or*, or *not* to expand or limit my search?

- Can I use quotation marks to search for exact phrases?

- Is the material published by a well-established source or expert author?

- Is the material up-to-date or based on the most current information?

- Is the material factual, and can it be verified by another source?

- Are there discrepancies between the information presented in different sources?

Please note that excerpts and passages in the StudySync® library and this workbook are intended as touchstones to generate interest in an author's work. The excerpts and passages do not substitute for the reading of entire texts, and StudySync® strongly recommends that students seek out and purchase the whole literary or informational work in order to experience it as the author intended. Links to online resellers are available in our digital library. In addition, complete works may be ordered through an authorized reseller by filling out and returning to StudySync® the order form enclosed in this workbook.

Reading & Writing
Companion

111

YOUR TURN

Read the sentences below. Then, complete the chart by sorting the sentences into two categories: those that are credible and reliable and those that are not. Write the corresponding letter for each sentence in the appropriate column.

	Sentences
A	The article was published recently and uses up-to-date information.
B	The text uses only one viewpoint or relies on opinions instead of cited sources.
C	The text includes many viewpoints that are properly cited.
D	The article was published many years ago and uses statistics that may be outdated.
E	The article includes clear arguments and counterarguments that are supported by factual information.
F	The website is a personal blog or social media website.

Credible and Reliable	Not Credible or Reliable

↻ YOUR TURN

Complete the chart below by filling in the title and author of a source for your informative research essay and answering the questions about this source.

Questions	Answers
Source Title and Author:	
Reliability: Has the source material been published in a well-established book or periodical or on a well-established website? Is the source material up-to-date or based on the most current information?	
Accuracy: Is the source based on factual information that can be verified by another source? Are there any discrepancies between this source and others?	
Credibility: Is the source material written by a recognized expert on the topic? Is the source material published by a well-respected author or organization?	
Decision: Should I use this source in my research essay? Is it effective in answering the research question?	

Please note that excerpts and passages in the StudySync® library and this workbook are intended as touchstones to generate interest in an author's work. The excerpts and passages do not substitute for the reading of entire texts, and StudySync® strongly recommends that students seek out and purchase the whole literary or informational work in order to experience it as the author intended. Links to online resellers are available in our digital library. In addition, complete works may be ordered through an authorized reseller by filling out and returning to StudySync® the order form enclosed in this workbook.

Reading & Writing Companion

113

Skill:
Research and Notetaking

••• CHECKLIST FOR RESEARCH AND NOTETAKING

In order to conduct short as well as more sustained research projects to answer a question (including a self-generated question) or solve a problem, note the following:

- Answer a question for a research project, or think of your own question that you would like to have answered.

- Look up your topic in an encyclopedia to find general information.

- Find specific, up-to-date information in books and periodicals or on the Internet. If appropriate, conduct interviews with experts to get information.

- Narrow or broaden your inquiry when appropriate.

  > If you find dozens of books on a topic, your research topic may be too broad.

  > If it is difficult to write a research question, narrow your topic so it is more specific.

- Synthesize your information by organizing your notes from various sources to see what your sources have in common and how they differ.

To conduct short as well as more sustained research projects to answer a question (including a self-generated question) or solve a problem, consider the following questions:

- What is my research question?

- Where could I look to find information?

- How does new information I have found affect my research question?

- How can I demonstrate my understanding of the subject I am investigating?

YOUR TURN

Read each point from Rishal's note cards below. Then, complete the chart by sorting the points into two categories: those that support re-examining our relationship with recycling and those that support reducing waste consumption. Write the corresponding letter for each point in the appropriate column.

	Points
A	Source 5: Processing plastic for re-use provides low-quality material that can be used only for cheap products.
B	Source 3: A plastic soft drink bottle takes about 450 years to biodegrade, or break down.
C	Source 6: The Northeastern United States has run out of room for landfills.
D	Source 8: As NBC News footage of a recycling plant shows, recycling even a fraction of these 70 million tons is not a clean and easy process.
E	Source 4: The situation after China's ban on foreign garbage: "bales of mixed paper (cereal boxes, junk mail and the like) and plastics are piling up in warehouses up and down the state."
F	Source 7: "Plastic pollution is surpassing crisis levels in the world's oceans."

Re-examine Our Relationship with Recycling	Reduce Waste Consumption

✏ WRITE

Use the questions in the checklist to locate sources and synthesize the information about one point in a paragraph for your draft.

Research Writing Process: Draft

| PLAN | DRAFT | REVISE | EDIT AND PUBLISH |

You have already made progress toward writing your informative research essay. You have developed a research plan; selected a major research question; and located, evaluated, and synthesized information from a variety of sources. Before you begin drafting, you should take a moment to critique your research plan and implement any changes needed. For example, now that you have done your background reading and research, you may want to refine your thesis or claim or clarify the points you plan to make in your essay.

Now it is time to draft your informative research essay.

✏ WRITE

Use your plan and other responses in your Binder to draft your essay. You may also have new ideas as you begin drafting. Feel free to explore those new ideas as you have them. You can also ask yourself these questions to ensure that your writing is focused and organized and you have elaborated on your ideas:

Draft Checklist:

☐ **Purpose and Focus:** Have I made my claim clear to readers? Will they understand the purpose of my research? Have I included only relevant information and details and nothing extraneous that might confuse my readers?

☐ **Organization:** Does the organizational structure in my essay make sense? Will readers be engaged by the organization and interested in the way I present information and evidence?

☐ **Evidence and Elaboration:** Have I provided sufficient evidence and elaboration? Will my readers be able to follow my ideas and details?

Before you submit your draft, read it over carefully. You want to be sure that you've responded to all aspects of the prompt.

Here is Rishal's informative research essay draft. As you read, notice how Rishal develops his draft to be focused and organized, so it has relevant evidence and elaboration to support his claim. As he continues to revise and edit his informative research essay, he will find and improve weak spots in his writing, as well as correct any language or punctuation mistakes.

☰ STUDENT MODEL: FIRST DRAFT

 NOTES

Nurture Nature

~~Although nature isn't always a consideration when going through our daily routine, even the smallest decisions and behaviors can have a lasting impact on the environment, either positively or negatively. Modern society seems more focused on economic gain and "progress" at the expense of the environment. The great civilizations of the past, such as anchent Greece, celebrated nature instead of trying to dominate it. In the 1800s, Romantic writers praised nature and were sceptical of industrial development. With more and more damage being done to the environment, we need to take action to reduce the amount of trash that is dumped in the natural world.~~

A Damaging Relationship

Did you know that it takes on average 66 days to establish a habit? Yet, in today's fast-paced world, many people do not stop and think about how their daily habits impact the environment around them. Although nature isn't always a consideration when going through our daily routine, even the smallest decisions and behaviors can have a lasting impact on the environment, either positively or negatively. Humans did not always have such a damaging relationship with the environment. The great civilizations of the past, such as ancient Greece, celebrated nature instead of trying to dominate it. Things started to change during the Industrial Revolution. Nonetheless, during the 1800s, Romantic writers praised nature and were skeptical of industrial development. Two-hundred years later, the environment is rarely something we think about while going through our daily lives. With more and more damage being done to the environment, we need to take action to reduce the harmful daily burdens we place on the environment due to our behaviors, habits, and choices.

 Skill: Print and Graphic Features

Rishal adds a heading to signal to his readers what the paragraph will be about. As he rereads his draft, he will continue to add headings to help organize his information effectively.

When people think about how to reduce the amount of trash in their community, they usually think first of recycling. Many cities and towns have recycling containers in public places, and some even provide them individually to homes and office buildings. Americans recycle nearly 70 million tons of material per year (Albeck-Ripka).

~~We must produce less trash. When looking where to start trash reduction programs, we need look no further than plastic. Fish mistake the plastic for food and die after eating it. Plastic trash takes practically forever to biodegrade. When people are too lazy to be responsible and throw plastic waste into a recycle bin or even a garbage can, defenseless creatures are forced to suffer! Huge sections of the Pacific Ocean are covered with plastic trash that has drifted out to sea and been collected together by currents. Gross! This, in combination with climate change, has created huge hypoxic areas where there is little life near the ocean's surface. The plastic also interferes with the photosynthesis of phytoplankton, which form the base of the oceanic trophic pyramid.~~

Skill: Critiquing Research

As he revises, Rishal thinks about how to synthesize and integrate information from multiple sources. In this paragraph, he adds relevant information from the New Hampshire Department of Environmental Services.

Plastic trash takes the longest to biodegrade, or break down. For example, a plastic shopping bag takes at least ten years to break down. A plastic soft drink bottle takes about 450 years to biodegrade (New Hampshire Department of Environmental Services). When people don't throw plastic waste into a recycle bin or even a garbage can, nature can be seriously harmed. For instance, fish mistake the plastic for food and die after eating it. Huge sections of the Pacific Ocean are covered with plastic trash that has drifted out to sea and been collected together by currents. This, in combination with climate change, has created huge "dead zones" where there is little life near the ocean's surface. All of the marine life near the surface suffers from a lack of oxygen. The plastic also blocks out sunlight, interfering with photosynthesis in tiny plants called phytoplankton. These plants form the base of the oceanic food chain.

Another problem with plastic is that it does not recycle well. Most plastics can be recycled into awful material that is only fairly awful and only good for cheap products like sinthetick fabric and bumper stickers (*The Guardian*). And, factories that recycle plastics require a great deal of energy, often with greenhouse gases and other pollution. Although we should continue to recycle as much paper as we have factory space for, recycling plastic is much less effishient.

For example, the Northeast has to pay nayboring states to accept its trash. It's run out of room for it (Lakeshore Recycling Services). Many people do not even bother recycling plastics and other trash and just throw them in the garbage. The garbage is taken to landfills. It's now at the point that some parts of the United States are running out of space for landfills.

~~All of this means that our top priority should be programs that reduce the amount of plastic waste and some people have already started work on the problem because one of the most effective strategies is banning stores from giving out plastic shopping bags. In Kenya, a ban on plastic bags has resulted in cleaner waterways and a less contaminated food supply chain. After the state of California banned plastic shopping bags, there was a drop in the amount of litter on beaches. Manufacturers of plastic shopping bags have lobbyed heavily against these laws. Another campaign against plastic involves plastic straws. Seattle has banned plastic straws and plastic utensils in restaurants. Plastic pollution is serpassing crisis levels in the world's oceans, and I'm proud Seattle is leading the way and setting an example for the nation by enacting a plastic straw ban, Seattle Public Utilities General Manager Mami Hara said. The city was inspired by a similar ban in Great Britain. India has announced it will institute the same type of ban in several years. Each community that takes action against plastic waste inspires other communities to do the same.~~

One of the most effective strategies is banning stores from giving out plastic shopping bags. In Kenya, a ban on plastic bags has resulted in cleaner waterways and a less contaminated food supply chain (Watts). After the state of California banned plastic shopping bags, there was a drop in the amount of litter on beaches. Manufacturers of plastic shopping bags have lobbied heavily against these laws. Another campaign against plastic involves plastic straws. Seattle has banned plastic straws and plastic utensils in restaurants. "Plastic pollution is surpassing crisis levels in the world's oceans, and I'm proud Seattle is leading the way and setting an example for the nation by enacting a plastic straw ban," Seattle Public Utilities

**Skill:
Paraphrasing**

Rishal realizes that he forgot to use quotation marks in a citation. Since the statement from Mami Hara is a direct quotation, not a paraphrase, he puts quotation marks around it.

**Skill: Sources
and Citations**

Even though Rishal attributed the statement about Seattle's plastic straw ban to Mami Hara, he needs to cite the source of the remark. So he inserts a parenthetical citation. Since the source is electronic, he doesn't have to include a page number.

General Manager Mami Hara said (CBS News). The city was inspired by a similar ban in Great Britain. India has announced it will institute the same type of ban in several years. Each community that takes action against plastic waste inspires other communities to do the same.

As individuals, we shouldn't rely on our local leaders do all the work on waste. We can make a huge difference if we all change our daily routines. Take a reusable bag to the store when you shop. If you forget to take a reusable bag to the store when you shop, ask for a paper bag. You can also make a difference when you order carry out. When you order carry out, ask that no plastic utensils or straws be included. Support businesses that use biodegradable containers instead of plastic. Tell your friends and family members about the problem, and share ways to fix it with them.

Nature needs to taken care of. Nature should be a source of inspiration. We need to be advocates for nature, just as the Romantic writers were. William Wordsworth said it best: "Come forth into the light of things; let nature be your teacher."

Works Cited

Albeck-Ripka, Livia. "Your Recycling Gets Recycled, Right? Maybe, or Maybe Not," *The New York Times*, 29 May 2018, www.nytimes.com/2018/05/29/climate/ recycling-landfills-plastic-papers.html

CBS News. "Seattle Becomes First U.S. City to Ban Plastic Utensils and Straws," 2 Jul. 2018. www.cbsnews.com/news/seattle-becomes-first-u-s-city-to-ban-plastic-utensils-and-straws

Lakeshore Recycling Services. "Roundup of Successful Waste Reduction Campaigns by Cities." Blog, 4/25/2018. www.lrsrecycles.com/ roundup-successful-waste-reduction-campaigns-cities/

"California Has a Recycling Crisis." *Los Angeles Times Editorial Board*, 5/26/2018. www.latimes.com/opinion/editorials/la-ed-recycling-crisis-20180526-story.html

NBC News Archives Xpress. "Recycling Center." Accessed on Nov. 23, 2018. https://www.nbcnewsarchivesxpress.com/contentdetails/1937321

Scientific American. "'Dead' Sea of Plastic Bottles." Accessed 2 Oct. 2018. www.scientificamerican.com/article/ dead-sea-of-plastic-bottles/

Somerville, Madeleine. "Yes, You Recycle. But Until You Start Reducing, You're Still Killing the Planet." *The Guardian*, 19 May 2016, www.theguardian.com/lifeandstyle/ 2016/jan/19/ eco-friendly-living-sustainability-recycling-reducing-saving-the-planet

Watts, Jonathan. "Eight Months On, Is the World's Most Drastic Plastic Bag Ban Working?" *The Guardian*, 4/25/2018, www.theguardian.com/world/2018/apr/25/nairobi-clean-up-highs-lows-kenyas-plastic-bag-ban.

Skill:
Critiquing Research

••• CHECKLIST FOR CRITIQUING RESEARCH

In order to conduct short or sustained research projects to answer a question or solve a problem, drawing on several sources, do the following:

- narrow or broaden the question or inquiry as necessary when researching your topic

- use advanced search terms effectively when looking for information online, such as using unique terms that are specific to your topic (i.e., "daily life in Jamestown, Virginia" rather than just "Jamestown, Virginia")

- assess the strengths and limitations of each source in terms of the task, purpose, and audience

- synthesize and integrate information from multiple sources to maintain a flow of ideas, and avoid overly relying on one single source

- quote or paraphrase the information you have found without plagiarizing, or copying your source

- provide information about your sources in a bibliography or another standard format for citations

To evaluate and use relevant information while conducting short or sustained research projects, consider the following questions:

- Did I narrow or broaden my research inquiry as needed?

- Have I successfully synthesized and integrated information from multiple sources on my topic to maintain a flow of ideas and avoided overly relying on one single source?

- Did I quote or paraphrase information without plagiarizing?

YOUR TURN

Choose the best answer to each question.

1. Below is the introduction from a student's draft, which explains why conservation is important. As he researches, the student discovers that restoration ecology may be more effective for saving endangered species. How should he replace his underlined thesis statement?

> Biodiversity is the variety of life in an environment. A healthy ecosystem needs to be biodiverse. When one species go extinct, other species often follow. Scientists had not realized that extinction occurs until late in the eighteenth century, so the concept was still relatively new to Romantics. Even so, they realized the threat extinction posed to nature, and so they began the conservation movement to protect rare plants and animals. <u>Conservation has been successful in rescuing many species, but it is important to maintain efforts to protect the environment.</u>

- A. Conservation has been ineffective in preventing extinction in many cases.
- B. Humans are the primary cause of extinction in the modern world.
- C. Biodiversity is essential to our understanding of how environments work.
- D. However, it is not enough to conserve; damaged ecosystems need to be restored.

2. Rishal came across the following information and source in his research about recycling. What should he do?

> Recycled products contain the energies of previous products, and their previous uses will determine the characteristic of the new product that will be made from the recycled material.
>
> Source: www.conspiracy.blog.com

- A. Modify his research question.
- B. Consider if the source is appropriate.
- C. Rewrite his thesis using the new information.
- D. Revise his research plan.

 WRITE

Use the questions in the checklist to critique your research process to determine whether you need to modify your major research question, revise your research plan, or change any other aspect of your informative research essay.

Skill:
Paraphrasing

••• CHECKLIST FOR PARAPHRASING

In order to integrate information into your research essay, note the following:

- make sure you understand what the author is saying after reading the text carefully; note:

  > any words or expressions that are unfamiliar

  > words and phrases that are important to include in a paraphrase to maintain the meaning of the text

- avoid plagiarism by acknowledging all sources for both paraphrased and quoted material, and avoid overly relying on any one source

- integrate information selectively to maintain a logical flow of ideas

To integrate information into your research essay, consider the following questions:

- Do I understand the meaning of the text? Have I determined the meanings of any words in the text that are unfamiliar to me?

- Does my paraphrase of the text maintain the text's original meaning? Have I missed any key points or details?

- Have I avoided plagiarism by acknowledging all my sources for both paraphrased and quoted material and avoided overly relying on any one source?

- Did I integrate information selectively to maintain a logical flow of ideas?

YOUR TURN

Read the quotation below from one of Rishal's sources for his informative research essay. Then, answer the multiple-choice questions.

> "Portland keeps an impressive seventy percent of its waste out of landfills. The city cooperates with more than three dozen independent haulers of trash and recycling, which actually makes this milestone even more impressive." (Lakeshore Recycling Systems)

1. What is incorrect about this paraphrase of the quotation from Lakeshore Recycling Systems?

> Portland works with three dozen independent haulers to keep an impressive seventy percent of its waste out of landfills.

- ○ A. It is incorrect because it summarizes the information, rather than paraphrasing it.
- ○ B. It is incorrect because it quotes much of the text directly, rather than paraphrasing it.
- ○ C. It is incorrect because the original meaning of the text is not maintained.
- ○ D. It is incorrect because key points are missing, and this alters the original meaning.

2. What would be the most accurate and complete paraphrase of the source?

- ○ A. The city of Portland works with various companies to keep seventy percent of its waste away from landfills.
- ○ B. The city of Portland has many recycling programs to support waste disposal, which is helpful to residents.
- ○ C. Thirty-six companies that specialize in waste management and recycling move over 50% of waste into landfills.
- ○ D. 70% of waste is kept out of landfills in Oregon thanks to the city of Portland's excellent recycling program.

 WRITE

Use the questions in the checklist to paraphrase information from a source and integrate it into a paragraph of your informative research essay.

Please note that excerpts and passages in the StudySync® library and this workbook are intended as touchstones to generate interest in an author's work. The excerpts and passages do not substitute for the reading of entire texts, and StudySync® strongly recommends that students seek out and purchase the whole literary or informational work in order to experience it as the author intended. Links to online resellers are available in our digital library. In addition, complete works may be ordered through an authorized reseller by filling out and returning to StudySync® the order form enclosed in this workbook.

Reading & Writing Companion   **125**

Skill:
Sources and Citations

••• CHECKLIST FOR SOURCES AND CITATIONS

In order to gather relevant information from multiple authoritative print and digital sources and to cite the sources correctly, do the following:

- gather information from a variety of print and digital sources, using search terms effectively to narrow your search

- find information on authors to see if they are experts on a topic

- avoid relying on any one source, and synthesize information from a variety of books, publications, and online resources

- quote or paraphrase the information you find, and cite it to avoid plagiarism

- integrate information selectively to maintain a logical flow of ideas in your essay, using transitional words and phrases

- include all sources in a bibliography, following a standard format:

    > Halall, Ahmed. *The Pyramids of Ancient Egypt*. New York: Central Publishing, 2016.

    > for a citation, footnote, or endnote, include the author, title, and page number

To check that you have gathered information and cited sources correctly, consider the following questions:

- Did I cite the information I found using a standard format to avoid plagiarism?

- Did I include all my sources in my bibliography?

YOUR TURN

Choose the best answer to each question.

1. Below is a section from a previous draft of Rishal's research paper. What change should Rishal make to improve the clarity of his citations?

> According to Megan Forbes on the National Oceanic and Atmospheric Administration (NOAA) Ocean Podcast episode "Garbage Patches: How Gyres Take Our Trash Out to Sea," there are at least three major patches of "concentrated (and mostly plastic) marine debris" in our oceans (Forbes).

   ○ A. Add the page number after the author in the parentheses.
   ○ B. Remove the citation in parentheses after the quotation.
   ○ C. Remove the quotation marks around the cited material.
   ○ D. No change needs to be made.

2. Below is a section from a previous draft of Rishal's works cited page in the MLA format. Which revision best corrects his style errors?

> Thompson, James. *Landfill Waste Costs Continued to Rise in 2016. Solid Waste Environmental Excellence Protocol*, 12 Jan. 2017. https://nrra.net/sweep/cost-to-landfill-waste-continues-to-rise-through 2016/

   ○ A. Thompson, James. "Landfill Waste Costs Continued to Rise in 2016." Solid Waste Environmental Excellence Protocol, 12 Jan 2017. https://nrra.net/sweep/cost-to-landfill-waste-continues-to-rise-through-2016/
   ○ B. *Landfill Waste Costs Continued to Rise in 2016.* by James Thompson. *Solid Waste Environmental ExcellenceProtocol*, 12 Jan 2017. https://nrra.net/sweep/cost-to-landfill-waste-continues-to-rise-through-2016/
   ○ C. "Landfill Waste Costs Continued to Rise in 2016." by James Thompson. *Solid Waste Environmental Excellence Protocol,* 12 Jan. 2017. https://nrra.net/sweep/cost-to-landfill-waste-continues-to-rise-through-2016/
   ○ D. Thompson, James. "Landfill Waste Costs Continued to Rise in 2016." *Solid Waste Environmental Excellence Protocol*, 12 Jan. 2017, https://nrra.net/sweep/cost-to-landfill-waste-continues-to-rise-through-2016/. Accessed 31 Dec. 2018.

✎ **WRITE**

Use the questions in the checklist to create or revise your in-text citations and works cited list.

Please note that excerpts and passages in the StudySync® library and this workbook are intended as touchstones to generate interest in an author's work. The excerpts and passages do not substitute for the reading of entire texts, and StudySync® strongly recommends that students seek out and purchase the whole literary or informational work in order to experience it as the author intended. Links to online resellers are available in our digital library. In addition, complete works may be ordered through an authorized reseller by filling out and returning to StudySync® the order form enclosed in this workbook.

Reading & Writing Companion   127

Skill:
Print and Graphic Features

••• CHECKLIST FOR PRINT AND GRAPHIC FEATURES

First, reread your draft and ask yourself the following questions:

- To what extent would including formatting, graphics, or multimedia be effective in achieving my purpose?
- Which formatting, graphics, or multimedia seem most important in conveying information to the reader?
- How is the addition of the formatting, graphics, or multimedia useful in aiding comprehension?

To include formatting, graphics, and multimedia, use the following questions as a guide:

- How can I use formatting to better organize information? Consider adding:
  - titles
  - headings
  - subheadings
  - bullets
  - boldface and italicized terms

- How can I use graphics to better convey information? Consider adding:
  - charts
  - graphs
  - tables
  - timelines
  - diagrams
  - figures and statistics

- How can I use multimedia to add interest and variety? Consider adding a combination of:
  - photographs
  - art
  - audio
  - video

Copyright © BookheadEd Learning, LLC

YOUR TURN

Choose the best answer to each question.

1. Reread the paragraph from Rishal's draft. Which of the following headings best represents the content of the passage and would aid his audience's comprehension of the main idea?

> We must produce less trash. When looking where to start trash reduction programs, we need look no further than plastic. Fish mistake the plastic for food and die after eating it. Plastic trash takes practically forever to biodegrade. When people are too lazy to be responsible and throw plastic waste into a recycle bin or even a garbage can, defenseless creatures are forced to suffer! Huge sections of the Pacific Ocean are covered with plastic trash that has drifted out to sea and been collected together by currents. Gross! This, in combination with climate change, has created huge hypoxic areas where there is little life near the ocean's surface. The plastic also interferes with the photosynthesis of phytoplankton, which form the base of the oceanic trophic pyramid.

- ○ A. Stop the Plastics Lobby Today
- ○ B. The Most Harmful Everyday Material
- ○ C. Oceans are not Landfills
- ○ D. Climate Change and Recycling

2. Rishal also considers adding an image, graph, or table to help his audience understand how extensive plastic waste is. Which of the following graphic elements would be most helpful to readers?

- ○ A. An image of a water bottle floating in the ocean, with wildlife nearby
- ○ B. A table depicting the increase in recycling facilities worldwide
- ○ C. A graphic displaying the effect of climate change on the world's oceans
- ○ D. An image showing large quantities of plastic waste in the ocean

 WRITE

Use the questions in the checklist to add at least three headings, two graphics, and one piece of multimedia to your research essay.

Research Writing Process: Revise

| PLAN | DRAFT | REVISE | EDIT AND PUBLISH |

You have written a draft of your informative research essay. You have also received input from your peers about how to improve it. Now you are going to revise your draft.

◀◀ REVISION GUIDE

Examine your draft to find areas for revision. Keep in mind your purpose and audience as you revise for clarity, development, organization, and style. Use the guide below to help you review.

Review	Revise	Example
Clarity		
Reread the concluding paragraph of your informative research essay.	Make sure you rephrase your thesis or claim in a new way to remind readers of the purpose of your research and topic.	Nature needs to ~~taken care of~~ be nurtured. Nature provides us with food, water, and the air we breathe. Yet, in return, some of our choices and behaviors damage it. Nature should be a source of inspiration. We need to be advocates for nature, just as the Romantic writers were. William Wordsworth said it best: "Come forth into the light of things; let nature be your teacher."

Review	Revise	Example
Development		
Highlight a key detail used to support your claim.	Strengthen your essay by supporting key details with evidence from reputable sources. Make sure to include any additional sources in your works cited list.	Plastic trash takes ~~practically forever~~ the longest to biodegrade, or break down. For example, a plastic shopping bag takes at least ten years to break down. A plastic soft drink bottle takes about 450 years to biodegrade (New Hampshire Department of Environmental Services). When people ~~are too lazy to be responsible and~~ don't throw plastic waste into a recycle bin or even a garbage can, ~~defenseless creatures are forced to suffer!~~ nature can be seriously harmed.
Organization		
Review your body paragraphs. Are they organized? Does information flow from one paragraph to the next? Identify and annotate any sentences within and across paragraphs that don't flow in a clear and logical way.	Rewrite the sentences so they appear in a clear and logical order. Eliminate sentences that are repetitive or complicate the clear organization of your paragraph.	For example, the Northeast has to pay nayboring states to accept its trash. ~~It's run out of room for it~~ because the region no longer has adequate space to manage its own landfills (Lakeshore Recycling Services). ~~Many people do not even bother recycling plastics and other trash and just throw them in the garbage. The garbage is taken to landfills. It's now at the point that some parts of the United States are running out of space for landfills.~~

Please note that excerpts and passages in the StudySync® library and this workbook are intended as touchstones to generate interest in an author's work. The excerpts and passages do not substitute for the reading of entire texts, and StudySync® strongly recommends that students seek out and purchase the whole literary or informational work in order to experience it as the author intended. Links to online resellers are available in our digital library. In addition, complete works may be ordered through an authorized reseller by filling out and returning to StudySync® the order form enclosed in this workbook.

Reading & Writing Companion **131**

Review	Revise	Example
Style: Word Choice		
Identify any weak adjectives or verbs.	Replace weak adjectives and verbs with strong, descriptive adjectives and verbs.	~~Tell your friends and family members about the problem, and share ways to fix it with them.~~ By sharing your research and the strategies you've implemented, you can support your friends and family members in understanding the problem and help them value nature in a more sustainable, beneficial manner.
Style: Sentence Fluency		
Read aloud your writing and listen to the way the text sounds. Does it sound choppy? Or does it flow smoothly with rhythm, movement, and emphasis on important details and events?	Rewrite a key passage, making your sentences longer or shorter to achieve a better flow of writing. Remove repetitive phrases.	We can make a huge difference if we all change our daily routines. ~~Take a reusable bag to the store when you shop. If you forget to take a reusable bag to the store when you shop, ask for a paper bag. You can also make a difference when you order carry out. When you order carry out, ask that no plastic utensils or straws be included.~~ Individuals can take easy and immediate action and make better decisions when it comes to their impact on nature, especially when it comes to recycling. For example, when you order carry-out, ask that no plastic utensils or straws be included.

✎ WRITE

Use the revision guide, as well as your peer reviews, to help you evaluate your informative research essay to determine places that should be revised.

Skill:
Using a Style Guide

••• CHECKLIST FOR USING A STYLE GUIDE

In order to make sure that your writing conforms to the guidelines in a style manual, do the following:

- Determine which style guide you should use before you write your draft.

  > Follow the guidelines chosen by a teacher, for example.

  > Familiarize yourself with that guide, and check your writing against the guide when you edit.

- Use the style guide for the overall formatting of your paper, citation style, bibliography format, and other style considerations for reporting research.

- As you draft, use an additional style guide, such as *Artful Sentences: Syntax as Style* by Virginia Tufte, to help you vary your syntax, or the grammatical structure of sentences.

  > Use a variety of simple, compound, complex, and compound-complex sentences to convey information.

  > Be sure to punctuate your sentences correctly.

  > Follow standard English language conventions to help you maintain a formal style for formal papers.

To edit your work so that it conforms to the guidelines in a style manual, consider the following questions:

- Have I followed the conventions for spelling, punctuation, capitalization, sentence structure, and formatting, according to the style guide?

- Have I varied my syntax to make my information clear for readers?

- Do I have an entry in my works cited or bibliography for each reference I used?

- Have I followed the correct style, including the guidelines for capitalization and punctuation, in each entry in my works cited or bibliography?

YOUR TURN

Read the types of information below. Then, complete the chart by sorting them into two categories: those that are found in a style guide and those that are not. Write the corresponding letter for each type of information in the appropriate column.

Types of Information			
A	a list of possible research topics	**F**	the definition of a word
B	how to select a thesis	**G**	when to use italics
C	how to cite internet sources	**H**	synonyms for a word
D	how to write an outline	**I**	when to use a hyphen
E	how to format a bibliography	**J**	proper punctuation for quotations

In a Style Guide	Not in a Style Guide

WRITE

Use the checklist to help you choose a convention that you have found challenging to follow. Use a credible style guide to check and correct any errors related to that convention in your research essay.

Grammar:
Contested Usage

For most formal writing, it is probably advisable to follow the traditional rules of grammar. In most cases, following the rules will improve both the clarity and effectiveness of your communication. However, there are a number of grammar "rules" that can be broken if you do it deliberately to improve the effectiveness of your writing.

Contested Rules	Text
• Never begin a sentence with *And* or *But*. • A paragraph must always consist of more than one sentence. • Never end a sentence with a preposition. • Dialogue should be set off by quotation marks.	**And** now Miss Emily had gone to join the representatives of those august names where they lay in the cedar-bemused cemetery among the ranked and anonymous graves of Union and Confederate soldiers who fell at the battle of Jefferson. A Rose for Emily, by William Faulkner

People, and even references, often disagree about word usage. For one thing, new words enter the language all the time. An example of a current debate regarding usage involves the word *literally*. This word is sometimes used to emphasize a statement or description that is not literally true or possible. Some sources argue against this usage, explaining that it is illogical to use the word *literally* to mean "figuratively." And yet, even Mark Twain used the word *literally* to describe things that could not be literally true. For instance:

Text	Contested Usage
And when the middle of the afternoon came, from being a poor poverty-stricken boy in the morning, Tom was **literally** rolling in wealth. The Adventures of Tom Sawyer, by Mark Twain	The character Tom Sawyer was not literally tumbling around in piles of money.

If you are unsure whether it is acceptable to break a rule or if you want to resolve questions you may have about usage, you can always check a reference work on the subject. Several worth recommending are Merriam-Webster's *Dictionary of English Usage*, Bryan A. Garner's *Garner's Modern American Usage*, and Theodore M. Bernstein's *Miss Thistlebottom's Hobgoblins*. The *Merriam-Webster Dictionary* online also includes a Usage Guide for words that have been the subject of contested usage. For instance, if you look up the word *affect*, you will find a Usage Guide on the different uses of the word *affect* versus *effect*.

⟳ YOUR TURN

1. What rule of usage has been deliberately broken in the sentence below?

> Dost thou love life? Then do not squander time, for that is the stuff life is made of.
> —Benjamin Franklin

○ A. Never begin a sentence with *Then*.

○ B. Never end a sentence with a preposition.

2. What evidence or source justifies the use of the word *ginormous* in the sentence below?

> Can you really eat that <u>ginormous</u> sandwich?

○ A. The dictionary includes the word *ginormous* and recommends it for informal and humorous contexts.

○ B. Most grammar resources tell users to avoid using slang in formal writing.

3. Does the following sentence break the rules of grammar in an effective way?

> Knowledge of a particular time in history will help you better understand what an essay written during that time period is about.

○ A. Yes, the sentence ends with a preposition, which makes the last part of the sentence "what an essay written during that time period is about" clear and easy to read.

○ B. No, it would be clearer and more effective to follow the rules of grammar and change the last part of the sentence to "the content of an essay written during that time period."

4. Read the dialogue below. What rule of grammar does this excerpt violate?

> What is it, Papa?
>
> It's a treat. For you.
>
> What is it?
>
> Here. Sit down.
>
> from *The Road*, by Cormac McCarthy

○ A. Every line of dialogue needs to identify the speaker.

○ B. Dialogue needs to be set off by quotation marks.

DASHES AND HYPHENS
HYPHENS
sync•skills

Grammar: Hyphens

Hyphens are mostly used to combine words, but they can also be used to divide words.

Rule	Text
You may use a hyphen in a compound adjective that precedes a noun.	That **yearned-for** golden age became even more golden in the imaginations of later medieval writers, who enhanced Geoffrey's legend. Unsolved Mysteries of History
Usually, hyphens are not needed to join a prefix to a word, but there are a few exceptions. • Use a hyphen after any prefix joined to a proper noun or a proper adjective. • Use a hyphen after the prefixes *all-, ex-* (meaning "former"), and *self-*. • Generally, hyphens are used to avoid confusion, such as in words beginning with *re-* that could be mistaken for another word. • Use a hyphen after the prefix *anti-* when it is joined to a word beginning with *i-*.	No complete parallel for the Cadbury fortification has been found anywhere else in **post-Roman** Britain. Conversation with Geoffrey Ashe
Hyphens can be used to create compound nouns by joining words and giving them a unified meaning.	She had once been a lowly **maid-of-all-work** just like Amelia. After the Ball
Hyphenate any compound word that is a spelled-out cardinal number (such as *twenty-one*) or ordinal number (such as *twenty-first*) up to *ninety-nine* or *ninety-ninth*. Hyphenate any spelled-out fraction.	She was **forty-six** years old, of average height and bearing, with an unremarkable face. American Jezebel

YOUR TURN

1. How should this sentence be changed?

> The world's population is growing at an alarming rate—fast enough to double in only forty-three years!

- ○ A. The world's population is—growing at an alarming rate—fast enough to double in only forty-three years!
- ○ B. The world's population is growing at an alarming rate—fast enough to double in only forty three years!
- ○ C. The world's population is growing at an alarming rate-fast enough to double in only forty-three years!
- ○ D. No change needs to be made to this sentence.

2. How should this sentence be changed?

> The op-ed article—the one printed in the local paper—suggested that anti intellectual attitudes were threatening democracy.

- ○ A. The op—ed article—the one printed in the local paper—suggested that anti intellectual attitudes were threatening democracy.
- ○ B. The op-ed article-the one printed in the local paper-suggested that anti intellectual attitudes were threatening democracy.
- ○ C. The op-ed article—the one printed in the local paper—suggested that anti-intellectual attitudes were threatening democracy.
- ○ D. No change needs to be made to this sentence.

3. How should this sentence be changed?

> John F. Kennedy was president of the United States from 1961 to 1963.

- ○ A. John F. Kennedy was president of the United States from 1961-to-1963.
- ○ B. John F. Kennedy was president of the United-States from 1961 to 1963.
- ○ C. John-F.-Kennedy was president of the United States from 1961 to 1963.
- ○ D. No change needs to be made to this sentence.

Research Writing Process: Edit and Publish

| PLAN | DRAFT | REVISE | EDIT AND PUBLISH |

You have revised your informative research essay based on your peer feedback and your own examination.

Now, it is time to edit your informative research essay. When you revised, you focused on the content of your essay. You probably critiqued your research and made sure you paraphrased sources correctly and avoided plagiarism. When you edit, you focus on the mechanics of your essay, paying close attention to things like grammar and punctuation.

Use the checklist below to guide you as you edit:

☐ Have I followed all the rules for hyphens?

☐ Can I defend any contested usage I have chosen? (Consult a style guide, such as *Artful Sentences: Syntax as Style* by Virginia Tufte, as appropriate.)

☐ Do I have any sentence fragments or run-on sentences?

☐ Have I spelled everything correctly?

Notice some edits Rishal has made:

- Hyphenated a compound adjective preceding a noun

- Corrected spelling errors

- Corrected a citation to match the MLA style

- Started a sentence with a conjunctive adverb, instead of the conjunction *and*

Another problem with plastic is that it does not recycle well. Most plastics can be recycled into ~~awful~~ lower-quality material that is only useful for cheap products like ~~sinthetick~~ synthetic fabric and bumper stickers (*The Guardian* Somerville). ~~And~~ In addition, factories that recycle plastics require a great deal of energy, often generating greenhouse gases and other pollution. Although we should continue to recycle as much paper as we have factory space for, recycling plastic is much less ~~effishient~~ efficient.

✏ WRITE

Use the questions in the checklist, as well as your peer reviews, to help you evaluate your informative research essay to determine areas that need editing. Then, edit your informative research essay to correct those errors.

Once you have made all your corrections, you are ready to publish your work. You can distribute your writing to family and friends, hang it on a bulletin board, or post it on your blog. If you publish online, share the link with your family, friends, and classmates.

A Golden Coin

POETRY

Introduction

In the early 1800s, President Thomas Jefferson sent Lewis and Clark on an expedition to explore the unknown western part of the country. Fortunately they hired a Native American woman to guide them. How did she help? How is she remembered today?

VOCABULARY

antique
very old and valuable

counselor
a person who gives advice and helps others

tribute
something that shows respect and admiration for someone

endure
suffer pain or difficulty over a period of time

survivor
someone who lives through very difficult circumstances

NOTES

☰ READ

1 Sleeping in grandfather's **antique** coinbox
2 are silver men of fame
3 long past Presidents.

4 Golden coins, mixed in, show bearded men,
5 names known only to history teachers.
6 Half hidden, a coin shows a golden woman,
7 sleeping infant tied to her back.
8 Despite her coinbox destiny,
9 her **tribute** should be greater.

10 "She deserves better," I say.
11 "Sacagawea of the Shoshone tribe,
12 this **survivor**.
13 She was an admirable ambassador,
14 a peacemaker,
15 a gentle guide,
16 and a **counselor**."

NOTES

17 Could you

18 **endure** floods,

19 cold, heat,

20 swarms of mosquitos like hungry armies?

21 Could you

22 be resourceful in the face of starvation,

23 all with a baby on your back?

24 She was young,

25 friend to Clark, adviser to Lewis.

26 She led them west,

27 speaking to the natives in their languages. They trusted her.

28 A woman and infant, journeying with white men, means peace.

29 I turn the coin over. I see a golden bird in full flight,

30 perhaps an eagle, perhaps a dove,

31 perhaps a symbol for the Shoshone

32 called, by some, "bird woman."

First Read

Read "A Golden Coin." After you read, complete the Think Questions below.

☁ THINK QUESTIONS

1. Who is the subject of the poem?

   The subject of the poem is _____.

2. Why does the speaker think that Sacagawea deserves better?

   The speaker thinks Sacagawea deserves better because _____

   _____ _____.

3. How did Sacagawea help Lewis and Clark? Include a line from the poem to support your response.

   In line _____ Sacagawea helped Lewis and Clark

   by _____.

4. Use context to confirm the meaning of the word *antique* as it is used in "A Golden Coin." Write your definition of *antique* here.

   Antique means _____.

   A context clue is _____.

5. What is another way to ask if someone could *endure* floods, cold, and heat like Sacagawea did?

   Could you _____ floods, cold, heat?

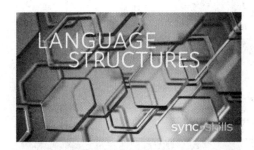

Skill:
Language Structures

★ DEFINE

In every language, there are rules that tell how to **structure** sentences. These rules define the correct order of words. In the English language, for example, a **basic** structure for sentences is subject, verb, and object. Some sentences have more **complicated** structures.

You will encounter both basic and complicated **language structures** in the classroom materials you read. Being familiar with language structures will help you better understand the text.

••• CHECKLIST FOR LANGUAGE STRUCTURES

To improve your comprehension of language structures, do the following:

✓ Monitor your understanding.

- Ask yourself: Why do I not understand this sentence? Is it because I do not understand some of the words? Or is it because I do not understand the way the words are ordered in the sentence?

✓ Break down the sentence into its parts.

- In English, adjectives almost always come before the noun. Example: He had a **big dog**.

  > A **noun** names a person, place, thing, or idea.

  > An **adjective** modifies, or describes, a noun or a pronoun.

  > If there is more than one adjective, they usually appear in the following order separated by a comma: quantity or number, quality or opinion, size, age, shape, color.
    Example: He had a **big, brown dog**.

  > If there is more than one adjective from the same category, include the word *and*.
    Example: He had **a brown and white dog**.

- Ask yourself: What are the nouns in this sentence? What adjectives describe them? In what order are the nouns and adjectives?

✓ Confirm your understanding with a peer or teacher.

Please note that excerpts and passages in the StudySync® library and this workbook are intended as touchstones to generate interest in an author's work. The excerpts and passages do not substitute for the reading of entire texts, and StudySync® strongly recommends that students seek out and purchase the whole literary or informational work in order to experience it as the author intended. Links to online resellers are available in our digital library. In addition, complete works may be ordered through an authorized reseller by filling out and returning to StudySync® the order form enclosed in this workbook.

Reading & Writing
Companion

145

⟳ YOUR TURN

Read each phrase in the chart below. Then complete the chart by sorting the words and images into the adjective, noun, and image columns.

Words and Images	
A	ambassador
B	gentle
C	[image of a smiling person pointing to a path]
D	armies
E	admirable
F	[image of many military people eating in a cafeteria]
G	guide
H	[image of a smiling teenage ambassador, wearing a coat with shiny pins, standing in front of a foreign flag]
I	hungry

Phrase	Adjective	Noun	Image
"She was an admirable ambassador. . ."			
". . .a peacemaker, a gentle guide, and a counselor."			
". . .swarms of mosquitos like hungry armies?"			

Skill: Analyzing and Evaluating Text

★ DEFINE

Analyzing and **evaluating** a text means reading carefully to understand the author's **purpose** and **message**. In informational texts, authors may provide information or opinions on a topic. They may be writing to inform or persuade a reader. In fictional texts, the author may be **communicating** a message or lesson through their story. They may write to entertain, or to teach the reader something about life.

Sometimes authors are clear about their message and purpose. When the message or purpose is not stated directly, readers will need to look closer at the text. Readers can use textual evidence to make inferences about what the author is trying to communicate. By analyzing and evaluating the text, you can form your own thoughts and opinions about what you read.

••• CHECKLIST FOR ANALYZING AND EVALUATING TEXT

In order to analyze and evaluate a text, do the following:

✓ Look for details that show why the author is writing.

- Ask yourself: Is the author trying to inform, persuade, or entertain? What are the main ideas of this text?

✓ Look for details that show what the author is trying to say.

- Ask yourself: What is the author's opinion about this topic? Is there a lesson I can learn from this story?

✓ Form your own thoughts and opinions about the text.

- Ask yourself: Do I agree with the author? Does this message apply to my life?

YOUR TURN

Read lines 4–20 of "A Golden Coin." Then, using the Checklist on the previous page, answer the multiple-choice questions.

---

from **"A Golden Coin"**

Golden coins, mixed in, show bearded men,
names known only to history teachers.
Half hidden, a coin shows a golden woman,
sleeping infant tied to her back.
Despite her coinbox destiny,
her tribute should be greater.

"She deserves better," I say.
"Sacagawea of the Shoshone tribe,
this survivor.
She was an admirable ambassador,
a peacemaker,
a gentle guide,
and a counselor."

Could you
endure floods,
cold, heat,
swarms of mosquitos like hungry armies?

---

1. What is the message or lesson of this poem?

    ○ A. Only images of presidents should be on silver United States coins.
    ○ B. Students would benefit from more facts about historical figures.
    ○ C. The Shoshone tribe became a well-known tribe in history.
    ○ D. Mosquitos are a big problem in the United States.

2. A detail that best supports this conclusion is—

    ○ A. "Golden coins, mixed in, show bearded men, names known only to history teachers."
    ○ B. "She deserves better," I say.
    ○ C. "She was an admirable ambassador, a peacemaker, a gentle guide, and a counselor."
    ○ D. "Could you endure floods, cold, heat, swarms of mosquitos like hungry armies?"

3. Which line from the poem suggests that the poet is trying to relate to the reader?

    ○ A. "Sleeping in grandfather's antique coinbox are silver men of fame long past Presidents."
    ○ B. "Golden coins, mixed in, show bearded men, names known only to history teachers."
    ○ C. "Sacagawea of the Shoshone tribe, this survivor."
    ○ D. "Could you endure floods, cold, heat, swarms of mosquitos like hungry armies?"

Please note that excerpts and passages in the StudySync® library and this workbook are intended as touchstones to generate interest in an author's work. The excerpts and passages do not substitute for the reading of entire texts, and StudySync® strongly recommends that students seek out and purchase the whole literary or informational work in order to experience it as the author intended. Links to online resellers are available in our digital library. In addition, complete works may be ordered through an authorized reseller by filling out and returning to StudySync® the order form enclosed in this workbook.

Reading & Writing Companion   **149**

Close Read

✏ WRITE

INFORMATIONAL: In the poem "A Golden Coin," the author claims that Sacagawea's "tribute" should be greater than a coin in a coinbox. How does Sacagawea's life merit a greater tribute? Write a paragraph in which you explain why Sacagawea's life deserves to be celebrated and remembered. Pay attention to and edit for *ea* and *a+consonant+e* spelling rules.

Use the checklist below to guide you as you write.

☐ Why is Sacagawea considered an important historical figure?

☐ What details about Sacagawea's life should be celebrated?

☐ How should Modern Americans remember Sacagawea?

Use the sentence frames to organize and write your argument.

Modern Americans should remember Sacagawea because _____.

Sacagawea should be celebrated because _____.

For example, _____.

Sacagawea should be remembered as a symbol of _____

because she was "_____."

I _____ with the poet because _____

_____.

A Modern Man

Introduction

Charles Dickens is probably best known for being an author of novels like *A Christmas Carol* and *Oliver Twist*. However, his influence in our society today expands well beyond the pages of a book. Charles Dickens inspired people to make changes by using his talent of writing. For example, his works have inspired improvements for people with disabilities, people living in poverty, as well as the conditions of communities suffering from pollution. Although Dickens will always be known for his entertaining writing, today we have him to thank for many of society's advancements.

VOCABULARY

influence

to affect or have an impact on

industrialization

the development of different businesses and types of work on a large scale

pollution

the presence of something harmful or poisonous in one's environment

condition

a state of something, especially regarding its quality

NOTES

☰ READ

A Modern Man from the 1800s: The Influential Life of Charles Dickens

1   "Bah! Humbug!" Perhaps you have heard someone say this phrase around the holiday season. This person is probably tired of waiting in long lines at the store, hearing the same songs on the radio, and spending money on gifts for others. We often call this person a "scrooge."

2   Scrooge was originally a character in Charles Dickens's famous novel *A Christmas Carol*. This reference is extremely popular in modern-day society even though the novel it comes from was written in 1843. Today, Dickens is well-known for his literature, but he has **influenced** society in many other ways as well. Using his talent for writing, Charles Dickens was able to enlighten his readers on the issues threatening England during the 19th century. Without his influence, our lives would have been very different today. Charles Dickens was a writer living in the 1800s, but he is considered a modern man for improving society as we know it.

3   Four of Charles Dickens's novels in particular inspired great change in 19th-century England that we still see today. The following novels served as the catalysts for improving the lives of people with disabilities, lending a helping hand to those living in poverty, reigniting the Christmas spirit, and creating laws concerning **pollution**.

NOTES

The Pickwick Papers, 1836

4   *The Pickwick Papers* was the first novel that Charles Dickens published. In this story, a character named Joe is an overweight boy who has trouble staying awake. He falls asleep at random times, no matter what he is doing. When Dickens wrote about Joe's disability in 1836, there was not a name for it. However, over 100 years later, doctors decided that Joe's sleeping problem described in *The Pickwick Papers* was an actual medical **condition**. In fact, today, when people experience the same symptoms as Joe, they are often diagnosed with "Pickwickian Syndrome." Thanks to Charles Dickens, this disability has a name. As a result of Dickens's novel, Pickwickian Syndrome was recognized as a legitimate condition, and now people can get the help they need.

Oliver Twist, 1837

5   In *Oliver Twist*, the main character is a poor, hungry orphan who steals in order to survive. This popular story shocked many people in 19th-century England. The upper class, or members of society who had money, didn't know that children were living like this on the streets of England in real life. Inspired by the novel *Oliver Twist*, many wealthy people realized that charity begins at home.

Brook Street Ragged and Industrial School, Hampstead Road, London

This prompted the upper class to donate food, clothing, and money to help those in need. In addition, Charles Dickens's story led to the creation of "ragged schools," which were schools that were built in poor communities. These schools helped to educate children who previously had no access to a school. Today, all students can receive an education in the public school system, no matter if they are rich or poor.

A Christmas Carol, 1843

6   Arguably Dickens's most famous story, *A Christmas Carol*, defined the holiday season as we know it. During the **industrialization** of England throughout the early 1800s, Christmas was not celebrated like it is today. In fact, most people worked on Christmas day. People didn't think of Christmas as a time with family, for getting presents, or eating food. However, that all changed after Charles Dickens wrote *A Christmas Carol* in 1843. His novel showed Christmas as a

Mr. Fezziwig's Ball from *A Christmas Carol*, 1843. Artist: John Leech

NOTES

party with loved ones, a lavish feast, and even snow! Once this novel became popular, the celebration of Christmas changed and became more like the holiday season we know today. For this reason, Charles Dickens is known as "The Man Who Invented Christmas."

7   Similar to Dickens's novel *The Pickwick Papers*, *A Christmas Carol* also inspired members of society to view people with disabilities more positively. In *A Christmas Carol*, a character named Tiny Tim has a physical disability that prevents him from walking without his crutches. Tiny Tim touched the hearts of many due to his kind nature and loving spirit. This fictional character really inspired a man named William Treloar. Treloar decided to open a college and hospital in England for people with disabilities. Thanks to Dickens's writing, more people like William Treloar started to accept and help people with disabilities. Through his writing, Dickens encouraged society to develop resources for people with disabilities. This idea is still popular today. Now, it is easy to find and support charities and events for people with disabilities, such as the Special Olympics.

Bleak House, 1852

8   Charles Dickens wrote the novel *Bleak House* in 1852. In this story, a character named Jo is a sweeper who cleans the polluted streets of England. Like *Oliver Twist*, this book inspired many citizens of England to address the filthy living conditions in their own communities. Thanks to *Bleak House*, the conditions of the roads and neighborhoods greatly improved. Also, this book brought attention to the importance of hygiene and cleanliness worldwide.

9   Dickens helped with the pollution problem in the streets of England, but a man named Charles Babbage wanted his help with a different kind of pollution: noise pollution. Babbage was an inventor and engineer who lived in London, and he had a problem with the excessive noise coming from the street musicians outside of his home. Since Babbage knew that Charles Dickens was such an inspirational man, he enlisted his help in this fight against noise. Sure enough, actions spoke louder than words, or in this case, noise. Working together, Dickens and Babbage helped pass a law against noise disturbances. Babbage even wrote a book about his quest to end unnecessary noise in the streets of England, and Dickens contributed to it. In one line, Dickens wrote that he was "daily interrupted, harassed, worried, wearied, driven nearly mad, by street musicians." This law against excessive street noise is still enforced today.

10   If Charles Dickens had not written his famous novels, our world would be very different today. His works inspired charity, education, acceptance, celebration, cleanliness, and even some peace and quiet. Dickens's legacy can inspire us to speak up about the issues affecting our modern-day society. Charles Dickens was an author living in 19th-century England, but his relevance still lives strong today.

First Read

Read "A Modern Man from the 1800s: The Influential Life of Charles Dickens." After you read, complete the Think Questions below.

☁ **THINK QUESTIONS**

1. Who is Charles Dickens? When did he live?

   Charles Dickens is _____.

   He lived _____.

2. Write two or three sentences describing how *A Christmas Carol* affected society.

   A Chistmas Carol affected society _____

   _____

   _____.

3. How did Dickens help make the world a better place? Include a line from the text to support your response.

   In paragraph _____ Dickens _____.

4. Use context to confirm the meaning of the word *condition* as it is used in "A Modern Man from the 1800s: The Influential Life of Charles Dickens." Write your definition of *condition* here.

   Condition means _____.

   A context clue is _____.

5. What is another way to say that someone has "influenced" society?

   Someone has _____.

Skill:
Analyzing Expressions

 DEFINE

When you read, you may find English expressions that you do not know. An **expression** is a group of words that communicates an idea. Three types of expressions are idioms, sayings, and figurative language. They can be difficult to understand because the meanings of the words are different from their **literal**, or usual, meanings.

An **idiom** is an expression that is commonly known among a group of people. For example, "It's raining cats and dogs" means it is raining heavily. **Sayings** are short expressions that contain advice or wisdom. For instance, "Don't count your chickens before they hatch" means do not plan on something good happening before it happens. **Figurative** language is when you describe something by comparing it with something else, either directly (using the words *like* or *as*) or indirectly. For example, "I'm as hungry as a horse" means I'm very hungry. None of the expressions are about actual animals.

••• CHECKLIST FOR ANALYZING EXPRESSIONS

To determine the meaning of an expression, remember the following:

✓ If you find a confusing group of words, it may be an expression. The meaning of words in expressions may not be their literal meaning.

- Ask yourself: Is this confusing because the words are new? Or because the words do not make sense together?

✓ Determining the overall meaning may require that you use one or more of the following:

- context clues

- a dictionary or other resource

- teacher or peer support

✓ Highlight important information before and after the expression to look for clues.

YOUR TURN

Read the conversations in the chart below. Then use the context clues to match the correct meaning to the excerpts.

Meanings	
A	Do not criticize other people for doing the same bad things that you have done.
B	Things that other people have always seem better than the things that you have.
C	You can give a person knowledge and resources, but you cannot force them to do something.

Excerpts	Meaning
Alex: "I already told you how to make a grilled cheese sandwich. Everything you need is in the kitchen. It's easy." Donny: "No, I can't do it. Just do it for me." Alex: "I guess **you can lead a horse to water but you can't make him drink**, huh?"	
Kerry: "You're so lucky to have a sister!" Linda: "What? No, I would rather have a little brother like you do!" Kerry: "I guess **the grass is always greener on the other side.**"	
Dan: "Gary said I cheated at a card game last night. Then he got quiet when I explained that he was caught cheating on a test last week." Samantha: "He needs to learn that **people who live in glass houses should not throw stones!**"	

Skill: Visual and Contextual Support

★ DEFINE

Visual support is an image or an object that helps you understand a text. **Contextual support** is a **feature** that helps you understand a text. By using visual and contextual supports, you can develop your vocabulary so you can better understand a variety of texts.

First, preview the text to identify any visual supports. These might include illustrations, graphics, charts, or other objects in a text. Then, identify any contextual supports. Examples of contextual supports are titles, headers, captions, and boldface terms. Write down your **observations**.

Then, write down what those visual and contextual supports tell you about the meaning of the text. Note any new vocabulary that you see in those supports. Ask your peers and your teacher to **confirm** your understanding of the text.

••• CHECKLIST FOR VISUAL AND CONTEXTUAL SUPPORT

To use visual and contextual support to understand texts, do the following:

✓ Preview the text. Read the title, headers, and other features. Look at any images and graphics.

✓ Write down the visual and contextual supports in the text.

✓ Write down what those supports tell you about the text.

✓ Note any new vocabulary that you see in those supports.

✓ Create an illustration for the reading and write a descriptive caption.

✓ Confirm your observations with your peers and teacher.

YOUR TURN

Read the examples below. Then, complete the chart by sorting the examples into those that are visual supports and those that are contextual supports.

Examples	
A	graphics
B	titles
C	boldface terms
D	captions
E	headers
F	photographs
G	illustrations
H	charts

Visual Supports	Contextual Supports

Please note that excerpts and passages in the StudySync® library and this workbook are intended as touchstones to generate interest in an author's work. The excerpts and passages do not substitute for the reading of entire texts, and StudySync® strongly recommends that students seek out and purchase the whole literary or informational work in order to experience it as the author intended. Links to online resellers are available in our digital library. In addition, complete works may be ordered through an authorized reseller by filling out and returning to StudySync® the order form enclosed in this workbook.

Reading & Writing Companion   **159**

Close Read

✎ WRITE

PERSONAL NARRATIVE: The author of "A Modern Man from the 1800s: The Influential Life of Charles Dickens" claims that Charles Dickens has influenced modern society in several ways. How has an author or piece of fiction influenced you in your personal life? Describe a time when you acted or thought differently after reading a piece of literature. Pay attention to and edit for main and helping verbs.

Use the checklist below to guide you as you write.

☐ What author or piece of fiction has influenced you to change?

☐ How did you think or act before you read the story?

☐ How did you think or act afterward? Why?

Use the sentence frames to organize and write your personal narrative.

I (acted / thought) _____ differently after reading _____ .

I was influenced by _____ .

The (lesson / theme / main idea) _____ of the text _____

Before I read the story, I _____ .

After I read the story, I _____ .

The story changed the way I _____ .

studysync®

ASSIGNMENTS   BINDER   LIBRARY

Fractured Selves

UNIT 5

Fractured Selves

What causes individuals to feel alienated?

Genre Focus: ARGUMENTATIVE

Texts

 Paired Readings

166   Literary Focus: Modernism

174   The Great Figure
       POETRY   William Carlos Williams

177   The Love Song of J. Alfred Prufrock
       POETRY   T.S. Eliot

190   miss rosie
       POETRY   Lucille Clifton

192   The Idler
       POETRY   Alice Dunbar-Nelson

195   A Cup of Tea
       FICTION   Katherine Mansfield

210   The Glass Menagerie
       DRAMA   Tennessee Williams

227   A Room of One's Own
       ARGUMENTATIVE TEXT   Virginia Woolf

231   The New Dress
       FICTION   Virginia Woolf

239   Hurricane Season
       POETRY   Fareena Arefeen

242   Be Ye Men of Valour
       ARGUMENTATIVE TEXT   Winston Churchill

254   The Pearl Divers' Daughters
       POETRY   Marcia Calabretta Cancio-Bello

257   Killers of the Dream
       INFORMATIONAL TEXT   Lillian Smith

261   Shooting an Elephant
       INFORMATIONAL TEXT   George Orwell

Extended Writing Project and Grammar

277 | **Plan**

Reasons and Relevant Evidence
Thesis Statement
Organizing Argumentative Writing

289 | **Draft**

Introductions
Transitions
Conclusions

302 | **Revise**

Using a Style Guide
Grammar: Commonly Misspelled Words
Grammar: Pronoun Case and Reference

311 | **Edit and Publish**

English Language Learner Resources

313 | **Fear of Missing Out**
INFORMATIONAL TEXT

322 | **The Ribbons**
FICTION

What causes individuals to feel alienated?

FAREENA AREFEEN

High schooler Fareena Arefeen was Houston's Youth Poet Laureate in 2016. Her one-year term included delivering public readings in the area and representing her city's youth, and she received a book deal and a scholarship to college. Arefeen, who moved to Texas from Bangladesh with her mother and sister, sees a mission beyond personal recognition in her role. "I want to tell other immigrants, like me, that their stories matter," she says. She plans to attend New York University.

MARCI CALABRETTA CANCIO-BELLO

Miami-based poet Marci Calabretta Cancio-Bello (b. 1989) was born in South Korea and adopted as a baby to a family in upstate New York. The idea for a poem published in her award-winning collection *Hour of the Ox* (2016) came to Cancio-Bello in the process of researching her Korean heritage. She became fascinated to learn about the dying art of pearl diving and wondered if she could be descended from its early practitioners.

WINSTON CHURCHILL

Twice the prime minister of the United Kingdom, Winston Churchill (1874–1965) led a successful Allied strategy with the United States and the Soviet Union to defeat Nazi Germany in World War II. He won the Nobel Prize for Literature in 1953 "for his mastery of historical and biographical description as well as for brilliant oratory in defending exalted human values." He remains one of the most quoted figures in English-speaking history and is credited for coining the word *summit* in 1950.

LUCILLE CLIFTON

American poet Lucille Clifton (1936–2010) is known for her concise language, carefully wrought lines, and the complexity she draws through straightforward images. Her poems confront and celebrate African American experience, capturing the lives of heroes and everyday characters alike. Clifton's work received many awards in her lifetime, and in 1987 she earned the distinction of the first author to ever have two books of poetry nominated for the Pulitzer Prize in the same year.

ALICE DUNBAR-NELSON

The writer Alice Dunbar-Nelson (1875–1935) was born in New Orleans. Her African American, Anglo, Creole, and Native American heritage offered Dunbar-Nelson, according to her writing, a racially ambiguous appearance, which in turn allowed her mobility among various social classes and ethnicities. Dunbar-Nelson published poetry, plays, fiction, essays, and journalism in her lifetime. She is also one of the few African American diarists of the 20th century in the published record.

T. S. ELIOT

Author of "The Waste Land," which is widely considered the most influential work of 20th-century literature, T. S. Eliot (1888–1965) was born in St. Louis, Missouri. After earning his undergraduate degree at Harvard, Eliot moved to England, becoming a British citizen in 1927. He worked as a bank clerk as well as a literary critic and publisher. His poetry was noted as radical and innovative in style, as he gave expression to the dissatisfaction his generation felt in the wake of World War I.

KATHERINE MANSFIELD

Katherine Mansfield (1888–1923) was born in New Zealand and died in France at the age of thirty-four from tuberculosis. In her brief life, she was known as a pioneer of the Modernist short story. Mansfield was very prolific in her final years, and at the time of her death, much of her work had yet to be published. Upon hearing the news of her death, her friend and contemporary Virginia Woolf wrote in her diary, "I was jealous of her writing—the only writing I have ever been jealous of."

GEORGE ORWELL

"What I have most wanted to do," wrote the English author George Orwell (1903–1950), "is make political writing into an art." Born in Myanmar (known as Burma at the time) and raised in England, Orwell knew he wanted to be a writer from a young age. His experiences working as a colonial police officer in India and fighting in the Spanish Civil War inform many of his stories and essays, which critique social inequality and totalitarianism.

LILLIAN SMITH

American author Lillian Smith (1897–1966) critiqued the values upheld by her community of white Southerners in the era of Jim Crow, stating, "segregation is evil." Her 1944 novel *Strange Fruit*, which features an interracial love story, was so controversial that the United States Postal Service refused to mail it. She was an early and ardent supporter of the civil rights movement, and continued to write until her death from cancer in 1966.

TENNESSEE WILLIAMS

American playwright Tennessee Williams (1911-1983) grew up in Columbus, Mississippi and St. Louis, Missouri, and recalls a childhood scarred by his parents' tense marriage. He began to write during this time, and would later base characters like Amanda Wingfield in *The Glass Menagerie* and Big Daddy in *Cat on a Hot Tin Roof* on his mother and father. Williams' plays are known for transforming American theater by bringing forth characters more dark and complex than had ever been seen before.

WILLIAM CARLOS WILLIAMS

The American Modernist poet William Carlos Williams (1883–1963) worked as a family doctor in Rutherford, New Jersey, scribbling lines on his prescription blanks in between patient visits. He crafted the language in his poems to mirror the patterns of everyday speech, which he saw as a distinctly American project. In his epic poem *Paterson,* Williams writes, "Any poem that has any worth expresses the whole life of the poet."

VIRGINIA WOOLF

The work of Virginia Woolf (1882–1941) received renewed attention long after her lifetime in the second wave of feminism in the 1970s. Woolf was a prominent writer of essays and Modernist novels in London during the period between World War I and World War II. Woolf's fiction employed stream-of-consciousness and female-driven narrative. Her book-length essay *A Room of One's Own* (1929) argued for the importance of creating space for women writers in a male-dominated literary tradition.

Modernism

Introduction

This informational text provides readers with historical and cultural information about the early 20th century and the formation of Modernism. The onset of the Great War and the breakdown of colonialism led to unprecedented work among artists who were intent on defying old rules and values. Modernist painters, such as Pablo Picasso, and writers, such as T. S. Eliot, were disillusioned by the manipulation of power and technology and the dreadful effects that the Great War had had on society. Modernists attempted to deal with their frightening reality by creating work that challenged age-old institutions and principles.

"Inspiring heroes and happy endings were no longer a requirement for good writing."

1   Throughout the history of storytelling, animals have been used to impart lessons to audiences. There are the trickster gods of various cultures, like the western Native Americans' Coyote, India's Hanuman the monkey, and Anansi the spider from West Africa. Aesop used animal characters so frequently in his fables that it became a defining characteristic of the genre. More recent stories with animal characters are Rudyard Kipling's collection *The Jungle Book,* published in 1894, and George Orwell's *Animal Farm,* published in 1945. Despite the surface similarities, however, these two works send remarkably different messages. In *The Jungle Book,* Mowgli, a human raised by wolves, learns to obey the "law of the jungle" and find his place in their social order. In *Animal Farm,* a group of farm animals overthrows the human farmers and tries to set up their own society. Under the guise of furthering equality, the cunning pigs compete with one another to take over, ultimately creating a horrifying dictatorship. In less than fifty years, popular books went from praising the virtues of societies to making sharp condemnations of their oppressive elements. This sudden change reflects the cultural revolution of Modernism, a movement that broke all the rules by creating new aesthetic forms that departed from the past.

A Shrinking Empire

2   Rudyard Kipling and George Orwell are two of Britain's best known writers. Both were born in India and lived in British colonies for parts of their childhoods and adult lives. Both experienced British **imperialism** firsthand, but they had completely opposite opinions of it. This difference can be attributed to the dominant cultures of their generations. Kipling was born in 1865, and so his views are representative of the late Victorian era. Kipling thought imperialism fueled growth and progress and, like many in the Victorian era, he sincerely believed that the British were civilizing the world. He became known as a strong supporter of British colonialism.

NOTES

Storming of Delhi, Thomas H. Sherratt & Matthew Somerville Morgan (1857). Depiction of the Sepoy uprising (1857–1858) against British rule, known as the Indian Mutiny.

3   Orwell was born in 1903. He didn't witness the explosive growth of the British Empire or see how it brought new resources and wealth to the United Kingdom. Instead, he witnessed its human costs. As a young man, Orwell worked for the Indian Imperial Police in Burma (now Myanmar). He saw growing resentment from the Burmese people living under British rule. He saw the British Empire taking advantage of their labor and resources while enforcing a social hierarchy where the colonists were on top and the indigenous people were on the bottom. Orwell was so ashamed of the role he played in this injustice that he eventually resigned from his job and turned to writing.

4   When the British Empire peaked in the early twentieth century, it controlled about a quarter of the world's population. In the coming decades, however, its control would begin to shrink. The shrinking of the empire began close to home. All but six of the counties of Ireland, Britain's first colony, broke off from the United Kingdom to form the Irish Free State in 1922. India and Pakistan followed in 1947, then Sri Lanka and Burma in 1948, Ghana in 1957, to name a few. Several factors allowed these countries to free themselves from British rule. There was a growth in nationalism and a desire for independence within the colonies. There was also a growing distaste for imperialism among the British. More and more people living under British rule were siding with George Orwell in the belief that "civilizing the world" while pillaging its resources and exploiting indigenous people was wrong. A key part of the Modernist movement was a rebellion against older traditions, including colonialism, and this was partially due to a strong sense of disillusionment, particularly after World War I.

World at War

5   The United Kingdom of Great Britain and Northern Ireland was the strongest empire of the time leading up to World War I, but not the only one. France, having recovered from a series of revolutions and regime changes, began

competing with Britain for control of Africa. Russia, the Ottoman Empire, and Austro-Hungarian Empire competed for control of Eastern Europe. In the middle of all of this, Germany gained power with such rapidity that Great Britain made alliances with Russia and France, despite their being historical enemies. Borders shifted, governments rose and fell, and alliances formed and broke. When a Serbian assassin killed Archduke Franz Ferdinand of Austria-Hungary, it sparked a **conflagration.** Country after country declared war to support their allies or oppose their enemies. World War I had begun.

Battle of Ypres, (1915) by Achille Beltrame.
The effects of poison gases in World War I.

6   The Great War, as it was called at the time, was brutal. Young soldiers had grown up on stories of glorious charges into the enemy line to fight with rifles and bayonets. They were unprepared for machine guns and mustard gas. They did not expect to spend weeks hiding in filthy trenches while listening to the sounds of gunshots and explosions. By the end of the war in 1919, 8.5 million soldiers were dead. More people were killed in WWI than in every previous European conflict combined. The scale of the bloodshed and destruction disillusioned a generation of artists and thinkers who would be central to Modernism. The Central Powers, consisting of the German, Austro-Hungarian, and Ottoman Empires, had all broken up. The Russian Empire also dissolved and was replaced by the Soviet Union. Germany suffered two economic crises while trying to pay reparations, which led to feelings of resentment. This fueled extremism, leading to the rise of Adolf Hitler and the Second World War.

7   World War II was even more brutal than its predecessor, leaving 40–50 million dead. The United Kingdom was among the victors, but it had suffered immensely from the war. Germany used a tactic they called *Blitzkrieg,* literally "lightning war." From September 1940 to May 1941, the German Air Force, or *Luftwaffe,* conducted nighttime bombing raids targeting London and other major British cities. By targeting civilians, they had hoped to demoralize

Please note that excerpts and passages in the StudySync® library and this workbook are intended as touchstones to generate interest in an author's work. The excerpts and passages do not substitute for the reading of entire texts, and StudySync® strongly recommends that students seek out and purchase the whole literary or informational work in order to experience it as the author intended. Links to online resellers are available in our digital library. In addition, complete works may be ordered through an authorized reseller by filling out and returning to StudySync® the order form enclosed in this workbook.

Reading & Writing
Companion

169

Britain and force them out of the war. Germany failed to kill the British spirit, but they did do severe damage to their cities and infrastructure. Also, with so many young people dead, the government needed to organize a way to care for the unemployed, the sick, and the elderly. Under the Labour Party, the UK government created a system of national health care. Between this and rebuilding, the United Kingdom had little money left for running an empire. Most of the remaining colonies of the British Empire gained independence in quick succession. Some of the British felt embarrassed by this loss of stature, but others were relieved to be finished with imperialism.

A New World

8   The seeds of Modernism began to sprout before the First World War, but it was between the wars that the movement truly flourished. War had not only devastated the world physically, it was a shock to the psyche as well. The British—as well as Continental Europeans—began to question whether imperialism was really spreading civilization. They also realized that the world was not as beautiful or polite as the Romantics and Victorians had claimed. Improved technology had promised better communication and more productive lives, but it was used to create unimaginable destruction during the war. Suddenly, people felt that everything they thought they knew about the world was wrong. Modernism was a search for a new way to look at the world. Modernists felt that the old forms of art depicting Western civilization needed to be recreated in order to still have meaning. Their movement was a rebellion against old traditions and conventions.

Modernist painter Pablo Picasso posing with paintings and ceramics.

9   Modernism took hold in visual arts before it spread to literature. Artists became less interested in trying to create realistic depictions of the world around them. Cubism, developed by Georges Braque and Pablo Picasso, rejected conventions of perspective, foreshortening, modeling, and chiaroscuro, or contrasting light and shade. Instead, Cubists used sharp, geometric angles to create a fragmented vision of the world. They would show multiple sides of a subject at the same time, creating a new view of reality. **Surrealism** also became popular. Surrealist art, influenced by Sigmund Freud and his system of psychoanalysis, intentionally defied reason by combining dreamlike images and reality. Other Modernist art movements include Futurism, Expressionism, Post-impressionism, Constructivism, de Stijl, and Abstract Expressionism. These various movements did not try to directly replicate a visual scene; they tried to capture movement, thought, emotion, and other abstractions that can't normally be portrayed on a canvas.

10   The artistic and literary communities of Modernism mingled frequently. Gertrude Stein, a writer and leader within the Modernist movement, hosted artists in her Paris salon such as Picasso, Braque, and Henri Matisse, and writers like Ernest Hemingway, F. Scott Fitzgerald, Ezra Pound, and Sherwood Anderson. It was inevitable that Modernist rebellions would spread to the written word. For example, Imagist poetry, which presents an image and lets the reader interpret it freely, has parallels to the Cubist method of presenting a subject from multiple perspectives. Futurism, an artistic movement that captured dynamic movement in a single image, can be compared to stream-of-consciousness writing. **Stream of consciousness,** pioneered by Virginia Woolf and James Joyce, mimics the free-flowing thoughts, feelings, and memories of a person's internal monologue. This style often seems chaotic and ignores strict rules of grammar, since a person's thoughts are not normally as clean and ordered as most prose writing.

11   Modernist writers also broke the rules when it came to themes and subject matter. They would openly discuss sexuality, criticize religion, and violate other taboos. Nothing was off-limits, and this openness was refreshing for many. Many people were reeling from the horrors of war and experiencing a sense of **alienation** from modern life. The public related to stories of flawed protagonists who were overwhelmed by despair. Inspiring heroes and happy endings were no longer a requirement for good writing. This can be seen clearly in T. S. Eliot's poem *The Waste Land,* which reflects the widespread feelings of disillusionment and disgust that followed World War I. Modernist writers broke away from traditional literary forms and values to create the classics of a new literature, wherein reality might be redefined not by fidelity to exterior appearances but by the patterns of myth or the flow of the subconscious mind.

12 **Major Concepts**

- **Class, Colonialism, and War**—In the first half of the century, Britain's power was challenged by conflict between the upper and lower classes, resistance to colonialism abroad, and the outbreak of World War I. These years brought a deep sense of disillusionment that permeated British writing, as writers responded to the profound changes in Britain's life and culture leading up to World War II.

- **Women's Rights**—Women comprised another disaffected group who sought greater political power in the early twentieth century. The suffrage movement in Britain, which had long been working peacefully to secure votes for women, took a bold new direction, and British suffragettes used unusual publicity stunts to call attention to their demands. The British government finally relented and gave women over thirty the right to vote in 1918; ten years later, the voting age was lowered to twenty-one.

Style and Form

13 **Modernist Literature**

- Modernist writing was about breaking traditions, both literary and social. For instance, poets used free verse instead of rhyme and meter, and writers challenged social norms regarding social class and women's traditional roles.

- Modernist writers did not view reality as a recognizable constant; rather, reality depended on each person's fragmented or subjective perception of it. "Look within," suggested Virginia Woolf. Woolf and other writers, including Katherine Mansfield and James Joyce, concentrated on writing about "an ordinary mind on an ordinary day."

- Sigmund Freud's system of psychoanalysis contributed to the focus on the internal life of a character and spurred Surrealism and related literary innovations, and his influence is felt in stream-of-consciousness writing focusing on the internal psychological struggles within characters.

14 The twentieth century was a traumatic time for many. Technology, philosophy, international relations: almost every aspect of life was turned on its head. Modernism was a new movement for a new world. The old rules had lost their credibility, so artists and writers needed to find new ways to view and comprehend reality. Modernist writers pioneered a variety of styles and techniques that writers use today. What are some examples of writers, filmmakers, musicians, and artists who continue to break conventions?

Copyright © BookheadEd Learning, LLC

Literary Focus

Read "Literary Focus: Modernism." After you read, complete the Think Questions below.

☁ THINK QUESTIONS

1. How do the lives and writings of Rudyard Kipling and George Orwell reflect the change in attitudes in the early 20th century? Use evidence from the text to support your answer.

2. How did the World Wars shape the Modernist movement? Use evidence from the text to support your answer.

3. What are some of the ways Modernism broke conventions? Use evidence from the text to support your answer.

4. Use context clues to determine the meaning of the word **imperialism**. Write your best definition here, along with the words and phrases that were most helpful in determining the word's meaning. Then, check a dictionary to confirm your understanding.

5. The word *alienation* likely stems from the Latin *alienatus*, meaning "separated." With this information in mind, write your best definition of the word **alienation** as it is used in this text. Cite any words or phrases that were particularly helpful in coming to your conclusion.

Please note that excerpts and passages in the StudySync® library and this workbook are intended as touchstones to generate interest in an author's work. The excerpts and passages do not substitute for the reading of entire texts, and StudySync® strongly recommends that students seek out and purchase the whole literary or informational work in order to experience it as the author intended. Links to online resellers are available in our digital library. In addition, complete works may be ordered through an authorized reseller by filling out and returning to StudySync® the order form enclosed in this workbook.

Reading & Writing Companion   **173**

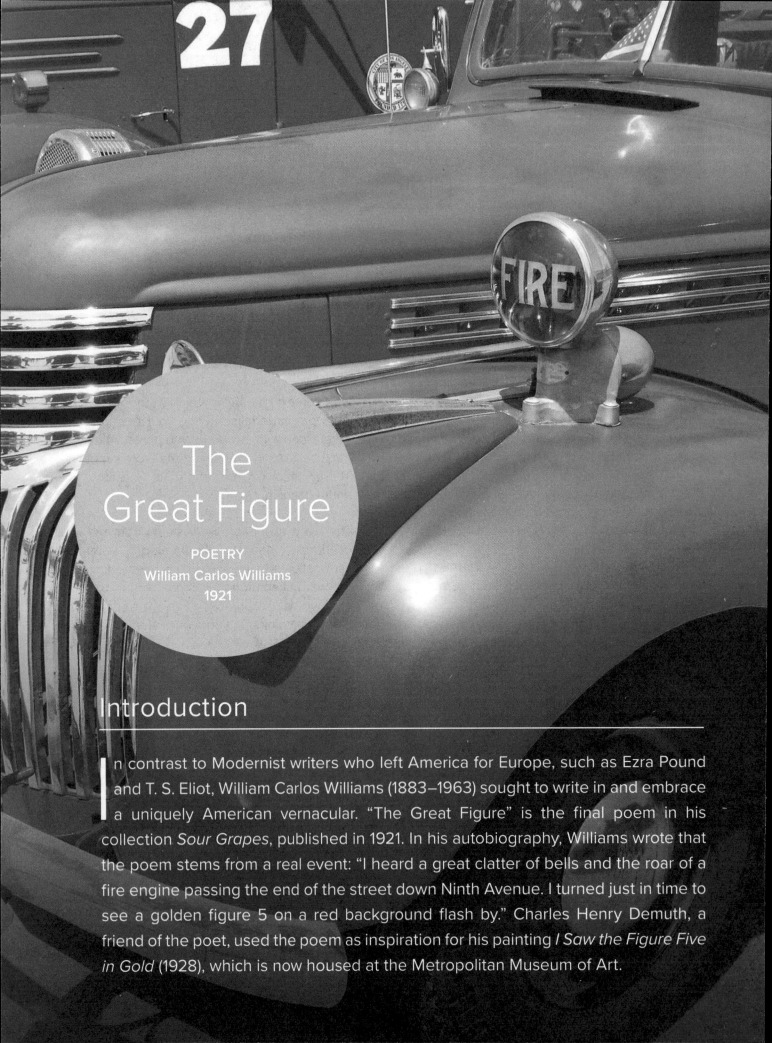

The Great Figure

POETRY
William Carlos Williams
1921

Introduction

In contrast to Modernist writers who left America for Europe, such as Ezra Pound and T. S. Eliot, William Carlos Williams (1883–1963) sought to write in and embrace a uniquely American vernacular. "The Great Figure" is the final poem in his collection *Sour Grapes*, published in 1921. In his autobiography, Williams wrote that the poem stems from a real event: "I heard a great clatter of bells and the roar of a fire engine passing the end of the street down Ninth Avenue. I turned just in time to see a golden figure 5 on a red background flash by." Charles Henry Demuth, a friend of the poet, used the poem as inspiration for his painting *I Saw the Figure Five in Gold* (1928), which is now housed at the Metropolitan Museum of Art.

"Among the rain / and lights / I saw the figure 5"

1   Among the rain
2   and lights
3   I saw the figure 5
4   in gold
5   on a red
6   firetruck
7   moving
8   with weight and **urgency**
9   **tense**
10 **unheeded**
11 to **gong** clangs
12 siren howls
13 and wheels rumbling
14 through the dark city.

I Saw the Figure 5 in Gold, by Charles Demuth (1928) was inspired by William Carlos Williams' poem, "The Great Figure."

Williams, William Carlos. "The Great Figure." *Sour Grapes*. Boston: The Four Seas Company, 1921.

Please note that excerpts and passages in the StudySync® library and this workbook are intended as touchstones to generate interest in an author's work. The excerpts and passages do not substitute for the reading of entire texts, and StudySync® strongly recommends that students seek out and purchase the whole literary or informational work in order to experience it as the author intended. Links to online resellers are available in our digital library. In addition, complete works may be ordered through an authorized reseller by filling out and returning to StudySync® the order form enclosed in this workbook.

Reading & Writing Companion   175

WRITE

PERSONAL NARRATIVE: Write about a seemingly minor event that affected you enough that you continue to remember it. Your response can be a poem, short story, or personal narrative. Be sure to provide specific details about the sights and sounds of the event, as Williams does in "The Great Figure." You may also include your thoughts and emotions about the event and why you continue to remember it.

The Love Song of J. Alfred Prufrock

POETRY
T.S. Eliot
1915

Introduction

Born in St. Louis to an old New England family, T. S. Eliot (1888–1965) was educated at Harvard, the Sorbonne, and Oxford, and received the Nobel Prize for Literature in 1948 for his boldly innovative and influential style. "The Love Song of J. Alfred Prufrock" demonstrates Eliot's characteristic stream of consciousness and versatility with diction. The poem marked a shift in poetic tradition from Romantic verse and Georgian lyrics to Modernism. Filled with allusions to other written works, Elliot takes the reader on a sentimental journey of a gentleman as he questions his life and worth.

"I should have been a pair of ragged claws Scuttling across the floors of silent seas."

NOTES

Skill:
Poetic Elements
and Structure

Eliot begins the poem with an epigraph that is in another language. This epigraph is most likely from another literary work. Eliot assumes that his reader can read this other language or is familiar with the work.

"The Love Song of J. Alfred Prufrock"

1 *S'io credesse che mia risposta fosse*
2 *A persona che mai tornasse al mondo,*
3 *Questa fiamma staria senza piu scosse.*
4 *Ma perciocche giammai di questo fondo*
5 *Non torno vivo alcun, s'i'odo il vero,*
6 *Senza tema d'infamia ti rispondo.*

7 Let us go then, you and I,
8 When the evening is spread out against the sky
9 Like a patient **etherized** upon a table;
10 Let us go, through certain half-deserted streets,
11 The muttering retreats
12 Of restless nights in one-night cheap hotels
13 And sawdust restaurants with oyster-shells:
14 Streets that follow like a **tedious** argument
15 Of **insidious** intent
16 To lead you to an overwhelming question . . .
17 Oh, do not ask, "What is it?"
18 Let us go and make our visit.

19 In the room the women come and go
20 Talking of Michelangelo[1].

21 The yellow fog that rubs its back upon the window-panes,
22 The yellow smoke that rubs its muzzle on the window-panes
23 Licked its tongue into the corners of the evening,
24 Lingered upon the pools that stand in drains,
25 Let fall upon its back the soot that falls from chimneys,
26 Slipped by the terrace, made a sudden leap,

T.S. Eliot

1. **Michelangelo** Michelangelo di Lodovico Buonarroti Simoni (1475–1564), Renaissance artist and sculptor, whose most famous works include David and the ceiling of the Sistine Chapel in Rome

27 And seeing that it was a soft October night,
28 Curled once about the house, and fell asleep.

29 And indeed there will be time
30 For the yellow smoke that slides along the street,
31 Rubbing its back upon the window panes;
32 There will be time, there will be time
33 To prepare a face to meet the faces that you meet
34 There will be time to murder and create,
35 And time for all the works and days of hands
36 That lift and drop a question on your plate;
37 Time for you and time for me,
38 And time yet for a hundred indecisions,
39 And for a hundred visions and revisions,
40 Before the taking of a toast and tea.

41 In the room the women come and go
42 Talking of Michelangelo.

43 And indeed there will be time
44 To wonder, "Do I dare?" and, "Do I dare?"
45 Time to turn back and descend the stair,
46 With a bald spot in the middle of my hair—
47 (They will say: "How his hair is growing thin!")
48 My morning coat, my collar mounting firmly to the chin,
49 My necktie rich and modest, but asserted by a simple pin—
50 (They will say: "But how his arms and legs are thin!")
51 Do I dare
52 Disturb the universe?
53 In a minute there is time
54 For decisions and revisions which a minute will reverse.

55 For I have known them all already, known them all:
56 Have known the evenings, mornings, afternoons,
57 I have measured out my life with coffee spoons;
58 I know the voices dying with a dying fall
59 Beneath the music from a farther room.
60 So how should I presume?

61 And I have known the eyes already, known them all—
62 The eyes that fix you in a formulated phrase,
63 And when I am formulated, sprawling on a pin,
64 When I am pinned and wriggling on the wall,
65 Then how should I begin
66 To spit out all the butt-ends of my days and ways?
67 And how should I presume?

Skill:
Poetic Elements
and Structure

Eliot uses repetition and rhyming couplets to give details about Prufrock's appearance. He is dressed well, but he worries about what people say about him, imagining they focus on his "bald spot" and thin arms and legs.

68   And I have known the arms already, known them all—
69   Arms that are braceleted and white and bare
70   (But in the lamplight, downed with light brown hair!)
71   Is it perfume from a dress
72   That makes me so digress?
73   Arms that lie along a table, or wrap about a shawl.
74   And should I then presume?
75   And how should I begin?

. . .

Skill:
Poetic Elements
and Structure

76   Shall I say, I have gone at dusk through narrow streets
77   And watched the smoke that rises from the pipes
78   Of lonely men in shirt-sleeves, leaning out of windows?

79   I should have been a pair of ragged claws
80   Scuttling across the floors of silent seas.

*The metaphor shows
that Prufrock feels he
should have been a
creature at the bottom
of the sea. The "lonely
men" that Prufrock
sees support the sense
of isolation. Each line
ends in "s" and the "s"
sound is repeated
throughout.*

. . .

81   And the afternoon, the evening, sleeps so peacefully!
82   Smoothed by long fingers,
83   Asleep . . . tired . . . or it **malingers**.
84   Stretched on the floor, here beside you and me.
85   Should I, after tea and cakes and ices,
86   Have the strength to force the moment to its crisis?
87   But though I have wept and fasted, wept and prayed,
88   Though I have seen my head (grown slightly bald) brought in upon a platter,
89   I am no prophet—and here's no great matter;
90   I have seen the moment of my greatness flicker,
91   And I have seen the eternal Footman[2] hold my coat, and snicker,
92   And in short, I was afraid.

93   And would it have been worth it, after all,
94   After the cups, the marmalade, the tea,
95   Among the porcelain, among some talk of you and me,
96   Would it have been worth while,
97   To have bitten off the matter with a smile,
98   To have squeezed the universe into a ball
99   To roll it toward some overwhelming question,
100   To say: "I am Lazarus[3], come from the dead,
101   Come back to tell you all, I shall tell you all"—

2. **footman** a house servant who attends to guests, as a porter might in a hotel
3. **Lazarus** Biblical figure raised from the dead by Jesus Christ

102 If one, settling a pillow by her head,

103 Should say: "That is not what I meant at all;

105 That is not it, at all."

105 And would it have been worth it, after all,

106 Would it have been worth while,

107 After the sunsets and the dooryards and the sprinkled streets,

108 After the novels, after the teacups, after the skirts that trail along the floor—

109 And this, and so much more?—

110 It is impossible to say just what I mean!

111 But as if a magic lantern threw the nerves in patterns on a screen:

112 Would it have been worth while

113 If one, settling a pillow or throwing off a shawl,

114 And turning toward the window, should say:

115 "That is not it at all,

116 That is not what I meant, at all."

. . .

177 No! I am not Prince Hamlet, nor was meant to be;

118 Am an attendant lord, one that will do

119 To swell a progress, start a scene or two,

120 Advise the prince; no doubt, an easy tool,

121 Deferential, glad to be of use,

122 Politic, cautious, and meticulous;

123 Full of high sentence, but a bit obtuse;

124 At times, indeed, almost ridiculous—

125 Almost, at times, the Fool[4].

126 I grow old . . . I grow old . . .

127 I shall wear the bottoms of my trousers rolled.

128 Shall I part my hair behind? Do I dare to eat a peach?

129 I shall wear white flannel trousers, and walk upon the beach.

130 I have heard the mermaids singing, each to each.

131 I do not think that they will sing to me.

132 I have seen them riding seaward on the waves

133 Combing the white hair of the waves blown back

134 When the wind blows the water white and black.

135 We have lingered in the chambers of the sea

136 By sea-girls wreathed with seaweed red and brown

137 Till human voices wake us, and we drown.

Skill:
Language, Style, and Audience

The speaker's allusion to Shakespeare's Hamlet *effectively shows that he views himself as absurd and awkward. He was not "meant to be" a prince like Hamlet, but instead thinks of himself as "the Fool."*

---

4. **the Fool** a character in a Tarot deck—a counterpart to the Joker in a deck of playing cards—
   depicted by an illustration of a young man at the edge of a cliff

First Read

Read "The Love Song of J. Alfred Prufrock." After you read, complete the Think Questions below.

☁ THINK QUESTIONS

1. What phrases or lines are repeated in the poem? What do these repetitions tell you about the speaker of the poem? Support your response with evidence from the text.

2. How is the speaker's appearance described? What can you infer about Prufrock from these descriptions? Support your response with evidence from the text.

3. Write two or three sentences summarizing the events of the poem. What seems to occur in the time span of the poem? Use evidence from the text to support your response.

4. Use context clues to determine the meaning of the word **malingers** as it is used in "The Love Song of J. Alfred Prufrock." Write your definition of *malingers* here and explain how you arrived at this definition.

5. Use context clues to determine the meaning of the word **deferential** as it is used in "The Love Song of J. Alfred Prufrock." Write your definition of *deferential* here and explain how you arrived at this definition.

Skill:
Language, Style, and Audience

Use the Checklist to analyze Language, Style, and Audience in "The Love Song of J. Alfred Prufrock." Refer to the sample student annotations about Language, Style, and Audience in the text.

••• CHECKLIST FOR LANGUAGE, STYLE, AND AUDIENCE

In order to determine an author's style and possible intended audience, do the following:

- ✓ identify language that is particularly fresh, engaging, or beautiful

- ✓ analyze the surrounding words and phrases as well as the context in which the specific words are being used

- ✓ note the audience—both intended and unintended—and possible reactions to the author's word choice and style

- ✓ note any allusions the author makes to texts written by other authors

- ✓ examine your reaction to the author's word choice and how the author's choice affected your reaction

To analyze the impact of a specific word choice on meaning including words with multiple meanings or language that is particularly fresh, engaging, or beautiful, consider the following questions:

- ✓ How does the author's use of fresh, engaging, or beautiful language enhance or change what is being described? How would a specific phrase or sentence sound different or shift in meaning if a synonym were used?

- ✓ How does the rhyme scheme, meter, and other poetic language affect the meaning?

- ✓ How does word choice, including different possible meanings from other countries, help determine meaning?

- ✓ How does the author use poetic techniques, multiple meaning words, and language that appeals to emotions to craft a message or idea?

- ✓ How would the text be different if another type of technique or other words were used?

Skill:
Language, Style, and Audience

Reread Lines 105–116 of "The Love Song of J. Alfred Prufrock." Then, using the Checklist on the previous page, answer the multiple-choice questions below.

↻ YOUR TURN

1. What is the most likely interpretation of "But as if a magic lantern threw the nerves in patterns on a screen"?

   ○ A. Prufrock can explain himself so clearly that it is like being able to read words on a screen.

   ○ B. Prufrock's emotions are so clear to him that it is like seeing his nervous system on a screen.

   ○ C. Prufrock's nervousness is so intense that it seems his nerves are being projected onto a screen.

   ○ D. Prufrock sees himself as a magician who can make patterns seem to appear and change on a screen.

2. Which statement best evaluates how the author's use of language affects the reader's perception of Prufrock in these lines?

   ○ A. The author's choice to use repetition emphasizes Prufrock's uncertainty about how to communicate what he is trying to say.

   ○ B. The author's choice to include a sentence that asks a question is effective because the purpose of the poem is to make a request of readers.

   ○ C. The language in line 113 helps readers understand that Prufrock is lying in bed as he writes the poem.

   ○ D. The author's lists in lines 107 and 108 are distracting because readers do not know enough about the events he is referencing.

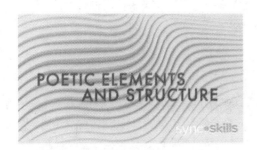

Skill:
Poetic Elements and Structure

Use the Checklist to analyze Poetic Elements and Structure in "The Love Song of J. Alfred Prufrock." Refer to the sample student annotations about Poetic Elements and Structure in the text.

••• CHECKLIST FOR POETIC ELEMENTS AND STRUCTURE

In order to analyze a poet's choices concerning how to structure specific parts of a poem, note the following:

- ✓ the form and overall structure of the poem

- ✓ the rhyme, rhythm, and meter, if present

- ✓ lines and stanzas in the poem that suggest its meanings and aesthetic impact

- ✓ how the poet began or ended the poem

- ✓ if the poet provided a comedic or tragic resolution

To analyze how an author's choices concerning how to structure specific parts of a poem contribute to its overall structure and meaning as well as its aesthetic impact, consider the following questions:

- ✓ How does the poet structure the poem? What is the structure of specific parts?

- ✓ How do the poet's choices contribute to the poem's overall structure, meaning, and aesthetic impact?

Please note that excerpts and passages in the StudySync® library and this workbook are intended as touchstones to generate interest in an author's work. The excerpts and passages do not substitute for the reading of entire texts, and StudySync® strongly recommends that students seek out and purchase the whole literary or informational work in order to experience it as the author intended. Links to online resellers are available in our digital library. In addition, complete works may be ordered through an authorized reseller by filling out and returning to StudySync® the order form enclosed in this workbook.

Reading & Writing Companion   **185**

Skill:
Poetic Elements and Structure

Reread lines 127–138 of "The Love Song of J. Alfred Prufrock." Then, using the Checklist on the previous page, answer the multiple-choice questions below.

⟳ YOUR TURN

1. This question has two parts. First, answer Part A. Then, answer Part B.

   Part A: Which statement best describes the rhyme scheme of these lines?

   ○ A. Eliot mainly uses couplets with some lines that break the pattern.

   ○ B. Eliot does not use a consistent rhyme scheme, even though some words rhyme.

   ○ C. Eliot follows a traditional rhyme scheme of *aabba*, which is usually found in sonnets.

   ○ D. Eliot uses blank verse to allude to the work of famous English poets who came before him.

   Part B: Which statement explains why Eliot would choose to use the rhyme scheme in Part A?

   ○ A. Eliot wanted to write a poem that completely rejected traditional poetic structures.

   ○ B. Eliot wanted to align himself with famous English writers like Shakespeare and Milton.

   ○ C. Eliot wanted to draw the reader's attention to the lines that do not fit the rhyme scheme.

   ○ D. Eliot wanted to help the reader follow the poem's conclusion by using a set rhyme scheme.

2. Which statement best explains a possible reason Eliot ended the poem as he did?

   ○ A. After focusing on Prufrock's regrets and insecurities, Eliot ended the poem on a hopeful note.

   ○ B. Prufrock is mostly unable to take action, but Eliot ends the poem with Prufrock in love.

   ○ C. The poem's conclusion offers Eliot's answer to Prufrock's question about how to begin.

   ○ D. Eliot wanted to highlight that Prufrock is unable to change by the poem's conclusion.

Skill:
Compare and Contrast

Use the Checklist to analyze Compare and Contrast in "The Love Song of J. Alfred Prufrock."

••• CHECKLIST FOR COMPARE AND CONTRAST

In order to determine how to compare and contrast texts from the same period, and how these texts treat similar themes or topics, use the following steps:

- ✓ first, identify two or more foundational works of American literature written during the eighteenth-, nineteenth- or early-twentieth-century

- ✓ next, identify the topic and theme in each work, and any central or recurring topics the author presents

- ✓ after, explain how each text reflects and represents the time period in which it was written, including its historical events, customs, beliefs, or social norms

- ✓ finally, explain the similarities or differences between two or more texts that are written during the same time period and address related themes and topics

To demonstrate knowledge of eighteenth-, nineteenth- and early-twentieth-century foundational works of American literature, consider the following questions:

- ✓ Are the texts from the same time period in American literature?

- ✓ In what ways does each text reflect and represent the time period in which it was written?

- ✓ How does each work treat themes or topics representative of the time period in which it was written?

- ✓ How is the treatment of the themes or topics in these literary works similar and different?

Skill:
Compare and Contrast

Reread lines 7–18 of "The Love Song of J. Alfred Prufrock" and the entirety of "The Great Figure." Then, answer the multiple-choice questions that follow.

↻ YOUR TURN

1. What theme, common to Modernism, do you see in these lines from both poems?

   ○ A. The chaos of modern life can sometimes make one feel isolated and overwhelmed.
   ○ B. One should be fearful of the technology and industrialization at the center of modern life.
   ○ C. Those who are tasked with protecting others grow accustomed to chaotic experiences.
   ○ D. The world seems forever dark and cold to those who are too afraid to love.

2. Which statement best compares the use of sentence structure in both poems?

   ○ A. Both poems reject traditional punctuation to allow readers to follow the flow of ideas.
   ○ B. Both poems experiment with sentence structure to show the positive outlook of the speaker.
   ○ C. Both poems use a combination of very short and very long sentences to highlight main ideas.
   ○ D. Both poems use long and fragmented sentence structure to show new thoughts entering the text.

Close Read

Reread "The Love Song of J. Alfred Prufrock." As you reread, complete the Skills Focus questions below. Then use your answers and annotations from the questions to help you complete the Write activity.

◎ SKILLS FOCUS

1. Highlight a section in the beginning of the poem in which the speaker uses multiple meanings or engaging language to describe the evening. Describe the effect the poet's word choice has on the reader's understanding of the scene.

2. Identify a section in which the poet includes a description that evokes at least one of the five senses. Explain why this description is effective and how it shapes your perception of the text.

3. Identify a section in which the poet uses unconventional sentence or poetic structure. Explain why this unconventional structure is effective and how it shapes your perception of the text.

4. Highlight a section in which the speaker is shown to be overwhelmed. Using your memory of "The Great Figure," explain how the speaker's behavior reflects the poem's literary period.

5. The title "The Love Song of J. Alfred Prufrock" might seem misleading after reading the poem. Identify two moments in which the speaker of the poem expresses a feeling of alienation. What causes his alienation? Why is this poem called a "Love Song"?

✏ WRITE

LITERARY ANALYSIS: Some critics claim that the speaker in "The Love Song of J. Alfred Prufrock" describes an atmosphere that is his own personal hell. What evidence in the poem do you find to support this claim? What is it about Prufrock's existence that seems hellish, and how does that existence help define this poem as a Modernist poem? Write a response that answers these questions, using evidence from the text to support your ideas.

Please note that excerpts and passages in the StudySync® library and this workbook are intended as touchstones to generate interest in an author's work. The excerpts and passages do not substitute for the reading of entire texts, and StudySync® strongly recommends that students seek out and purchase the whole literary or informational work in order to experience it as the author intended. Links to online resellers are available in our digital library. In addition, complete works may be ordered through an authorized reseller by filling out and returning to StudySync® the order form enclosed in this workbook.

Reading & Writing Companion   189

miss rosie

POETRY
Lucille Clifton
1987

Introduction

Twice a finalist for the Pulitzer Prize in Poetry, American poet and educator Lucille Clifton (1936–2010) was born in Depew, New York. In addition to offering acute insight into family dynamics, community, and the African American experience, Clifton's work is often heralded for its exploration of the enduring strength and dignity of those who live on the margins of society. One such poem, "miss rosie," tells the story of someone who, on the surface, appears to be a homeless woman whom people might pass by, leaving her forlorn and forgotten. Yet, as we learn from the speaker, people are more than their present circumstances.

"through your destruction / i stand up"

NOTES

1 when i watch you
2 wrapped up like garbage
3 sitting, surrounded by the smell
4 of too old potato peels
5 or
6 when i watch you
7 in your old man's shoes
8 with the little toe cut out
9 sitting, waiting for your mind
10 like next week's grocery
11 i say
12 when i watch you
13 you wet brown bag of a woman
14 who used to be the best looking gal in georgia
15 used to be called the Georgia Rose
16 i stand up
17 through your destruction
18 i stand up

Lucille Clifton, "miss rosie" from The Collected Poems of Lucille Clifton. Copyright © 1987 by Lucille Clifton. Reprinted with the permission of The Permissions Company, Inc., on behalf of BOA Editions, Ltd., www.boaeditions.org.

✏ WRITE

LITERARY ANALYSIS: The poem "miss rosie" follows a dramatic structure as the speaker recounts the life of a person that society often ignores. Write a short response in which you analyze the effect the dramatic structure has on the meaning of the poem. In your essay, consider and respond to questions such as the following: What story does this poem tell? What relationship does the speaker of the poem have with Miss Rosie? How would the story be different if Miss Rosie were telling her own story? What message is being conveyed by this story? Remember to use textual evidence to support your response.

Please note that excerpts and passages in the StudySync® library and this workbook are intended as touchstones to generate interest in an author's work. The excerpts and passages do not substitute for the reading of entire texts, and StudySync® strongly recommends that students seek out and purchase the whole literary or informational work in order to experience it as the author intended. Links to online resellers are available in our digital library. In addition, complete works may be ordered through an authorized reseller by filling out and returning to StudySync® the order form enclosed in this workbook.

Reading & Writing Companion 191

The Idler

POETRY
Alice Dunbar-Nelson
1895

Introduction

Poet, essayist, diarist, and activist Alice Dunbar-Nelson (1875–1935) was born in New Orleans, Louisiana, the daughter of a once-enslaved Louisiana woman named Patricia Wright. Identity, family and oppression are subjects Dunbar-Nelson often explored in her work, including the groundbreaking collections *Violets and Other Tales* and *The Goodness of St. Rocque and Other Stories*. In "The Idler," the speaker observes an idler on the road who dreams all day and yet seems content.

"To be a happy idler, to lounge and sun, And dreaming, pass his long-drawn days away."

1   An idle lingerer on the wayside's road,
2   He gathers up his work and yawns away;
3   A little longer, ere the tiresome load
4   Shall be **reduced** to ashes or to clay.

5   No matter if the world has marched along,
6   And scorned his slowness as it quickly passed;
7   No matter, if amid the busy **throng**,
8   He greets some face, **infantile** at the last.

9   His mission? Well, there is but one,
10 And if it is a mission he knows it, nay,
11 To be a happy idler, to lounge and sun,
12 And dreaming, pass his long-drawn days away.

13 So dreams he on, his happy life to pass
14 **Content**, without ambitions painful sighs,
15 Until the sands run down into the glass;
16 He smiles—content—unmoved and dies.

17 And yet, with all the pity that you feel
18 For this poor mothling of that flame, the world;
19 Are you the better for your desperate deal,
20 When you, like him, into **infinitude** are hurled?

Alice Ruth Moore Dunbar Nelson

Please note that excerpts and passages in the StudySync® library and this workbook are intended as touchstones to generate interest in an author's work. The excerpts and passages do not substitute for the reading of entire texts, and StudySync® strongly recommends that students seek out and purchase the whole literary or informational work in order to experience it as the author intended. Links to online resellers are available in our digital library. In addition, complete works may be ordered through an authorized reseller by filling out and returning to StudySync® the order form enclosed in this workbook.

Reading & Writing Companion   **193**

WRITE

DISCUSSION: What is the speaker's opinion of the idler's approach to life? What makes you think so? Support your interpretation with textual evidence. What are your own thoughts about the idler's way of living? Discuss with your classmates what you would want to tell him. Describe any personal experiences that led to your beliefs.

A Cup of Tea

FICTION
Katherine Mansfield
1922

Introduction

Katherine Mansfield (1888–1923) was a Modernist fiction writer from New Zealand who gained widespread recognition after the publication *In a German Pension*, her first collection of short stories. She soon became friends with other famous Modernist writers, such as D.H. Lawrence and Virginia Woolf. The short story "A Cup of Tea" describes a not so typical day in the life of Rosemary Fell, delving into themes of class, gender, beauty, and materialism in London high society.

"'Philip,' she whispered, and she pressed his head against her bosom, 'am I pretty?'"

Katherine Mansfield

1   Rosemary Fell was not exactly beautiful. No, you couldn't have called her beautiful. Pretty? Well, if you took her to pieces . . . But why be so cruel as to take anyone to pieces? She was young, brilliant, extremely modern, exquisitely well dressed, amazingly well read in the newest of the new books, and her parties were the most delicious mixture of the really important people and . . . artists—**quaint** creatures, discoveries of hers, some of them too terrifying for words, but others quite presentable and amusing.

2   Rosemary had been married two years. She had a duck of a boy. No, not Peter—Michael. And her husband absolutely adored her. They were rich, really rich, not just comfortably well off, which is odious and stuffy and sounds like one's grandparents. But if Rosemary wanted to shop she would go to Paris as you and I would go to Bond Street. If she wanted to buy flowers, the car pulled up at that perfect shop in Regent Street, and Rosemary inside the shop just gazed in her dazzled, rather exotic way, and said: "I want those and those and those. Give me four bunches of those. And that jar of roses. Yes, I'll have all the roses in the jar. No, no lilac. I hate lilac. It's got no shape." The attendant bowed and put the lilac out of sight, as though this was only too true; lilac was dreadfully shapeless. "Give me those stumpy little tulips. Those red and white ones." And she was followed to the car by a thin shopgirl staggering under an immense white paper armful that looked like a baby in long clothes . . .

3   One winter afternoon she had been buying something in a little antique shop in Curzon Street. It was a shop she liked. For one thing, one usually had it to oneself. And then the man who kept it was ridiculously fond of serving her. He beamed whenever she came in. He clasped his hands; he was so gratified he could scarcely speak. **Flattery**, of course. All the same, there was something . . .

NOTES

4   "You see, madam," he would explain in his low respectful tones, "I love my things. I would rather not part with them than sell them to someone who does not appreciate them, who has not that fine feeling which is so rare . . ." And, breathing deeply, he unrolled a tiny square of blue velvet and pressed it on the glass counter with his pale finger-tips.

5   To-day it was a little box. He had been keeping it for her. He had shown it to nobody as yet. An exquisite little enamel box with a glaze so fine it looked as though it had been baked in cream. On the lid a minute creature stood under a flowery tree, and a more minute creature still had her arms round his neck. Her hat, really no bigger than a geranium petal, hung from a branch; it had green ribbons. And there was a pink cloud like a watchful cherub floating above their heads. Rosemary took her hands out of her long gloves. She always took off her gloves to examine such things. Yes, she liked it very much. She loved it; it was a great duck. She must have it. And, turning the creamy box, opening and shutting it, she couldn't help noticing how charming her hands were against the blue velvet. The shopman, in some dim cavern of his mind, may have dared to think so too. For he took a pencil, leant over the counter, and his pale, bloodless fingers crept timidly towards those rosy, flashing ones, as he murmured gently: "If I may venture to point out to madam, the flowers on the little lady's bodice."

6   "Charming!" Rosemary admired the flowers. But what was the price? For a moment the shopman did not seem to hear. Then a murmur reached her. "Twenty-eight guineas[1], madam."

7   "Twenty-eight guineas." Rosemary gave no sign. She laid the little box down; she buttoned her gloves again. Twenty-eight guineas. Even if one is rich . . . She looked vague. She stared at a plump tea-kettle like a plump hen above the shopman's head, and her voice was dreamy as she answered: "Well, keep it for me – will you? I'll . . ."

8   But the shopman had already bowed as though keeping it for her was all any human being could ask. He would be willing, of course, to keep it for her for ever.

9   The **discreet** door shut with a click. She was outside on the step, gazing at the winter afternoon. Rain was falling, and with the rain it seemed the dark came too, spinning down like ashes. There was a cold bitter taste in the air, and the new-lighted lamps looked sad. Sad were the lights in the houses opposite. Dimly they burned as if regretting something. And people hurried by, hidden under their hateful umbrellas. Rosemary felt a strange pang. She pressed her muff against her breast; she wished she had the little box, too, to

---

1. **guinea** a unit of British currency until the early 19th century

Skill:
Summarizing

The protagonist, Rosemary is a rich woman on a shopping trip who wants a jewelry box, but leaves it at the shop.

Rosemary doesn't say what's on her mind.

She seems more concerned about how she looks and behaves, than anything else.

NOTES

cling to. Of course the car was there. She'd only to cross the pavement. But still she waited. There are moments, horrible moments in life, when one emerges from shelter and looks out, and it's awful. One oughtn't to give way to them. One ought to go home and have an extra-special tea. But at the very instant of thinking that, a young girl, thin, dark, shadowy—where had she come from?—was standing at Rosemary's elbow and a voice like a sigh, almost like a sob, breathed: "Madam, may I speak to you a moment?"

10   "Speak to me?" Rosemary turned. She saw a little battered creature with enormous eyes, someone quite young, no older than herself, who clutched at her coat-collar with reddened hands, and shivered as though she had just come out of the water.

11   "M-madam," stammered the voice. "Would you let me have the price of a cup of tea?"

12   "A cup of tea?" There was something simple, sincere in that voice; it wasn't in the least the voice of a beggar. "Then have you no money at all?" asked Rosemary.

13   "None, madam," came the answer.

14   "How extraordinary!" Rosemary peered through the dusk, and the girl gazed back at her. How more than extraordinary! And suddenly it seemed to Rosemary such an adventure. It was like something out of a novel by Dostoevsky, this meeting in the dusk. Supposing she took the girl home? Supposing she did do one of those things she was always reading about or seeing on the stage, what would happen? It would be thrilling. And she heard herself saying afterwards to the amazement of her friends: "I simply took her home with me," as she stepped forward and said to that dim person beside her: "Come home to tea with me."

15   The girl drew back startled. She even stopped shivering for a moment. Rosemary put out a hand and touched her arm. "I mean it," she said, smiling. And she felt how simple and kind her smile was. "Why won't you? Do. Come home with me now in my car and have tea."

16   "You—you don't mean it, madam," said the girl, and there was pain in her voice.

17   "But I do," cried Rosemary. "I want you to. To please me. Come along."

18   The girl put her fingers to her lips and her eyes devoured Rosemary. "You're—you're not taking me to the police station?" she stammered.

19   "The police station!" Rosemary laughed out. "Why should I be so cruel? No, I only want to make you warm and to hear—anything you care to tell me."

Copyright © BookheadEd Learning, LLC

20 Hungry people are easily led. The footman held the door of the car open, and a moment later they were skimming through the dusk.

21 "There!" said Rosemary. She had a feeling of triumph as she slipped her hand through the velvet strap. She could have said, "Now I've got you," as she gazed at the little captive she had netted. But of course she meant it kindly. Oh, more than kindly. She was going to prove to this girl that—wonderful things did happen in life, that—fairy godmothers were real, that—rich people had hearts, and that women were sisters. She turned impulsively, saying: "Don't be frightened. After all, why shouldn't you come back with me? We're both women. If I'm the more fortunate, you ought to expect . . ."

22 But happily at that moment, for she didn't know how the sentence was going to end, the car stopped. The bell was rung, the door opened, and with a charming, protecting, almost embracing movement, Rosemary drew the other into the hall. Warmth, softness, light, a sweet scent, all those things so familiar to her she never even thought about them, she watched that other receive. It was fascinating. She was like the rich little girl in her nursery with all the cupboards to open, all the boxes to unpack.

23 "Come, come upstairs," said Rosemary, longing to begin to be generous. "Come up to my room." And, besides, she wanted to spare this poor little thing from being stared at by the servants; she decided as they mounted the stairs she would not even ring for Jeanne, but take off her things by herself. The great thing was to be natural!

24 And "There!" cried Rosemary again, as they reached her beautiful big bedroom with the curtains drawn, the fire leaping on her wonderful lacquer[2] furniture, her gold cushions and the primrose[3] and blue rugs.

25 The girl stood just inside the door; she seemed dazed. But Rosemary didn't mind that.

26 "Come and sit down," she cried, dragging her big chair up to the fire, "in this comfy chair. Come and get warm. You look so dreadfully cold."

27 "I daren't, madam," said the girl, and she edged backwards.

28 "Oh, please,"—Rosemary ran forward—"you mustn't be frightened, you mustn't, really. Sit down, when I've taken off my things we shall go into the next room and have tea and be cosy. Why are you afraid?" And gently she half pushed the thin figure into its deep cradle.

Skill:
Word Patterns and
Relationships

I infer that the -ed at the ending indicates mounted is a verb.

The word might have something to do with climbing because the word sounds like "mountain," and that would make sense given the context.

2. **lacquer** a liquid used to make wood shiny
3. **primrose** a European flowering plant that produces flowers with small yellow petals

29   But there was no answer. The girl stayed just as she had been put, with her hands by her sides and her mouth slightly open. To be quite sincere, she looked rather stupid. But Rosemary wouldn't acknowledge it. She leant over her, saying: "Won't you take off your hat? Your pretty hair is all wet. And one is so much more comfortable without a hat, isn't one?"

30   There was a whisper that sounded like "Very good, madam," and the crushed hat was taken off.

31   "And let me help you off with your coat, too," said Rosemary.

32   The girl stood up. But she held onto the chair with one hand and let Rosemary pull. It was quite an effort. The other scarcely helped her at all. She seemed to stagger like a child, and the thought came and went through Rosemary's mind, that if people wanted helping they must respond a little, just a little, otherwise it became very difficult indeed. And what was she to do with the coat now? She left it on the floor, and the hat too. She was just going to take a cigarette off the mantelpiece when the girl said quickly, but so lightly and strangely: "I'm very sorry, madam, but I'm going to faint. I shall go off, madam, if I don't have something."

33   "Good heavens, how thoughtless I am!" Rosemary rushed to the bell.

34   "Tea! Tea at once! And some brandy immediately!"

35   The maid was gone again, but the girl almost cried out: "No, I don't want no brandy. I never drink brandy. It's a cup of tea I want, madam." And she burst into tears.

36   It was a terrible and fascinating moment. Rosemary knelt beside her chair.

37   "Don't cry, poor little thing," she said. "Don't cry." And she gave the other her lace handkerchief. She really was touched beyond words. She put her arm round those thin, bird-like shoulders.

38   Now at last the other forgot to be shy, forgot everything except that they were both women, and gasped out: "I can't go on no longer like this. I can't bear it. I can't bear it. I shall do away with myself. I can't bear no more."

39   "You shan't have to. I'll look after you. Don't cry any more. Don't you see what a good thing it was that you met me? We'll have tea and you'll tell me everything. And I shall arrange something. I promise. Do stop crying. It's so exhausting. Please!"

40   The other did stop just in time for Rosemary to get up before the tea came. She had the table placed between them. She plied the poor little creature

with everything, all the sandwiches, all the bread and butter, and every time her cup was empty she filled it with tea, cream and sugar. People always said sugar was so nourishing. As for herself she didn't eat; she smoked and looked away tactfully so that the other should not be shy.

41 And really the effect of that slight meal was marvelous. When the tea-table was carried away a new being, a light, frail creature with tangled hair, dark lips, deep, lighted eyes, lay back in the big chair in a kind of sweet **languor**, looking at the blaze. Rosemary lit a fresh cigarette; it was time to begin.

42 "And when did you have your last meal?" she asked softly.

43 But at that moment the door-handle turned.

44 "Rosemary, may I come in?" It was Philip.

45 "Of course."

46 He came in. "Oh, I'm so sorry," he said, and stopped and stared.

47 "It's quite all right," said Rosemary, smiling. "This is my friend, Miss—"

48 "Smith, madam," said the languid figure, who was strangely still and unafraid.

49 "Smith," said Rosemary. "We are going to have a little talk."

50 "Oh yes," said Philip. "Quite," and his eye caught sight of the coat and hat on the floor. He came over to the fire and turned his back to it. "It's a beastly afternoon," he said curiously, still looking at that **listless** figure, looking at its hands and boots, and then at Rosemary again.

51 "Yes, isn't it?" said Rosemary enthusiastically. "Vile."

52 Philip smiled his charming smile. "As a matter of fact," said he, "I wanted you to come into the library for a moment. Would you? Will Miss Smith excuse us?"

53 The big eyes were raised to him, but Rosemary answered for her: "Of course she will." And they went out of the room together.

54 "I say," said Philip, when they were alone. "Explain. Who is she? What does it all mean?"

55 Rosemary, laughing, leaned against the door and said: "I picked her up in Curzon Street. Really. She's a real pick-up. She asked me for the price of a cup of tea, and I brought her home with me."

Please note that excerpts and passages in the StudySync® library and this workbook are intended as touchstones to generate interest in an author's work. The excerpts and passages do not substitute for the reading of entire texts, and StudySync® strongly recommends that students seek out and purchase the whole literary or informational work in order to experience it as the author intended. Links to online resellers are available in our digital library. In addition, complete works may be ordered through an authorized reseller by filling out and returning to StudySync® the order form enclosed in this workbook.

Reading & Writing Companion   201

56   "But what on earth are you going to do with her?" cried Philip.

57   "Be nice to her," said Rosemary quickly. "Be frightfully nice to her. Look after her. I don't know how. We haven't talked yet. But show her—treat her—make her feel—"

58   "My darling girl," said Philip, "you're quite mad, you know. It simply can't be done."

59   "I knew you'd say that," retorted Rosemary. "Why not? I want to. Isn't that a reason? And besides, one's always reading about these things. I decided—"

60   "But," said Philip slowly, and he cut the end of a cigar, "she's so astonishingly pretty."

61   "Pretty?" Rosemary was so surprised that she blushed. "Do you think so? I—I hadn't thought about it."

62   "Good Lord!" Philip struck a match. "She's absolutely lovely. Look again, my child. I was bowled over when I came into your room just now. However . . . I think you're making a ghastly mistake. Sorry, darling, if I'm **crude** and all that. But let me know if Miss Smith is going to dine with us in time for me to look up *The Milliner's Gazette*[4]."

63   "You absurd creature!" said Rosemary, and she went out of the library, but not back to her bedroom. She went to her writing-room and sat down at her desk. Pretty! Absolutely lovely! Bowled over! Her heart beat like a heavy bell. Pretty! Lovely! She drew her cheque-book towards her. But no, cheques would be no use, of course. She opened a drawer and took out five pound notes, looked at them, put two back, and holding the three squeezed in her hand, she went back to her bedroom.

64   Half an hour later Philip was still in the library, when Rosemary came in.

65   "I only wanted to tell you," said she, and she leaned against the door again and looked at him with her dazzled exotic gaze, "Miss Smith won't dine with us to-night."

66   Philip put down the paper. "Oh, what's happened? Previous engagement?"

67   Rosemary came over and sat down on his knee. "She insisted on going," said she, "so I gave the poor little thing a present of money. I couldn't keep her against her will, could I?" she added softly.

---

4. ***The Milliner's Gazette*** Hill's Milliner's Gazette was a trade paper published in London for hatmakers, an occupation associated with prostitution

68   Rosemary had just done her hair, darkened her eyes a little and put on her pearls. She put up her hands and touched Philip's cheeks.

69   "Do you like me?" said she, and her tone, sweet, husky, troubled him.

70   "I like you awfully," he said, and he held her tighter. "Kiss me."

71   There was a pause.

72   Then Rosemary said dreamily: "I saw a fascinating little box to-day. It cost twenty-eight guineas. May I have it?"

73   Philip jumped her on his knee. "You may, little wasteful one," said he.

74   But that was not really what Rosemary wanted to say.

75   "Philip," she whispered, and she pressed his head against her bosom, "am I *pretty*?"

Skill:
Summarizing

Rosemary directs her husband's attention to her, and away from the girl. She seems insecure.

At the end of the story, Rosemary returns to what she really wanted all along.

A CUP OF TEA

First Read

Read "A Cup of Tea." After you read, complete the Think Questions below.

 THINK QUESTIONS

1. Why does Rosemary want to take the girl from the street home with her? Is it really just to offer her a cup of tea? Cite evidence from the text to support your answer.

2. Why does Rosemary like the enamel box she discovers at the antique shop? Cite evidence from the text to support your answer.

3. How does Rosemary react when Philip comments that the girl Rosemary brought home is "astonishingly pretty"? Why does she react this way? Cite evidence from the text to support your answer.

4. Which context clues helped you determine the meaning of the word **discreet** as it is used in the text? Write your definition of *discreet* here, and indicate which clues helped you figure out the meaning of the word.

5. The Latin word *crudus* means "raw or rough." With this in mind, write your best definition of the word **crude** as it is used in the text. Indicate which context clues helped you determine the word's meaning.

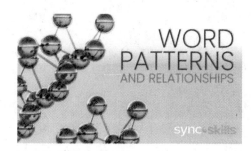

Skill: Word Patterns and Relationships

Use the Checklist to analyze Word Patterns and Relationships in "A Cup of Tea." Refer to the sample student annotations about Word Patterns and Relationships in the text.

••• CHECKLIST FOR WORD PATTERNS AND RELATIONSHIPS

In order to identify patterns of word changes to indicate different meanings or parts of speech, do the following:

- ✓ determine the word's part of speech

- ✓ when reading, use context clues to make a preliminary determination of the meaning of the word

- ✓ when writing a response to a text, check that you understand the meaning and part of speech and that it makes sense in your sentence

- ✓ consult a dictionary to verify your preliminary determination of the meanings and parts of speech

- ✓ be sure to read all of the definitions, and then decide which definition, form, and part of speech makes sense within the context of the text

To identify and correctly use patterns of word changes that indicate different meanings or parts of speech, consider the following questions:

- ✓ What is the intended meaning of the word?

- ✓ Do I know that this word form is the correct part of speech? Do I understand the word patterns for this particular word?

- ✓ When I consult a dictionary, can I confirm that the meaning I have determined for this word is correct? Do I know how to use it correctly?

Please note that excerpts and passages in the StudySync® library and this workbook are intended as touchstones to generate interest in an author's work. The excerpts and passages do not substitute for the reading of entire texts, and StudySync® strongly recommends that students seek out and purchase the whole literary or informational work in order to experience it as the author intended. Links to online resellers are available in our digital library. In addition, complete works may be ordered through an authorized reseller by filling out and returning to StudySync® the order form enclosed in this workbook.

Reading & Writing   205
Companion

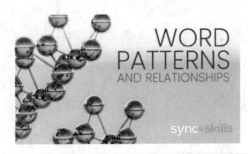

Skill: Word Patterns and Relationships

Reread paragraph 21 of "A Cup of Tea." Then, using the Checklist on the previous page, answer the multiple-choice questions below.

⟳ YOUR TURN

1. What part of speech is "impulsively"?

   ○ A. noun

   ○ B. verb

   ○ C. adjective

   ○ D. adverb

2. Given the definitions provided, what is most likely the meaning of *impulsively*?

   > **Impulsive**
   > /ɪmˈpʌlsɪv/
   > *noun*
   > 1. act in the moment
   > 2. related to electrical energy
   > 3. a force

   ○ A. To cause electrical energy

   ○ B. To act without thinking

   ○ C. To perform actions without one's consent

   ○ D. To consider the consequences well in advance

Skill:
Summarizing

Use the Checklist to analyze Summarizing in "A Cup of Tea." Refer to the sample student annotations about Summarizing in the text.

••• CHECKLIST FOR SUMMARIZING

In order to determine how to write an objective summary of a text, note the following:

✓ answers to the basic questions *who, what, where, when, why,* and *how*

✓ in literature or nonfiction, note how two or more themes or central ideas are developed over the course of the text, and how they interact and build on one another to produce a complex account

✓ stay objective, and do not add your own personal thoughts, judgments, or opinions to the summary

To provide an objective summary of a text, consider the following questions:

✓ What are the answers to basic *who, what, where, when, why,* and *how* questions in literature and works of nonfiction?

✓ Does my summary include how two or more themes or central ideas are developed over the course of the text, and how they interact and build on one another in my summary?

✓ Is my summary objective, or have I added my own thoughts, judgments, and personal opinions?

Please note that excerpts and passages in the StudySync® library and this workbook are intended as touchstones to generate interest in an author's work. The excerpts and passages do not substitute for the reading of entire texts, and StudySync® strongly recommends that students seek out and purchase the whole literary or informational work in order to experience it as the author intended. Links to online resellers are available in our digital library. In addition, complete works may be ordered through an authorized reseller by filling out and returning to StudySync® the order form enclosed in this workbook.

Reading & Writing Companion   **207**

Skill:
Summarizing

Reread paragraphs 9–13 of "A Cup of Tea." Then, using the Checklist on the previous page, answer the multiple-choice questions below.

↻ YOUR TURN

1. The following is a sentence that a student wrote to summarize this passage of the text. What feedback would you give to help improve this summary?

> "Rosemary feels sad because she can't afford the antique she feels she is entitled to, when a young girl approaches her in the street."

○ A. The summary of the passage is incomplete because it does not mention the "extra-special tea."

○ B. The summary does not provide basic information, such as Rosemary's last name or where she is shopping.

○ C. This is an analysis, not an objective summary, because the text does not explicitly say that Rosemary is sad.

○ D. The summary is not objective because the word "entitled" has negative connotations, and this is not implied in the passage.

2. If you were to write a summary of this passage, what two themes do you notice are repeated in this paragraph?

○ A. Having too much wealth and being lonely

○ B. Being homesick and knowing where you belong

○ C. Isolation in one's own world and dissatisfaction

○ D. The wealthy are hypocritical and insecurity

Close Read

Reread "A Cup of Tea." As you reread, complete the Skills Focus questions below. Then use your answers and annotations from the questions to help you complete the Write activity.

◎ SKILLS FOCUS

1. Reread paragraph 48. Highlight the word *languid*, and, in your annotation, use your knowledge of word patterns and relationships to answer the following questions: What part of speech is this word? How do you know? What do you think this word means and why?

2. Identify details about the economic setting that contrast Rosemary's wealth and Miss Smith's poverty, and explain why it might be important to include these details in a summary of the story.

3. Identify a passage that shows Rosemary has conflicting feelings toward Miss Smith, and explain how these feelings contribute to the theme of materialism among the upper classes.

4. Identify a comment Philip makes about Miss Smith's beauty and in brief summary explain two possible reasons why Philip discourages his wife from helping Miss Smith.

5. This story revolves around the character of Rosemary as she seeks a connection with someone or something. What details in the story help you understand why Rosemary might feel so alienated? What about her life has caused this?

✏ WRITE

COMPARE AND CONTRAST: Write a response in which you compare and contrast the ideas and attitudes expressed about wealth and poverty in "miss rosie," "The Idler," and "A Cup of Tea." Remember to use textual evidence from "A Cup of Tea" to support your response.

Please note that excerpts and passages in the StudySync® library and this workbook are intended as touchstones to generate interest in an author's work. The excerpts and passages do not substitute for the reading of entire texts, and StudySync® strongly recommends that students seek out and purchase the whole literary or informational work in order to experience it as the author intended. Links to online resellers are available in our digital library. In addition, complete works may be ordered through an authorized reseller by filling out and returning to StudySync® the order form enclosed in this workbook.

Reading & Writing Companion   **209**

The Glass Menagerie

DRAMA
Tennessee Williams
1944

Introduction

Thomas Lanier ("Tennessee") Williams III was one of America's most influential 20th century playwrights, and it was his semi-autobiographical work *The Glass Menagerie* that launched him to fame after years of obscurity. Here, in the fifth scene from the play, frustrated would-be poet Tom Wingfield responds to his mother Amanda's inquiries about the gentleman caller he has invited over to meet Laura, his painfully shy younger sister.

"A fire escape landing's a poor excuse for a porch."

SCENE FIVE

1. *Legend on the screen:* "**Annunciation**."

2. *Music is heard as the light slowly comes on.*

3. *It is early dusk of a spring evening. Supper has just been finished in the Wingfield apartment. Amanda and Laura, in light-colored dresses, are removing dishes from the table in the dining room, which is shadowy, their movements formalized almost as a dance or ritual, their moving forms as pale and silent as moths. Tom, in white shirt and trousers, rises from the table and crosses toward the fire escape.*

4. AMANDA [*as he passes her*]: Son, will you do me a favor?

5. TOM: What?

6. AMANDA: Comb your hair! You look so pretty when your hair is combed!

7. [*Tom slouches on the sofa with the evening paper. Its enormous headline reads: "Franco Triumphs[1]."*]

8. There is only one respect in which I would like you to **emulate** your father.

9. TOM: What respect is that?

10. AMANDA: The care he always took of his appearance. He never allowed himself to look untidy.

11. [*He throws down the paper and crosses to the fire escape.*]

12. Where are you going?

---

1. **Franco Triumphs** eventual Spanish dictator Francisco Franco fought for the Nationalists in the Spanish Civil War, who were eventually victorious and installed him as leader from 1939 to 1975.

13   TOM: I'm going out to smoke.

14   AMANDA: You smoke too much. A pack a day at fifteen cents a pack. How much would that amount to in a month? Thirty times fifteen is how much, Tom? Figure it out and you will be astounded at what you could save. Enough to give you a night-school course in accounting at Washington U.! Just think what a wonderful thing that would be for you, son!

15   [*Tom is unmoved by the thought.*]

16   TOM: I'd rather smoke. [*He steps out on the landing, letting the screen door slam.*]

17   AMANDA [*sharply*]: I know! That's the tragedy of it. . . . [*Alone, she turns to look at her husband's picture.*]

18   [*Dance music: "The World Is Waiting for the Sunrise!"*]

Skill:
Media

The radio play is immediately different from the script: Tom's soliloquy sets the scene, and there is no stage direction or dialogue before it.

Tom sounds different than I imagined. He is more casual in the radio version.

19   TOM [*to the audience*]: Across the alley from us was the Paradise Dance Hall. On evenings in spring the windows and doors were open and the music came outdoors. Sometimes the lights were turned out except for a large glass sphere that the hung from the ceiling. It would turn slowly about and filter the dusk with delicate rainbow colors. Then the orchestra played a waltz or a tango, something that had a slow and sensuous rhythm. Couples would come outside, to the relative privacy of the alley. You could see them kissing behind ash pits and telephone poles. This was the compensation for lives that passed like mine, without any change or adventure. Adventure and change were imminent this year. They were waiting around the corner for all these kids. Suspended in the mist over Berchtesgaden[2], caught in the folds of Chamberlain's umbrella[3]. In Spain there was Guernica![4] But here there was only hot swing music and liquor, dance halls, bars, and movies, and sex that hung in the gloom like a chandelier and flooded the world with brief, deceptive rainbows. . . . All the world was waiting for bombardments!

Skill:
Dramatic Elements and Structure

Amanda is clearly out of place in this city. The stage directions provide needed clues about who she is as a character and reveal that she is not at home in the city setting.

20   [*Amanda turns from the picture and comes outside.*]

21   AMANDA [*sighing*]; A fire escape landing's a poor excuse for a porch. [*She spreads a newspaper on a step and sits down, gracefully and demurely as if she were settling into a swing on a Mississippi veranda.*] What are you looking at?

---

2. **Berchtesgaden** a small German town in the Alps
3. **Chamberlain's umbrella** a figure of speech used to describe England's prime minister Neville Chamberlain's failure to appease Hitler at the Munich Conference in 1938
4. **Guernica** a large oil painting by Pablo Picasso depicting the bombing of the Spanish town of Guernica during the Spanish Civil War

22 TOM: The moon.

23 AMANDA: Is there a moon this evening?

24 TOM: It's rising over Garfinkel's Delicatessen.

25 AMANDA: So it is! A little silver slipper of a moon. Have you made a wish on it yet?

Skill:
Media

The audiobook is more similar to the script. The actor changes his voice to play the characters. But it sounds unnatural when he says "Um-hum", perhaps because this interpretation is meant to be an exact reading of the script.

26 TOM: Um-hum.

27 AMANDA: What did you wish for?

28 TOM: That's a secret.

29 AMANDA: A secret, huh? Well, I won't tell mine either. I will be just as mysterious as you.

30 TOM: I bet I can guess what yours is.

31 AMANDA: Is my head so transparent?

32 TOM: You're not a **sphinx**.

33 AMANDA: No, I don't have secrets. I'll tell you what I wished for on the moon. Success and happiness for my precious children! I wish for that whenever there's a moon, and when there isn't a moon, I wish for it, too.

34 TOM: I thought perhaps you wished for a gentleman caller.

35 AMANDA: Why do you say that?

36 TOM: Don't you remember asking me to fetch one?

37 AMANDA: I remember suggesting that it would be nice for your sister if you brought home some nice young man from the warehouse. I think that I've made that suggestion more than once.

38 TOM: Yes, you have made it repeatedly.

39 AMANDA: Well?

40 TOM: We are going to have one.

41 AMANDA: *What?*

42 TOM: A gentleman caller!

43 [*The annunciation is celebrated with music.*]

44 [*Amanda rises.*]

45 [*Image on screen:* A caller with a bouquet.]

46 AMANDA: You mean you have asked some nice young man to come over?

47 TOM: Yep. I've asked him to dinner.

48 AMANDA: You really did?

49 TOM: I did!

50 AMANDA: You did, and did he—*accept?*

51 TOM: He did!

52 AMANDA: Well, well—well, well! That's—lovely!

53 TOM: I thought that you would be pleased.

54 AMANDA: It's definite then?

55 TOM: Very definite.

56 AMANDA: Soon?

57 TOM: Very soon.

58 AMANDA: For heaven's sake, stop putting on and tell me some things, will you?

59 TOM: What things do you want me to tell you?

60 AMANDA: *Naturally* I would like to know when he's *coming!*

61 TOM: He's coming tomorrow.

62 AMANDA: *Tomorrow?*

63 TOM: Yep. Tomorrow.

64 AMANDA: But, Tom!

Skill:
Media

Amanda is stuttering, which is not in the script. This is the actor's interpretation. In the script, I thought she seemed more accusatory than nervous. Nervousness might be easier to communicate over the radio.

65   TOM: Yes, Mother?

66   AMANDA: Tomorrow gives me no time!

67   TOM: Time for what?

68   AMANDA: Preparations! Why didn't you phone me at once, as soon as you asked him, the minute that he accepted? Then, don't you see, I could have been getting ready!

69   TOM: You don't have to make any fuss.

70   AMANDA: Oh, Tom, Tom, Tom, of course I have to make a fuss! I want things nice, not sloppy! Not thrown together. I'll certainly have to do some fast thinking, won't I?

71   TOM: I don't see why you have to think at all.

72   AMANDA: You just don't know. We can't have a gentleman caller in a pigsty! All my wedding silver has to be polished, the monogrammed table linen ought to be laundered! The windows have to be washed and fresh curtains put up. And how about clothes? We have to *wear* something, don't we?

73   TOM: Mother, this boy is no one to make a fuss over!

74   AMANDA: Do you realize he's the first young man we've introduced to your sister? It's terrible, dreadful, disgraceful that poor little sister has never received a single gentleman caller! Tom, come inside! [*She opens the screen door.*]

75   TOM: What for?

76   AMANDA: I want to ask you some things.

77   TOM: If you're going to make such a fuss, I'll call it off, I'll tell him not to come!

78   AMANDA: You certainly won't do anything of the kind. Nothing offends people worse than broken engagements. It simply means I'll have to work like a Turk! We won't be brilliant, but we will pass inspection. Come on inside.

79   [*Tom follows her inside, groaning.*]

80   Sit down.

81   TOM: Any particular place you would like me to sit?

NOTES

82   AMANDA: Thank heavens I've got that new sofa! I'm also making payments on a floor lamp I'll have sent out! And put the chintz covers on, they'll brighten things up! Of course I'd hoped to have these walls re-papered. . . . What is the young man's name?

83   TOM: His name is O'Connor.

84   AMANDA: That, of course, means fish—tomorrow is Friday! I'll have that salmon loaf—with Durkee's dressing! What does he do? He works at the warehouse?

85   TOM: Of course! How else would I—

86   AMANDA: Tom, he—doesn't drink?

87   TOM: Why do you ask me that?

88   AMANDA: Your father *did!*

89   TOM: Don't get started on that!

90   AMANDA: He *does* drink, then?

91   TOM: Not that I know of!

92   AMANDA: Make sure, be certain! The last thing I want for my daughter's a boy who drinks!

93   TOM: Aren't you being a little premature? Mr. O'Connor has not yet appeared on the scene!

94   AMANDA: But will tomorrow. To meet your sister, and what do I know about his character? Nothing! Old maids are better off than wives of drunkards!

95   TOM: Oh, my God!

96   AMANDA: Be still!

97   TOM: [*leaning forward to whisper*]: Lots of fellows meet girls whom they don't marry!

98   AMANDA: Oh, talk sensibly, Tom—and don't be sarcastic! [*She has gotten a hairbrush.*]

99   TOM: What are you doing?

100   AMANDA: I'm brushing that cowlick down! [*She attacks his hair with the brush.*] What is this young man's position at the warehouse?

101   TOM [*submitting grimly to the brush and interrogation*]: This young man's position is that of a shipping clerk, Mother.

102   AMANDA: Sounds to me like a fairly responsible job, the sort of a job *you* would be in if you had more *get-up*. What is his salary? Have you any idea?

103   TOM: I would judge it to be approximately eighty-five dollars a month.

104   AMANDA: Well—not princely, but—

105   TOM: Twenty more than I make.

106   AMANDA: Yes, how well I know! But for a family man, eighty-five dollars a month is not much more than you can just get by on. . . .

107   TOM: Yes, but Mr. O'Connor is not a family man.

108   AMANDA: He might be, mightn't he? Some time in the future?

109   TOM: I see. Plans and provisions.

110   AMANDA: You are the only young man that I know of who ignores the fact that the future becomes the present, the present the past, and the past turns into everlasting regret if you don't plan for it!

111   TOM: I will think that over and see what I can make of it.

112   AMANDA: Don't be **supercilious** with your mother! Tell me some more about this—what do you call him?

113   TOM: James D. O'Connor. The D. is for Delaney.

114   AMANDA: Irish on *both* sides! *Gracious!* And doesn't drink?

115   TOM: Shall I call him up and ask him right this minute?

116   AMANDA: The only way to find out about those things is to make discreet inquiries at the proper moment. When I was a girl in Blue Mountain and it was suspected that a young man drank, the girl whose attentions he had been receiving, if any girl *was*, would sometimes speak to the minister of his church, or rather her father would if her father was living, and sort of feel him out on the young man's character. That is the way such things are discreetly handled to keep a young woman from making a tragic mistake!

NOTES

117 TOM: Then how did you happen to make a tragic mistake?

118 AMANDA: That innocent look of your father's had everyone fooled! He *smiled*—the world was *enchanted!* No girl can do worse than put herself at the mercy of a handsome appearance! I hope that Mr. O'Connor is not too good-looking.

119 TOM: No, he's not too good-looking. He's covered with freckles and hasn't too much of a nose.

120 AMANDA: He's not right-down **homely**, though?

121 TOM: Not right-down homely. Just medium homely, I'd say.

122 AMANDA: Character's what to look for in a man.

123 TOM: That's what I've always said, Mother.

124 AMANDA: You've never said anything of the kind and I suspect you would never give it a thought.

125 TOM: Don't be so suspicious of me.

126 AMANDA: At least I hope he's the type that's up and coming.

127 TOM: I think he really goes in for self-improvement.

128 AMANDA: What reason have you to think so?

129 TOM: He goes to night school.

130 AMANDA: [*beaming*]: Splendid! What does he do, I mean study?

131 TOM: Radio engineering and public speaking!

132 AMANDA: Then he has visions of being advanced in the world! Any young man who studies public speaking is aiming to have an executive job some day! And radio engineering? A thing for the future! Both of these facts are very illuminating. Those are the sort of things that a mother should know concerning any young man who comes to call on her daughter. Seriously or—not.

133 TOM: One little warning. He doesn't know about Laura. I didn't let on that we had dark ulterior motives. I just said, why don't you come and have dinner with us? He said okay and that was the whole conversation.

Skill:
Dramatic Elements
and Structure

Was Tom worried James would not come to dinner if he knew about his sister? Or does he really think these are "dark ulterior motives"?

Amanda makes fun of Tom in a kind way by calling him eloquent as an oyster.

134   AMANDA: I bet it was! You're eloquent as an oyster. However, he'll know about Laura when he gets here. When he sees how lovely and sweet and pretty she is, he'll thank his lucky stars he was asked to dinner.

135   TOM: Mother, you mustn't expect too much of Laura.

136   AMANDA: What do you mean?

137   TOM: Laura seems all those things to you and me because she's ours and we love her. We don't even notice she's crippled any more.

138   AMANDA: Don't say crippled! You know that I never allow that word to be used!

139   TOM: But face facts, Mother. She is and—that's not all—

140   AMANDA: What do you mean "not all"?

141   TOM: Laura is very different from other girls.

142   AMANDA: I think the difference is all to her advantage.

143   TOM: Not quite all—in the eyes of others—strangers—she's terribly shy and lives in a world of her own and those things make her seem a little peculiar to people outside the house.

144   AMANDA: Don't say peculiar.

145   TOM: Face the facts. She is.

146   [*The dance hall music changes to a tango that has a minor and somewhat ominous tone.*]

147   AMANDA: In what way is she peculiar—may I ask?

148   TOM [*gently*]: She lives in a world of her own—a world of little glass ornaments, Mother. . . .

149   [*He gets up. Amanda remains holding the brush, looking at him, troubled.*]

150   She plays old phonograph records and—that's about all—

151   [*He glances at himself in the mirror and crosses to the door.*]

152   AMANDA [*sharply*]: Where are you going?

153 TOM: I'm going to the movies. [*He goes out the screen door.*]

154 AMANDA: Not to the movies, every night to the movies! [*She follows quickly to the screen door.*] I don't believe you always go to the movies!

155 [*He is gone. Amanda look worriedly after him for a moment. Then vitality and optimism return and she turns from the door, crossing to the portieres.*]

156 Laura! Laura!

157 [*Laura answers from the kitchenette.*]

158 LAURA: Yes, Mother.

159 AMANDA: Let those dishes go and come in front!

160 [*Laura appears with a dish towel. Amanda speaks to her gaily.*]

161 Laura, come here and make a wish on the moon!

162 [*Screen image:* The Moon.]

163 LAURA [*entering*]: Moon—moon?

164 AMANDA: A little silver slipper of a moon. Look over your left shoulder, Laura, and make a wish!

165 [*Laura looks faintly puzzled as if called out of sleep. Amanda seizes her shoulders and turns her at an angle by the door.*]

166 Now! Now, darling, *wish!*

167 LAURA: What shall I wish for, Mother?

168 AMANDA [*her voice trembling and her eyes suddenly filling with tears*]: Happiness! Good fortune!

169 [*The sound of the violin rises and the stage dims out.*]

First Read

Read *The Glass Menagerie*. After you read, complete the Think Questions below.

☁ THINK QUESTIONS

1. What does Tom remember as he steps out onto the fire escape? Describe his memories using details from the text. What does this memory suggest about his feelings about his own life at that moment? Support your inference with a quotation from the text.

2. What ideas or feelings does the moon inspire in Amanda? What can you infer about Amanda based on the wish she expresses when seeing the moon and her behavior throughout this scene? Cite details from the text to support your inferences.

3. How does Amanda react when Tom reveals that he has invited a "gentleman caller" to dinner? What sorts of qualities does she ask about? What does her reaction suggest about her character and her relationship to her children? Support your answer with textual evidence.

4. Use context to determine the meaning of the word **emulate** as it is used in *The Glass Menagerie*. Write your definition of "emulate" here and tell how you found it.

5. Use context to determine the meaning of the word **homely** as it is used in *The Glass Menagerie*. Write your definition of "homely" here and tell how you found it.

Skill: Dramatic Elements and Structure

Use the Checklist to analyze Dramatic Elements and Structure in "The Glass Menagerie." Refer to the sample student annotations about Dramatic Elements and Structure in the text.

••• CHECKLIST FOR DRAMATIC ELEMENTS AND STRUCTURE

In order to determine the author's choices regarding the development of a drama, note the following:

- ✓ how character choices and dialogue affect the plot

- ✓ the stage directions and how they are used to reveal character and plot development

- ✓ the names of all the characters, and their relationships with one another

- ✓ character development, including personality traits, motivations, decisions they make, and actions they take

- ✓ the setting(s) of the story and how it influences the characters and the events of the plot

To analyze the impact of the author's choices regarding how to develop and relate elements of a story or drama, consider the following questions:

- ✓ How does the setting affect the characters and plot?

- ✓ How do the characters' actions help develop the theme or message of the play?

- ✓ How does the order of events in the play affect the development of the drama?

- ✓ How do the choices the characters make help advance the plot?

Skill: Dramatic Elements and Structure

Reread paragraphs 152–169 of *The Glass Menagerie*. Then, using the Checklist on the previous page, answer the multiple-choice questions below.

♻ YOUR TURN

1. What is the most likely reason that Laura is introduced at the end of the scene?

   ○ A. To show how dialogue between Laura and Amanda differs from conversations that Amanda had with Tom.

   ○ B. To allow the audience to finally see Laura and determine why Tom and Amanda seem so worried about her.

   ○ C. To provide details about Laura's personality traits to the audience that show how wrong Tom and Amanda are about her.

   ○ D. To reinforce the relationship between mother and daughter, and show that Tom is the outcast of the family.

2. Which of the following best describes the effect of the final stage direction in this scene?

   ○ A. It uses music to add a specific emotion to the closing dialogue in the scene.

   ○ B. It provides resolution to the scene through the character's actions.

   ○ C. It provides background music and necessary information to the audience.

   ○ D. It uses music to create tension so the audience wants to know what happens next.

Please note that excerpts and passages in the StudySync® library and this workbook are intended as touchstones to generate interest in an author's work. The excerpts and passages do not substitute for the reading of entire texts, and StudySync® strongly recommends that students seek out and purchase the whole literary or informational work in order to experience it as the author intended. Links to online resellers are available in our digital library. In addition, complete works may be ordered through an authorized reseller by filling out and returning to StudySync® the order form enclosed in this workbook.

Reading & Writing Companion   223

Skill:
Media

Use the Checklist to analyze Media in *The Glass Menagerie*. Refer to the sample student annotations about Media in the text.

••• CHECKLIST FOR MEDIA

In order to identify multiple interpretations of a story, drama, or poem, do the following:

✓ note the similarities and differences in different media, such as the live production of a play or a recorded novel or poetry

✓ evaluate how each version interprets the source text

✓ consider how, within the same medium, a story can have multiple interpretations if told by writers from different time periods and cultures

✓ consider how stories told in the same medium will likely reflect the specific objectives as well as the respective ideas, concerns, and values of each writer

To analyze multiple interpretations of a story, drama, or poem, evaluating how each version interprets the source text, consider the following questions:

✓ What medium is being used, and how does it affect the interpretation of the source text?

✓ What are the main similarities and differences between the two (or more) versions?

✓ If each version is from a different time period and/or culture, what does each version reveal about the author's objectives and the time period and culture in which it was written?

Skill:
Media

Reread lines 97–114 of *The Glass Menagerie* and review the radio and audiobook clips in the digital lesson. Then, using the Checklist on the previous page, answer the multiple-choice questions below.

↻ YOUR TURN

1. What is the most likely reason that the audiobook reads some stage directions from this passage and not others?

   ○ A. Some stage directions were removed due to time constraints in the audiobook version of the play.

   ○ B. Each interpretation varies given the time period and culture, and stage directions are less popular in 2018.

   ○ C. The stage directions are read only when the audience of the audiobook version needs the additional information.

   ○ D. The playwright omitted some stage directions because the actors did not need the instructions in the audiobook version.

2. In what way is the first line in this clip from the 1951 radio play different from the script?

   ○ A. The radio play removes the reference to marriage that is included in the script.

   ○ B. The radio play does not use the original words from the script in the first line.

   ○ C. The actor does not whisper as instructed by the stage direction.

   ○ D. The actor is devoid of emotion, unlike instructions in the script.

3. What is one effect of having a live studio audience for the radio play?

   ○ A. The live studio audience reaction influences the actor's interpretation of the play.

   ○ B. The playwright adjusts the script to accomodate for the audience reaction.

   ○ C. The live studio audience sees the stage directions in action and tell the listener what is happening.

   ○ D. The actors occasionally have to pause for the laughter to subside so that they can be heard.

Please note that excerpts and passages in the StudySync® library and this workbook are intended as touchstones to generate interest in an author's work. The excerpts and passages do not substitute for the reading of entire texts, and StudySync® strongly recommends that students seek out and purchase the whole literary or informational work in order to experience it as the author intended. Links to online resellers are available in our digital library. In addition, complete works may be ordered through an authorized reseller by filling out and returning to StudySync® the order form enclosed in this workbook.

Reading & Writing Companion   225

Close Read

Reread *The Glass Menagerie*. As you reread, complete the Skills Focus questions below. Then use your answers and annotations from the questions to help you complete the Write activity.

◎ SKILLS FOCUS

1. Reread the stage directions. How do music and lighting cues contribute to the text? How do they affect your understanding of what happens in the scene and why the events are important to the story? Highlight textual evidence and make annotations to explain your choices.

2. In this scene, Williams offers indirect characterization of Laura through dialogue between Amanda and Tom. What can readers infer about Laura based on their descriptions? How do Laura's actions at the end of the scene compare and contrast with readers' expectations? Support your answer with textual evidence and make annotations to explain your answer choices.

3. Identify places in the text where Amanda shows concern about appearances. What sorts of things is she worried about and why? How does her portrayal in the radio play and in the audio book reflect the character's perspective on the importance of appearances? Highlight textual evidence and make annotations to support your explanation.

4. Compare and contrast the portrayals of Tom in the radio play and in the audiobook. How do the actors' portrayals compare to your first impressions of Tom in Williams's original text? Highlight your textual evidence and make annotations to explain your choices.

5. *The Glass Menagerie* is a "memory play" loosely based on Williams's own experiences with his mother and sister. How does the character of Tom represent feelings of alienation? What might be causing those feelings? Highlight textual evidence and make annotations to explain your ideas.

✏ WRITE

COMPARE AND CONTRAST: Listen to the audio clips of *The Glass Menagerie*. How do these two versions differ from each other? How does each version interpret the source text of the play, making the dramatic elements work for that specific medium? Choose at least one substantial difference between the two versions, and explain and evaluate how each version interprets the source material. Support your writing with textual evidence and both audio recordings.

A Room Of One's Own

ARGUMENTATIVE TEXT
Virginia Woolf
1929

Introduction

Virginia Woolf (1882–1941) was one of the most important Modernist authors of the early 20th century. Best remembered for her lyrical, experimental novels, including *Mrs. Dalloway* and *To the Lighthouse*, Woolf also wrote a book-length essay entitled "A Room of One's Own," in which she muses on women as writers and as characters in fiction, describing the many challenges women face in their paths to self-actualization. In this excerpt, Woolf speculates about what might have happened if Shakespeare had had a talented and strong-willed author for a sister. Through this hypothetical scenario, Woolf illustrates the limited opportunities that had historically been available to women.

"She had no chance of learning grammar and logic, let alone of reading Horace and Virgil."

From Chapter Three

1   Let me imagine, since the facts are so hard to come by, what would have happened had Shakespeare had a wonderfully gifted sister, called Judith, let us say. Shakespeare himself went, very probably—his mother was an heiress—to the grammar school, where he may have learnt Latin—Ovid, Virgil and Horace[1]—and the elements of grammar and **logic**. He was, it is well known, a wild boy who **poached** rabbits, perhaps shot a deer, and had, rather sooner than he should have done, to marry a woman in the neighborhood, who bore him a child rather quicker than was right. That escapade sent him to seek his fortune in London. He had, it seemed, a taste for the theatre; he began by holding horses at the stage door. Very soon he got work in the theatre, became a successful actor, and lived at the hub of the universe, meeting everybody, knowing everybody, practicing his art on the boards, exercising his wits in the streets, and even getting access to the palace of the queen. Meanwhile his extraordinarily gifted sister, let us suppose, remained at home. She was as adventurous, as imaginative, as agog to see the world as he was. But she was not sent to school. She had no chance of learning grammar and logic, let alone of reading Horace and Virgil. She picked up a book now and then, one of her brother's perhaps, and read a few pages. But then her parents came in and told her to mend the stockings or mind the stew and not moon about with books and papers. They would have spoken sharply but kindly, for they were **substantial** people who knew the conditions of life for a woman and loved their daughter—indeed, more likely than not she was the apple of her father's eye. Perhaps she scribbled some pages up in an apple loft[2] on the sly, but was careful to hide them or set fire to them. Soon, however, before she was out of her teens, she was to be betrothed to the son of a neighboring wool-stapler. She cried out that marriage was hateful to her, and for that she was severely beaten by her father. Then he ceased to scold her. He begged her instead not to hurt him, not to shame him in this matter of her marriage. He would give her a chain of beads or a fine petticoat, he said; and there were tears in his eyes. How could she disobey him? How could she

1. **Ovid, Virgil, and Horace** three of the most famous poets of ancient Rome
2. **apple loft** an open second storey of a barn

break his heart? The force of her own gift alone drove her to it. She made up a small parcel of her belongings, let herself down by a rope one summer's night and took the road to London. She was not seventeen. The birds that sang in the hedge were not more musical than she was. She had the quickest fancy, a gift like her brother's, for the tune of words. Like him, she had a taste for the theatre. She stood at the stage door; she wanted to act, she said. Men laughed in her face. The manager—a fat, loose-lipped man—guffawed. He bellowed something about poodles dancing and women acting—no woman, he said, could possibly be an actress. He hinted—you can imagine what. She could get no training in her craft. Could she even seek her dinner in a tavern or roam the streets at midnight? Yet her genius was for fiction and lusted to feed abundantly upon the lives of men and women and the study of their ways. At last—for she was very young, oddly like Shakespeare the poet in her face, with the same grey eyes and rounded brows—at last Nick Greene the actor-manager took pity on her; she found herself with child by that gentleman and so—who shall measure the heat and violence of the poet's heart when caught and tangled in a woman's body?—killed herself one winter's night and lies buried at some crossroads where the omnibuses now stop outside the Elephant and Castle[3].

2   That, more or less, is how the story would run, I think, if a woman in Shakespeare's day had had Shakespeare's genius. But for my part, I agree with the deceased bishop[4], if such he was—it is unthinkable that any woman in Shakespeare's day should have had Shakespeare's genius. For genius like Shakespeare's is not born among labouring, uneducated, **servile** people. It was not born in England among the Saxons and the Britons. It is not born today among the working classes. How, then, could it have been born among women whose work began, according to Professor Trevelyan, almost before they were out of the nursery, who were forced to it by their parents and held to it by all the power of law and custom? Yet genius of a sort must have existed among women as it must have existed among the working classes. Now and again an Emily Bronte or a Robert Burns[5] blazes out and proves its presence. But certainly it never got itself on to paper. When, however, one reads of a witch being ducked, of a woman possessed by devils, of a wise woman selling herbs, or even of a very remarkable man who had a mother, then I think we are on the track of a lost novelist, a suppressed poet, of some mute and inglorious Jane Austen, some Emily Bronte who dashed her brains out on the moor or mopped and mowed about the highways crazed with the torture that her gift had put her to. Indeed, I would venture to guess that

3. **outside the Elephant and Castle** a road and Underground transportation hub in the Southwark borough of London
4. **the deceased bishop** Virginia Woolf remembers a bishop who wrote that no woman could ever become as smart or accomplished as Shakespeare
5. **Emily Brontë or a Robert Burns** Emily Brontë (1818–1848), author of the classic novel Wuthering Heights; Robert Burns (1759–1796), national poet of Scotland, writer of "Auld Lang Syne"

NOTES

Anon, who wrote so many poems without signing them, was often a woman. It was a woman Edward Fitzgerald[6], I think, suggested who made the ballads and the folk-songs, crooning them to her children, beguiling her spinning with them, on the length of the winter's night.

3 This may be true or it may be false—who can say?—but what is true in it, so it seemed to me, reviewing the story of Shakespeare's sister as I had made it, is that any woman born with a great gift in the sixteenth century would certainly have gone crazed, shot herself, or ended her days in some lonely cottage outside the village, half witch, half wizard, feared and mocked at. For it needs little skill in psychology to be sure that a highly gifted girl who had tried to use her gift for poetry would have been so thwarted and hindered by other people, so tortured and pulled **asunder** by her own contrary instincts, that she must have lost her health and sanity to a certainty.

Excerpted from *A Room of One's Own* by Virginia Woolf, published by Mariner Books.

✎ WRITE

ARGUMENTATIVE: Woolf states: "Genius like Shakespeare's is not born among labouring, uneducated, servile people." Do you think this statement still holds true today? In an essay response, discuss whether you think "genius" among the "working classes" is possible in today's society, and why or why not. How might this have been different in the time in which Woolf lived, and why?

6. **woman Edward Fitzgerald** Lady Edward FitzGerald (1809–1883), translated quatrains ascribed to the 11th century Persian poet Omar Khayyam that became very popular; later investigations strongly suggested his *Rubáiyát* was largely of FitzGerald's own invention

The New Dress

FICTION
Virginia Woolf
1927

Introduction

English author Virginia Woolf (1882–1941) is widely considered one of the most important literary figures of the 20th century. Woolf was a pioneer in her use of stream-of-consciousness, a narrative technique that follows a character's flow of thoughts. Her short story "The New Dress" was first published in the May 1927 issue of *Forum*, a New York City magazine. Some literary critics suspect that the short story was originally meant as a chapter for *Mrs. Dalloway*, Woolf's best-known novel. Both texts share some of the same characters and were written within three years of one another. In the story, Mabel wears a new handmade yellow dress to one of Mrs. Dalloway's cocktail parties. Deeply self-conscious, Mabel is convinced she is being mocked by the other partygoers.

"What's Mabel wearing? What a fright she looks!"

1   Mabel had her first serious suspicion that something was wrong as she took her cloak off and Mrs. Barnet, while handing her the mirror and touching the brushes and thus drawing her attention, perhaps rather markedly, to all the appliances for tidying and improving hair, complexion, clothes, which existed on the dressing table, confirmed

Virginia Woolf

the suspicion—that it was not right, not quite right, which growing stronger as she went upstairs and springing at her, with conviction as she greeted Clarissa Dalloway, she went straight to the far end of the room, to a shaded corner where a looking-glass hung and looked. No! It was not RIGHT. And at once the misery which she always tried to hide, the **profound** dissatisfaction—the sense she had had, ever since she was a child, of being inferior to other people—set upon her, relentlessly, remorselessly, with an intensity which she could not beat off, as she would when she woke at night at home, by reading Borrow or Scott[1]; for oh these men, oh these women, all were thinking— "What's Mabel wearing? What a fright she looks! What a hideous new dress!"— their eyelids flickering as they came up and then their lids shutting rather tight. It was her own appalling inadequacy; her cowardice; her mean, water-sprinkled blood that depressed her. And at once the whole of the room where, for ever so many hours, she had planned with the little dressmaker how it was to go, seemed **sordid**, repulsive; and her own drawing-room so shabby, and herself, going out, puffed up with vanity as she touched the letters on the hall table and said: "How dull!" to show off—all this now seemed unutterably silly, paltry, and provincial. All this had been absolutely destroyed, shown up, exploded, the moment she came into Mrs. Dalloway's drawing-room.

---

1. **Borrow or Scott** George Henry Borrow (1803–1881), travel writer, lived with English gypsies and wrote romantically about their lifestyle; Sir Walter Scott (1771–1832) author of the popular 1819 novel *Ivanhoe*, which presented a romanticized, unrealistic version of England in the Middle Ages

Copyright © BookheadEd Learning, LLC

2   What she had thought that evening when, sitting over the teacups, Mrs. Dalloway's invitation came, was that, of course, she could not be fashionable. It was absurd to pretend it even—fashion meant cut, meant style, meant thirty guineas at least—but why not be original? Why not be herself, anyhow? And, getting up, she had taken that old fashion book of her mother's, a Paris fashion book of the time of the Empire, and had thought how much prettier, more dignified, and more womanly they were then, and so set herself—oh, it was foolish—trying to be like them, pluming herself in fact, upon being modest and old-fashioned, and very charming, giving herself up, no doubt about it, to an orgy of self-love, which deserved to be **chastised**, and so rigged herself out like this.

3   But she dared not look in the glass. She could not face the whole horror—the pale yellow, idiotically old-fashioned silk dress with its long skirt and its high sleeves and its waist and all the things that looked so charming in the fashion book, but not on her, not among all these ordinary people. She felt like a dressmaker's dummy standing there, for young people to stick pins into.

4   "But, my dear, it's perfectly charming!" Rose Shaw said, looking her up and down with that little satirical pucker of the lips which she expected—Rose herself being dressed in the height of the fashion, precisely like everybody else, always.

5   We are all like flies trying to crawl over the edge of the saucer, Mabel thought, and repeated the phrase as if she were crossing herself, as if she were trying to find some spell to annul this pain, to make this agony endurable. Tags of Shakespeare, lines from books she had read ages ago, suddenly came to her when she was in agony, and she repeated them over and over again. "Flies trying to crawl," she repeated. If she could say that over often enough and make herself see the flies, she would become numb, chill, frozen, dumb. Now she could see flies crawling slowly out of a saucer of milk with their wings stuck together; and she strained and strained (standing in front of the looking-glass, listening to Rose Shaw) to make herself see Rose Shaw and all the other people there as flies, trying to hoist themselves out of something, or into something, meagre, insignificant, toiling flies. But she could not see them like that, not other people. She saw herself like that—she was a fly, but the others were dragonflies, butterflies, beautiful insects, dancing, fluttering, skimming, while she alone dragged herself up out of the saucer. (Envy and spite, the most detestable of the vices, were her chief faults.)

6   "I feel like some dowdy, decrepit, horribly dingy old fly," she said, making Robert Haydon stop just to hear her say that, just to reassure herself by furbishing up a poor weak-kneed phrase and so showing how detached she was, how witty, that she did not feel in the least out of anything. And, of course, Robert Haydon answered something, quite polite, quite insincere, which she

saw through instantly, and said to herself, directly he went (again from some book), "Lies, lies, lies!" For a party makes things either much more real, or much less real, she thought; she saw in a flash to the bottom of Robert Haydon's heart; she saw through everything. She saw the truth. THIS was true, this drawing-room, this self, and the other false. Miss Milan's little workroom was really terribly hot, stuffy, sordid. It smelt of clothes and cabbage cooking; and yet, when Miss Milan put the glass in her hand, and she looked at herself with the dress on, finished, an extraordinary bliss shot through her heart. Suffused with light, she sprang into existence. Rid of cares and wrinkles, what she had dreamed of herself was there—a beautiful woman. just for a second (she had not dared look longer, Miss Milan wanted to know about the length of the skirt), there looked at her, framed in the scrolloping mahogany, a grey-white, mysteriously smiling, charming girl, the core of herself, the soul of herself; and it was not vanity only, not only self-love that made her think it good, tender, and true. Miss Milan said that the skirt could not well be longer; if anything the skirt, said Miss Milan, puckering her forehead, considering with all her wits about her, must be shorter; and she felt, suddenly, honestly, full of love for Miss Milan, much, much fonder of Miss Milan than of any one in the whole world, and could have cried for pity that she should be crawling on the floor with her mouth full of pins, and her face red and her eyes bulging—that one human being should be doing this for another, and she saw them all as human beings merely, and herself going off to her party, and Miss Milan pulling the cover over the canary's cage, or letting him pick a hemp-seed from between her lips, and the thought of it, of this side of human nature and its patience and its endurance and its being content with such miserable, scanty, sordid, little pleasures filled her eyes with tears.

7   And now the whole thing had vanished. The dress, the room, the love, the pity, the scrolloping looking-glass, and the canary's cage—all had vanished, and here she was in a corner of Mrs. Dalloway's drawing-room, suffering tortures, woken wide awake to reality.

8   But it was all so paltry, weak-blooded, and petty-minded to care so much at her age with two children, to be still so utterly dependent on people's opinions and not have principles or convictions, not to be able to say as other people did, "There's Shakespeare! There's death! We're all weevils in a captain's biscuit"—or whatever it was that people did say.

9   She faced herself straight in the glass; she pecked at her left shoulder; she issued out into the room, as if spears were thrown at her yellow dress from all sides. But instead of looking fierce or tragic, as Rose Shaw would have done—Rose would have looked like Boadicea[2]—she looked foolish and self-

2. **Boadicea** tribal queen of the indigenous Celtic Iceni, who led a rebellion against Roman occupation 60–61 CE

conscious, and simpered like a schoolgirl and slouched across the room, positively slinking, as if she were a beaten mongrel, and looked at a picture, an engraving. As if one went to a party to look at a picture! Everybody knew why she did it—it was from shame, from humiliation.

10   "Now the fly's in the saucer," she said to herself, "right in the middle, and can't get out, and the milk," she thought, rigidly staring at the picture, "is sticking its wings together."

11   "It's so old-fashioned," she said to Charles Burt, making him stop (which by itself he hated) on his way to talk to some one else.

12   She meant, or she tried to make herself think that she meant, that it was the picture and not her dress, that was old-fashioned. And one word of praise, one word of affection from Charles would have made all the difference to her at the moment. If he had only said, "Mabel, you're looking charming to-night!" it would have changed her life. But then she ought to have been truthful and direct. Charles said nothing of the kind, of course. He was malice itself. He always saw through one, especially if one were feeling particularly mean, paltry, or feeble-minded.

13   "Mabel's got a new dress!" he said, and the poor fly was absolutely shoved into the middle of the saucer. Really, he would like her to drown, she believed. He had no heart, no fundamental kindness, only a **veneer** of friendliness. Miss Milan was much more real, much kinder. If only one could feel that and stick to it, always. "Why," she asked herself—replying to Charles much too pertly, letting him see that she was out of temper, or "ruffled" as he called it ("Rather ruffled?" he said and went on to laugh at her with some woman over there)—"Why," she asked herself, "can't I feel one thing always, feel quite sure that Miss Milan is right, and Charles wrong and stick to it, feel sure about the canary and pity and love and not be whipped all round in a second by coming into a room full of people?" It was her odious, weak, vacillating character again, always giving at the critical moment and not being seriously interested in conchology, etymology, botany, archeology, cutting up potatoes and watching them fructify like Mary Dennis, like Violet Searle.

14   Then Mrs. Holman, seeing her standing there, bore down upon her. Of course a thing like a dress was beneath Mrs. Holman's notice, with her family always tumbling downstairs or having the scarlet fever. Could Mabel tell her if Elmthorpe was ever let for August and September? Oh, it was a conversation that bored her unutterably!—it made her furious to be treated like a house agent or a messenger boy, to be made use of. Not to have value, that was it, she thought, trying to grasp something hard, something real, while she tried to answer sensibly about the bathroom and the south aspect and the hot water to the top of the house; and all the time she could

see little bits of her yellow dress in the round looking-glass which made them all the size of boot-buttons or tadpoles; and it was amazing to think how much humiliation and agony and self-loathing and effort and passionate ups and downs of feeling were contained in a thing the size of a threepenny bit. And what was still odder, this thing, this Mabel Waring, was separate, quite disconnected; and though Mrs. Holman (the black button) was leaning forward and telling her how her eldest boy had strained his heart running, she could see her, too, quite detached in the looking-glass, and it was impossible that the black dot, leaning forward, gesticulating, should make the yellow dot, sitting solitary, self-centred, feel what the black dot was feeling, yet they pretended.

15   "So impossible to keep boys quiet"—that was the kind of thing one said.

16   And Mrs. Holman, who could never get enough sympathy and snatched what little there was greedily, as if it were her right (but she deserved much more for there was her little girl who had come down this morning with a swollen knee-joint), took this miserable offering and looked at it suspiciously, grudgingly, as if it were a halfpenny when it ought to have been a pound and put it away in her purse, must put up with it, mean and miserly though it was, times being hard, so very hard; and on she went, creaking, injured Mrs. Holman, about the girl with the swollen joints. Ah, it was tragic, this greed, this clamour of human beings, like a row of cormorants, barking and flapping their wings for sympathy—it was tragic, could one have felt it and not merely pretended to feel it!

17   But in her yellow dress to-night she could not wring out one drop more; she wanted it all, all for herself. She knew (she kept on looking into the glass, dipping into that dreadfully showing-up blue pool) that she was condemned, despised, left like this in a backwater, because of her being like this a feeble, vacillating creature; and it seemed to her that the yellow dress was a penance which she had deserved, and if she had been dressed like Rose Shaw, in lovely, clinging green with a ruffle of swansdown, she would have deserved that; and she thought that there was no escape for her—none whatever. But it was not her fault altogether, after all. It was being one of a family of ten; never having money enough, always skimping and paring; and her mother carrying great cans, and the linoleum worn on the stair edges, and one sordid little domestic tragedy after another—nothing catastrophic, the sheep farm failing, but not utterly; her eldest brother marrying beneath him but not very much—there was no romance, nothing extreme about them all. They petered out respectably in seaside resorts; every watering-place had one of her aunts even now asleep in some lodging with the front windows not quite facing the sea. That was so like them—they had to squint at things always. And she had done the same—she was just like her aunts. For all her dreams of living in India, married to some hero like Sir Henry

Lawrence[3], some empire builder (still the sight of a native in a turban filled her with romance), she had failed utterly. She had married Hubert, with his safe, permanent underling's job in the Law Courts, and they managed tolerably in a smallish house, without proper maids, and hash when she was alone or just bread and butter, but now and then—Mrs. Holman was off, thinking her the most dried-up, unsympathetic twig she had ever met, absurdly dressed, too, and would tell every one about Mabel's fantastic appearance—now and then, thought Mabel Waring, left alone on the blue sofa, punching the cushion in order to look occupied, for she would not join Charles Burt and Rose Shaw, chattering like magpies and perhaps laughing at her by the fireplace—now and then, there did come to her delicious moments, reading the other night in bed, for instance, or down by the sea on the sand in the sun, at Easter—let her recall it—a great tuft of pale sand-grass standing all twisted like a shock of spears against the sky, which was blue like a smooth china egg[4], so firm, so hard, and then the melody of the waves—"Hush, hush," they said, and the children's shouts paddling—yes, it was a divine moment, and there she lay, she felt, in the hand of the Goddess who was the world; rather a hard-hearted, but very beautiful Goddess, a little lamb laid on the altar (one did think these silly things, and it didn't matter so long as one never said them). And also with Hubert sometimes she had quite unexpectedly—carving the mutton for Sunday lunch, for no reason, opening a letter, coming into a room—divine moments, when she said to herself (for she would never say this to anybody else), "This is it. This has happened. This is it!" And the other way about it was equally surprising—that is, when everything was arranged—music, weather, holidays, every reason for happiness was there—then nothing happened at all. One wasn't happy. It was flat, just flat, that was all.

18 Her wretched self again, no doubt! She had always been a fretful, weak, unsatisfactory mother, a wobbly wife, lolling about in a kind of twilight existence with nothing very clear or very bold, or more one thing than another, like all her brothers and sisters, except perhaps Herbert—they were all the same poor water-veined creatures who did nothing. Then in the midst of this creeping, crawling life, suddenly she was on the crest of a wave. That wretched fly—where had she read the story that kept coming into her mind about the fly and the saucer?—struggled out. Yes, she had those moments. But now that she was forty, they might come more and more seldom. By degrees she would cease to struggle any more. But that was deplorable! That was not to be **endured**! That made her feel ashamed of herself!

---

3. **Sir Henry Lawrence** Brigadier General Sir Henry Montgomery Lawrence (1806–1857), a British colonial administrator in India who was killed at the Siege of Lucknow
4. **china egg** a decorative egg made of porcelain

NOTES

19 She would go to the London Library to-morrow. She would find some wonderful, helpful, astonishing book, quite by chance, a book by a clergyman, by an American no one had ever heard of; or she would walk down the Strand and drop, accidentally, into a hall where a miner was telling about the life in the pit, and suddenly she would become a new person. She would be absolutely transformed. She would wear a uniform; she would be called Sister Somebody; she would never give a thought to clothes again. And for ever after she would be perfectly clear about Charles Burt and Miss Milan and this room and that room; and it would be always, day after day, as if she were lying in the sun or carving the mutton. It would be it!

20 So she got up from the blue sofa, and the yellow button in the looking-glass got up too, and she waved her hand to Charles and Rose to show them she did not depend on them one scrap, and the yellow button moved out of the looking-glass, and all the spears were gathered into her breast as she walked towards Mrs. Dalloway and said "Good night."

21 "But it's too early to go," said Mrs. Dalloway, who was always so charming.

22 "I'm afraid I must," said Mabel Waring. "But," she added in her weak, wobbly voice which only sounded ridiculous when she tried to strengthen it, "I have enjoyed myself enormously."

23 'I have enjoyed myself," she said to Mr. Dalloway, whom she met on the stairs.

24 "Lies, lies, lies!" she said to herself, going downstairs, and "Right in the saucer!" she said to herself as she thanked Mrs. Barnet for helping her and wrapped herself, round and round and round, in the Chinese cloak she had worn these twenty years.

✏ WRITE

NARRATIVE: Compose a brief passage of a short story focusing on a character whose outward appearance does not match his or her feelings. Use "The New Dress" as a model, because the main character in the story secretly thinks she looks hideous while she tries to put a brave face on her situation. Consider how it might affect a person to hide his or her true feelings at a party or with a single person who is important to him or her.

Hurricane Season

POETRY
Fareena Arefeen
2016

Introduction

In September of 2008, Hurricane Ike roared through Haiti and Cuba, traveled up the Gulf of Mexico, and barreled into Texas with increasing velocity, causing broken windows, flooded streets and numerous casualties. Houston-area poet Fareena Arefeen channels her own memories of the city's natural disasters in "Hurricane Season," an energetic meditation on her connection to Houston as a first-generation immigrant and her desire to wield language to create art. While a junior at Houston's High School for Performing and Visual Arts, Arefeen was named the city's second Youth Poet Laureate in 2016.

"I only came into my skin after I grew into this city"

NOTES

1 My mother tells me that I was born outside of the eye of a hurricane,
2 where the storm is strong and moves quickly in **radials**.
3 I think I am a series of low pressure systems and winds that can carry **bayous**.

4 I've heard that a child playing on the coast in Africa
5 can cause the start of a hurricane in the Atlantic and maybe
6 a working immigrant in Toronto can be the origin of a poet in Houston.

7 My ninth birthday was suspended in the space between **cyclone** and serene.
8 I watched my city build itself up again after Hurricane Ike and
9 I guess we are both having growing pains.

10 I've learned that my purpose is flooding.
11 I want to form inundacions of words and earn
12 the title of a Category Four[1]. Drought relief and filler of bayou banks.
13 Hurricanes bring heat energy from the tropics
14 the way I would like to bring light to the city that taught me how to hold
   rainwater in the form of letters.

15 On my thirteenth birthday, I watched the bayou
16 spill into this dizzy headed space city
17 like a push of blood to the lungs.

18 Inhaling **atmospheric** pressure of a tropical storm
19 in the eye of hurricane season felt like bayou backwash
20 of building Rothko[2] layers.

21 Maybe if I could say that brown is my favorite color,
22 I would finally see the whirlpools that rest in my skin and in the Buffalo Bayou.
23 And someday I could love the greens hidden in browns hidden in **labyrinths**
   of color.

---

1. **Category Four** hurricanes or cyclones are measured for force on a five-level scale, five being the most powerful
2. **Rothko** Mark Rothko (1903–1970), abstract expressionist painter and creator of Houston's Rothko Chapel

24 I only came into my skin
25 after I grew into this city and they both happened like storm clouds; rolling in and all at once.

26 Now, I find impressions of myself in the silt
27 as there are maps of this city pressed into my hands like footsteps on wet ground.

28 On my seventeenth birthday, the clouds broke light rays
29 the way I want to leave fractures in my city
30 that can be filled with the work of new artists and immigrants to take my place.

31 My favorite smell is rain
32 falling through concrete and cumin[3] because they combine homes.
33 I can be a drop of water falling in multiple places.

34 I am stuck to the city I've learned to call my own
35 like humidity on skin that can finally
36 hold its own storm.

By Fareena Arefeen, 2016. Used by permission of Fareena Arefeen.

✎ WRITE

LITERARY ANALYSIS: Arefeen uses the image of a hurricane to express a wide variety of personal experiences; at times the speaker seems to be the hurricane itself, while at other times the speaker seems to be in the midst of experiencing a hurricane. Is the image of a hurricane in this poem creative, destructive, or both? Cite textual evidence to support your argument.

---

3. **cumin** a powdery spice derived from the crushed seeds of a flowering plant, commonly used in Bengali cuisine

Be Ye Men of Valour

ARGUMENTATIVE TEXT
Winston Churchill
1940

Introduction

Delivered on May 19, 1940, "Be Ye Men of Valour" was Winston Churchill's (1874–1965) first radio address as British Prime Minister. In the speech, Churchill acknowledges that German military aggression would likely soon be directed at Great Britain, and tells his countrymen not to be intimidated. Instead, he urges them to prepare to do whatever is necessary to defeat a formidable adversary.

"Our task is not only to win the battle—but to win the war."

1   I speak to you for the first time as Prime Minister in a solemn hour for the life of our country, of our empire, of our allies, and, above all, of the cause of freedom. A tremendous battle is raging in France and Flanders[1]. The Germans, by a remarkable combination of air bombing and heavily armored tanks, have broken through the French defenses north of the Maginot Line[2], and strong columns of their armored vehicles are ravaging the open country, which for the first day or two was without defenders. They have penetrated deeply and spread alarm and confusion in their track. Behind them there are now appearing infantry in lorries[3], and behind them, again, the large **masses** are moving forward. The re-groupment of the French armies to make head against, and also to strike at, this intruding wedge has been proceeding for several days, largely assisted by the magnificent efforts of the Royal Air Force.

British prime minister Winston Churchill (1874–1965) inspects bomb damage outside the London offices of the British Equitable Assurance after a World War II air raid, 10th September 1940.

NOTES

Skill:
Central or
Main Idea

While there is a lot of other information here, the main idea of this first paragraph is that war is raging and Britain (Churchill's audience) is in great danger. The additional details describe what is happening with the war.

2   We must not allow ourselves to be intimidated by the presence of these armored vehicles in unexpected places behind our lines. If they are behind our Front, the French are also at many points fighting actively behind theirs. Both sides are therefore in an extremely dangerous position. And if the French Army and our own Army are well handled, as I believe they will be, if the French retain that genius for recovery and counter-attack for which they have so long been famous, and if the British Army shows the dogged endurance and solid fighting power of which there have been so many examples in the past, then a sudden transformation of the scene might spring into being.

1. **Flanders** the northern area of Belgium, encompassing Brussels
2. **the Maginot Line** a line of fortifications built in the 1930s along the French border to prevent German invasion
3. **lorry** (British) truck

NOTES

Skill:
Word Meaning

What does *grapples* mean? It appears to be an action taken "with the enemy" by a man, an officer, a brigade, or a division, so I'm guessing it's a verb. It also looks a bit like "grape," but I'm not sure about that connection.

Skill:
Informational
Text Structure

Early in his speech, Churchill appeals to pathos, presenting images of "ruin and slavery . . . turned upon us." With listeners in an emotional state, he unfolds his thesis: Britain is ready to fight and will do everything to win.

3   Now it would be foolish, however, to disguise the gravity of the hour. It would be still more foolish to lose heart and courage or to suppose that well-trained, well-equipped armies numbering three or four millions of men can be overcome in the space of a few weeks, or even months, by a scoop, or raid of mechanized vehicles, however **formidable**. We may look with confidence to the stabilization of the Front in France, and to the general engagement of the masses, which will enable the qualities of the French and British soldiers to be matched squarely against those of their adversaries. For myself, I have invincible confidence in the French Army and its leaders. Only a very small part of that splendid Army has yet been heavily engaged; and only a very small part of France has yet been invaded. There is a good evidence to show that practically the whole of the specialized and mechanized forces of the enemy have been already thrown into the battle; and we know that very heavy losses have been inflicted upon them. No officer or man, no brigade or division, which grapples at close quarters with the enemy, wherever encountered, can fail to make a worthy contribution to the general result. The Armies must cast away the idea of resisting attack behind concrete lines or natural obstacles, and must realize that mastery can only be regained by furious and unrelenting assault. And this spirit must not only animate the High Command, but must inspire every fighting man.

4   In the air—often at serious odds, often at odds hitherto thought overwhelming—we have been clawing down three or four to one of our enemies; and the relative balance of the British and German Air Forces is now considerably more favorable to us than at the beginning of the battle. In cutting down the German bombers, we are fighting our own battle as well as that of France. My confidence in our ability to fight it out to the finish with the German Air Force has been strengthened by the fierce encounters which have taken place and are taking place. At the same time, our heavy bombers are striking nightly at the tap-root of German mechanized power, and have already inflicted serious damage upon the oil refineries on which the Nazi effort to dominate the world directly depends.

5   We must expect that as soon as stability is reached on the Western Front, the bulk of that hideous apparatus of aggression which gashed Holland into ruin and slavery in a few days will be turned upon us. I am sure I speak for all when I say we are ready to face it, to endure it, and to retaliate against it to any extent that the unwritten laws of war permit. There will be many men and many women in this Island who, when the ordeal comes upon them, as come it will, will feel comfort, and even a pride, that they are sharing the perils of our lads at the Front—soldiers, sailors, and airmen—God bless them—and are drawing away from them a part at least of the onslaught they have to bear. Is not this the appointed time for all to make the utmost exertions in their power? If the battle is to be won, we must provide our men with ever-increasing quantities of the weapons and ammunition they need. We must have, and have quickly, more aeroplanes, more tanks, more shells, more guns. There is imperious need for

these vital munitions. They increase our strength against the powerfully armed enemy. They replace the wastage of the obstinate struggle—and the knowledge that wastage will speedily be replaced enables us to draw more readily upon our reserves and throw them in now that everything counts so much.

6   Our task is not only to win the battle—but to win the war. After this battle in France **abates** its force, there will come the battle for our Island—for all Britain is, and all that Britain means. That will be the struggle. In that supreme emergency we shall not hesitate to take every step, even the most drastic, to call forth from our people the last ounce and the last inch of effort of which they are capable. The interests of property, the hours of labor, are nothing compared to the struggle for life and honor, for right and freedom, to which we have vowed ourselves.

7   I have received from the Chiefs of the French Republic, and in particular from its indomitable Prime Minister, Monsieur Reynaud, the most sacred pledges that whatever happens they will fight to the end, be it bitter or be it glorious. Nay, if we fight to the end, it can only be glorious.

8   Having received His Majesty's **commission**, I have formed an Administration of men and women of every Party and of almost every point of view. We have differed and quarreled in the past, but now one bond unites us all: to wage war until victory is won, and never to surrender ourselves to servitude and shame, whatever the cost and the agony may be. This is one of the most awe-striking periods in the long history of France and Britain. It is also beyond doubt the most sublime. Side by side, unaided except by their kith and kin in the great Dominions[4] and by the wide empires which rest beneath their shield—side by side the British and French peoples have advanced to rescue not only Europe but mankind from the foulest and most soul-destroying tyranny which has ever darkened and stained the pages of history. Behind them, behind us, behind the Armies and Fleets of Britain and France, gather a group of shattered States and bludgeoned races: the Czechs, the Poles, the Norwegians, the Danes, the Dutch, the Belgians—upon all of whom the long night of barbarism will descend, unbroken even by a star of hope, unless we conquer, as conquer we must, as conquer we shall.

9   Today is Trinity Sunday[5]. Centuries ago words were written to be a call and a spur to the faithful servants of truth and justice:

10   Arm yourselves, and be ye men of **valour**, and be in readiness for the conflict; for it is better for us to perish in battle than to look upon the outrage of our nation and our altars. As the will of God is in Heaven, even so let it be.

---

4. **the great Dominions** referring to the colonized lands of the British Empire in Africa, India, Southeast Asia, the Pacific and the Caribbean
5. **Trinity Sunday** the eighth Sunday after Easter in the Christian liturgical calendar, celebrating the Trinity of God, Jesus, and the Holy Spirit

Skill:
Informational
Text Structure

Churchill continues his appeal to pathos here, saying "all Britain" could be lost. He then reasserts his position that Britain needs to "take every step" and that Britons will need to accept "even the most drastic" efforts.

Skill:
Central or
Main Idea

All the way through to the conclusion, the main ideas from the beginning are supported: Although the situation is legitimately dangerous, there is hope. But only if Britain acts with bravery and determination.

First Read

Read "Be Ye Men of Valour." After you read, complete the Think Questions below.

1. What is the current state of the war, and why does Churchill feel such a sense of urgency? Use details from the text to support your inferences.

2. How is what Churchill says about France in paragraph 1 different from what he says in paragraph 3? What reaction do you infer he hopes to elicit from his audience by making these two conflicting points? Support your inferences with evidence from the text.

3. Who are the "group of shattered States and bludgeoned races"? What image of Britain and France does Churchill hope to convey with this reference? Support your answer with evidence from the text.

4. Use context clues to find the definition of **formidable** as it is used in the text. Write your definition here, and explain which clues helped you arrive at it.

5. Write your definition for the word **commission** as it appears in the text. Then use a print or online dictionary to confirm the definition.

Skill:
Informational Text Structure

Use the Checklist to analyze Informational Text Structure in "Be Ye Men of Valour." Refer to the sample student annotations about Informational Text Structure in the text.

••• CHECKLIST FOR INFORMATIONAL TEXT STRUCTURE

In order to determine the structure an author uses in his or her exposition or argument, note the following:

✓ where the author introduces and clarifies their argument

✓ sentences and paragraphs that reveal the text structure the author uses to frame the argument

✓ whether the text structure is effective in presenting all sides of the argument, and makes his or her points clear, convincing and engaging

To analyze and evaluate the effectiveness of the structure an author uses in his or her exposition or argument, including whether the structure makes points clear, convincing, and engaging, consider the following questions:

✓ Did I have to read a particular sentence or phrase over again? Where?

✓ Did I find myself distracted or uninterested while reading the text? When?

✓ Did the structure the author used make their points clear, convincing, and engaging? Why or why not?

✓ Was the author's exposition or argument effective? Why or why not?

Please note that excerpts and passages in the StudySync® library and this workbook are intended as touchstones to generate interest in an author's work. The excerpts and passages do not substitute for the reading of entire texts, and StudySync® strongly recommends that students seek out and purchase the whole literary or informational work in order to experience it as the author intended. Links to online resellers are available in our digital library. In addition, complete works may be ordered through an authorized reseller by filling out and returning to StudySync® the order form enclosed in this workbook.

Reading & Writing Companion   247

Skill:
Informational Text Structure

Reread paragraph 8 of "Be Ye Men of Valour." Then, using the Checklist on the previous page, answer the multiple-choice questions below.

⟳ YOUR TURN

1. This question has two parts. First, answer Part A. Then, answer Part B.

   Part A: The central argument of this excerpt can best be described as—

   ○ A. "The Danes have been soundly defeated by the Nazis."
   ○ B. "Britain and France both have very large empires."
   ○ C. "Britain and France must and will defeat the Nazis."
   ○ D. "To defeat the Nazis, Britain and France must act as tyrants."

   Part B: Which of the following sentences or phrases from the text best supports your answer to Part A.

   ○ A. "This is one of the most awe-striking periods in the long history of France and Britain."
   ○ B. "Behind them, behind us, behind the Armies and Fleets of Britain and France, gather a group of shattered States and bludgeoned races."
   ○ C. "upon all of whom the long night of barbarism will descend, unbroken even by a star of hope"
   ○ D. "as conquer we must, as conquer we shall"

2. In using the phrase "foulest and most soul-destroying tyranny," Churchill is most clearly—

   ○ A. making an appeal to his audience's reason.
   ○ B. making an appeal to his audience's emotions.
   ○ C. explaining that Britain has no chance of winning the war.
   ○ D. explaining that Britain and France are very close friends.

Skill:
Central or Main Idea

Use the Checklist to analyze Central or Main Idea in "Be Ye Men of Valour." Refer to the sample student annotations about Central or Main Idea in the text.

••• CHECKLIST FOR CENTRAL OR MAIN IDEA

In order to identify two or more central ideas of a text, note the following:

- ✓ the main idea in each paragraph or group of paragraphs

- ✓ key details in each paragraph or section of text, distinguishing what they have in common

- ✓ whether the details contain information that could indicate more than one main idea in a text

  - a science text, for example, may provide information about a specific environment and also a message on ecological awareness

  - a biography may contain equally important ideas about a person's achievements, influence, and the time period in which the person lives or lived

- ✓ when each central idea emerges

- ✓ ways that the central ideas interact and build on one another

To determine two or more central ideas of a text and analyze their development over the course of the text, including how they interact and build on one another to provide a complex analysis, consider the following questions:

- ✓ What main idea(s) do the details in each paragraph explain or describe?

- ✓ What central or main ideas do all the paragraphs support?

- ✓ How do the central ideas interact and build on one another? How does that affect when they emerge?

- ✓ How might you provide an objective summary of the text? What details would you include?

Please note that excerpts and passages in the StudySync® library and this workbook are intended as touchstones to generate interest in an author's work. The excerpts and passages do not substitute for the reading of entire texts, and StudySync® strongly recommends that students seek out and purchase the whole literary or informational work in order to experience it as the author intended. Links to online resellers are available in our digital library. In addition, complete works may be ordered through an authorized reseller by filling out and returning to StudySync® the order form enclosed in this workbook.

Reading & Writing Companion   249

Skill:
Central or Main Idea

Reread paragraph 8 of "Be Ye Men of Valour." Then, using the Checklist on the previous page, answer the multiple-choice questions below.

⟳ YOUR TURN

1. This question has two parts. First, answer Part A. Then, answer Part B.

   Part A: Which of the following is the best restatement of the central idea of this paragraph?

   ○ A. Regardless of the cost, Britain will sacrifice everything to protect the rest of Europe from Nazi domination.

   ○ B. Regardless of the cost, France and Britain together must save humankind from the evils of Nazi domination.

   ○ C. Although Britain has had some internal strife, it is time to put all that aside and bond together to fight Nazi Germany.

   ○ D. Although it is unlikely that France and Germany will defeat Nazi Germany, they must try for the good of humankind.

   Part B: Which content from the paragraph best supports the answer to Part A?

   ○ A. "Having received His Majesty's commission, I have formed an Administration of men and women of every Party and of almost every point of view."

   ○ B. "We have differed and quarreled in the past, but now one bond unites us all . . ."

   ○ C. "This is one of the most awe-striking periods in the long history of France and Britain."

   ○ D. ". . . side by side the British and French peoples have advanced to rescue not only Europe but mankind from the foulest and most soul-destroying tyranny . . ."

Skill:
Word Meaning

Use the Checklist to analyze Word Meaning in "Be Ye Men of Valour." Refer to the sample student annotations about Word Meaning in the text.

••• CHECKLIST FOR WORD MEANING

In order to find the pronunciation of a word or determine or clarify its precise meaning, do the following:

- ✓ determine the word's part of speech

- ✓ use context clues to make an inferred meaning of the word or phrase

- ✓ consult a dictionary to verify your preliminary determination of the meaning of a word or phrase

- ✓ be sure to read all of the definitions, and then decide which definition makes sense within the context of the text

In order to determine or clarify a word's part of speech, do the following:

- ✓ determine what the word is describing

- ✓ identify how the word is being used in the phrase or sentence

In order to determine the etymology of a word, or its origin or standard usage, do the following:

- ✓ use reference materials, such as a dictionary, to determine the word's origin and history

- ✓ consider how the historical context of the word clarifies its usage

To determine or clarify the etymology or standard usage of a word, consider the following questions:

- ✓ How formal or informal is this word?

- ✓ What is the word describing? What inferred meanings can I make?

- ✓ In what context is the word being used?

- ✓ Is this slang? An example of vernacular? In what other contexts might this word be used?

- ✓ What is the etymology of this word?

Skill:
Word Meaning

Reread the first sentence of paragraph 4 of "Be Ye Men of Valour." Then, using the Checklist on the previous page, answer the multiple-choice questions below.

↻ YOUR TURN

1. What part of speech is the word *favorable*? How do you know?

   ○ A. It is a verb because it describes how the British Air Force is "clawing down" three or four Germans plans for every one British plan that the Germans are shooting down.

   ○ B. It is an adverb because it describes how the British Air Force is "clawing down" three or four Germans plans for every one British plan that the Germans are shooting down.

   ○ C. It is an adjective because it describes the relative balance of the British and German Air Forces at the time of the speech compared with at the beginning of the battle.

   ○ D. It is a noun because it describes the relative balance of the British and German Air Forces at the time of the speech compared with at the beginning of the battle.

2. Which of the following definitions of *favorable* is most accurate for this context?

   ○ A. expressing approval or support

   ○ B. giving consent; allowing something to happen

   ○ C. giving advantage to someone or something

   ○ D. suggesting a good outcome

Close Read

Reread "Be Ye Men of Valour." As you reread, complete the Skills Focus questions below. Then use your answers and annotations from the questions to help you complete the Write activity.

◎ SKILLS FOCUS

1. Highlight the first sentence of Churchill's speech. What is the most likely meaning of *solemn* in this context? What part of speech is this word, and how do you know? Refer to a dictionary. What is the best definition of this word, given its usage in this passage?

2. Highlight a call to action Churchill makes to his listeners, and explain why it is an effective text structure to help him achieve his purpose.

3. Identify a passage that gives details about events in Europe. Explain how these details support the main idea of Churchill's speech.

4. Identify a passage that reveals Churchill's main idea, and explain how his word choice effectively communicates that idea to his audience.

5. Churchill's speech takes place during one of the most important turning points in modern history. Highlight two examples of Churchill discussing division and alienation, and two examples of Churchill discussing bonding and collaboration. What were the causes of the division? Why is coming together so important at this time?

✏ WRITE

RHETORICAL ANALYSIS: Informational text structure can be used skillfully to compose ideas in a way that heightens the persuasive power of a speech or written work. Write a response in which you summarize the main argument of Churchill's speech and evaluate the structure of the speech. In your response, address the following question: Does the arrangement of ideas make the speech more persuasive? Remember to support your response with textual evidence.

Please note that excerpts and passages in the StudySync® library and this workbook are intended as touchstones to generate interest in an author's work. The excerpts and passages do not substitute for the reading of entire texts, and StudySync® strongly recommends that students seek out and purchase the whole literary or informational work in order to experience it as the author intended. Links to online resellers are available in our digital library. In addition, complete works may be ordered through an authorized reseller by filling out and returning to StudySync® the order form enclosed in this workbook.

Reading & Writing Companion   253

The Pearl Divers' Daughters

POETRY
Marci Calabretta Cancio-Bello
2016

Introduction

———————————————

Marci Calabretta Cancio-Bello (b. 1989) was a John S. and James L. Knight Fellow at Florida International University before the publication of her first book, *Hour of the Ox*, which won the 2015 Donald Hall Prize for Poetry. She is a teacher and editor, and her poetry has been featured in dozens of journals and anthologies, including *Best New Poets 2015*, a collection featuring 50 up-and-coming young poets. "The Pearl Divers' Daughters" explores the lives and legacy of haenyeo, the legendary female divers of South Korea's Jeju province.

"... pearl divers whose songs build and blossom like barrel-fires or anemones."

1 We are the pearl divers' daughters
2 skinning the ocean of her abalone[1] scales,
3 planting oyster seeds in each other's vertebrae.

4 Our mothers carved veins into the sea
5 with **reinvented** air, wrists scarred in rows and rings—
6 octopi and coral—legs scissoring against the sun,

7 the space between their thighs **profound** as trenches.
8 Haenyeo, we name them, pearl divers whose songs build
9 and blossom like barrel-fires or anemones[2].

10 They press our shoulders against the ribs
11 of whale sharks, our palms on dotted black rays.
12 We graze our fingers through damselfish[3] schools,

13 but our appetites are as **insatiate** as the sea is for land.
14 We gnaw the shore, legs wound in seaweed,
15 skin flayed by the tongues of clams, pulling, pushing.

16 Arirang[4], our mothers say patriotically, and cities
17 bloom from our spines, rooting us to **cartographies**,
18 thumbing our eyes into sand-locked jewels.

---

1. **abalone** a general name for sea snails, eaten cooked and raw all over the world
2. **anemones** sea invertebrates resembling the flowering plant for which they are named; they are sedentary or slow-moving and capture fish and marine animals for food
3. **damselfish** brightly hued fish of the family Pomacentridae, often characterized by two contrasting colors that meet horizontally along the middle of the body
4. **Arirang** traditional Korean folk song about a tragic romance that is the national anthem of both North and South Korea

19 We are the pearl divers' daughters,

20 our sisters' skirts are **hemmed** in coral,

21 our brothers are cloud-eyed eels.

22 Arirang, we say, our futures pearled

23 into every empty shell, our tongues pressed

24 against the words until we become them.

A group of 'Haenyeo' on South Korea's southern island of Jeju. Haenyeo, or 'sea women', refers to women who use free-diving to retrieve shell fish from the sea floor.

"The Pearl Divers' Daughters" from *Hour of the Ox*, by Marci Calabretta Cancio-Bello, © 2016. All rights are controlled by the University of Pittsburgh Press, Pittsburgh, PA 15260. Used by permission of the University of Pittsburgh Press.

✏ WRITE

EXPLANATORY: Marci Calabretta Cancio-Bello weaves references to pearl diving in the Korean province of Jeju throughout her poem "The Pearl Divers' Daughters." Analyze the images she presents to determine the actions and tasks that these pearl divers undertake as part of their job. Then, conduct informal research about pearl diving in another particular culture or time period. How do the methods and customs of pearl diving described in "The Pearl Divers' Daughters" align with or depart from those of the culture or time period you researched? Remember to use textual evidence and your research to support your response.

Killers Of The Dream

INFORMATIONAL TEXT
Lillian Smith
1949

Introduction

Lillian Smith (1897–1966) wrote *Killers Of The Dream*, her 1949 memoir, to challenge Southern taboos and unpack the moral and psychological costs of segregation. Written before the American civil rights movement of the 1950s and 60s, her critique of social mores about race and sin influenced those who would later stand up for racial equality. In this excerpt from the first chapter of her book, she reveals that she learned to discriminate as a child, and that these destructive lessons about maintaining white privilege were taught to her by people she loved and trusted—her own parents.

"This haunted childhood belongs to every southerner of my age."

1   Even its children knew that the South was in trouble. No one had to tell them; no words said aloud. To them, it was a vague thing weaving in and out of their play, like a ghost haunting an old graveyard or whispers after the household sleeps—fleeting mystery, vague menace to which each responded in his own way. Some learned to screen out all except the soft and the soothing; others denied even as they saw plainly, and heard. But all knew that under quiet words and warmth and laughter, under the slow ease and tender concern about small matters, there was a heavy burden on all of us and as heavy a refusal to confess it. The children knew this "trouble" was bigger than they, bigger than their family, bigger than their church, so big that people turned away from its size. They had seen it flash out and shatter a town's peace, had felt it tear up all they believed in. They had measured its giant strength and felt weak when they remembered.

2   This haunted childhood belongs to every southerner of my age. We ran away from it but we came back like a hurt animal to its wound, or a murderer to the scene of his sin. The human heart dares not stay away too long from that which hurt it most. There is a return journey to anguish that few of us are released from making.

3   We who were born in the South called this mesh of feeling and memory "loyalty." We thought of it sometimes as "love." We identified with the South's trouble as if we, individually, were responsible for all of it. We defended the sins and the sorrow of three hundred years as if each sin had been committed by us alone and each sorrow had cut across our heart. We were as hurt at criticism of our region as if our own name had been called aloud by the critic. We knew guilt without understanding it, and there is no tie that binds men closer to the past and each other than that.

4   It is a strange thing, this umbilical cord uncut. In times of ease, we do not feel its pull, but when we are threatened with change, suddenly it draws the wholewhite South together in a collective fear and fury that wipe our minds clear of reason and we are blocked from sensible contact with the world we live in.

5   To keep this resistance strong, wall after wall was thrown up in the southern mind against criticism from without and within. Imaginations closed tight against the hurt of others; a regional armoring that took place to ward off the "enemies" who would make our trouble different—or maybe rid us of it completely. For it was a trouble that we did not want to give up. We were as involved with it as a child who cannot be happy at home and cannot bear to tear himself away, or as a grownup who has fallen in love with his own disease. We southerners had identified with the long sorrowful past on such deep levels of love and hate and guilt that we did not know how to break old bonds without pulling our lives down. *Change* was the evil word, a shrill clanking that made us know too well our servitude. *Change* meant leaving one's memories, one's sins, one's **ambivalent** pleasures, the room where one was born.

6   In this South I lived as a child and now live. And it is of it that my story is made. I shall not tell, here, of experiences that were different and special and belonged only to me, but those most white southerners born at the turn of the century share with each other. Out of the intricate weaving of unnumbered threads, I shall pick out a few strands, a few designs that have to do with what we call color and race . . . and politics . . . and money and how it is made . . . and religion . . . and sex and the body image . . . and love . . . and dreams of the Good and the killers of dreams.

7   A southern child's basic lessons were woven of such **dissonant** strands as these; sometimes the threads tangled into a terrifying mess; sometimes **archaic**, startling designs would appear in the weaving; sometimes a design was left broken while another was completed with minute care. Bewildered teachers, bewildered pupils in home and on the street, driven by an invisible Authority, learned their lessons:

8   The mother who taught me what I know of tenderness and love and compassion taught me also the bleak rituals of keeping Negroes in their "place." The father who rebuked me for an air of superiority toward schoolmates from the mill and rounded out his rebuke by gravely reminding me that "all men are brothers," trained me in the steel-rigid **decorums** I must demand of every colored male. They who so gravely taught me to split my body from my mind and both from my "soul," taught me also to split my conscience from my acts and Christianity from southern tradition.

9   Neither the Negro nor sex was often discussed at length in our home. We were given no formal instruction in these difficult matters but we learned our lessons well. We learned the intricate system of taboos, of **renunciations** and compensations, of manners, voice modulations, words, feelings, along with our prayers, our toilet habits, and our games. I do not remember how or when, but by the time I had learned that God is love, that Jesus is His Son and came to give us more abundant life, that all men are brothers with a common

Please note that excerpts and passages in the StudySync® library and this workbook are intended as touchstones to generate interest in an author's work. The excerpts and passages do not substitute for the reading of entire texts, and StudySync® strongly recommends that students seek out and purchase the whole literary or informational work in order to experience it as the author intended. Links to online resellers are available in our digital library. In addition, complete works may be ordered through an authorized reseller by filling out and returning to StudySync® the order form enclosed in this workbook.

Reading & Writing
Companion

259

Father, I also knew that I was better than a Negro, that all black folks have their place and must be kept in it, that sex has its place and must be kept in it, that a terrifying disaster would befall the South if I ever treated a Negro as my social equal and as terrifying a disaster would befall my family if ever I were to have a baby outside of marriage. I had learned that God so loved the world that He gave His only begotten Son so that we might have segregated churches in which it was my duty to worship each Sunday and on Wednesday at evening prayers. I had learned that white southerners are a hospitable, courteous, tactful people who treat those of their own group with consideration and who as carefully segregate from all the richness of life "for their own good and welfare" thirteen million people whose skin is colored a little differently from my own.

Excerpted from *Killers Of The Dream* by Lillian Smith, published by W.W. Norton & Company.

✏ WRITE

PERSONAL RESPONSE: Near the beginning of the passage, Smith says "The human heart dares not stay away too long from that which hurt it most." Do you agree with this claim? Do you think people are somehow drawn back to places, events, or circumstances that have hurt them in the past? Present your response to this idea using textual evidence as well as experiences of people you have researched or learned about.

Shooting an Elephant

INFORMATIONAL TEXT
George Orwell
1936

Introduction

A British novelist, essayist and social commentator, George Orwell (1903–1950) often wrote about the complex and sometimes destructive relationship between a nation's government and its citizens. One of Orwell's most famous and influential works is *1984*, a dystopian novel set in a future where a totalitarian regime exerts almost complete control over the actions, feelings, and thoughts of its citizens. While touching on similar themes and political undertones, "Shooting an Elephant" is a short, autobiographical piece depicting Orwell's experiences living and working in Burma (known commonly today as Myanmar) in the early 1920s. These experiences would forever inform Orwell's views on imperialism, totalitarianism, and what it means to be truly free.

"In a job like that you see the dirty work of Empire at close quarters."

1   In Moulmein, in Lower Burma[1], I was hated by large numbers of people—the only time in my life that I have been important enough for this to happen to me. I was sub-divisional police officer of the town, and in an aimless, petty kind of way anti-European feeling was very bitter. No one had the guts to raise a riot, but if a European woman went through the bazaars[2] alone somebody would probably spit betel juice[3] over her dress. As a

Changing quarters in Upper Burma: baggage elephants arriving in camp, engraving by Paul Naumann from The Illustrated London News, No 2585, November 3, 1888.

police officer I was an obvious target and was baited whenever it seemed safe to do so. When a nimble Burman tripped me up on the football field and the referee (another Burman) looked the other way, the crowd yelled with hideous laughter. This happened more than once. In the end the sneering yellow faces of young men that met me everywhere, the insults hooted after me when I was at a safe distance, got badly on my nerves. The young Buddhist[4] priests were the worst of all. There were several thousands of them in the town and none of them seemed to have anything to do except stand on street corners and jeer at Europeans.

2   All this was perplexing and upsetting. For at that time I had already made up my mind that imperialism was an evil thing and the sooner I chucked up my job and got out of it the better. Theoretically—and secretly, of course—I was all for the Burmese and all against their **oppressors**, the British. As for the job

1. **Lower Burma** the coastal area of Myanmar, formerly Burma, incorporated into the British Empire in 1852
2. **bazaar** open public market where small producers, growers, and craftspeople sell their wares
3. **betel juice** the resulting liquid that is regularly spit out in the popular Southeast Asian habit of chewing betel leaves
4. **Buddhist** a follower of Buddhism, a variety of spiritual practices based on teachings of Gautama Buddha, an Indian monk who lived between the 6th and 4th centuries BCE

I was doing, I hated it more bitterly than I can perhaps make clear. In a job like that you see the dirty work of Empire at close quarters. The wretched prisoners huddling in the stinking cages of the lock-ups, the grey, cowed faces of the long-term convicts, the scarred buttocks of the men who had been flogged with bamboos—all these oppressed me with an intolerable sense of guilt. But I could get nothing into perspective. I was young and ill-educated and I had had to think out my problems in the utter silence that is imposed on every Englishman in the East. I did not even know that the British Empire is dying, still less did I know that it is a great deal better than the younger empires that are going to supplant it. All I knew was that I was stuck between my hatred of the empire I served and my rage against the evil-spirited little beasts who tried to make my job impossible. With one part of my mind I thought of the British Raj[5] as an unbreakable tyranny, as something clamped down, *in saecula saeculorum*[6], upon the will of **prostrate** peoples; with another part I thought that the greatest joy in the world would be to drive a bayonet into a Buddhist priest's guts. Feelings like these are the normal by-products of imperialism; ask any Anglo-Indian official, if you can catch him off duty.

3   One day something happened which in a roundabout way was enlightening. It was a tiny incident in itself, but it gave me a better glimpse than I had had before of the real nature of imperialism— the real motives for which despotic governments act. Early one morning the sub-inspector at a police station the other end of the town rang me up on the phone and said that an elephant was ravaging the bazaar. Would I please come and do something about it? I did not know what I could do, but I wanted to see what was happening and I got on to a pony and started out. I took my rifle, an old .44 Winchester and much too small to kill an elephant, but I thought the noise might be useful *in terrorem*[7]. Various Burmans stopped me on the way and told me about the elephant's doings. It was not, of course, a wild elephant, but a tame one which had gone "must." It had been chained up, as tame elephants always are when their attack of "must" is due, but on the previous night it had broken its chain and escaped. Its mahout, the only person who could manage it when it was in that state, had set out in pursuit, but had taken the wrong direction and was now twelve hours' journey away, and in the morning the elephant had suddenly reappeared in the town. The Burmese population had no weapons and were quite helpless against it. It had already destroyed somebody's bamboo hut, killed a cow and raided some fruit-stalls and devoured the stock; also it had met the municipal rubbish van and, when the driver jumped out and took to his heels, had turned the van over and inflicted violences upon it.

---

5. **the British Raj** the administration of the British Empire in colonial India, which consisted of the modern states of India, Pakistan, Afghanistan, Bangladesh and Myanmar (Burma) from 1858 to 1947
6. *in saecula saeculorum* a Latin phrase from the New Testament meaning "forever and ever"
7. *in terrorem* from the Latin, a threat or clause compelling someone to withdraw or avoid action

Skill:
Author's Purpose and Point of View

Orwell's purpose is to tell the truth about imperialism. The repetition of "real" shows he learned something he was trying to convince his readers of, too. This excerpt works because Orwell makes his intentions clear.

NOTES

4   The Burmese sub-inspector and some Indian constables were waiting for me in the quarter where the elephant had been seen. It was a very poor quarter, a labyrinth of squalid bamboo huts, thatched with palmleaf, winding all over a steep hillside. I remember that it was a cloudy, stuffy morning at the beginning of the rains. We began questioning the people as to where the elephant had gone and, as usual, failed to get any definite information. That is invariably the case in the East; a story always sounds clear enough at a distance, but the nearer you get to the scene of events the vaguer it becomes. Some of the people said that the elephant had gone in one direction, some said that he had gone in another, some professed not even to have heard of any elephant. I had almost made up my mind that the whole story was a pack of lies, when we heard yells a little distance away. There was a loud, scandalized cry of "Go away, child! Go away this instant!" and an old woman with a switch in her hand came round the corner of a hut, violently shooing away a crowd of naked children. Some more women followed, clicking their tongues and exclaiming; evidently there was something that the children ought not to have seen. I rounded the hut and saw a man's dead body sprawling in the mud. He was an Indian, a black Dravidian coolie[8], almost naked, and he could not have been dead many minutes. The people said that the elephant had come suddenly upon him round the corner of the hut, caught him with its trunk, put its foot on his back and ground him into the earth. This was the rainy season and the ground was soft, and his face had scored a trench a foot deep and a couple of yards long. He was lying on his belly with arms crucified and head sharply twisted to one side. His face was coated with mud, the eyes wide open, the teeth bared and grinning with an expression of unendurable agony. (Never tell me, by the way, that the dead look peaceful. Most of the corpses I have seen looked devilish.) The friction of the great beast's foot had stripped the skin from his back as neatly as one skins a rabbit. As soon as I saw the dead man I sent an orderly to a friend's house nearby to borrow an elephant rifle. I had already sent back the pony, not wanting it to go mad with fright and throw me if it smelt the elephant.

5   The orderly came back in a few minutes with a rifle and five cartridges, and meanwhile some Burmans had arrived and told us that the elephant was in the paddy fields below, only a few hundred yards away. As I started forward practically the whole population of the quarter flocked out of the houses and followed me. They had seen the rifle and were all shouting excitedly that I was going to shoot the elephant. They had not shown much interest in the elephant when he was merely ravaging their homes, but it was different now that he was going to be shot. It was a bit of fun to them, as it would be to an English crowd; besides they wanted the meat. It made me vaguely uneasy. I had no intention of shooting the elephant—I had merely sent for the rifle to defend myself if necessary—and it is always unnerving to have a crowd following you. I marched down the hill, looking and feeling a fool, with the rifle over my shoulder and an ever-growing army of people **jostling** at my heels. At the bottom, when you got

---

Skill:
Figurative
Language

Orwell uses a simile here to help readers visualize what the dead man's back looked like. This also has the effect of demeaning the dead man and personifying the elephant, making its actions seem intentional and methodical.

---

8. **coolie** (derogatory) an indentured laborer

Copyright © BookheadEd Learning, LLC

away from the huts, there was a metalled road and beyond that a **miry** waste of paddy fields a thousand yards across, not yet ploughed but soggy from the first rains and dotted with coarse grass. The elephant was standing eight yards from the road, his left side towards us. He took not the slightest notice of the crowd's approach. He was tearing up bunches of grass, beating them against his knees to clean them and stuffing them into his mouth.

6   I had halted on the road. As soon as I saw the elephant I knew with perfect certainty that I ought not to shoot him. It is a serious matter to shoot a working elephant—it is comparable to destroying a huge and costly piece of machinery—and obviously one ought not to do it if it can possibly be avoided. And at that distance, peacefully eating, the elephant looked no more dangerous than a cow. I thought then and I think now that his attack of "must" was already passing off; in which case he would merely wander harmlessly about until the mahout came back and caught him. Moreover, I did not in the least want to shoot him. I decided that I would watch him for a little while to make sure that he did not turn savage again, and then go home.

7   But at that moment I glanced round at the crowd that had followed me. It was an immense crowd, two thousand at the least and growing every minute. It blocked the road for a long distance on either side. I looked at the sea of yellow faces above the garish clothes-faces all happy and excited over this bit of fun, all certain that the elephant was going to be shot. They were watching me as they would watch a conjurer about to perform a trick. They did not like me, but with the magical rifle in my hands I was momentarily worth watching. And suddenly I realized that I should have to shoot the elephant after all. The people expected it of me and I had got to do it; I could feel their two thousand wills pressing me forward, irresistibly. And it was at this moment, as I stood there with the rifle in my hands, that I first grasped the hollowness, the futility of the white man's dominion in the East. Here was I, the white man with his gun, standing in front of the unarmed native crowd—seemingly the leading actor of the piece; but in reality I was only an absurd puppet pushed to and fro by the will of those yellow faces behind. I perceived in this moment that when the white man turns tyrant it is his own freedom that he destroys. He becomes a sort of hollow, posing dummy, the conventionalized figure of a sahib[9]. For it is the condition of his rule that he shall spend his life in trying to impress the "natives," and so in every crisis he has got to do what the "natives" expect of him. He wears a mask, and his face grows to fit it. I had got to shoot the elephant. I had committed myself to doing it when I sent for the rifle. A sahib has got to act like a sahib; he has got to appear resolute, to know his own mind and do definite things. To come all that way, rifle in hand, with two thousand people marching at my heels, and then to trail feebly away, having done nothing—no, that was impossible. The crowd would laugh at me. And my whole life, every white man's life in the East, was one long struggle not to be laughed at.

___

9. **Sahib** an honorific term used a sign of respect in British India, derived from Arabic, meaning "young prince"

Skill:
Figurative
Language

Here Orwell compares the elephant to two things: machinery and a cow. Like machinery, the elephant is very valuable in Burmese society. And like a cow, the elephant does not appear to be a threat.

Skill:
Connotation
and Denotation

I know condition can mean the state of something, such as how well it functions. While this meaning works here, it seems Orwell is trying to connote or denote another meaning because the previous sentence has a negative tone.

NOTES

8 But I did not want to shoot the elephant. I watched him beating his bunch of grass against his knees, with that preoccupied grandmotherly air that elephants have. It seemed to me that it would be murder to shoot him. At that age I was not squeamish about killing animals, but I had never shot an elephant and never wanted to. (Somehow it always seems worse to kill a large animal.) Besides, there was the beast's owner to be considered. Alive, the elephant was worth at least a hundred pounds; dead, he would only be worth the value of his tusks, five pounds, possibly. But I had got to act quickly. I turned to some experienced-looking Burmans who had been there when we arrived, and asked them how the elephant had been behaving. They all said the same thing: he took no notice of you if you left him alone, but he might charge if you went too close to him.

9 It was perfectly clear to me what I ought to do. I ought to walk up to within, say, twenty-five yards of the elephant and test his behavior. If he charged, I could shoot; if he took no notice of me, it would be safe to leave him until the mahout came back. But also I knew that I was going to do no such thing. I was a poor shot with a rifle and the ground was soft mud into which one would sink at every step. If the elephant charged and I missed him, I should have about as much chance as a toad under a steam-roller. But even then I was not thinking particularly of my own skin, only of the watchful yellow faces behind. For at that moment, with the crowd watching me, I was not afraid in the ordinary sense, as I would have been if I had been alone. A white man mustn't be frightened in front of "natives"; and so, in general, he isn't frightened. The sole thought in my mind was that if anything went wrong those two thousand Burmans would see me pursued, caught, trampled on and reduced to a grinning corpse like that Indian up the hill. And if that happened it was quite probable that some of them would laugh. That would never do.

10 There was only one alternative. I shoved the cartridges into the magazine and lay down on the road to get a better aim. The crowd grew very still, and a deep, low, happy sigh, as of people who see the theatre curtain go up at last, breathed from innumerable throats. They were going to have their bit of fun after all. The rifle was a beautiful German thing with cross-hair sights. I did not then know that in shooting an elephant one would shoot to cut an imaginary bar running from ear-hole to ear-hole. I ought, therefore, as the elephant was sideways on, to have aimed straight at his ear-hole, actually I aimed several inches in front of this, thinking the brain would be further forward.

11 When I pulled the trigger I did not hear the bang or feel the kick—one never does when a shot goes home—but I heard the devilish roar of glee that went up from the crowd. In that instant, in too short a time, one would have thought, even for the bullet to get there, a mysterious, terrible change had come over the elephant. He neither stirred nor fell, but every line of his body had altered. He looked suddenly stricken, shrunken, immensely old, as though the frightful impact of the bullet had paralysed him without knocking him down. At last, after what seemed a long time —it might have been five seconds, I dare

Skill:
Author's Purpose and Point of View

I thought he would be most afraid of being "trampled on" by the elephant. Instead, he's more concerned with being humiliated than being killed. This point of view is effective because it is unexpected, which makes it memorable.

say—he sagged flabbily to his knees. His mouth slobbered. An enormous senility seemed to have settled upon him. One could have imagined him thousands of years old. I fired again into the same spot. At the second shot he did not collapse but climbed with desperate slowness to his feet and stood weakly upright, with legs sagging and head drooping. I fired a third time. That was the shot that did for him. You could see the agony of it jolt his whole body and knock the last remnant of strength from his legs. But in falling he seemed for a moment to rise, for as his hind legs collapsed beneath him he seemed to tower upward like a huge rock toppling, his trunk reaching skyward like a tree. He trumpeted, for the first and only time. And then down he came, his belly towards me, with a crash that seemed to shake the ground even where I lay.

12   I got up. The Burmans were already racing past me across the mud. It was obvious that the elephant would never rise again, but he was not dead. He was breathing very rhythmically with long rattling gasps, his great mound of a side painfully rising and falling. His mouth was wide open—I could see far down into caverns of pale pink throat. I waited a long time for him to die, but his breathing did not weaken. Finally I fired my two remaining shots into the spot where I thought his heart must be. The thick blood welled out of him like red velvet, but still he did not die. His body did not even jerk when the shots hit him, the tortured breathing continued without a pause. He was dying, very slowly and in great agony, but in some world remote from me where not even a bullet could damage him further. I felt that I had got to put an end to that dreadful noise. It seemed dreadful to see the great beast lying there, powerless to move and yet powerless to die, and not even to be able to finish him. I sent back for my small rifle and poured shot after shot into his heart and down his throat. They seemed to make no impression. The tortured gasps continued as steadily as the ticking of a clock.

13   In the end I could not stand it any longer and went away. I heard later that it took him half an hour to die. Burmans were bringing dahs and baskets even before I left, and I was told they had stripped his body almost to the bones by the afternoon.

14   Afterwards, of course, there were endless discussions about the shooting of the elephant. The owner was furious, but he was only an Indian and could do nothing. Besides, legally I had done the right thing, for a mad elephant has to be killed, like a mad dog, if its owner fails to control it. Among the Europeans opinion was divided. The older men said I was right, the younger men said it was a damn shame to shoot an elephant for killing a coolie, because an elephant was worth more than any damn Coringhee coolie[10]. And afterwards I was very glad that the coolie had been killed; it put me legally in the right and it gave me a sufficient **pretext** for shooting the elephant. I often wondered whether any of the others grasped that I had done it solely to avoid looking a fool.

---

10. **Coringhee coolie** a laborer who has migrated from Southern India, or Coringhee

First Read

Read "Shooting an Elephant." After you read, complete the Think Questions below.

☁ THINK QUESTIONS

1. According to Orwell, he was "hated by large numbers of people" during his time in Burma. Why was he so hated? Support your answer using textual evidence.

2. Referring to information that is directly stated or implied, what does Orwell mean when he says he "had to think out my problems in utter silence?"

3. In two or three sentences, explain why Orwell was "very glad" the elephant had killed someone.

4. Use context clues to determine the meaning of the word **oppressors** as it is used in the text. Write your definition of *oppressors* here and explain how you figured it out.

5. Keeping in mind that the Old Norse word *myrr* means "bog" or "swamp," determine the meaning of **miry** as it is used in the text. Write your definition of *miry* here. Then check your inferred meaning in a print or digital library.

Skill: Author's Purpose and Point of View

Use the Checklist to analyze Author's Purpose and Point of View in "Shooting an Elephant." Refer to the sample student annotations about Author's Purpose and Point of View in the text.

••• CHECKLIST FOR AUTHOR'S PURPOSE AND POINT OF VIEW

In order to identify author's purpose and point of view, note the following:

- ✓ whether the writer is attempting to establish trust by citing his or her experience or education

- ✓ whether the evidence the author provides is convincing and that the argument or position is logical

- ✓ what words and phrases the author uses to appeal to the emotions

- ✓ the author's use of rhetoric, or the art of speaking and writing persuasively, such as the use of repetition to drive home a point as well as allusion and alliteration

- ✓ the author's use of rhetoric to contribute to the power, persuasiveness, or beauty of the text

To determine the author's purpose and point of view, consider the following questions:

- ✓ How does the author try to convince me that he or she has something valid and important for me to read?

- ✓ What words or phrases express emotion or invite an emotional response? How or why are they effective or ineffective?

- ✓ What words and phrases contribute to the power, persuasiveness, or beauty of the text? Is the author's use of rhetoric successful? Why or why not?

Skill: Author's Purpose and Point of View

Reread paragraphs 12–14 of "Shooting an Elephant." Then, using the Checklist on the previous page, answer the multiple-choice questions below.

⟳ YOUR TURN

1. Orwell's point of view in paragraphs 12–13 is effective because—

   ○ A. it shows the reader how awful it was to watch the elephant die.

   ○ B. it gets the reader to understand that killing elephants requires great skill.

   ○ C. it explains to the reader why it was essential to kill the elephant.

   ○ D. it invites the reader to share Orwell's excitement upon seeing the elephant.

2. How does the information in Paragraph 14 reinforce Orwell's purpose for writing this text?

   ○ A. Orwell explains how the older and younger European men he talked to had different opinions about his actions.

   ○ B. Orwell explains how he was justified in killing the elephant because its owner had not done a good job of controlling it.

   ○ C. Orwell reinforces the horrible reality of colonialism by reducing the killing of the elephant to being a legal issue.

   ○ D. Orwell reinforces his point that Europeans and Burmans have different opinions on colonialism.

Skill:
Connotation and Denotation

Use the Checklist to analyze Connotation and Denotation in "Shooting an Elephant ." Refer to the sample student annotations about Connotation and Denotation in the text.

••• CHECKLIST FOR CONNOTATION AND DENOTATION

In order to identify the denotative meanings of words, use the following steps:

✓ first, note unfamiliar words and phrases, key words used to describe important individuals, events, or ideas, or words that inspire an emotional reaction

✓ next, determine and note the denotative meaning of words by consulting a reference material such as a dictionary, glossary, or thesaurus

✓ finally, analyze nuances in the meaning of words with similar denotations

To better understand the meaning of words and phrases as they are used in a text, including connotative meanings, use the following questions as a guide:

✓ What is the genre or subject of the text? Based on context, what do you think the meaning of the word is intended to be?

✓ Is your inference the same or different from the dictionary definition?

✓ Does the word create a positive, negative, or neutral emotion?

✓ What synonyms or alternative phrasing help you describe the connotative meaning of the word?

To determine the meaning of words and phrases as they are used in a text, including connotative meanings, use the following questions as a guide:

✓ What is the denotative meaning of the word? Is that denotative meaning correct in context?

✓ What possible positive, neutral, or negative connotations might the word have, depending on context?

✓ What textual evidence signals a particular connotation for the word?

Skill:
Connotation and Denotation

Reread paragraph 8 of "Shooting an Elephant ." Then, using the Checklist on the previous page, answer the multiple-choice questions below.

⟳ YOUR TURN

1. What is the most likely connotation of "preoccupied grandmotherly air"?

   ○ A. Negative: The elephant is being described as annoying.

   ○ B. Positive: The elephant is being described as gentle and caring.

   ○ C. Positive: The elephant is being described as wise and funny.

   ○ D. Neutral: The elephant is being described simply as an animal.

2. What is the most likely reason Orwell uses "beast" to describe the elephant?

   ○ A. Orwell wants to convey that the elephant could still be used to help the villagers.

   ○ B. Orwell wants to convey that the elephant has been terribly mistreated by the mahout.

   ○ C. After personifying the elephant, Orwell is telling the reader that it is still evil.

   ○ D. After personifying the elephant, Orwell is reminding the reader that it is still an animal.

Skill:
Figurative Language

Use the Checklist to analyze Figurative Language in "Shooting an Elephant ." Refer to the sample student annotations about Figurative Language in the text.

••• CHECKLIST FOR FIGURATIVE LANGUAGE

In order to determine the meaning of figurative language in context, note the following:

✓ words that mean one thing literally and suggest something else

✓ similes, metaphors, or personification

✓ figures of speech, including

- paradoxes, or a seemingly contradictory statement that when further investigated or explained proves to be true, such as

  > a character described as "a wise fool"

  > a character stating, "I must be cruel to be kind"

- hyperbole, or exaggerated statements not meant to be taken literally, such as

  > a child saying, "I'll be doing this homework until I'm 100!"

  > a claim such as, "I'm so hungry I could eat a horse!"

In order to interpret figurative language in context and analyze its role in the text, consider the following questions:

✓ Where is there figurative language in the text and what seems to be the purpose of the author's use of it?

✓ Why does the author use a figure of speech rather than literal language?

✓ What impact does exaggeration or hyperbole have on your understanding of the text?

✓ Where are there examples of paradoxes and how do they affect the meaning in the text?

✓ Which phrases contain references that seem contradictory?

✓ Where are contradictory words and phrases used to enhance the reader's understanding of the character, object, or idea?

✓ How does the figurative language develop the message or theme of the literary work?

Skill:
Figurative Language

Reread paragraph 7 of "Shooting an Elephant ." Then, using the Checklist on the previous page, answer the multiple-choice questions below.

⟳ YOUR TURN

1. What is the best explanation of the simile "as they would watch a conjurer about to perform a trick"?

   ○ A. The Burmese people are treating this experience as a kind of entertainment.

   ○ B. The Burmese people are hoping that Orwell will make the elephant disappear.

   ○ C. The Burmese people believe that Orwell is a kind of magician.

   ○ D. The Burmese people believe that rifles are magical tools.

2. This question has two parts. First, answer Part A. Then, answer Part B.

   Part A: What does the figurative language in this paragraph indicate the speaker is feeling at this moment?

   ○ A. The speaker feels that the elephant is in complete control of the situation and is about to attack him.

   ○ B. The speaker feels that he has lost control of the situation and is about to be attacked by the Burmese people.

   ○ C. The speaker feels that the situation is in his control rather than in the control of the Burmese people.

   ○ D. The speaker feels that the situation is in the control of the Burmese people rather than in his control.

   Part B: Which simile or metaphor best supports your answer to Part A?

   ○ A. ". . . with the magical rifle in my hands I was momentarily worth watching."

   ○ B. ". . . the futility of the white man's dominion in the East."

   ○ C. "Here was I, the white man with his gun, standing in front of the unarmed native crowd . . ."

   ○ D. "I was only an absurd puppet pushed to and fro by the will of those yellow faces behind."

SHOOTING
AN
ELEPHANT

Close Read

Reread "Shooting an Elephant." As you reread, complete the Skills Focus questions below. Then use your answers and annotations from the questions to help you complete the Write activity.

◎ SKILLS FOCUS

1. Highlight a passage in which Orwell describes the moral dilemma he is facing. Summarize the dilemma and what it reveals about the theme.

2. Identify a passage in Paragraph 2 in which Orwell describes his strong negative feelings toward both imperialism and the Burmese people. Explain how Orwell's use of language in this passage adds to the effectiveness of the text.

3. Find a section of the text in which the elephant serves as a symbol or metaphor for something else. Explain what the elephant symbolizes.

4. In Paragraph 11, highlight a description of the elephant after Orwell has shot it. Explain the point of view the author is conveying in this passage; then evaluate the effectiveness of the description in communicating that point of view.

5. Throughout the essay, Orwell describes ways in which he feels alienated and separate from everyone around him. Highlight two examples of this, and explain what is causing his alienation.

✎ WRITE

EXPLANATORY ESSAY: What do you think is the point of view Orwell is expressing in his essay "Shooting an Elephant"? Analyze the literary elements and figurative language in the text to determine the author's point of view. Then write a short essay, responding to this question. Remember to use textual evidence to support your response.

Extended
Writing
Project and
Grammar

EXTENDED
WRITING
PROJECT
LITERARY ANALYSIS
WRITING

Literary Analysis Writing Process: Plan

PLAN	DRAFT	REVISE	EDIT AND PUBLISH

At first glance, a poem about an indecisive man, a short story about a woman wearing a new dress, and an essay about shooting an elephant might not seem to have much in common. However, each of these selections is an example of Modernist literature that features themes relating to isolation and alienation.

WRITING PROMPT

Why is alienation such a common theme in Modernist literature?

Consider all the texts you have read in this unit, and reflect on how alienation impacts those who experience it. Then, select three characters or speakers from the texts. Write a literary analysis essay to examine how the authors explore the theme of alienation through these three characters or speakers. In your conclusion, synthesize the ideas in these texts about alienation in the modern world. Regardless of which selections you choose, be sure your literary analysis includes the following:

- an introduction
- a thesis statement
- coherent body paragraphs
- reasons and relevant evidence
- a conclusion

Please note that excerpts and passages in the StudySync® library and this workbook are intended as touchstones to generate interest in an author's work. The excerpts and passages do not substitute for the reading of entire texts, and StudySync® strongly recommends that students seek out and purchase the whole literary or informational work in order to experience it as the author intended. Links to online resellers are available in our digital library. In addition, complete works may be ordered through an authorized reseller by filling out and returning to StudySync® the order form enclosed in this workbook.

Reading & Writing Companion   **277**

Introduction to Literary Analysis Writing

A literary analysis is a form of argumentative writing that tries to persuade readers to accept the writer's interpretation of a literary text. Good literary analysis writing builds an argument with a strong claim, convincing reasons, relevant textual evidence, and a clear structure with an introduction, body, and conclusion. The characteristics of literary analysis writing include:

- an introduction
- a thesis statement
- textual evidence
- transitions
- a formal style
- a conclusion

In addition to these characteristics, writers of literary analyses also carefully craft their work through their use of a strong, confident tone and compelling syntax, or sentence structure, which help to make the text more persuasive. Effective arguments combine these genre characteristics and elements of the writer's craft to engage and convince the reader.

As you continue with this Extended Writing Project, you'll receive more instruction and practice in crafting each of the characteristics of literary analysis writing to create your own literary analysis.

Before you get started on your own literary analysis, read this literary analysis that one student, Emma, wrote in response to the writing prompt. As you read the Model, highlight and annotate the features of literary analysis writing that Emma included in her literary analysis.

≡ STUDENT MODEL

Alienation in a Post-War Society

1 In the early 20th century, the world was in flux. New technology led to destruction as war raged in Europe. At the same time, many challenged traditional norms of gender and class. For example, women's suffrage movements gained traction in both Great Britain and the United States. The world people thought they knew was changing, and as a result men and women of all levels of society felt lost. Writers and artists reacted by challenging old conventions and social norms. They created new styles and sought to represent individuals' subjective points of view. Alienation is a common theme in modernist literature because uncertainty was a by-product of the rapidly changing society. Modernist works such as "The Love Song of J. Alfred Prufrock," "The New Dress," and "A Cup of Tea" show that feelings of alienation stretched across lines of gender and class.

2 Although he was born in the United States, poet T. S. Eliot moved to England in 1914 while World War I raged in Europe. His poem "The Love Song of J. Alfred Prufrock," published the following year, reflects the disillusionment and uncertainty Europeans felt as the world changed around them. The first images in the poem create tension as a familiar scene turns ominous: "Let us go then, you and I, / When the evening is spread out against the sky / Like a patient etherized upon a table" (7–9). An evening stroll under the night sky is typically a romantic or serene image, but Eliot uses it differently. By comparing the evening to a patient about to have surgery, Eliot upends expectations. This makes readers uncomfortable because they do not know what will happen on the journey on which they are about to embark with the poem's speaker.

3 Uncertainty and alienation are also reflected in the speaker himself. He constantly doubts his own worth and place in the world. Instead of simply interacting with people, he stops to ask, "Do I dare / Disturb the universe?" (51–52). The entire poem takes place in the speaker's

own mind. There are no outside forces preventing him from engaging with others. The speaker's own hesitancy and insecurity prevent him from participating in society. In this way, "The Love Song of J. Alfred Prufrock" shows that alienation can be a product of our own making.

4   The protagonist of Virginia Woolf's short story "The New Dress" is also a victim of her own insecurities. Like the speaker of Eliot's poem, Mabel Waring wants to participate in society but is instead alienated by her own feelings of inadequacy. Mabel is so worried that the other guests will judge her that she cannot enjoy herself at a party:

> And at once the misery which she always tried to hide, the profound dissatisfaction—the sense she had had, ever since she was a child, of being inferior to other people—set upon her, relentlessly, remorselessly, with an intensity which she could not beat off, as she would when she woke at night at home, by reading Borrow or Scott; for oh these men, oh these women, all were thinking—"What's Mabel wearing? What a fright she looks! What a hideous new dress!"—their eyelids flickering as they came up and then their lids shutting rather tight. It was her own appalling inadequacy; her cowardice; her mean, water-sprinkled blood that depressed her.

Mabel's uncertainty is directly tied to her perception of society's expectations. She worries that, as a member of a slightly lower social class, she cannot measure up to other guests' expectations, and it makes her doubt her worth. Later, when a fellow party guest points out that Mabel has bought a new dress, it causes her to unravel: "'Why,' she asked herself, 'can't I . . . feel sure about the canary and pity and love and not be whipped all round in a second by coming into a room full of people?'" Instead of enjoying her social interactions, Mabel allows a single comment to send her into a spiral of anxiety and shame. In the end, she leaves the party early, too embarrassed by her appearance to remain in the company of others. "The New Dress" shows that alienation can be a product of society's expectations.

5   Rosemary Fell, the protagonist in Katherine Mansfield's "A Cup of Tea," is the opposite of Mabel in several key ways. Rosemary is a member of London's high society and is extremely wealthy. She is also well-respected and sure of her place in the world. Yet, Rosemary

NOTES

also fails to connect with the people around her. When she decides to invite a penniless young woman, Miss Smith, home for tea, she does so in order to make herself feel like a benefactor instead of out of a genuine desire to make a friend: "She was going to prove to this girl that—wonderful things did happen in life, that—fairy godmothers were real, that—rich people had hearts, and that women *were* sisters." The class difference between the characters prevents Rosemary from seeing Miss Smith as a whole person. Instead, she views the interaction as a game to keep herself entertained on a rainy day. This becomes clear when she abruptly throws Miss Smith out after her husband, Philip, comments on the young woman's beauty. Just as the guest's comment affects Mabel in "The New Dress," this passing commentary sends Rosemary into a spiral as the words echo in her head: "Pretty! Absolutely lovely! Bowled over! Her heart beat like a heavy bell." Rosemary abandons Miss Smith at the first sign that their friendship could lead to a rivalry for her husband's attention. Later, Rosemary asks her husband to reassure her. "'Philip,' she whispered, and she pressed his head against her bosom, 'am I *pretty*?'" As the story concludes, Miss Smith has been alienated by the woman who claimed to be her benefactor, and Rosemary feels insecure in her relationship with her husband. "A Cup of Tea" shows that alienation can occur when issues relating to class and gender complicate individual relationships between two people.

6   The characters in these modernist works come from different backgrounds and have different experiences, but the results of their attempted interactions with others are similar. Hindered by their own insecurities, the speaker in "The Love Song of J. Alfred Prufrock" and the protagonists in "The New Dress" and "A Cup of Tea" are left alone and afraid. Alienation is a common theme in these modernist works because in a post-war, ever-changing world, it is human nature to ask, "Am I good enough?"

WRITE

Writers often take notes about their ideas for a literary analysis before they sit down to write. Think about what you've learned so far about literary analysis writing to help you begin prewriting.

- **Purpose:** What selections do you want to write about, and how do they develop themes relating to alienation?

- **Audience:** Who is your audience, and what idea do you want to express to them?

- **Introduction:** How will you introduce your topic? How will you engage an audience and preview what you plan to argue in your essay?

- **Thesis Statement:** What is your claim about the selections you've chosen? How can you word your claim so it is clear to readers?

- **Textual Evidence:** What evidence will you use to support your claim? What facts, details, examples, and quotations will persuade your audience to agree with your claim?

- **Transitions:** How will you smoothly transition from one idea to another within and across paragraphs?

- **Formal Style:** How can you create and maintain a formal style and an objective tone as you build your argument?

- **Conclusion:** How will you wrap up your argument? How can you restate the main ideas in your argument without being redundant?

Response Instructions

Use the questions in the bulleted list to write a one-paragraph summary. Your summary should describe what you will argue in your literary analysis.

Don't worry about including all of the details now; focus only on the most essential and important elements. You will refer to this short summary as you continue through the steps of the writing process.

Skill: Reasons and Relevant Evidence

••• CHECKLIST FOR REASONS AND RELEVANT EVIDENCE

As you determine the reasons and relevant evidence you will need to support your claim, use the following questions as a guide:

- What is my claim (or claims)? What are the strengths and limitations of my claim(s)?
- What relevant evidence do I have? Where could I add more support for my claim(s)?
- What do I know about the audience's:
  - > knowledge about my topic?
  - > concerns and values?
  - > possible biases toward the subject matter?

Use the following steps to help you develop claims fairly and thoroughly:

- establish a claim. Then, evaluate:
  - > its strengths and limitations
  - > any biases you have
  - > any gaps in support for your claim, so that your support can be more thorough
- consider your audience and their perspective on your topic. Determine:
  - > their probable prior knowledge about the topic
  - > their concerns and values
  - > any biases they may have toward the subject matter
- find the most relevant evidence that supports the claim

Copyright © BookheadEd Learning, LLC

YOUR TURN

Read the quotations from "A Cup of Tea" below. Then, complete the chart by sorting the quotations into two categories: those that serve as relevant evidence to support Emma's claim and those that do not. Write the corresponding letter for each quotation in the appropriate column.

	Quotations
A	"Rosemary had been married two years. She had a duck of a boy. No, not Peter—Michael. And her husband absolutely adored her."
B	"Half an hour later Philip was still in the library, when Rosemary came in."
C	"Rosemary Fell was not exactly beautiful. No, you couldn't have called her beautiful. Pretty? Well, if you took her to pieces. . . But why be so cruel as to take anyone to pieces?"
D	"'Do you like me?' said she, and her tone, sweet, husky, troubled him."
E	"She went to her writing-room and sat down at her desk. Pretty! Absolutely lovely! Bowled over! Her heart beat like a heavy bell."
F	"The other did stop just in time for Rosemary to get up before the tea came. She had the table placed between them."

Supports Claim	Does Not Support Claim

✏ **WRITE**

Use the questions in the checklist to draft your claim and select reasons and relevant evidence for your argumentative literary analysis essay.

Skill:
Thesis Statement

••• CHECKLIST FOR THESIS STATEMENT

Before you begin writing your thesis statement, ask yourself the following questions:

- What is the prompt asking me to write about?
- What claim do I want to make about the topic of this essay?
- Is my claim precise and informative?
- How is my claim specific to my topic? How does it inform the reader about my topic?
- Does my thesis statement introduce the body of my essay?
- Where should I place my thesis statement?

Here are some methods for introducing and developing a topic as well as a precise and informative claim:

- think about your central claim of your essay
  - > identify a clear claim you want to introduce, thinking about:
    - o how closely your claim is related to your topic and how specific it is to your supporting details
    - o how your claim includes necessary information to guide the reader through the topic
  - > identify as many claims as you intend to prove
- your thesis statement should:
  - > let the reader anticipate the content of your essay
  - > help you begin your essay in an organized manner
  - > present your opinion clearly
  - > respond completely to the writing prompt
- consider the best placement for your thesis statement
  - > if your response is short, you may want to present your thesis statement in the first sentence of the essay
  - > if your response is longer (as in a formal essay), you can place it at the end of your introductory paragraph

Please note that excerpts and passages in the StudySync® library and this workbook are intended as touchstones to generate interest in an author's work. The excerpts and passages do not substitute for the reading of entire texts, and StudySync® strongly recommends that students seek out and purchase the whole literary or informational work in order to experience it as the author intended. Links to online resellers are available in our digital library. In addition, complete works may be ordered through an authorized reseller by filling out and returning to StudySync® the order form enclosed in this workbook.

Reading & Writing Companion **285**

YOUR TURN

Read the thesis statements below. Then, complete the chart by sorting them into two categories: effective thesis statements and ineffective thesis statements. Write the corresponding letter for each statement in the appropriate column.

	Thesis Statements
A	"The New Dress" and "A Cup of Tea" both offer harsh criticism of traditional gender roles.
B	In *A Room of One's Own,* Virginia Woolf argues that women have been negatively affected by unfair limitations.
C	"The New Dress" and "A Cup of Tea" were both written by women in the early 20th century.
D	Virginia Woolf's *A Room of One's Own* includes a long passage that hypothesizes about what might have happened if Shakespeare had had an equally talented sister.
E	T. S. Eliot's "The Love Song of J. Alfred Prufrock" is a difficult poem for most readers to understand.
F	T. S. Eliot's poem "The Love Song of J. Alfred Prufrock" warns readers that time is fleeting.

Effective Thesis Statements	Ineffective Thesis Statements

WRITE

Use the questions in the checklist to plan and write your thesis statement.

Skill: Organizing Argumentative Writing

••• CHECKLIST FOR ORGANIZING ARGUMENTATIVE WRITING

As you consider how to organize your writing for your argumentative essay, use the following questions as a guide:

- What kinds of evidence could I find that would support my claim?
- Did I choose an organizational structure that establishes clear relationships between claims and supporting reasons and evidence?

Follow these steps to organize your argumentative essay in a way that logically sequences claim(s), reasons, and evidence:

- identify your precise, or specific, claim or claims and the evidence that supports them
- establish the significance of your claim

  > find what others may have written about the topic, and learn why they feel it is important

  > look for possible consequences or complications if something is done or is not accomplished

- choose an organizational structure that logically sequences and establishes clear relationships among claims, opposing claims or counterclaims, and the evidence presented to support the claims

Please note that excerpts and passages in the StudySync® library and this workbook are intended as touchstones to generate interest in an author's work. The excerpts and passages do not substitute for the reading of entire texts, and StudySync® strongly recommends that students seek out and purchase the whole literary or informational work in order to experience it as the author intended. Links to online resellers are available in our digital library. In addition, complete works may be ordered through an authorized reseller by filling out and returning to StudySync® the order form enclosed in this workbook.

Reading & Writing Companion   **287**

⟳ YOUR TURN

Read the thesis statements below. Then, complete the chart by writing the organizational structure that would be most appropriate for the purpose, topic, and context of the corresponding essay, as well as the audience.

Organizational Structure Options		
order of importance	cause and effect	compare and contrast

Thesis Statement	Organizational Structure
The devastation of the world wars led to a sense of isolation among authors and readers.	
Modernists had more in common with Victorian writers than one might think.	
Many factors led Romantics to idolize nature, but the Industrial Revolution had the strongest influence.	

⟳ YOUR TURN

Complete the outline by writing an introductory statement, thesis statement, and three main ideas as well as supporting evidence for the body paragraphs of your argumentative essay. Make sure your ideas are appropriate for the purpose, topic, and context of your essay, as well as your audience.

Outline	Summary
Introductory Statement	
Thesis	
Body Paragraph 1	
Supporting Evidence 1	
Body Paragraph 2	
Supporting Evidence 2	
Body Paragraph 3	
Supporting Evidence 3	

Literary Analysis Writing Process: Draft

PLAN	DRAFT	REVISE	EDIT AND PUBLISH

You have already made progress toward writing your literary analysis. Now it is time to draft your literary analysis.

✏ WRITE

Use your plan and other responses in your Binder to draft your literary analysis. You may also have new ideas as you begin drafting. Feel free to explore those new ideas as you have them. You can also ask yourself these questions to ensure that your writing is focused and organized and has appropriate evidence and elaboration to support your thesis:

Draft Checklist:

☐ **Purpose and Focus:** Have I made my topic and claim clear to readers? Have I included only relevant information and details and nothing extraneous that might confuse my readers?

☐ **Organization:** Is the organizational structure of my essay appropriate for my purpose, audience, topic, and context? Are my ideas presented in a way that persuades readers?

☐ **Evidence and Elaboration:** Will my readers be able to easily understand the connection between my ideas and supporting evidence?

Before you submit your draft, read it over carefully. You want to be sure that you've responded to all aspects of the prompt.

Please note that excerpts and passages in the StudySync® library and this workbook are intended as touchstones to generate interest in an author's work. The excerpts and passages do not substitute for the reading of entire texts, and StudySync® strongly recommends that students seek out and purchase the whole literary or informational work in order to experience it as the author intended. Links to online resellers are available in our digital library. In addition, complete works may be ordered through an authorized reseller by filling out and returning to StudySync® the order form enclosed in this workbook.

Reading & Writing Companion **289**

Here is Emma's literary analysis draft. As you read, notice how Emma develops her draft to be focused and organized, so it has relevant evidence and elaboration to support her ideas. As she continues to revise and edit her literary analysis, she will find and improve weak spots in her writing, as well as correct any language or punctuation mistakes.

 NOTES

☰ STUDENT MODEL: FIRST DRAFT

Alienation in a Post-War Society

~~In the early 20th century, the world was in flux. The world people thought they knew was changing, and as a result men and women of all levels of society felt lost. Old conventions and social norms were challenged by writers and artists. They created new styles, and these same writers and artists sought to represent individuals' subjective points of view. "The Love Song of J. Alfred Prufrock," "The New Dress," and "A Cup of Tea" show that feelings of alienation can affect anyone.~~

 Skill:
Introductions

Emma decides to provide more context in the beginning of her introduction by adding details to show why the world was changing. She then adds a sentence about alienation to connect her introductory sentences and her thesis statement. Finally, she rephrases her thesis to give her essay a more precise focus.

In the early 20th century, the world was in flux. New technology led to destruction as war raged in Europe. At the same time, many challenged traditional norms of gender and class. For example, women's suffrage movements gained traction in both Great Britain and the United States. The world people thought they knew was changing, and as a result men and women of all levels of society felt lost. Writers and artists reacted by challenging old conventions and social norms. They created new styles and sought to represent individuals' subjective points of view. Alienation is a common theme in modernist literature because uncertainty was a by-product of the rapidly changing society. Modernist works such as "The Love Song of J. Alfred Prufrock," "The New Dress," and "A Cup of Tea" show that feelings of alienation stretched across lines of gender and class.

Poet T. S. Eliot moved to England in 1914 while World War I was going on in Europe. Although he was born in the United States. T. S. Eliot's poem "The Love Song of J. Alfred Prufrock," published in 1915, reflects the uncertainty Europeans felt as the world changed around them. The first images in the poem create tension as a familiar scene turns ominous:

> Let us go then, you and I,
> When the evening is spread out against the sky
> Like a patient etherized upon a table.

An evening stroll under the night sky is typically a romantic or serene image, but Eliot uses it differently. By comparing the evening to a patient about to have surgery, Eliot goes against the reader's expectations for how natural imagery will work in the poem. This makes readers uncomfortable because they do not know what will happen on the journey on which they are about to embarck with him. Uncertainty and alienation are apparent in the speaker himself. He constantly doubts his own worth and place in the world. Instead of simply interacting with people, he stops to ask: Do I dare Disturb the universe? The entire poem takes place in the speaker's own mind. Because of insecurity, the speaker struggles to participate in society. In this way, "The Love Song of J. Alfred Prufrock" shows that alienation can be a product of our own making.

The person in Virginia Woolf's short story is also a victim of insecurities, like the speaker of Eliot's poem, she wants to participate in society but is instead alienated by her own feelings of inadequacy. In "The New Dress," Mabel Waring is so worried that the other guests will judge her that she cannot enjoy herself at a party:

> And at once the misery which she always tried to hide, the profound dissatisfaction—the sense she had had, ever since she was a child, of being inferior to other people—set upon her, relentlessly, remorselessly, with an intensity which she could not beat off, as she would when she woke at night at home, by reading Borrow or Scott; for oh these men, oh these women, all were thinking—"What's Mabel wearing? What a fright she looks! What a hideous new dress!"—their eyelids flickering as they came up and then their lids shutting rather tight. It was her own appalling inadequacy; her cowardice; her mean, water-sprinkled blood that depressed her.

Later, when a fellow party guest points out that Mabel has bought a new dress, it causes her to unravel. Instead of enjoying her social interactions, Mabel allows a single comment to send her into a spiral of anxiety and shame. In the end, she leaves the party early, too embarrassed by her appearance to remain in the company of others. "The New Dress" is a story about society's expectations.

Rosemary Fell, the protagonist in Katherine Mansfield's "A Cup of Tea" is a member of London's high society and is extremely wealthy.

~~She is also well-respected and sure of her place in the world. Yet, Rosemary also fails to connect with the people around her. When she decides to invite a penniless young woman home for tea, she does so in order to make herself feel like a benefactor instead of out of a genuine desire to make a friend. Rosemary is kept from seeing Miss Smith as a whole person by the class difference. Instead, she views the interaction as a game to keep herself entertained on a rainy day, which becomes clear when she abruptly throws Miss Smith out after husband, Philip, comments on the young woman's beauty. Like Mabel's experience, this sends Rosemary into a spiral as the words echo in her head, "Pretty! Absolutely lovely! Bowled over! Her heart beat like a heavy bell." Rosemary asks her husband to reassure her. "'Philip,' she whispered, and she pressed his head against her bosom, 'am I pretty?'" Rosemary abandons Miss Smith at the first sign of that their friendship could lead to a rivalry for her husband's attention. Miss Smith has been alienated by the woman who claimed to be her benefactor, and Rosemary feels insecure in her relationship with her husband.~~

The protagonist of Virginia Woolf's short story "The New Dress" is also a victim of her own insecurities. Like the speaker of Eliot's poem, Mabel Waring wants to participate in society but is instead alienated by her own feelings of inadequacy. Mabel is so worried that the other guests will judge her that she cannot enjoy herself at a party:

> And at once the misery which she always tried to hide, the profound dissatisfaction—the sense she had had, ever since she was a child, of being inferior to other people—set upon her, relentlessly, remorselessly, with an intensity which she could not beat off, as she would when she woke at night at home, by reading Borrow or Scott; for oh these men, oh these women, all were thinking—"What's Mabel wearing? What a fright she looks! What a hideous new dress!"—their eyelids flickering as they came up and then their lids shutting rather tight. It was her own appalling inadequacy; her cowardice; her mean, water-sprinkled blood that depressed her.

Mabel's uncertainty is directly tied to her perception of society's expectations. She worries that, as a member of a slightly lower social class, she cannot measure up to other guests' expectations, and it

**Skill:
Transitions**

To connect her discussion of the two stories, Emma focuses on how the authors approach the same theme from different perspectives. She modifies the concluding sentence of her paragraph about "The New Dress" to summarize her analysis of this theme in the story. She then creates a transition to her discussion of "A Cup of Tea" by contrasting the two protagonists in her new topic sentence about that work.

makes her doubt her worth. Later, when a fellow party guest points out that Mabel has bought a new dress, it causes her to unravel: "'Why,' she asked herself, 'can't I . . . feel sure about the canary and pity and love and not be whipped all round in a second by coming into a room full of people?'" Instead of enjoying her social interactions, Mabel allows a single comment to send her into a spiral of anxiety and shame. In the end, she leaves the party early, too embarrassed by her appearance to remain in the company of others. "The New Dress" shows that alienation can be a product of society's expectations.

Rosemary Fell, the protagonist in Katherine Mansfield's "A Cup of Tea," is the opposite of Mabel in several key ways. Rosemary is a member of London's high society and is extremely wealthy. She is also well-respected and sure of her place in the world. Yet, Rosemary also fails to connect with the people around her. When she decides to invite a penniless young woman, Miss Smith, home for tea, she does so in order to make herself feel like a benefactor instead of out of a genuine desire to make a friend: "She was going to prove to this girl that—wonderful things did happen in life, that—fairy godmothers were real, that—rich people had hearts, and that women *were* sisters." The class difference between the characters prevents Rosemary from seeing Miss Smith as a whole person. Instead, she views the interaction as a game to keep herself entertained on a rainy day. This becomes clear when she abruptly throws Miss Smith out after her husband, Philip, comments on the young woman's beauty. Just as the guest's comment affects Mabel in "The New Dress," this passing commentary sends Rosemary into a spiral as the words echo in her head: "Pretty! Absolutely lovely! Bowled over! Her heart beat like a heavy bell." Rosemary abandons Miss Smith at the first sign that their friendship could lead to a rivalry for her husband's attention. Later, Rosemary asks her husband to reassure her. "'Philip,' she whispered, and she pressed his head against her bosom, 'am I *pretty*?'" As the story concludes, Miss Smith has been alienated by the woman who claimed to be her benefactor, and Rosemary feels insecure in her relationship with her husband. "A Cup of Tea" shows that alienation can occur when issues relating to class and gender complicate individual relationships between two people.

~~"The Love Song of J. Alfred Prufrock," "The New Dress," and "A Cup of Tea" prove that feelings of alienation were common during~~

NOTES

Skill:
Conclusions

Emma strengthens her conclusion by revising the beginning and end of the paragraph. She rephrases her thesis in the first sentence. Then she adds a closing question, which helps her connect with her audience and make her idea memorable.

~~Modernism. Bewildered by their own feelings, the speaker in "The Love Story of J. Alfred Prufrock" and the protagonists in "The New Dress" and "A Cup of Tea" are left alone and afraid. Alienation is a common theme in these modernist works because in a post-war, ever-changing world art, gender, and class needed redefining.~~

The characters in these modernist works come from different backgrounds and have different experiences, but the results of their attempted interactions with others are similar. Hindered by their own insecurities, the speaker in "The Love Song of J. Alfred Prufrock" and the protagonists in "The New Dress" and "A Cup of Tea" are left alone and afraid. Alienation is a common theme in these modernist works because in a post-war, ever-changing world, it is human nature to ask, "Am I good enough?"

Skill:
Introductions

••• CHECKLIST FOR INTRODUCTIONS

Before you write your introduction, ask yourself the following questions:

- What is my claim? In addition:

  > How can I make it more precise and informative?

  > Have I included why my claim is significant to discuss? How does it help the reader understand the topic better? What does it contribute to the conversation on my topic?

- How can I introduce my topic? Have I organized complex ideas, concepts, and information so that each new element builds on the previous element and creates a unified whole?

- How will I "hook" my reader's interest? I might:

  > start with an attention-grabbing statement

  > begin with an intriguing question

  > use descriptive words to set a scene

Here are two strategies to help you introduce your precise claim and topic clearly in an introduction:

- Peer Discussion

  > Talk about your topic with a partner, explaining what you already know and your ideas about your topic.

  > Write notes about the ideas you have discussed and any new questions you may have.

  > Review your notes, and think about what your claim or controlling idea will be.

  > Briefly state your precise and informative claim, establishing why it is important—or what ideas you are contributing to your topic—and how it is different from other claims about your topic.

  > Write a possible "hook."

Freewriting

> Freewrite for 10 minutes about your topic. Don't worry about grammar, punctuation, or having fully formed ideas. The point of freewriting is to discover ideas.

> Review your notes, and think about what your claim or controlling idea will be.

> Briefly state your precise and informative claim, establishing why it is important—or what ideas you are contributing to your topic—and how it is different from other claims about your topic.

> Write a possible "hook."

⟳ YOUR TURN

Choose the best answer to the question.

Below is a passage from a previous draft of Emma's introduction. The underlined sentence is inappropriate for the context of an academic essay and does not clearly introduce the topic of the paper. How should Emma revise the sentence to better suit the topic and context?

> <u>Feeling alienated is the worst.</u> Imagine going to a party and being ridiculed by the other guests because you are wearing a new dress, or having your husband tell you that your new friend is more beautiful than you are. How would that make you feel? Alienation is a common theme in modernist literature because writers began to fight back against the unfair social restrictions set on women during this time.

- ○ A. Women in the early 20th century faced criticism if they did not conform to societal expectations.
- ○ B. Virginia Woolf and Katherine Mansfield were Modernist writers who examined societal expectations.
- ○ C. Feeling like an outsider can be a real bummer, and this was a very common feeling for Modernist women.
- ○ D. Society is way more critical of women than of men, and this was definitely on Virginia Woolf's mind.

✎ WRITE

Use the questions in the checklist to revise the introduction of your literary analysis essay.

Please note that excerpts and passages in the StudySync® library and this workbook are intended as touchstones to generate interest in an author's work. The excerpts and passages do not substitute for the reading of entire texts, and StudySync® strongly recommends that students seek out and purchase the whole literary or informational work in order to experience it as the author intended. Links to online resellers are available in our digital library. In addition, complete works may be ordered through an authorized reseller by filling out and returning to StudySync® the order form enclosed in this workbook.

Reading & Writing Companion   297

Skill:
Transitions

••• CHECKLIST FOR TRANSITIONS

Before you revise your current draft to include transitions, think about:

- the key ideas you discuss in your body paragraphs
- the relationships among your claim(s), reasons, and evidence
- the logical progression of your argument

Next, reread your current draft and note places in your essay where:

- the relationships between your claim(s), reasons, and evidence are unclear
- you could add linking words, vary sentence structure (or syntax), or use other transitional devices to make your argument more cohesive. Look for:

  > sudden jumps in your ideas

  > places where the ideas in a paragraph do not logically follow from the points in the previous paragraph

  > repetitive sentence structures

Revise your draft to use words, phrases, and clauses as well as varied syntax to link the major sections of your essay, create cohesion, and clarify the relationships between claim(s) and reasons and between reasons and evidence, using the following questions as a guide:

- Are there unifying relationships among the claims, reasons, and evidence in my argument?
- Have I clarified these relationships?
- How can I link major sections of my essay using words, phrases, clauses, and varied syntax?

⟳ YOUR TURN

Choose the best answer to each question.

1. Below is a paragraph from a previous draft of Emma's argumentative literary analysis essay. The main idea of the paragraph is unclear. Which sentence should Emma add to the beginning of the paragraph to improve the focus of the paragraph?

> Once she arrives at the party, she cannot stand to look at herself: "But she dared not look in the glass. She could not face the whole horror—the pale yellow, idiotically old-fashioned silk dress with its long skirt and its high sleeves and its waist and all the things that looked so charming in the fashion book, but not on her, not among all these ordinary people." Mabel is very critical of herself.

- ○ A. The main character, Mabel, buys a new dress and goes to a party.
- ○ B. The main character in "The New Dress" is Mabel Waring.
- ○ C. Mabel's internal reflections show that she feels inadequate.
- ○ D. Have you ever felt self-conscious at a party, just like Mabel?

2. Emma wants to improve the transition between two paragraphs in a previous draft of her literary analysis essay by replacing the underlined sentence. Which sentence would be the best transition to include at the beginning of the second paragraph?

> When Mabel's confidence is shaken, she turns to others to buck up her spirits: "one word of affection from Charles would have made all the difference to her at the moment. If he had only said, 'Mabel, you're looking charming to-night!' it would have changed her life." She needs the approval of other people, and whether or not she feels affirmed can deeply impact her mood.
>
> Rosemary Fell, the protagonist of Katherine Mansfield's "A Cup of Tea" is very insecure.

- ○ A. Charles does not respond by giving Mabel a compliment, and this is very similar to what happens in Katherine Mansfield's "A Cup of Tea," which is another Modernist short story.
- ○ B. Even though her economic status is different, Rosemary Fell, the protagonist of Katherine Mansfield's "A Cup of Tea," also feels alienated when she does not feel affirmed by others.
- ○ C. This brief exchange between characters is a pivotal moment in Woolf's short story, so paying close attention to the relationship between Mabel and her husband is very revealing.
- ○ D. The narrator continues, "Charles said nothing of the kind, of course. He was malice itself," emphasizing that Mabel is truly on her own and alienated from even her husband.

✎ WRITE

Use the questions in the checklist to revise your use of transitions in a section of your literary analysis essay.

Skill:
Conclusions

Copyright © BookheadEd Learning, LLC

••• CHECKLIST FOR CONCLUSIONS

Before you write your conclusion, ask yourself the following questions:

- How can I rephrase the thesis or main idea in my conclusion? What impression can I make on my reader?
- How can I write my conclusion so that it supports and follows logically from my argument?
- How can I conclude with a memorable comment?

Below are two strategies to help you provide a concluding statement or section that follows from and supports your argument:

- Peer Discussion

  > After you have written your introduction and body paragraphs, talk with a partner about what you want readers to remember, writing notes about your discussion.

  > Review your notes, and think about what you wish to express in your conclusion.

  > Do not simply restate your claim or thesis statement. Rephrase your main idea to show the depth of your knowledge and the importance of your claim.

  > Write your conclusion.

- Freewriting

  > Freewrite for 10 minutes about what you might include in your conclusion. Don't worry about grammar, punctuation, or having fully formed ideas. The point of freewriting is to discover ideas.

  > Review your notes, and think about what you wish to express in your conclusion.

  > Do not simply restate your claim or thesis statement. Rephrase your main idea to show the depth of your knowledge and the importance of your claim.

  > Write your conclusion.

↻ YOUR TURN

Choose the best answer to the question.

Below is a passage from a previous draft of Emma's conclusion. She wants to add a sentence to clarify her purpose and leave her audience with a memorable thought. Which sentence should she add?

> Taking a close look at modernist texts shows that doubt and isolation were common feelings during the early 20th century. "The Love Song of J. Alfred Prufrock," "The New Dress," and "A Cup of Tea" reflect how rapid social and political changes made people feel helpless and disconnected at this time in history.

○ A. No one likes feeling helpless and disconnected from other people, especially when so much change is happening in the world.

○ B. *The Catcher in the Rye* reveals that people still felt this way in the mid-20th century and that the best way to fight this feeling was to find purpose in life.

○ C. While isolation was a common feeling, Modernist authors collectively proved that there was nothing left to do but reimagine art, gender, and class.

○ D. Modernist authors like T. S. Eliot, Virginia Woolf, and Katherine Mansfield also developed themes that questioned social norms.

✎ WRITE

Use the questions in the checklist to revise the conclusion of your literary analysis.

Please note that excerpts and passages in the StudySync® library and this workbook are intended as touchstones to generate interest in an author's work. The excerpts and passages do not substitute for the reading of entire texts, and StudySync® strongly recommends that students seek out and purchase the whole literary or informational work in order to experience it as the author intended. Links to online resellers are available in our digital library. In addition, complete works may be ordered through an authorized reseller by filling out and returning to StudySync® the order form enclosed in this workbook.

Reading & Writing Companion   **301**

Literary Analysis Writing Process: Revise

PLAN	DRAFT	REVISE	EDIT AND PUBLISH

You have written a draft of your argumentative literary analysis essay. You have also received input from your peers about how to improve it. Now you are going to revise your draft.

⬅ REVISION GUIDE

Examine your draft to find areas for revision. Use the guide below to help you review:

Review	Revise	Example
Clarity		
Scan your body paragraphs. Annotate any sentences where the connection between your ideas is unclear.	Add details so the relationship between your ideas is clear.	The entire poem takes place in the speaker's own mind. There are no outside forces preventing him from engaging with others. ~~Because of insecurity, the speaker struggles to participate in society.~~ The speaker's own hesitancy and insecurity prevent him from participating in society.

Review	Revise	Example
Development		
Identify the reasons that support your claims. Annotate places where you feel there is not enough evidence or explanation to support your claims.	Focus on a single idea or claim and add support, such as textual evidence or explanation.	Yet, Rosemary also fails to connect with the people around her. When she decides to invite a penniless young woman, Miss Smith, home for tea, she does so in order to make herself feel like a benefactor instead of out of a genuine desire to make a friend:: "She was going to prove to this girl that— wonderful things did happen in life, that—fairy godmothers were real, that—rich people had hearts, and that women *were* sisters."
Organization		
Review your body paragraphs. Identify and annotate any sentences that don't flow in a clear and logical way.	Rewrite the sentences so they appear in a logical sequence. Include transitions that clarify the organization of your ideas. Delete details that are repetitive or not essential to support the claim.	Rosemary abandons Miss Smith at the first sign that their friendship could lead to a rivalry for her husband's attention. Later, Rosemary asks her husband to reassure her. "'Philip,' she whispered, and she pressed his head against her bosom, 'am I *pretty*?'" ~~Rosemary abandons Miss Smith at the first sign of that their friendship could lead to a rivalry for her husband's attention.~~ As the story concludes, Miss Smith has been alienated by the woman who claimed to be her benefactor, and Rosemary feels insecure in her relationship with her husband.

Review	Revise	Example
Style: Word Choice		
Identify any sentences that use informal diction. Look for everyday words and phrases that could be replaced with more formal terms.	Replace everyday language with formal, academic language.	By comparing the evening to a patient about to have surgery, Eliot ~~goes against the reader's~~ upends expectations ~~for how natural imagery will work in the poem~~.
Style: Sentence Fluency		
Read your literary analysis essay aloud. Annotate places where the sentences do not flow naturally.	Revise choppy sentences by linking them together. Shorten longer, unfocused sentences to make the key idea clear.	Instead, she views the interaction as a game to keep herself entertained on a rainy day~~., which~~ This becomes clear when she abruptly throws Miss Smith out after her husband, Philip, comments on the young woman's beauty.

✏ WRITE

Use the revision guide, as well as your peer reviews, to help you evaluate your argumentative literary analysis essay to determine areas that should be revised.

Skill:
Using a Style Guide

••• CHECKLIST FOR USING A STYLE GUIDE

In order to ensure that your work conforms to the guidelines in a style manual, do the following:

- Determine which style guide you should use.
- Use the style guide for the overall formatting of your paper, citation style, bibliography format, and other style considerations for reporting research.
- As you draft, use an additional style guide, such as *Artful Sentences: Syntax as Style* by Virginia Tufte or *The Elements of Style* by William Strunk Jr. and E. B. White, to help you vary your syntax, or the grammatical structure of sentences.

  > Use a variety of simple, compound, complex, and compound-complex sentences to convey information.

  > Be sure to punctuate your sentences correctly.

  > Follow standard English language conventions to help you maintain a formal style for formal papers.

To edit your work so that it conforms to the guidelines in a style manual, consider the following questions:

- Have I followed the conventions for spelling, punctuation, capitalization, sentence structure, and formatting, according to the style guide?
- Have I varied my syntax to make my paper engaging for readers?
- Do I have an entry in my works cited or bibliography for each reference I used?
- Have I followed the correct style, including the guidelines for capitalization and punctuation, in each entry in my works cited or bibliography?

↻ YOUR TURN

Read the style questions in the chart below. Then, complete the chart by identifying the header for a section of a style guide that would most likely contain the information needed to answer the question. Write the corresponding letter for each header in the appropriate row.

Style Guide Section Headers	
A	How to Cite Information If No Page Numbers Are Available
B	Words and Expressions Commonly Misused
C	Omit Needless Words
D	How to Cite Plays
E	Form the Singular Possessive of Nouns

Style Question	Section Header
Should I use *affect* or *effect*?	
How do I format dialogue from a drama?	
Should I write "Charles's friend" or "Charles' friend"?	
How do I cite information from a website?	
How do I make my writing more succinct?	

✎ WRITE

Use the checklist to help you choose a convention that has been challenging for you to follow. Use a credible style guide to correct any errors related to that convention in your essay.

Grammar:
Commonly Misspelled Words

By following a few simple steps, you can learn how to spell new words—even words that are unfamiliar or difficult. As you write, keep a list of words that you have trouble spelling. Refer to online or print resources for pronunciation, Latin or Greek roots, and other information that may help you remember how the words are spelled. Then, use the steps below to learn the spelling of those words.

Say it. Look at the word again, and say it aloud. Say it again, pronouncing each syllable clearly.

See it. Close your eyes. Picture the word. Visualize it letter by letter.

Write it. Look at the word again, and write it two or three times. Then, write the word without looking at the printed version.

Check it. Check your spelling. Did you spell it correctly? If not, repeat each step until you can spell it easily.

Here are some words that can sometimes confuse even strong spellers.

Commonly Misspelled Words		
abundant	accompaniment	against
apparatus	arctic	behavior
business	calendar	cemetery
circumstantial	deference	definite
exhibition	financier	forty
magnificence	metaphor	necessity
playwright	reference	repetitive
seize	sufficient	surprise
transparent	undoubtedly	unnecessary
vaccine	versatile	villain

Please note that excerpts and passages in the StudySync® library and this workbook are intended as touchstones to generate interest in an author's work. The excerpts and passages do not substitute for the reading of entire texts, and StudySync® strongly recommends that students seek out and purchase the whole literary or informational work in order to experience it as the author intended. Links to online resellers are available in our digital library. In addition, complete works may be ordered through an authorized reseller by filling out and returning to StudySync® the order form enclosed in this workbook.

Reading & Writing Companion   **307**

YOUR TURN

1. How should this sentence be changed?

> No matter what the calender says today's date is, the weather feels absolutely arctic.

○ A. No matter what the calander says today's date is, the weather feels absolutely arctic.
○ B. No matter what the calendar says today's date is, the weather feels absolutely arctic.
○ C. No matter what the calaendar says today's date is, the weather feels absolutely artic.
○ D. No change needs to be made to this sentence.

2. How should this sentence be changed?

> Aunt Polly, who had gotten her degree in poetry, was always quick to seize upon a metaphor.

○ A. Aunt Polly, who had gotten her degree in poetry, was always quick to sieze upon a metaphor.
○ B. Aunt Polly, who had gotten her degree in poetry, was always quick to seise upon a metafor.
○ C. Aunt Polly, who had gotten her degree in poetry, was always quick to seize upon a metaphore.
○ D. No change needs to be made to this sentence.

3. How should this sentence be changed?

> Dr. Mason insists that the vacine against influenza is an important part of an annual checkup.

○ A. Dr. Mason insists that the vaccene agenst influenza is an important part of an annual checkup.
○ B. Dr. Mason insists that the vaccine against influenza is an important part of an annual checkup.
○ C. Dr. Mason insists that the vacine aggainst influenza is an important part of an annual checkup.
○ D. No change needs to be made to this sentence.

4. How should this sentence be changed?

> Undoubtedley in deferense to my grandfather's wishes, my family planned to hold his birthday dinner at his favorite restaurant.

○ A. Undoutedley in defence to my grandfather's wishes, my family planned to hold his birthday dinner at his favorite restaurant.
○ B. Undoubtedley in defrence to my grandfather's wishes, my family planned to hold his birthday dinner at his favorite restaurant.
○ C. Undoubtedly in deference to my grandfather's wishes, my family planned to hold his birthday dinner at his favorite restaurant.
○ D. No change needs to be made to this sentence.

Grammar: Pronoun Case and Reference

Pronouns have four properties: number, person, gender, and case. There are three cases: subject (or nominative), object (or objective), and possessive case. Writers frequently make pronoun-case errors when there are multiple subjects (compound subjects) or multiple objects (compound objects) in a sentence.

Correctly Edited	Incorrect	Explanation
He and Joseph started a charity to help stray cats.	Him and Joseph started a charity to help stray cats.	"Him and Joseph" are the *subjects* of this sentence. "Him" is incorrect because "Him" is in the *object* case.
Read this book and tell Mr. Tannenbaum and **me** what you think.	Read this book and tell Mr. Tannenbaum and I what you think.	"Mr. Tannenbaum and I" are *objects* in this sentence. "I" is incorrect because "I" is in the *subject* case.
I know that **she** and her sister traveled through South America last year.	I know that her and her sister traveled through South America last year.	"Her and her sister" are the *subjects* in a clause. The first "her" is incorrect because "her" is in the *object* case. The second "her," however, is correct because it is in the *possessive* case, showing a relationship to the sister.

Sentences that use pronouns can become confusing for a reader if the pronouns do not have clear antecedents. Strong writing avoids ambiguity.

Correctly Edited	Incorrect	Strategy for Revision
The team captain told Karen to take **the captain's** guard position.	The team captain told Karen to take her guard position.	Replace a pronoun with a noun.
Lock the car after you put it in the garage.	When you put the car in the garage, don't forget to lock it.	Rewrite the sentence to make the antecedent clear.

⟳ YOUR TURN

1. How should this sentence be changed?

> The committee awarded the band, the female vocalist, and him a music trophy.

- ○ A. They awarded the band, the female vocalist, and him a music trophy.
- ○ B. The committee awarded the band, she, and him a music trophy.
- ○ C. The committee awarded the band, the female vocalist, and he a music trophy.
- ○ D. No change needs to be made to this sentence.

2. How should this sentence be changed?

> The exam that Ms. Standjord is giving to us on Wednesday will be simple for you and I.

- ○ A. The exam that Ms. Standjord is giving to we on Wednesday will be simple for you and I.
- ○ B. The exam that Ms. Standjord is giving to us on Wednesday will be simple for you and me.
- ○ C. The exam that Ms. Standjord is giving to us on Wednesday will be simple for she and I.
- ○ D. No change needs to be made to this sentence.

3. How should this sentence be changed?

> Charlotte emailed Olivia, who was away on a business trip, to say that her mother had been in an automobile accident.

- ○ A. Charlotte emailed she, who was away on a business trip, to say that her mother had been in an automobile accident.
- ○ B. Charlotte emailed Olivia, who was away on a business trip, to say that Olivia's mother had been in an automobile accident.
- ○ C. She emailed Olivia, who was away on a business trip, to say that her mother had been in an automobile accident.
- ○ D. No change needs to be made to this sentence.

Literary Analysis Writing Process: Edit and Publish

| PLAN | DRAFT | REVISE | EDIT AND PUBLISH |

You have revised your literary analysis based on your peer feedback and your own examination.

Now, it is time to edit your literary analysis. When you revised, you focused on the content of your literary analysis. You probably looked at your essay's claim and thesis statement, your organization, and your supporting evidence. When you edit, you focus on the mechanics of your literary analysis, paying close attention to things like grammar and punctuation.

Use the checklist below to guide you as you edit:

- [ ] Have I followed relevant rules in the style guide?

- [ ] Do my pronouns reflect the correct case and have clear antecedents?

- [ ] Do I have any sentence fragments or run-on sentences?

- [ ] Have I spelled everything correctly?

Notice some edits Emma has made:

- Fixed a spelling error

- Replaced an unclear pronoun with a noun

- Added a slash to show a line break in a quotation from a poem, and cited line numbers

Please note that excerpts and passages in the StudySync® library and this workbook are intended as touchstones to generate interest in an author's work. The excerpts and passages do not substitute for the reading of entire texts, and StudySync® strongly recommends that students seek out and purchase the whole literary or informational work in order to experience it as the author intended. Links to online resellers are available in our digital library. In addition, complete works may be ordered through an authorized reseller by filling out and returning to StudySync® the order form enclosed in this workbook.

Reading & Writing Companion **311**

By comparing the evening to a patient about to have surgery, Eliot upends expectations. This makes readers uncomfortable because they do not know what will happen on the journey on which they are about to ~~embarck~~ embark with ~~him~~ the poem's speaker.

Uncertainty and alienation are also reflected in the speaker himself. He constantly doubts his own worth and place in the world. Instead of simply interacting with people, he stops to ask:~~,~~ ~~Do I dare Disturb the universe?~~ "Do I dare / Disturb the universe?" (51-52).

✏ WRITE

Use the questions in the checklist, as well as your peer reviews, to help you evaluate your literary analysis to determine places that need editing. Then, edit your literary analysis to correct those errors.

Once you have made all your corrections, you are ready to publish your work. You can distribute your writing to family and friends, hang it on a bulletin board, or post it on your blog. If you publish online, share the link with your family, friends, and classmates.

Fear of Missing Out

INFORMATIONAL TEXT

Introduction

With countless dating websites and apps, single people have plenty of opportunities to meet their soul mates. But psychologists say that all this choice might not be helpful after all. This article explains the paradox of choice and how it might influence dating in the 21st century.

VOCABULARY

myriad

large number; multitude

paralyze

to make someone or something unable to move

anxiety

a painful or uneasy feeling about something

compatibility

the state of being able to get along without conflict

paradox

a statement that is seemingly contradictory or impossible and yet often reveals a larger truth

 NOTES

READ

1   Imagine you are on a date. The person is nice and attractive. You're having a good time. But you wonder if you could be having a better time with someone else. Besides, this person doesn't share your love of 90s hip-hop! Time to use that matchmaking app to find a different date for next weekend.

2   Such is the state of dating in the 21st century. There are more ways than ever to meet people, from dating sites to matchmaking services to location-based apps. That means there are always countless people out there just waiting to meet you. Why settle down when you can swipe right?

3   Making choices is hard. Not only do we struggle to choose from a **myriad** of options, but we also stress after the decision is made over whether or not it was the right one. For example, if you go to a grocery store that has only one type of breakfast cereal available, you buy it. If it's bad, then it's the store's fault for carrying only that one item. But if you buy a bad box from a store chock-full of cereal varieties, whose fault is it? Yours. And that causes **anxiety**.

NOTES

4   The same goes for online dating. The sheer number of potential online matches can leave daters second-guessing their choices. They wonder if they could have done better. Having two or more equally enticing options causes stress and anxiety. Sometimes people are unable to make any choice at all. If you do choose, you live in constant fear that the other option was better. This condition is known as the **paradox** of choice.

5   Research supports the idea that choice is not always a good thing. In a famous experiment, conducted by Columbia University psychologist Sheena Iyengar, researchers set up a table in a grocery store. In two conditions, people were offered either six or 24 varieties of gourmet jam to taste and purchase. Researchers found that the number of varieties did not change how many people tasted the jam. Surprisingly, however, only three percent of people who were offered 24 varieties purchased a jar. But 30 percent of people offered six varieties purchased a jar. Researchers concluded that more options is not better for decision-making.

6   Likewise, researchers Amitai Shenhav and Randy Buckner put people in an fMRI scanner. They were asked to choose between two objects. The objects were either both high in value (for example, a camera and an MP3 player), both low in value (a bag of pretzels and a water bottle), or of opposite values (a camera and a bag of pretzels). The researchers found that when forced to choose between two high-value objects, people found the decision very hard. Afterward, they felt anxiety over whether they made the right choice.

7   And yet, online dating does lead to successful long-term relationships. According to a study from the University of Chicago, one third of U.S. couples who married between 2005 and 2012 met online. In addition, those couples were less likely to divorce. They were more likely to report being happy in their marriages.

8   Some experts use those statistics and others to show that the paradox of choice is overblown. They say that if having choices were really so **paralyzing** for people, why would we have entire aisles devoted to cereal varieties? In some cases, people seem to like having more options.

9   Some researchers theorize that the reason people go on dates with so many different online matches is not the number of available daters. Rather, it's because of the type of information on online dating profiles. It's not what potential partners really need to know for **compatibility**. A dating profile cannot realistically reflect personality. It cannot show how you interact with others. You must meet someone in person for that. A picture and a location is no substitute for chemistry.

First Read

Read "Fear of Missing Out." After you read, complete the Think Questions below.

☁ THINK QUESTIONS

1. What is the paradox of choice? Explain in your own words. Use textual evidence to support your explanation.

   Paradox of choice is_____

   _____.

2. How has technology changed dating? Cite textual evidence to support your answer.

   Technology has changed dating _____

   _____.

3. Explain the jam study. What did researchers test, and what did they find? Support your answer with textual evidence.

   The jam study was _____.

   Researchers tested _____

4. Use context to determine the meaning of the word *myriad* as it is used in "Fear of Missing Out." Write your definition of *myriad* here.

   Myriad means _____.

   A context clue is _____.

5. Use context to determine the meaning of the word *anxiety* as it is used in "Fear of Missing Out." Write your definition of *anxiety* here.

   Anxiety means _____.

   A context clue is _____.

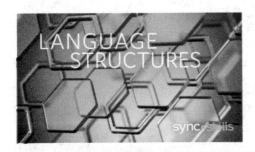

Skill:
Language Structures

★ DEFINE

In every language, there are rules that tell how to **structure** sentences. These rules define the correct order of words. In the English language, for example, a **basic** structure for sentences is subject, verb, and object. Some sentences have more **complicated** structures.

You will encounter both basic and complicated **language structures** in the classroom materials you read. Being familiar with language structures will help you better understand the text.

••• CHECKLIST FOR LANGUAGE STRUCTURES

To improve your comprehension of language structures, do the following:

 Monitor your understanding.

- Ask yourself: Why do I not understand this sentence? Is it because the sentence is long? Or is it because I do not understand the logical relationship between ideas in this sentence?

- Pay attention to coordinating conjunctions.

  > **Coordinating conjunctions** show an equal emphasis on the ideas in a sentence.

  > Some examples of coordinating conjunctions are and, but, and or.

- Pay attention to subordinating conjunctions.

  > **Subordinating conjunctions** show that one idea is more important and the other idea is less important, or subordinate.

  > Some examples of subordinating conjunctions are after, instead, and once.

- Break down the sentence into its parts.

- Ask yourself: How does the writer use conjunctions to combine sentences? Can I break the sentence down into two shorter sentences?

✓ Confirm your understanding with a peer or teacher.

YOUR TURN

Read each sentence below from "Fear of Missing Out." Then, complete the chart by sorting the sentences into those that use coordinating conjunctions and those that use subordinating conjunctions.

Sentences	
A	They say that if having choices were really so paralyzing for people, why would we have entire aisles devoted to cereal varieties?
B	Not only do we struggle to choose from a myriad of options, but we also stress after the decision is made over whether or not it was the right one.
C	The objects were either both high in value (for example, a camera and an MP3 player), both low in value (a bag of pretzels and a water bottle), or of opposite values (a camera and a bag of pretzels).
D	If it's bad, then it's the store's fault for carrying only that one item.

Coordinating Conjunctions	Subordinating Conjunctions

Skill:
Supporting Evidence

★ DEFINE

In some informational or argumentative texts, the author may share an opinion. This **opinion** may be the author's **claim** or **thesis**. The author must then provide readers with **evidence** that supports their opinion. Supporting evidence can be details, examples, or facts that agree with the author's claim or thesis.

Looking for supporting evidence can help you confirm your understanding of what you read. Finding and analyzing supporting evidence can also help you form your own opinions about the subject.

••• CHECKLIST FOR SUPPORTING EVIDENCE

In order to find and analyze supporting evidence, do the following:

✓ Identify the topic and the author's claim or thesis.

- Ask yourself: What is this mostly about? What is the author's opinion?

✓ Find details, facts, and examples that support the author's claim or thesis.

- Ask yourself: Is this detail important? How does this detail relate to the thesis or claim?

✓ Analyze the supporting evidence.

- Ask yourself: Is this evidence strong? Do I agree with the evidence?

Please note that excerpts and passages in the StudySync® library and this workbook are intended as touchstones to generate interest in an author's work. The excerpts and passages do not substitute for the reading of entire texts, and StudySync® strongly recommends that students seek out and purchase the whole literary or informational work in order to experience it as the author intended. Links to online resellers are available in our digital library. In addition, complete works may be ordered through an authorized reseller by filling out and returning to StudySync® the order form enclosed in this workbook.

Reading & Writing Companion   **319**

YOUR TURN

Read each line below from "Fear of Missing Out." Then, complete the chart by deciding if the text is a detail, a fact, or an example to support the claim.

	Lines from Text
A	The researchers found that when forced to choose between two high-value objects, people found the decision very hard.
B	The same goes for online dating. The sheer number of potential online matches can leave daters second-guessing their choices.
C	According to a study from the University of Chicago, one third of U.S. couples who married between 2005 and 2012 met online.
D	Imagine you are on a date. The person is nice and attractive. You're having a good time. But you wonder if you could be having a better time with someone else.
E	There are more ways than ever to meet people, from dating sites to matchmaking services to location-based apps.
F	It's not what potential partners really need to know for compatibility. A dating profile cannot realistically reflect personality.

Details	Facts	Examples

Close Read

✏ WRITE

ARGUMENTATIVE: Does online dating cause too much anxiety to be successful? Some say yes. Some say no. The article "Fear of Missing Out" explores this topic. Choose a side and write a paragraph explaining your point of view. Use evidence from the text to support your claim. Pay attention to and edit for plurals.

Use the checklist below to guide you as you write.

☐ Does online dating cause too much anxiety to be successful?

☐ What convinced you to support or disagree with the author's claim?

☐ What evidence supports your position?

Use the sentence frames to organize and write your personal response.

Online dating (does / does not) _____ cause _____.

Research shows that people _____.

According to paragraph_____, "_____".

With online dating, _____.

Other research shows _____.

Overall, the paradox of choice _____.

Please note that excerpts and passages in the StudySync® library and this workbook are intended as touchstones to generate interest in an author's work. The excerpts and passages do not substitute for the reading of entire texts, and StudySync® strongly recommends that students seek out and purchase the whole literary or informational work in order to experience it as the author intended. Links to online resellers are available in our digital library. In addition, complete works may be ordered through an authorized reseller by filling out and returning to StudySync® the order form enclosed in this workbook.

Reading & Writing Companion **321**

The Ribbons

FICTION

Introduction

In this fictional letter, a woman named Elizabeth tells a story of growing up in Pennsylvania in the 1820s. Her family is poor, but one day Elizabeth's mother gives her some money to spend as she likes. What will she do with this sudden windfall, and what lifelong lesson can be learned?

VOCABULARY

dismissive

feeling or showing that something or someone is not worth consideration

frivolous

unnecessary, serving no purpose

correspond

to write to someone

diminish

to be made smaller in size or importance

indulge

to give in to someone's whims or wishes

READ

NOTES

My dear Cora:

1   Thank you for your thoughtful and amusing letter. It brightened up an otherwise dreary day. I was especially intrigued by your story about your niece and her **dismissive** response to the new dresses that you so kindly brought her from Paris. I cannot believe she could only speak of how ugly her old dresses were without a compliment for the new ones. As you may recall, my own childhood was filled with love and laughter, but not money. What I wouldn't have given for dresses from Paris!

2   Because we have been **corresponding** for many years, you know that I love to tell stories of my youth in my small town. I am reminded of one such story now. If you **indulge** my memories, it might be of value to your churlish niece.

3   To help my family keep wood on the fire through the freezing Pennsylvania winters, my mother and I took in sewing. My brother would sit and read to us by candlelight as we sewed. On those nights, the sewing rarely felt like work,

Please note that excerpts and passages in the StudySync® library and this workbook are intended as touchstones to generate interest in an author's work. The excerpts and passages do not substitute for the reading of entire texts, and StudySync® strongly recommends that students seek out and purchase the whole literary or informational work in order to experience it as the author intended. Links to online resellers are available in our digital library. In addition, complete works may be ordered through an authorized reseller by filling out and returning to StudySync® the order form enclosed in this workbook.

Reading & Writing Companion   **323**

the cold seemed distant, and the hours rushed by. One spring, when the flowers started to grow a little earlier than usual, my family no longer needed extra candles and coal. My mother allowed me to keep some of the money in gratitude for my winter of work.

4   I had never before had any money to my own name. I was filled with excitement at the possibilities. I spent days dreaming about what I should buy with my riches. After a week of rolling the coins about in my hand, I took a ride with Father into town. I grasped my coin purse like I thought it would fall right through the wood cart. The day was bright with new beginnings. I was finally going to enter a shop and choose something for myself—not flour for Mother, nor laces for Father's boots, but something **frivolous** and only for me! As I walked across the square, my friend Mary greeted me. I invited her to join me in my shopping. I thought the presence of a friend would only enhance the joy of the day. As we walked down the road together, I saw a beautiful spool of ribbon in a shop window. I instantly knew I should buy it and use it to improve my favorite hat. I pointed the ribbon out to Mary and she said, "How beautiful! Those ribbons are much prettier than the dingy ones you're wearing now. It will be such a lovely improvement."

5   At that, I felt the color rising in my cheeks. I had been so excited for the new ribbons, but Mary's careless comment hurt me deeply. I bought the ribbons, and they were quite beautiful, but I could never quite recapture the joy I felt when I first saw them in the window. Later, in thinking back on the day, I thought of a line from a book that my brother had read to us that winter. The book was *Hope Leslie* by Catharine Maria Sedgwick: "But it is unnecessary to heighten the glory of day by comparing it with the preceding twilight." The glory of my day of wealth was only **diminished** by thinking of my previous poverty, not enhanced.

6   And that, my dear friend, is what you need to remind your niece. When she is given a new dress, she should not focus on the ratty old one that preceded it. We must all focus on the glory of the present day for its own shining sake, and not think of the darkness til we must.

With love,
Elizabeth

First Read

Read "The Ribbons." After you read, complete the Think Questions below.

☁ THINK QUESTIONS

1. Why does Elizabeth share the story of the ribbons?

    Elizabeth shares the story about the ribbons because _____.

2. Why did Mary's comment cause Elizabeth to feel embarrassed? Support your inference with textual evidence.

    Elizabeth felt embarrassed because _____

    _____.

3. What is Cora's niece supposed to learn from this story? Support your response with textual evidence.

    Cora's niece is supposed to learn that _____

    _____.

4. Use context to determine the meaning of the word *dismissive* as it is used in "The Ribbons." Write your definition of *dismissive* here.

    Dismissive means _____.

    A context clue is _____.

5. Use context to determine the meaning of the word *correspond* as it is used in "The Ribbons." Write your definition of *correspond* here.

    Correspond means _____.

    A context clue is _____.

Skill:
Analyzing Expressions

★ DEFINE

When you read, you may find English expressions that you do not know. An **expression** is a group of words that communicates an idea. Three types of expressions are idioms, sayings, and figurative language. They can be difficult to understand because the meanings of the words are different from their **literal**, or usual, meanings.

An **idiom** is an expression that is commonly known among a group of people. For example, "It's raining cats and dogs" means it is raining heavily. **Sayings** are short expressions that contain advice or wisdom. For instance, "Don't count your chickens before they hatch" means do not plan on something good happening before it happens. **Figurative** language is when you describe something by comparing it with something else, either directly (using the words *like* or *as*) or indirectly. For example, "I'm as hungry as a horse" means I'm very hungry. None of the expressions are about actual animals.

••• CHECKLIST FOR ANALYZING EXPRESSIONS

To determine the meaning of an expression, remember the following:

✓ If you find a confusing group of words, it may be an expression. The meaning of words in expressions may not be their literal meaning.

  ◦ Ask yourself: Is this confusing because the words are new? Or because the words do not make sense together?

✓ Determining the overall meaning may require that you use one or more of the following:

  • context clues

  ◦ a dictionary or other resource

  • teacher or peer support

✓ Highlight important information before and after the expression to look for clues.

⟳ YOUR TURN

Read the situations below. Then, complete the chart by matching the hyperbolic description that matches each situation.

	Hyperbolic Description
A	My brain is frozen!
B	I aged five years in that waiting room.
C	I nearly died laughing!
D	This hurts so bad that the doctor needs to remove my entire foot.

Situation	Hyperboles
You have to wait a long time at the dentist's office.	
You eat ice cream too fast and get a headache.	
You hit your little toe on a table leg.	
Someone tells you a very funny joke.	

Please note that excerpts and passages in the StudySync® library and this workbook are intended as touchstones to generate interest in an author's work. The excerpts and passages do not substitute for the reading of entire texts, and StudySync® strongly recommends that students seek out and purchase the whole literary or informational work in order to experience it as the author intended. Links to online resellers are available in our digital library. In addition, complete works may be ordered through an authorized reseller by filling out and returning to StudySync® the order form enclosed in this workbook.

Reading & Writing Companion   **327**

Skill: Visual and Contextual Support

 DEFINE

Visual support is an image or an object that helps you understand a text. **Contextual support** is a **feature** that helps you understand a text. By using visual and contextual supports, you can develop your vocabulary so you can better understand a variety of texts.

First, preview the text to identify any visual supports. These might include illustrations, graphics, charts, or other objects in a text. Then, identify any contextual supports. Examples of contextual supports are titles, headers, captions, and boldface terms. Write down your **observations**.

Then, write down what those visual and contextual supports tell you about the meaning of the text. Note any new vocabulary that you see in those supports. Ask your peers and your teacher to **confirm** your understanding of the text.

••• CHECKLIST FOR VISUAL AND CONTEXTUAL SUPPORT

To use visual and contextual support to understand texts, do the following:

- ✓ Preview the text. Read the title, headers, and other features. Look at any images and graphics.

- ✓ Write down the visual and contextual supports in the text.

- ✓ Write down what those supports tell you about the text.

- ✓ Note any new vocabulary that you see in those supports.

- ✓ Create an illustration for the reading and write a descriptive caption.

- ✓ Confirm your observations with your peers and teacher.

YOUR TURN

Read the following example of correspondence. Then, complete the multiple-choice questions below.

Dear Mom and Dad,

Hello from Camp! How are you? I am doing well but I am exhausted after each long day of activities. Today we defeated the counselors in a game of beach volleyball! They have been the defending champions for the last two weeks. It feels great to win! Now I need to learn chess in order to compete in next week's mind games.

The food in the cafeteria is getting better. They actually served pizza yesterday and it tasted delicious! Can we please go out to eat when I get home in two weeks? I love your cooking, mom, but I think we all deserve a night out!

I miss you,
Charlie

---

1. Which is an example of a *salutation*?

   ○ A. Today we defeated the counselors in a game of beach volleyball!

   ○ B. I miss you,

   ○ C. Dear Mom and Dad,

2. Which sentence is part of the *body* of the letter?

   ○ A. Dear Mom and Dad,

   ○ B. Now I need to learn chess in order to compete in next week's mind games.

   ○ C. I miss you, Charlie

3. Which is an example of a *signature*?

   ○ A. It feels great to win!

   ○ B. I miss you, Charlie

   ○ C. Dear Mom and Dad,

4. Which sentence is written in *first person*?

   ○ A. I am so happy that we decided to send Charlie to camp this summer.

   ○ B. They play so many sports at summer camp.

   ○ C. He learned how to play chess!

Close Read

PERSONAL NARRATIVE: The narrator in "The Ribbons" explores the memory of a lesson learned from a bittersweet experience. Write a letter to a friend or family member explaining your experience with this main idea from the text. Include specific details from your life for support. Pay attention to and edit for negatives and contractions.

Use the checklist below to guide you as you write.

☐ What bittersweet experience helped you learn a lesson?

☐ Who was involved in this experience?

☐ What did you learn from this experience?

Use the sentence frames to organize and write your personal narrative.

_____,

How are you? I heard that you _____.

Did you _____? I learned _____ when I _____.

One day _____ said, "_____"

I thought, "_____."

Unfortunately, I _____ and _____.

It was very _____.

I hope you learn from my experience!

_____

Copyright © BookheadEd Learning, LLC

:studysync®

Times of Transition

UNIT 6

Times of Transition

How are we shaped by change?

Genre Focus: FICTION

Texts

Paired Readings

336   Literary Focus: Postmodernism and Postcolonialism

342   The Mysterious Anxiety of Them and Us
POETRY   Ben Okri

352   Love After Love
POETRY   Derek Walcott

355   The Museum
FICTION   Leila Aboulela

371   A Temporary Matter
FICTION   Jhumpa Lahiri

394   Tryst with Destiny (Speech on the Eve of India's Independence)
ARGUMENTATIVE TEXT   Jawaharlal Nehru

398   A Small Place
INFORMATIONAL TEXT   Jamaica Kincaid

401   Ghosts
FICTION   Chimamanda Ngozi Adichie

419   ARK
FICTION   Ehud Lavski and Yael Nathan

429   Blindspot: Hidden Biases of Good People
ARGUMENTATIVE TEXT   Mahzarin Banaji and Anthony Greenwald

433   News Literacy in the Misinformation Age
INFORMATIONAL TEXT   The New Literacy Project in partnership with StudySync

441   Honesty on Social Media
ARGUMENTATIVE TEXT

454   Dawn Revisited
POETRY   Rita Dove

456   Commencement Address at the New School
ARGUMENTATIVE TEXT   Zadie Smith

Extended Oral Project and Grammar

473 | **Plan**

Organizing an Oral Presentation
Evaluating Sources
Considering Audience and Purpose
Persuasive Techniques

496 | **Draft**

Sources and Citations
Communicating Ideas
Reasons and Evidence
Engaging in Discourse

513 | **Revise**

Grammar: Parallel Structure
Grammar: Sentence Variety - Openings

520 | **Edit and Present**

English Language Learner Resources

522 | **Hope**
FICTION

533 | **When the World Sleeps**
DRAMA

547 | Text Fulfillment through StudySync

How are we shaped by change?

LEILA ABOULELA

Leila Aboulela (b. 1964) is a Sudanese writer of short stories and novels. She was born in Cairo, Egypt; was raised in Khartoum, Sudan; and has lived much of her adult life in Aberdeen, Scotland. All of her literary works carefully portray the faith and values of her characters, which often feature people who practice Islam and must negotiate ethical dilemmas. Aboulela sees fiction as a "gentle way of passing on information" about Islam to non-Muslim readers.

CHIMAMANDA NGOZI ADICHIE

Chimamanda Ngozi Adichie (b. 1977) writes short stories, novels, and essays and splits her time between Nigeria and the United States. Her education has included studies in medicine, communication, political science, African history, and creative writing. Adichie's family lived in the house once owned by the notable Nigerian author Chinua Achebe, a literary figure Adichie credits as her inspiration for becoming a writer.

MAHZARIN R. BANAJI

Harvard psychologist Mahzarin R. Banaji (b. 1956) was born and raised in Secunderabad, India, and moved to the United States to pursue her Ph.D. at Ohio State University. Banaji is best known for her work exploring the concept of implicit bias, or the prejudice that results from stereotypes and attitudes built in to our society. Along with her work at Harvard, Banaji runs the website Project Implicit, which aims to spread awareness of the role implicit bias plays in our daily lives.

RITA DOVE

American author Rita Dove (b. 1952) served as the United States Poet Laureate from 1993 to 1995, and as the Poet Laureate of Virginia from 2004 to 2006. In addition to poetry, she writes plays and fiction. Over the course of Dove's career, one major change in her approach to writing has been her sense of an audience. When she began writing, she did not yet have readers; now, after numerous publications and awards, she writes knowing that many people will read the ideas and perspectives she puts forth.

JAMAICA KINCAID

Jamaica Kincaid (b. 1949) moved from St. John's, Antigua at the age of sixteen to work as an au pair in Manhattan, and has lived in New York ever since. Her early writing career began as a journalist for a girls' magazine, and as her talent was recognized, she became employed as a staff writer for *The New Yorker*. Critics often struggle to categorize her work, which is by turns both political and personal, and like human experience itself: complex, beautiful, and resonant.

JHUMPA LAHIRI

Jhumpa Lahiri (b. 1967) says, "While I am American by virtue of the fact that I was raised in this country, I am Indian thanks to the efforts of two individuals." Lahiri's parents infused her Rhode Island childhood with the language, values, and traditions of their Bengali Indian origins, and the family took frequent trips to Kolkata, the capital of West Bengal. Lahiri's fiction and essays often feature characters who navigate multiple cultural identities, modeled after her own Indian American experience.

JAWAHARLAL NEHRU

Activist, lawyer, and politician Jawaharlal Nehru (1889–1964) was repeatedly imprisoned for civil disobedience in the 1920s and 1930s. A leader of the movement to establish Indian independence from the British administration, Nehru worked closely with Mahatma Gandhi and was recognized as his successor by the end of World War II. Named the first prime minister of India in 1947, Nehru went on to model the new government into a secular republic with democratic values.

BEN OKRI

Ben Okri (b. 1959) spent part of his childhood in London, and part in his home of Nigeria, where he experienced the Biafran War firsthand. He was once again living in London when he polished the final draft of *The Famished Road* (1991), which made Okri the youngest ever winner of the Man Booker Prize for Fiction. In prose and in verse, Okri's attention to the music of language and the art of storytelling reflects his lifelong love of literature and deep connection to his Urhobo culture.

ZADIE SMITH

Author Zadie Smith (b. 1975) grew up in London with a Jamaican mother and an English father. She liked to sing, dance, and write from an early age. When she was fourteen, Smith changed the spelling of her first name, Sadie, to its current spelling with a Z. Smith pitched her first novel to an agent while she was still in college in Cambridge, England; *White Teeth* (2000) became an instant bestseller. She writes fiction and essays and works as a professor of creative writing in New York City.

DEREK WALCOTT

The poetry of Derek Walcott (1930–2017) celebrates his Caribbean heritage and interrogates the influence of colonialism. Walcott was raised in the British colony of Saint Lucia in the West Indies, where he trained as a painter and began publishing poems at age fourteen. He later lived between Trinidad, New York City, Boston, and Saint Lucia as a poet, playwright, and professor. Walcott defined poetry as a form of survival, cohering the "fragmented memory" of individual and cultural histories.

EHUD LAVSKI AND YAEL NATHAN

Together, writer Ehud Lavski and illustrator Yael Nathan publish EL Comics, a science fiction–infused series of webcomics they describe as having "twisted endings." Lavski lives in Los Angeles and works primarily in film and television as a scriptwriter. Nathan lives in Tel Aviv and works in a wide range of design fields, producing images for graphic and interface design in addition to creating classical animation, character design, and illustration.

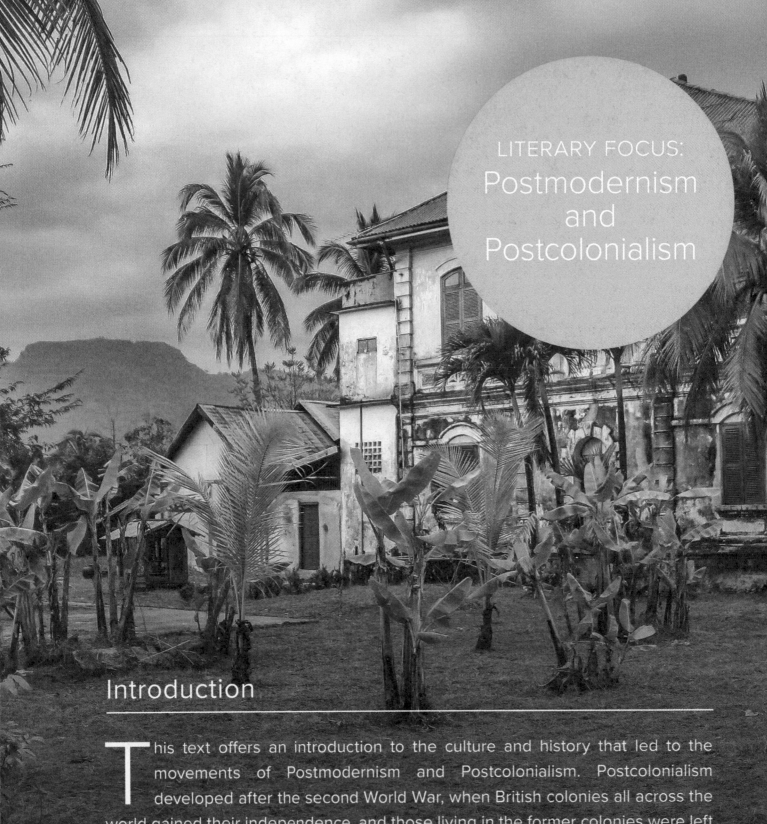

Postmodernism and Postcolonialism

Introduction

This text offers an introduction to the culture and history that led to the movements of Postmodernism and Postcolonialism. Postcolonialism developed after the second World War, when British colonies all across the world gained their independence, and those living in the former colonies were left to deal with the violent consequences of years of British rule. Postcolonial writers provided necessary new perspectives in literature from people previously silenced by the dominance of colonial powers. Postmodernism was a response to the end of World War II and the Modernist movement—a kind of rebellion that attempted to expand on literary tradition by exploding it from within.

"Colony by colony, the British Empire was dismantled."

NOTES

1   You may have heard the word *postmodern* used to describe unusual artwork, literature, music, or even experimental pop and rap stars. Another related term you may be familiar with is *postcolonialism*. Both words represent prominent literary movements of the twentieth and twenty-first centuries. Although you may not yet have a thorough understanding of these movements, more than likely you have noticed that both words have one detail in common: the prefix *post-*, meaning "after." As the word parts signify, **postmodernism** came after Modernism, and **postcolonialism** came after colonialism. Because both movements are reactions to previous historical, cultural, and literary events, it is important to begin by studying what led to these movements, specifically the end of Modernism, British colonialism, and World War II.

British Colonialism

2   During the nineteenth and early twentieth centuries, Britain colonized large portions of the world, with the aim of total control over vast territories. Although the British Empire did build railroads, telegraphs, schools, and hospitals in these territories, colonialism was based on economic exploitation and influenced by racist attitudes. Throughout the British Empire, government administrators and Christian missionaries often came into conflict with the people under colonial rule. Later, writers would describe the devastating effects of British colonialism and the imposition of Christianity on traditional

A meeting of British colonial administrators with tribal messengers from the interior in Lagos, Nigeria.

ways of life. One prominent example is Nigerian writer Chinua Achebe. Achebe's highly acclaimed and influential novel *Things Fall Apart* (1958) explored the experience of European colonization from the perspective of the Nigerians, at a time when most English literature reflected a European viewpoint.

The End of the Empire

3   To strengthen its economy after World War II, Britain had to reduce expenses abroad and, therefore, gradually agreed to many colonies' demands for independence. Colony by colony, the British Empire was dismantled. In Asia and Africa, the new nations created from former British colonies faced an array of **formidable** problems, including overpopulation, poverty, and ethnic and religious **strife.** For example, when India and Pakistan became independent in 1947, millions of people fled across new borders, with a majority of Hindus focusing on a newly free India and many Muslims streaming toward Pakistan. In such a chaotic atmosphere of divergent cultures and faiths, mass migration, and new governments, violence ensued and more than a million people perished. In Africa, many former British colonies achieved independence during the 1950s and 1960s, but their national stability was undermined by ethnic clashes often resulting from arbitrarily drawn borders. When building colonial empires, Britain and other European powers had drawn up the boundaries of African nations with little regard to the inhabitants' ethnic diversity or existing territories.

Postmodern and Postcolonial Literature

4   Most literary critics generally accept that the end of World War II marked the end of the Modernist movement and led the way toward Postmodernism and Postcolonialism. **Postmodern literature** refers to the literature that emerged after the war in reaction to the previous Modernist movement. In typical Modernist works, authors present a subjective point of view with a focus on one's inner experience, using a stream-of-consciousness narration. Modernist works deal with themes of alienation and uncertain identity. In contrast, Postmodernist works focus on the external world and may include an ironic narrator or even multiple narrators offering multiple perspectives on the same event. Themes often reflect collective voices, popular culture, and multicultural experiences.

5   Although it can be difficult to define, Postmodernist literature is known for its rebellious approach and willingness to test boundaries. Postmodern literary works reexamine literary tradition. For instance, such works may include a unique combination of multiple genres to comment on Postmodern life or demonstrate a self-awareness of the writing form through parody of other texts. One driving idea behind Postmodernism is that "everything has already been done" and artists can no longer be completely original. Therefore,

Sotheby's unveils Postmodern artist Banksy's newly-titled "Love Is in the Bin" at Sotheby's on October 12, 2018, in London, England. Originally titled "Girl with Balloon," the canvas passed through a hidden shredder seconds after it sold at Sotheby's London Contemporary Art Evening Sale on October 5, 2018, making it the first artwork in history to have been created live during an auction.

Postmodernists take a playful approach, drawing inspiration from existing texts, combining forms, and having fun with literary experimentation.

6   **Postcolonial literature** describes the genre of literature produced by writers of formerly colonized countries. Postcolonial writers describe the struggles of colonization and **decolonization** and often write about themes of identity, racism, and cultural dominance. Their writing challenges many of the assumptions of colonialism, particularly the assertion that European culture was superior and needed to spread to all corners of the earth. Many writers from former British colonies, including Chinua Achebe, Wole Soyinka, Derek Walcott, Salman Rushdie, and V. S. Naipaul, address the political and social problems that continued to plague their countries even after independence.

7   As contemporaneous movements, Postcolonial literature shares some similarities with Ppostmodernism, and some Postcolonial authors write in a Postmodern style. For example, Indian-born author Salman Rushdie has been hailed for his innovative Postmodern take on Indian history and independence in his novel *Midnight's Children* (1981). Nigerian poet and novelist Ben Okri is considered one of the foremost African authors of both Postmodernism and Postcolonialism, and his novel *The Famished Road* about a quest for identity won the Booker Prize in 1991.

8   Among the most obvious lasting effects of British colonialism is the large number of English speakers spread throughout the world. Postcolonial writers may have wrestled with the issue of using English, the language of their oppressors, but many choose English because it is so widely spoken and can

NOTES

reach large audiences. Writing in English, these authors reclaim and define their own identities and tell their own stories, from their perspectives.

Major Concepts

9 • **Multiple Perspectives**—Postcolonial writers express different viewpoints about colonization, history, social justice, and culture—and also challenge stereotypes.

• **Decolonization Struggles**—Postcolonial literature criticizes colonial powers but also exposes corruption in Postcolonial governments.

• **Self-referentiality**—Postmodernist literature frequently demonstrates self-awareness by referencing other works or even by directly acknowledging the reader or viewer, as when a character might speak directly to the camera about being "watched."

Style and Form

10 • Postmodern literature experiments with different literary forms and combines existing forms to create new styles of literature. As a result, writers have created variations and innovations upon traditional forms and themes.

• Postcolonial writers may use established narrative forms and the English language, even though it may not be their native language. This has broadened the scope of English literature in both subject matter and style, adding the voices and experiences of writers from cultures throughout the world.

11 The British Empire may have ended before the age of Postmodernism and Postcolonialism, but the world of literature has expanded enormously. By adding new perspectives and new voices, literature has become a platform for all narratives and literary experiments.

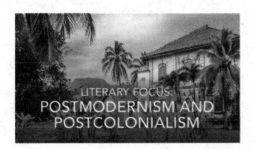

Literary Focus

Read "Literary Focus: Postmodernism and Postcolonialism." After you read, complete the Think Questions below.

☁ THINK QUESTIONS

1. What were the effects of imperialism? Cite evidence from the text to support your answer.

2. Why does Postmodernism rebel against tradition and authority? Cite evidence from the text to support your answer.

3. What effect did British colonialism have on the English language, and why is this important to literature? Cite evidence from the text to support your answers.

4. The word *postmodernism* contains the Latin prefix *post-*, meaning "after." With this information in mind, write your best definition of the word **Postmodernism** as it used in this text. Cite any words or phrases that were particularly helpful in coming to your conclusion.

5. Use context clues to determine the meaning of the word *postcolonialism*. Write your best definition here, along with the words and phrases that were most helpful in determining the word's meaning. Then, check a dictionary to confirm your understanding.

The Mysterious Anxiety of Them and Us

POETRY
Ben Okri
2006

Introduction

Ben Okri (b. 1959) is a writer of novels, poetry, short stories, and social commentary from Minna, Nigeria. During his youth, Okri was an avid reader of English literature and an avid listener to his mother's traditional African stories and myths. Okri's writing draws from both influences, often incorporating realism, folktales, mythology, as well as dream logic, or the feeling of being in a dream. In his book *Tales of Freedom*, Okri created a new form called the "stoku," which he described as "an amalgam of short story and haiku. It is a story as it inclines towards a flash of a moment, insight, vision or paradox." The invented style can be seen on full display in "The Mysterious Anxiety of Them and Us," a stoku set in a dream-like atmosphere where an arbitrary distinction engenders an almost surreal tension.

"While we had been eating it had often occurred to me that there was nothing to stop them from sticking knives into our backs."

1   We were in the magnificent grounds of our mysterious host. A feast had been laid out in the open air. There were many of us present. Some were already seated and some were standing behind those seated. In a way there were too many of us for the food served, or it felt like that.

Nigerian poet and novelist Ben Okri

NOTES

Skill:
Story Structure

The author uses vague descriptions to set up the allegory. This is an effective choice because it suggests that the stoku reflects abstract ideas instead of telling about concrete characters, settings, and plot events.

2   There was a moment when it seemed that everyone would rush at the food and we'd have to be **barbaric** and eat with our hands, fighting over the feast laid out on the lovely tables. The moment of tension lasted a long time.

3   Our host did nothing, and said nothing. No one was sure what to do. **Insurrection** brooded in the winds. Then something strange happened. Those who were at table served themselves, and began eating.

4   We ate calmly. My wife was sitting next to me. The food was wonderful.

5   We ate with some awareness of those behind us, who were not eating, and who did not move. They merely watched us eating.

Skill:
Context Clues

Barbaric and tension are more formal words compared to the rest of the author's diction. Perhaps the author does this to call the reader's attention to certain ideas in the story.

6   Did we who were eating feel guilty? It was a complex feeling. There is no way of resolving it as such. Those who were at table ate. That's it. That's all.

7   We ate a while. Then the people behind us began to murmur. One of them, in a low voice, said:

8   'The first person who offers us some food will receive . . .'

9   I was tempted to offer them some food. But how could I? Where would I start? The situation was impossible. If you turned around, you would see them all. Then your situation would be **polarized**. It would be you and them. But it was never that way to begin with. We were all at the feast. It's just that you were

Please note that excerpts and passages in the StudySync® library and this workbook are intended as touchstones to generate interest in an author's work. The excerpts and passages do not substitute for the reading of entire texts, and StudySync® strongly recommends that students seek out and purchase the whole literary or informational work in order to experience it as the author intended. Links to online resellers are available in our digital library. In addition, complete works may be ordered through an authorized reseller by filling out and returning to StudySync® the order form enclosed in this workbook.

Reading & Writing Companion   343

at the table, and you began to eat. They weren't at table and they didn't eat. They did nothing. They didn't even come over, take a plate, and serve themselves. No one told them, to just stand there watching us eat. They did it to themselves.

10   So to turn around and offer them food would automatically be to see them and treat them as inferior. When in fact they behaved in a manner that made things turn out that way. And so we continued to eat, and ignored the murmurs. Soon we had finished eating. We were satisfied, and took up the invitation to visit other parts of the estate. There was still plenty of food left, as it happened. My wife and I were almost the last to leave the table. As I got up, I looked behind us. I was surprised to see only three people there. Was that all? They had seemed like more, like a crowd. Maybe there had been more of them, but they'd drifted off, given up, or died. While we had been eating it had often occurred to me that there was nothing to stop them from sticking knives into our backs. My wife and I filed out with the others, towards the gardens, in the **sumptuous** grounds of that magnificent estate. It had been a dreamy day of rich sunlight.

Ben Okri, "The Mysterious Anxiety of Them and Us," from *Tales of Freedom*, first published by Rider, an imprint of the Ebury Group, 2009. Copyright © Ben Okri 2009. Reproduced by permission of Ben Okri c/o Georgina Capel Associates Ltd., 29 Wardour Street, London, W1D 6PS.

THE MYSTERIOUS ANXIETY
OF THEM AND US

First Read

Read "The Mysterious Anxiety of Them and Us." After you read, complete the Think Questions below.

 THINK QUESTIONS

1. In the middle of paragraph 3, the narrator says, "Then something strange happened." Citing evidence from the text, explain what happened. How does what occurred affect the narrator's feelings?

2. In paragraph 6, the narrator asks, "Did we who were eating feel guilty?" How does he respond to his own question? What does the way he answers tell you about him? Use examples from the text to support your answer.

3. How did you react to the last sentence, "It had been a dreamy day of rich sunlight"? Do you think it is consistent with the tone of the rest of the text? Use evidence from the text to support your answer.

4. What is the meaning of the word **insurrection** as it is used in the text? Write your best definition here, along with a brief explanation of how you arrived at its meaning.

5. Use context clues to determine the meaning of the word **sumptuous** as it is used in "The Mysterious Anxiety of Them and Us." Write your definition of *sumptuous* here, along with those words or phrases from the text that helped most. Then check a dictionary to confirm your understanding.

Skill:
Story Structure

Use the Checklist to analyze Story Structure in "The Mysterious Anxiety of Them and Us." Refer to the sample student annotations about Story Structure in the text.

••• CHECKLIST FOR STORY STRUCTURE

In order to identify the choices an author makes when structuring specific parts of a text, note the following:

✓ the choices an author makes to organize specific parts of a text such as where to begin and end a story, or whether the ending should be tragic, comic, or inconclusive

✓ the author's use of any literary devices, such as:

- pacing: how quickly or slowly the events of a story unfold
- allegory: a story or poem that conveys a hidden meaning which is usually moral or political

✓ how the overall structure of the text contributes to its meaning as well as its aesthetic impact, such as

- an allegorical story structure
- the creation of suspense through the use of pacing

To analyze how an author's choices concerning how to structure specific parts of a text contribute to its overall structure and meaning as well as its aesthetic impact, consider the following questions:

✓ How does the author structure the text overall? How does the author structure specific parts of the text?

✓ Does the author incorporate literary elements such as allegory? How do these elements affect the overall text structure and the aesthetic impact of the text?

✓ What is the literal or everyday meaning of the narrative? What would the allegorical meaning of the narrative be? How do the characters, setting, and plot work together to convey this message?

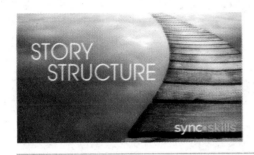

Skill:
Story Structure

Reread paragraph 9 of "The Mysterious Anxiety of Them and Us." Then, using the Checklist on the previous page, answer the multiple-choice questions below.

↻ YOUR TURN

1. What is the literal meaning of paragraph 9?

   ○ A. The people standing behind will eat after the people sitting are done.

   ○ B. The host created this situation as a test to see what the narrator would do.

   ○ C. The narrator thinks the best thing to do in this situation is not turn around.

   ○ D. The fact that some get more than others is universal and impossible to change.

2. What is the symbolic meaning of paragraph 9?

   ○ A. People need to take responsibility for their own life and wellbeing.

   ○ B. The events that happened at the feast could happen to anyone in real life.

   ○ C. The people standing behind have to wait their turn to eat because they arrived late.

   ○ D. Wealthy people avoid thinking about the poor because they do not want to feel guilty.

3. The language Okri uses to develop allegory in this paragraph is effective because it—

   ○ A. suggests that people are not responsible for their own actions.

   ○ B. reflects the way wealthy people rationalize their actions.

   ○ C. describes explicit conflict between two social groups.

   ○ D. emphasizes the struggles of people living in poverty.

Please note that excerpts and passages in the StudySync® library and this workbook are intended as touchstones to generate interest in an author's work. The excerpts and passages do not substitute for the reading of entire texts, and StudySync® strongly recommends that students seek out and purchase the whole literary or informational work in order to experience it as the author intended. Links to online resellers are available in our digital library. In addition, complete works may be ordered through an authorized reseller by filling out and returning to StudySync® the order form enclosed in this workbook.

Reading & Writing
Companion

347

Skill:
Context Clues

Use the Checklist to analyze Context Clues in "The Mysterious Anxiety of Them and Us." Refer to the sample student annotations about Context Clues in the text.

••• CHECKLIST FOR CONTEXT CLUES

In order to use context as a clue to the meaning of a word or phrase, note the following:

- ✓ clues about the word's part of speech

- ✓ clues in the surrounding text about the word's meaning

- ✓ words with similar denotations that seem to differ slightly in meaning

- ✓ signal words that cue a type of context clue, such as:

  - *comparably*, *related to*, or *similarly* to signal a comparison context clue

  - *on the other hand*, *however*, or *in contrast* to signal a contrast context clue

  - *by reason of*, *because*, or *as a result* to signal a cause-and-effect context clue

To determine the meaning of a word or phrase as they are used in a text, consider the following questions:

- ✓ What is the meaning of the overall sentence, paragraph, or text?

- ✓ How does the position of the word in the sentence help me define it?

- ✓ How does the word function in the sentence? What clues help identify the word's part of speech?

- ✓ What clues in the text suggest the word's definition?

- ✓ What do I think the word means?

To verify the preliminary determination of the meaning of the word or phrase based on context, consider the following questions:

- ✓ Does the definition I inferred make sense within the context of the sentence?

- ✓ Which of the dictionary's definitions makes sense within the context of the sentence?

Skill:
Context Clues

Reread paragraphs 6–8 of "The Mysterious Anxiety of Them and Us." Then, using the Checklist on the previous page, answer the multiple-choice questions below.

⟳ YOUR TURN

1. Using context clues, determine the part of speech for *murmur*.

   ○ A. *Murmur* is a noun.
   ○ B. *Murmur* is a verb.
   ○ C. *Murmur* is an adverb.
   ○ D. *Murmur* is an adjective.

2. This question has two parts. First, answer Part A. Then, answer Part B.

---

murmur
noun

1. a constant sound
2. condition related to issues with the heart

verb

1. to speak in a low, soft voice
2. to complain

Origin: Late Middle English: borrowed from Old French *murmure* meaning "sound of voices, from Latin, *murmur* meaning "humming" or "muttering."

Please note that excerpts and passages in the StudySync® library and this workbook are intended as touchstones to generate interest in an author's work. The excerpts and passages do not substitute for the reading of entire texts, and StudySync® strongly recommends that students seek out and purchase the whole literary or informational work in order to experience it as the author intended. Links to online resellers are available in our digital library. In addition, complete works may be ordered through an authorized reseller by filling out and returning to StudySync® the order form enclosed in this workbook.

Reading & Writing
Companion

349

Part A: What is the most likely definition of "murmur" given this context in this passage?

○ A. Definition 1.a

○ B. Definition 2.b

○ C. Definition 1.b

○ D. Definition 2.a

Part B: Which of the following context clues from the text **best** supports your answer to Part A?

○ A. "That's it. That's all."

○ B. "We ate a while"

○ C. "Then the people behind us began . . ."

○ D. "One of them, in a low voice, said . . ."

THE MYSTERIOUS ANXIETY
OF THEM AND US

Close Read

Reread "The Mysterious Anxiety of Them and Us." As you reread, complete the Skills Focus questions below. Then use your answers and annotations from the questions to help you complete the Write activity.

◎ SKILLS FOCUS

1. Identify a detail that is suggestive of a hidden meaning or abstract idea, and explain how it effectively contributes to the story's allegorical structure.

2. Identify an example of simple, plain writing in the text, and explain how the author's choice to use this diction and syntax contributes to the effectiveness of the allegory.

3. Identify a sentence that inspires readers to have an emotional response. Explain how this author's use of language effectively shapes the reader's perceptions of the narrator or events.

4. Re-read the final paragraph of the story. Using context clues, determine the part of speech and possible meaning of the word *magnificent*. Then, highlight the word and in your annotation explain why the author's choice to repeat this word at the beginning and end of the story is important in the final impact of the story.

5. Throughout this allegorical short story, the narrator describes changes in thinking and in feeling about this strange situation. Highlight two instances of these changes, and in your annotation describe the impact they have on you, the reader.

✏ WRITE

LITERARY ANALYSIS: This work is written in an allegorical, dreamlike structure with little explanation of what is happening and why. What do you think is the "mysterious anxiety"? Who do you think are the "them and us"? Write a brief literary analysis that explains the events and the theme as you see them, which may not be the way your classmates see them. Tell what you think of the narrator and point out connections between the text and the real world. Support your ideas with textual evidence when you can.

Love After Love

POETRY
Derek Walcott
1976

Introduction

Derek Walcott (1930–2017), professor, playwright and poet, won the Nobel Prize in Literature in 1992 in recognition of his poetry. In brief lyrical verse as well as epic poems, Walcott, who was born in Saint Lucia, wrote of the Caribbean experience with a perspective that shifted from one as intimate as its tiptoeing lizards to one as large-scale as the cultural scars of colonialism. "Love After Love" is one of the great 20th-century poet's most beloved works.

"You will love again the stranger who was your self."

 NOTES

1 The time will come
2 when, with **elation**
3 you will greet yourself arriving
4 at your own door, in your own mirror
5 and each will smile at the other's welcome,

6 and say, sit here. Eat.
7 You will love again the stranger who was your self.
8 Give wine. Give bread. Give back your heart
9 to itself, to the stranger who has loved you

10 all your life, whom you ignored
11 for another, who knows you by heart.
12 Take down the love letters from the bookshelf,

13 the photographs, the **desperate** notes,
14 peel your own image from the mirror.
15 Sit. Feast on your life.

Derek Walcott in Saint Malo, France

"After Love" ("work") from THE POETRY OF DEREK WALCOTT 1948-2013 by Derek Walcott, selected by Glyn Maxwell

WRITE

DISCUSSION: Derek Walcott's poem "Love After Love" is a free verse poem written in a conversational style that gives advice to readers. Work in pairs and groups to analyze the form, sound, and graphics of the poem. Notice the graphical elements of enjambment and punctuation as well as the repetition of words and phrases. Consider how these elements affect the sound of the poem. Have one volunteer read the poem aloud. Then work in pairs or as a group to change the graphical elements. For instance, you might take out the enjambment or rewrite the text to avoid a comma or period within a line. In other words, change the shape and look of the poem on the page. Then have another volunteer read aloud the revised poem. Finally, discuss the effects of a poet's choice of form and graphics on the sound of the poem and the expression of meaning.

The Museum

FICTION
Leila Aboulela
1999

Introduction

Much like Shadia, the main character in her award-winning story "The Museum," author Leila Aboulela (b. 1964) grew up in Khartoum, the capital of Sudan, before moving as a young woman to Aberdeen, Scotland. Experiencing firsthand the cultural divide between Islam and the West would serve as the inspiration for much of Aboulela's writing, which explores issues of identity, migration, and Islamic spirituality. "The Museum" is one of her earliest published stories, yet it displays all the hallmarks of her best work, which has been translated into 14 languages and even adapted into a series of plays by BBC Radio.

"We have 7UP in Africa, and some people, a few people, have bathrooms with golden taps . . ."

NOTES

1   At first Shadia was afraid to ask him for his notes. The earring made her afraid; the straight long hair that he had tied up with a rubber band. She had never seen a man with an earring and such long hair. But then she had never known such cold, so much rain. His silver earring was the strangeness of the West, another culture shock. She stared

Sudanese writer Leila Aboulela

at it during classes, her eyes straying from the white scribbles on the board. Most times she could hardly understand anything. Only the notation was familiar. But how did it all fit together? How did *this* formula lead to *this*? Her ignorance and the impending exams were horrors she wanted to escape. His long hair was a dull colour between yellow and brown. It reminded her of a doll she had when she was young. She had spent hours combing that doll's hair, stroking it. She had longed for such straight hair. When she went to Paradise she would have hair like that. When she ran it would fly behind her; if she bent her head down it would fall over her like silk and sweep the flowers on the grass. She watched his ponytail move as he wrote and then looked up at the board. She pictured her doll, vivid suddenly, after years, and felt sick that she was daydreaming in class, not learning a thing.

2   The first days of term, when the classes started for the M.Sc. in Statistics, she was like someone tossed around by monstrous waves—battered, as she lost her way to the different lecture rooms, fumbled with the photocopying machine, could not find anything in the library. She could scarcely hear or eat or see. Her eyes bulged with fright, watered from the cold. The course required a certain background, a background she didn't have. So she **floundered,** she and the other African students, the two Turkish girls, and the men from Brunei. Asafa, the short, round-faced Ethiopian, said, in his grave voice—as this collection from the Third World whispered their anxieties in grim Scottish corridors, the girls in nervous giggles – 'Last year, last year a Nigerian on this very same course committed suicide. *Cut his wrists.*'

3   Us and them, she thought. The ones who would do well, the ones who would crawl and sweat and barely pass. Two predetermined groups. Asafa, generous and wise (he was the oldest), leaned over and whispered to Shadia: 'The Spanish girl is good. Very good.' His eyes bulged redder than Shadia's. He cushioned his fears every night in the university pub; she only cried. Their countries were next-door neighbours but he had never been to Sudan, and Shadia had never been to Ethiopia. 'But we met in Aberdeen!' she had shrieked when this information was exchanged, giggling furiously. Collective fear had its **euphoria.**

4   'That boy Bryan,' said Asafa, 'is excellent.'

5   'The one with the earring?'

6   Asafa laughed and touched his own unadorned ear. 'The earring doesn't mean anything. He'll get the Distinction. He was an undergraduate here; got First Class Honours. That gives him an advantage. He knows all the lecturers, he knows the system.'

7   So the idea occurred to her of asking Bryan for the notes of his graduate year. If she strengthened her background in stochastic processes and time series, she would be better able to cope with the new material they were bombarded with every day. She watched him to judge if he was approachable. Next to the courteous Malaysian students, he was devoid of manners. He mumbled and slouched and did not speak with respect to the lecturers. He spoke to them as if they were his equals. And he did silly things. When he wanted to throw a piece of paper in the bin, he squashed it into a ball and aimed at the bin. If he missed, he muttered under his breath. She thought that he was immature. But he was the only one who was sailing through the course.

8   The glossy handbook for overseas students had explained about the 'famous British reserve' and hinted that they should be grateful, things were worse further south, less 'hospitable.' In the cafeteria, drinking coffee with Asafa and the others, the picture of 'hospitable Scotland' was something different. Badr, the Malaysian, blinked and whispered, 'Yesterday our windows got smashed; my wife today is afraid to go out.'

9   'Thieves?' asked Shadia, her eyes wider than anyone else's.

10 'Racists,' said the Turkish girl, her lipstick chic, the word tripping out like silver, like ice.

11 Wisdom from Asafa, muted, before the collective silence: 'These people think they own the world . . .' and around them the aura of the dead Nigerian student. They were ashamed of that brother they had never seen. He had weakened, caved in. In the cafeteria, Bryan never sat with them. They never

sat with him. He sat alone, sometimes reading the local paper. When Shadia walked in front of him he didn't smile. 'These people are strange . . . One day they greet you, the next day they don't . . .'

12 On Friday afternoon, as everyone was ready to leave the room after Linear Models, she gathered her courage and spoke to Bryan. He had spots on his chin and forehead, was taller than her, restless, as if he was in a hurry to go somewhere else. He put his calculator back in its case, his pen in his pocket. She asked him for his notes, and his blue eyes behind his glasses took on the blankest look she had ever seen in her life. What was all the surprise for? Did he think she was an insect? Was he surprised that she could speak?

13 A mumble for a reply, words strung together. So taken aback, he was. He pushed his chair back under the table with this foot.

14 'Pardon?'

15 He slowed down, separated each word. 'Ah'll have them for ye on Monday.'

16 'Thank you.' She spoke English better than he did! How pathetic. The whole of him was pathetic. He wore the same shirt every blessed day. Grey and white stripe.

. . .

17 On the weekends, Shadia never went out of the halls and, unless someone telephoned long-distance from home, she spoke to no one. There was time to remember Thursday nights in Khartoum: a wedding to go to with Fareed, driving in his red Mercedes. Or the club with her sisters. Sitting by the pool drinking lemonade with ice, the waiters all dressed in white. Sometimes people swam at night, dived in the water—dark like the sky above. Here, in this country's weekend of Saturday and Sunday, Shadia washed her clothes and her hair. Her hair depressed her. The damp weather made it frizz up after she straightened it with hot tongs. So she had given up and now wore it in a bun all the time, tightly pulled back away from her face, the curls held down by pins and Vaseline Tonic. She didn't like this style, her corrugated hair, and in the mirror her eyes looked too large. The mirror in the public bathroom, at the end of the corridor to her room, had printed on it: 'This is the face of someone with HIV.' She had written about this mirror to her sister, something foreign and sensational like hail, and cars driving on the left. But she hadn't written that the mirror made her feel as if she had left her looks behind in Khartoum.

18 On the weekends, she made a list of the money she had spent: the sterling enough to keep a family alive back home. Yet she might fail her exams after all that expense, go back home empty-handed without a degree. Guilt was cold like the fog of this city. It came from everywhere. One day she forgot to

pray in the morning. She reached the bus stop and then realized she hadn't prayed. That morning folded out like the nightmare she sometimes had, of discovering that she had gone out into the street without any clothes.

19 In the evening, when she was staring at multidimensional scaling, the telephone in the hall rang. She ran to answer it. Fareed's cheerful greeting: 'Here, Shadia, Mama and the girls want to speak to you.' His mother's endearments: 'They say it's so cold where you are . . .'

20 Shadia was engaged to Fareed. Fareed was a package that came with the 7UP franchise, the paper factory, the big house he was building, his sisters and widowed mother. Shadia was going to marry them all. She was going to be happy and make her mother happy. Her mother deserved happiness after the misfortunes of her life. A husband who left her for another woman. Six girls to bring up. People felt sorry for her mother. Six girls to educate and marry off. But your Lord is generous: each of the girls, it was often said, was lovelier than the other. They were clever too: dentist, pharmacist, architect, and all with the best of manners.

21 'We are just back from looking at the house.' Fareed's turn again to talk. 'It's coming along fine, they're putting the tiles down . . .'

22 'That's good, that's good,' her voice strange from not talking to anyone all day.

23 'The bathroom suites. If I get them all the same colour for us and the girls and Mama, I could get them on a discount. Blue, the girls are in favour of blue,' his voice echoed from one continent to another. Miles and miles.

24 'Blue is nice. Yes, better get them all the same colour.'

25 He was building a block of flats, not a house. The ground-floor flat for his mother and the girls until they married, the first floor for him and Shadia. When Shadia had first got engaged to Fareed, he was the son of a rich man. A man with the franchise for 7UP and the paper factory which had a monopoly[1] in ladies' sanitary towels. Fareed's sisters never had to buy sanitary towels; their house was abundant with boxes of *Pinky,* fresh from the production line. But Fareed's father died of an unexpected heart attack soon after the engagement party (five hundred guests at the Hilton). Now Shadia was going to marry the rich man himself. 'You are a lucky, lucky girl,' her mother had said, and Shadia had rubbed soap in her eyes so that Fareed would think she was weeping about his father's death.

26 There was no time to talk about her course on the telephone, no space for her anxieties. Fareed was not interested in her studies. He had said, 'I am

---

1. **monopoly** complete and exclusive control over something

NOTES

very broad-minded to allow you to study abroad. Other men would not have put up with this . . .' It was her mother who was keen for her to study, to get a postgraduate degree from Britain and then have a career after she got married. 'This way,' her mother had said, 'you will have your in-laws' respect. They have money but you have a degree. Don't end up like me. I left my education to marry your father and now . . .' Many conversations ended with her mother bitter; with her mother say, 'No one suffers like I suffer,' and making Shadia droop. At night her mother sobbed in her sleep, noises that woke Shadia and her sisters.

27 No, on the long-distance line, there was no space for her worries. Talk about the Scottish weather. Picture Fareed, generously perspiring, his stomach straining the buttons of his shirt. Often she had nagged him to lose weight, without success. His mother's food was too good; his sisters were both overweight. On the long-distance line, listen to the Khartoum gossip as if listening to a radio play.

28 On Monday, without saying anything, Bryan slid two folders across the table towards her as if he did not want to come near her, did not want to talk to her. She wanted to say, 'I won't take them till you hand them to me politely.' But smarting, she said, 'Thank you very much.' *She* had manners. *She* was well brought up.

29 Back in her room, at her desk, the clearest handwriting she had ever seen. Sparse on the pages, clean. Clear and rounded like a child's, the tidiest notes. She cried over them, wept for no reason. She cried until she wetted one of the pages, smudged the ink, blurred one of the formulas. She dabbed at it with a tissue but the paper flaked and became transparent. Should she apologize about the stain, say that she was drinking water, say that it was rain? Or should she just keep quiet, hope he wouldn't notice? She chided herself for all that concern. *He* wasn't concerned about wearing the same shirt every day. She was giving him too much attention thinking about him. He was just an immature and closed-in sort of character. He probably came from a small town, his parents were probably poor, low-class. In Khartoum, she never mixed with people like that. Her mother liked her to be friends with people who were higher up. How else were she and her sisters going to marry well? She must study the notes and stop crying over this boy's handwriting. His handwriting had nothing to do with her, nothing to do with her at all.

30 Understanding after not understanding is a fog lifting, pictures swinging into focus, missing pieces slotting into place. It is fragments gelling, a sound vivid whole, a basis to build on. His notes were the knowledge she needed, the gap filled. She struggled through them, not skimming them with the carelessness of incomprehension, but taking them in, making them a part of her, until in the depth of concentration, in the late hours of the nights, she lost awareness of time and place, and at last, when she slept she became epsilon

and gamma, and she became a variable, making her way through discrete space from state 'i' to state 'j'.

. . .

31   It felt natural to talk to him. As if now that she had spent hours and days with his handwriting, she knew him in some way. She forgot the offence she had taken when he had slid his folders across the table to her, all the times he didn't say hello.

32   In the computer room, at the end of the Statistical Packages class, she went to him and said: 'Thanks for the notes. They are really good. I think I might not fail, after all. I might have a chance to pass.' Her eyes were dry from all the nights she had stayed up. She was tired and grateful.

33   He nodded and they spoke a little about the Poisson distribution[2], queuing theory[3]. Everything was clear in his mind; his brain was a clear pane of glass where all the concepts were written out boldly and neatly. Today, he seemed more at ease talking to her, though he still shifted about from foot to foot, avoiding her eyes.

34   He said, 'Do ye want to go for a coffee?'

35   She looked up at him. He was tall and she was not used to speaking to people with blue eyes. Then she made a mistake. Perhaps because she had been up late last night, she made that mistake. Perhaps there were other reasons for that mistake. The mistake of shifting from one level to another.

36   She said, 'I don't like your earring.'

37   The expression in his eyes, a focusing, no longer shifting away. He lifted his hand to his ear and tugged the earring off. His earlobe without the silver looked red and scarred.

38   She giggled because she was afraid, because he wasn't smiling, wasn't saying anything. She covered her mouth with her hand, then wiped her forehead and eyes. A mistake had been made and it was too late to go back. She plunged ahead, careless now, reckless. 'I don't like your long hair.'

39   He turned and walked away.

. . .

---

2. **Poisson distribution** a probability distribution formula developed by French mathematician Siméon Denis Poisson (1781–1840) to predict the frequency of events in a fixed interval
3. **queuing theory** involving the mathematical study of queues, or lines

40   The next morning, Multivariate Analysis, and she came in late, dishevelled from running and the rain. The professor, whose name she wasn't sure of (there were three who were Mc-something), smiled, unperturbed. All the lecturers were relaxed and **urbane,** in tweed jackets and polished shoes. Sometimes she wondered how the incoherent Bryan, if he did pursue an academic career, was going to transform himself into a professor like that. But it was none of her business.

41   Like most of the other students, she sat in the same seat in every class. Bryan sat a row ahead which was why she could always look at his hair. But he had cut it, there was no ponytail today! Just his neck and the collar of the grey and white striped shirt.

42   Notes to take down. *In discriminant analysis, a linear combination of variables serves as the basis for assigning cases to groups.*

43   She was made up of layers. Somewhere inside, deep inside, under the crust of vanity, in the untampered-with essence, she would glow and be in awe, and be humble and think, this is just for me, he cut his hair for me. But there were other layers, bolder, more to the surface. Giggling. Wanting to catch hold of a friend. Guess what? You wouldn't *believe* what this idiot did!

44   *Find a weighted average of variables . . . The weights are estimated so that they result in the best separation between the groups.*

45   After the class he came over and said very seriously, without a smile, 'Ah've cut my hair.'

46   A part of her hollered with laughter, sang: 'You stupid boy, you stupid boy, I can see that, can't I?'

47   She said, 'It looks nice.' She said the wrong thing and her face felt hot and she made herself look away so that she would not know his reaction. It was true though, he did look nice; he looked decent now.

. . .

48   She should have said to Bryan, when they first held their coffee mugs in their hands and were searching for an empty table, 'Let's sit with Asafa and the others.' Mistakes follow mistakes. Across the cafeteria, the Turkish girl saw them together and raised her perfect eyebrows. Badr met Shadia's eyes and quickly looked away. Shadia looked at Bryan and he was different, different without the earring and the ponytail, transformed in some way. If he would put lemon juice on his spots . . . but it was none of her business. Maybe the boys who smashed Badr's windows looked like Bryan, but with fiercer eyes, no glasses. She must push him away from her. She must make him dislike her.

49   He asked her where she came from and when she replied, he said, 'Where's that?'

50   'Africa,' with sarcasm. 'Do you know where *that* is?'

51   His nose and cheeks under the rims of his glasses went red. Good, she thought, good. He will leave me now in peace.

52   He said, 'Ah know Sudan is in Africa, I meant where exactly in Africa.'

53   'Northeast, south of Egypt. Where are *you* from?'

54   'Peterhead. It's north of here. By the sea.'

55   It was hard to believe that there was anything north of Aberdeen. It seemed to her that they were on the northernmost corner of the world. She knew better now than to imagine suntanning and sandy beaches for his 'by the sea.' More likely dismal skies, pale, bad-tempered people shivering on the rocky shore.

56   'Your father works in Peterhead?'

57   'Aye, he does.'

58   She had grown up listening to the proper English of the BBC World Service only to come to Britain and find people saying 'yes' like it was said back home in Arabic: 'aye.'

59   'What does he do, your father?'

60   He looked surprised, his blue eyes surprised. 'Ma dad's a joiner.'

61   Fareed hired people like that to work on the house. Ordered them about.

62   'And your mother?' she asked.

63   He paused a little, stirred sugar in his coffee with a plastic spoon. 'She's a lollipop lady.'

64   Shadia smirked into her coffee, took a sip.

65   'My father,' she said proudly, 'is a doctor, a specialist.' Her father was a gynaecologist. The woman who was now his wife had been one of his patients. Before that, Shadia's friends had teased her about her father's job, crude jokes that made her laugh. It was all so sordid now.

66   'And my mother,' she blew the truth up out of proportion, 'comes from a very big family. A ruling family. If you British hadn't colonized us, my mother would have been a princess now.'

67   'Ye walk like a princess,' he said.

68   What a gullible, silly boy! She wiped her forehead with her hand and said, 'You mean I am **conceited** and proud?'

69   'No, Ah didnae mean that, no . . .' The packet of sugar he was tearing open tipped from his hand, its contents scattered over the table. 'Ah . . . sorry . . .' He tried to scoop up the sugar and knocked against his coffee mug, spilling a little on the table.

70   She took out a tissue from her bag, reached over and mopped up the stain. It was easy to pick up all the bits of sugar with the damp tissue.

71   'Thanks,' he mumbled and they were silent. The cafeteria was busy: full of the humming, buzzing sound of people talking to each other, trays and dishes. In Khartoum, she avoided being alone with Fareed. She preferred it when they were with others: their families, their many natural friends. If they were ever alone, she imagined that her mother or her sister was with them, could hear them, and she spoke to Fareed with that audience in mind.

72   Bryan was speaking to her, saying something about rowing on the River Dee. He went rowing on the weekends, he belonged to a rowing club.

73   To make herself pleasing to people was a skill Shadia was trained in. It was not difficult to please people. Agree with them, never dominate the conversation, be economical with the truth. Now, here was someone to whom all these rules needn't apply.

74   She said to him, 'The Nile is superior to the Dee. I saw your Dee, it is nothing, it is like a stream. There are two Niles, the Blue and the White, named after their colours. They come from the south, from two different places. They travel for miles over countries with different names, never knowing they will meet. I think they get tired of running alone, it is such a long way to the sea. They want to reach the sea so that they can rest, stop running. There is a bridge in Khartoum, and under this bridge the two Niles meet. If you stand on the bridge and look down you can see the two waters mixing together.'

75   'Do ye get homesick?' he asked. She felt tired now, all this talk of the river running to rest in the sea. She had never talked like this before. Luxury words, and this question he asked.

76   'Things I should miss I don't miss. Instead I miss things I didn't think I would miss. The *azan*, the Muslim call to prayer from the mosque. I don't know if you know about it. I miss that. At dawn it used to wake me up. I would hear 'prayer is better than sleep' and just go back to sleep. I never got up to pray.' She looked down at her hands on the table. There was no relief in confessions, only his smile, young, and something like wonder in his eyes.

NOTES

77 'We did Islam in school,' he said. 'Ah went on a trip to Mecca[4].' He opened out his palms on the table.

78 'What!'

79 'In a book.'

80 'Oh.'

81 The coffee was finished. They should go now. She should go to the library before the next lecture and photocopy previous exam papers. Asafa, full of helpful advice, had shown her where to find them.

82 'What is your religion?' she asked.

83 'Dunno, nothing I suppose.'

84 'That's terrible! That's really terrible!' Her voice was too loud, concerned.

85 His face went red again and he tapped his spoon against the empty mug.

86 Waive all politeness, make him dislike her. Badr had said, even before his windows got smashed, that here in the West they hate Islam. Standing up to go, she said **flippantly,** 'Why don't you become a Muslim then?'

87 He shrugged. 'Ah wouldnae mind travelling to Mecca, I was keen on that book.'

88 Her eyes filled with tears. They blurred his face when he stood up. In the West they hate Islam and he . . . She said, 'Thanks for the coffee,' and walked away, but he followed her.

89 'Shadiya, Shadiya,' he pronounced her name wrongly, three syllables instead of two, 'there's this museum about Africa. I've never been before. If you'd care to go, tomorrow . . .'

90 No sleep for the guilty, no rest, she should have said no, I can't go, no I have too much catching up to do. No sleep for the guilty, the memories come from another continent. Her father's new wife, happier than her mother, fewer worries. When Shadia visits she offers fruit in a glass bowl, icy oranges and guavas, soothing in the heat. Shadia's father hadn't wanted a divorce, hadn't wanted to leave them; he wanted two wives, not a divorce. But her mother had too much pride, she came from fading money, a family with a 'name.'

91 Tomorrow she need not show up at the museum, even though she said that she would. She should have told Bryan she was engaged to be married,

4. **Mecca** the holiest city of the Islamic religion, located in Saudi Arabia, which Muslims face during the regular call to prayer

mentioned it casually. What did he expect from her? Europeans had different rules, reduced, abrupt customs. If Fareed knew about this . . . her secret thoughts like snakes . . . Perhaps she was like her father, a traitor. Her mother said that her father was devious. Sometimes Shadia was devious. With Fareed in the car, she would deliberately say, 'I need to stop at the grocer, we need things at home.' At the grocer he would pay for all her shopping and she would say, 'No, you shouldn't do that, no, you are too generous, you are embarrassing me.' With the money she saved, she would buy a blouse for her mother, nail varnish for her mother, a magazine, imported apples.

. . .

92   It was strange to leave her desk, lock her room and go out on a Saturday. In the hall the telephone rang. It was Fareed. If he knew where she was going now . . . Guilt was like a hard boiled egg stuck in her chest. A large cold egg.

93   'Shadia, I want you to buy some of the fixtures for the bathrooms. Taps and towel hangers. I'm going to send you a list of what I want exactly and the money . . .'

94   'I can't, I can't.'

95   'What do you mean you can't? If you go into any large department store . . .'

96   'I can't, I wouldn't know where to put these things, how to send them.'

97   There was a rustle on the line and she could hear someone whispering, Fareed distracted a little. He would be at work this time in the day, glass bottles filling up with clear effervescent, the words 7UP written in English and Arabic, white against the dark green.

98   'You can get good things, things that aren't available here. Gold would be good. It would match . . .'

99   Gold. Gold toilet seats!

100   'People are going to burn in hell for eating out of gold dishes, you want to sit on gold!'

101   He laughed. He was used to getting his own way, not easily threatened. 'Are you joking with me?'

102   'No.'

103   In a quieter voice, 'This call is costing . . .'

104   She knew, she knew. He shouldn't have let her go away. She was not coping with the whole thing, she was not handling the stress. Like the Nigerian student.

105 ‘Shadia, gold-coloured, not gold. It's smart.’

106 ‘Allah is going to punish us for this, it's not right . . .’

107 ‘Since when have you become so religious!’

. . .

108 Bryan was waiting for her on the steps of the museum, familiar-looking against the strange grey of the city streets where cars had their headlamps on in the middle of the afternoon. He wore a different shirt, a navy-blue jacket. He said, not looking at her, ‘Ah was beginning to think you wouldnae turn up.’

109 There was no entry fee to the museum, no attendant handing out tickets. Bryan and Shadia walked on soft carpets; thick blue carpets that made Shadia want to take off her shoes. The first thing they saw was a Scottish man from Victorian times. He sat on a chair surrounded by possessions from Africa: overflowing trunks, an ancient map strewn on the floor of the glass cabinet. All the light in the room came from this and other glass cabinets and gleamed on the waxed floors. Shadia turned away; there was an ugliness in the lifelike wispiness of his hair, his determined expression, the way he sat. A hero who had gone away and come back, laden, ready to report.

110 Bryan began to conscientiously study every display cabinet, to read the posters on the wall. She followed him around and thought that he was studious, careful; that was why he did so well in his degree. She watched the intent expression on his face as he looked at everything. For her the posters were an effort to read, the information difficult to take in. It had been so long since she had read anything outside the requirements of the course. But she persevered, saying the words to herself, moving her lips . . . *‘During the 18th and 19th centuries, northeast Scotland made a disproportionate impact on the world at large by contributing so many skilled and committed individuals. In serving an empire they gave and received, changed others and were themselves changed and often returned home with tangible reminders of their experiences.’*

111 The tangible reminders were there to see, preserved in spite of the years. Her eyes skimmed over the disconnected objects out of place and time. Iron and copper, little statues. Nothing was of her, nothing belonged to her life at home, what she missed. Here was Europe's vision, the clichés about Africa: cold and odd.

112 She had not expected the dim light and the hushed silence. Apart from Shadia and Bryan, there was only a man with a briefcase, a lady who took down notes, unless there were others out of sight on the second floor. Something electrical, the heating of the lights, gave out a humming sound like that of an air conditioner. It made Shadia feel as if they were in an aeroplane without windows, detached from the world outside.

113 'He looks like you, don't you think?' she said to Bryan. They stood in front of a portrait of a soldier who died in the first year of the twentieth century. It was the colour of his eyes and his hair. But Bryan did not answer her, did not agree with her. He was preoccupied with reading the caption. When she looked at the portrait again, she saw that she was mistaken. That strength in the eyes, the purpose, was something Bryan didn't have. They had strong faith in those days long ago.

114 Biographies of explorers who were educated in Edinburgh; they knew what to take to Africa: doctors, courage, Christianity, commerce, civilization. They knew what they wanted to bring back: cotton—watered by the Blue Nile, the Zambezi River. She walked after Bryan, felt his concentration, his interest in what was before him and thought, 'In a photograph we would not look nice together.'

115 She touched the glass of a cabinet showing papyrus rolls, copper pots. She pressed her forehead and nose against the cool glass. If she could enter the cabinet, she would not make a good exhibit. She wasn't right, she was too modern, too full of mathematics.

116 Only the carpet, its petroleum blue, pleased her. She had come to this museum expecting sunlight and photographs of the Nile, something to relieve her homesickness: a comfort, a message. But the messages were not for her, not for anyone like her. A letter from West Africa, 1762, an employee to his employer in Scotland. An employee trading European goods for African curiosities. *It was difficult to make the natives understand my meaning, even by an interpreter, it being a thing so seldom asked of them, but they have all undertaken to bring something and laughed heartily at me and said, I was a good man to love their country so much . . .*

117 Love my country so much. She should not be here, there was nothing for her here. She wanted to see minarets[5], boats fragile on the Nile, people. People like her father. The times she had sat in the waiting room of his clinic, among pregnant women, a pain in her heart because she was going to see him in a few minutes. His room, the air conditioner and the smell of his pipe, his white coat. When she hugged him, he smelled of Listerine mouthwash. He could never remember how old she was, what she was studying; six daughters, how could he keep track. In his confusion, there was freedom for her, games to play, a lot of teasing. She visited his clinic in secret, telling lies to her mother. She loved him more than she loved her mother. Her mother who did everything for her, tidied her room, sewed her clothes from *Burda* magazine. Shadia was twenty-five and her mother washed everything for her by hand, even her pants and bras.

---

5. **minarets** a tower in the Islamic world built specifically for the adhan, or call to prayer, to be made

118 'I know why they went away,' said Bryan. 'I understand why they travelled.' At last he was talking. She had not seen him intense before. He spoke in a low voice. 'They had to get away, to leave here . . .'

119 'To escape from the horrible weather . . .' She was making fun of him. She wanted to put him down. The imperialists who had humiliated her history were heroes in his eyes.

120 He looked at her. 'To escape . . .' he repeated.

121 'They went to benefit themselves,' she said, 'people go away because they benefit in some way.'

122 'I want to get away,' he said.

123 She remembered when he had opened his palms on the table and said, 'I went on a trip to Mecca.' There had been pride in his voice.

124 'I should have gone somewhere else for the course,' he went on. 'A new place, somewhere down south.'

125 He was on a plateau, not like her. She was fighting and struggling for a piece of paper that would say she was awarded an M.Sc. from a British university. For him, the course was a continuation.

126 'Come and see,' he said, and he held her arm. No one had touched her before, not since she had hugged her mother goodbye. Months now in this country and no one had touched her.

127 She pulled her arm away. She walked away, quickly up the stairs. Metal steps rattled under her feet. She ran up the stairs to the next floor. Guns, a row of guns aiming at her. They had been waiting to blow her away. Scottish arms of centuries ago, gunfire in service of the empire.

128 Silver muzzles, a dirty grey now. They must have shone prettily once, under a sun far away. If they blew her away now, where would she fly and fall? A window that looked out at the hostile sky. She shivered in spite of the wool she was wearing, layers of clothes. Hell is not only blazing fire, a part of it is freezing cold, torturous ice and snow. In Scotland's winter you have a glimpse of this unseen world, feel the breath of it in your bones.

129 There was a bench and she sat down. There was no one here on this floor. She was alone with sketches of jungle animals, words on the wall. A diplomat away from home, in Ethiopia in 1903: Asafa's country long before Asafa was born. *It is difficult to imagine anything more satisfactory or better worth taking part in than a lion drive. We rode back to camp feeling very well indeed. Archie was quite right when he said that this was the first time since we have started*

that we have really been in Africa—the real Africa of jungle inhabited only by game, and plains where herds of antelope meet your eye in every direction.

130 'Shadiya, don't cry.' He still pronounced her name wrongly because she had not told him how to say it properly.

131 He sat next to her on the bench, the blur of his navy jacket blocking the guns, the wall-length pattern of antelope herds. She should explain that she cried easily, there was no need for the alarm on his face. His awkward voice: 'Why are ye crying?'

132 He didn't know, he didn't understand. He was all wrong, not a substitute . . .

133 'They are telling lies in this museum,' she said. 'Don't believe them. It's all wrong. It's not jungles and antelopes, it's people. We have things like computers and cars. We have 7UP in Africa, and some people, a few people, have bathrooms with golden taps . . . I shouldn't be here with you. You shouldn't talk to me . . .'

134 He said, 'Museums change, I can change . . .'

135 He didn't know it was a steep path she had no strength for. He didn't understand. Many things, years and landscapes, gulfs. If she had been strong she would have explained, and not tired of explaining. She would have patiently taught him another language, letters curved like the epsilon and gamma he knew from mathematics. She would have shown him that words could be read from the right to left. If she had not been small in the museum, if she had been really strong, she would have made his trip to Mecca real, not only in a book.

From *Coloured Lights* by Leila Aboulela. © Leila Aboulela, 2001. Reproduced with permission of Birlinn Limited via PLSclear.

 WRITE

DISCUSSION: Divide yourselves into groups of four or five. Discuss these questions: How do Shadia and Bryan view each other? What is the main reason they find it so hard to communicate with each other? Support your ideas with textual evidence. Take notes as answers are suggested, and be prepared to share your group's notes with the rest of the class. If you have time, talk about your own experiences with cross-cultural friendships.

A Temporary Matter

FICTION
Jhumpa Lahiri
1999

Introduction

Pulitzer Prize-winner Jhumpa Lahiri (b. 1967) often writes about the intricacies of love and expectation among Indian American families. In "A Temporary Matter," a story from Lahiri's debut collection, *Interpreter of Maladies*, a couple confronts the sadness they've long avoided. After their baby was stillborn, Shoba and Shukumar's marriage changed. No longer intimate with one another, Shoba spends her days outside of the house, while Shukumar barely leaves. A scheduled hour-long power outage for five consecutive evenings provides the couple with a strange gift. Instead of avoiding one another, they find themselves able to talk, using the rules of a game Shoba learned from her family in India.

"He learned not to mind the silences."

1   The notice informed them that it was a temporary matter: for five days their electricity would be cut off for one hour, beginning at eight P.M. A line had gone down in the last snowstorm, and the repairmen were going to take advantage of the milder evenings to set it right. The work would affect only the houses on the quiet tree-lined

Jhumpa Lahiri

street, within walking distance of a row of brick-faced stores and a trolley stop, where Shoba and Shukumar had lived for three years.

2   "It's good of them to warn us," Shoba conceded after reading the notice aloud, more for her own benefit than Shukumar's. She let the strap of her leather satchel, plump with files, slip from her shoulders, and left it in the hallway as she walked into the kitchen. She wore a navy blue poplin raincoat over gray sweatpants and white sneakers, looking, at thirty-three, like the type of woman she'd once claimed she would never resemble.

3   She'd come from the gym. Her cranberry lipstick was visible only on the outer reaches of her mouth, and her eyeliner had left charcoal patches beneath her lower lashes. She used to look this way sometimes, Shukumar thought, on mornings after a party or a night at a bar, when she'd been too lazy to wash her face, too eager to collapse into his arms. She dropped a sheaf of mail on the table without a glance. Her eyes were still fixed on the notice in her other hand. "But they should do this sort of thing during the day."

4   "When I'm here, you mean," Shukumar said. He put a glass lid on a pot of lamb, adjusting it so only the slightest bit of steam could escape. Since January he'd been working at home, trying to complete the final chapters of his dissertation on agrarian[1] revolts in India. "When do the repairs start?"

---

1. **agrarian** concerning the cultivation or distribution of land

5   "It says March nineteenth. Is today the nineteenth?" Shoba walked over to the framed corkboard that hung on the wall by the fridge, bare except for a calendar of William Morris wallpaper patterns. She looked at it as if for the first time, studying the wallpaper pattern carefully on the top half before allowing her eyes to fall to the numbered grid on the bottom. A friend had sent the calendar in the mail as a Christmas gift, even though Shoba and Shukumar hadn't celebrated Christmas that year.

6   "Today then," Shoba announced. "You have a dentist appointment next Friday, by the way."

7   He ran his tongue over the tops of his teeth; he'd forgotten to brush them that morning. It wasn't the first time. He hadn't left the house at all that day, or the day before. The more Shoba stayed out, the more she began putting in extra hours at work and taking on additional projects, the more he wanted to stay in, not even leaving to get the mail, or to buy fruit or wine at the stores by the trolley stop.

8   Six months ago, in September, Shukumar was at an academic conference in Baltimore when Shoba went into labor, three weeks before her due date. He hadn't wanted to go to the conference, but she had insisted; it was important to make contacts, and he would be entering the job market next year. She told him that she had his number at the hotel, and a copy of his schedule and flight numbers, and she had arranged with her friend Gillian for a ride to the hospital in the event of an emergency. When the cab pulled away that morning for the airport, Shoba stood waving good-bye in her robe, with one arm resting on the mound of her belly as if it were a perfectly natural part of her body.

9   Each time he thought of that moment, the last moment he saw Shoba pregnant, it was the cab he remembered most, a station wagon, painted red with blue lettering. It was cavernous compared to their own car. Although Shukumar was six feet tall, with hands too big ever to rest comfortably in the pockets of his jeans, he felt dwarfed in the back seat. As the cab sped down Beacon Street, he imagined a day when he and Shoba might need to buy a station wagon of their own, to cart their children back and forth from music lessons and dentist appointments. He imagined himself gripping the wheel, as Shoba turned around to hand the children juice boxes. Once, these images of parenthood had troubled Shukumar, adding to his anxiety that he was still a student at thirty-five. But that early autumn morning, the trees still heavy with bronze leaves, he welcomed the image for the first time.

10 A member of the staff had found him somehow among the identical convention rooms and handed him a stiff square of stationery. It was only a

Please note that excerpts and passages in the StudySync® library and this workbook are intended as touchstones to generate interest in an author's work. The excerpts and passages do not substitute for the reading of entire texts, and StudySync® strongly recommends that students seek out and purchase the whole literary or informational work in order to experience it as the author intended. Links to online resellers are available in our digital library. In addition, complete works may be ordered through an authorized reseller by filling out and returning to StudySync® the order form enclosed in this workbook.

Reading & Writing Companion   373

telephone number, but Shukumar knew it was the hospital. When he returned to Boston it was over. The baby had been born dead. Shoba was lying on a bed, asleep, in a private room so small there was barely enough space to stand beside her, in a wing of the hospital they hadn't been to on the tour for expectant parents. Her placenta had weakened and she'd had a cesarean[2], though not quickly enough. The doctor explained that these things happen. He smiled in the kindest way it was possible to smile at people known only professionally. Shoba would be back on her feet in a few weeks. There was nothing to indicate that she would not be able to have children in the future.

11   These days Shoba was always gone by the time Shukumar woke up. He would open his eyes and see the long black hairs she shed on her pillow and think of her, dressed, sipping her third cup of coffee already, in her office downtown, where she searched for typographical errors in textbooks and marked them, in a code she had once explained to him, with an assortment of colored pencils. She would do the same for his dissertation, she promised, when it was ready. He envied her the specificity of her task, so unlike the elusive nature of his. He was a mediocre student who had a facility for absorbing details without curiosity. Until September he had been **diligent** if not dedicated, summarizing chapters, outlining arguments on pads of yellow lined paper. But now he would lie in their bed until he grew bored, gazing at his side of the closet which Shoba always left partly open, at the row of the tweed jackets and corduroy trousers he would not have to choose from to teach his classes that semester. After the baby died it was too late to withdraw from his teaching duties. But his adviser had arranged things so that he had the spring semester to himself. Shukumar was in his sixth year of graduate school. "That and the summer should give you a good push," his adviser had said. "You should be able to wrap things up by next September."

12   But nothing was pushing Shukumar. Instead he thought of how he and Shoba had become experts at avoiding each other in their three-bedroom house, spending as much time on separate floors as possible. He thought of how he no longer looked forward to weekends, when she sat for hours on the sofa with her colored pencils and her files, so that he feared that putting on a record in his own house might be rude. He thought of how long it had been since she looked into his eyes and smiled, or whispered his name on those rare occasions they still reached for each other's bodies before sleeping.

2. **cesarean** a cesarean section, c-section, is a surgical procedure to deliver a baby through an incision in the abdomen

NOTES

13   In the beginning he had believed that it would pass, that he and Shoba would get through it all somehow. She was only thirty-three. She was strong, on her feet again. But it wasn't a consolation. It was often nearly lunchtime when Shukumar would finally pull himself out of bed and head downstairs to the coffeepot, pouring out the extra bit Shoba left for him, along with an empty mug, on the countertop.

14   Shukumar gathered onion skins in his hands and let them drop into the garbage pail, on top of the ribbons of fat he'd trimmed from the lamb. He ran the water in the sink, soaking the knife and the cutting board, and rubbed a lemon half along his fingertips to get rid of the garlic smell, a trick he'd learned from Shoba. It was seven-thirty. Through the window he saw the sky, like soft black pitch. Uneven banks of snow still lined the sidewalks, though it was warm enough for people to walk about without hats or gloves. Nearly three feet had fallen in the last storm, so that for a week people had to walk single file, in narrow trenches. For a week that was Shukumar's excuse for not leaving the house. But now the trenches were widening, and water drained steadily into grates in the pavement.

15   "The lamb won't be done by eight," Shukumar said. "We may have to eat in the dark."

16   "We can light candles," Shoba suggested. She unclipped her hair, coiled neatly at her nape during the days, and pried the sneakers from her feet without untying them. "I'm going to shower before the lights go," she said, heading for the staircase. "I'll be down."

17   Shukumar moved her satchel and her sneakers to the side of the fridge. She wasn't this way before. She used to put her coat on a hanger, her sneakers in the closet, and she paid bills as soon as they came. But now she treated the house as if it were a hotel. The fact that the yellow chintz armchair in the living room clashed with the blue-and-maroon Turkish carpet no longer bothered her. On the enclosed porch at the back of the house, a crisp white bag still sat on the wicker chaise, filled with lace she had once planned to turn into curtains.

18   While Shoba showered, Shukumar went into the downstairs bathroom and found a new toothbrush in its box beneath the sink. The cheap, stiff bristles hurt his gums, and he spit some blood into the basin. The spare brush was one of many stored in a metal basket. Shoba had bought them once when they were on sale, in the event that a visitor decided, at the last minute, to spend the night.

19   It was typical of her. She was the type to prepare for surprises, good and bad. If she found a skirt or a purse she liked she bought two. She kept the bonuses

Please note that excerpts and passages in the StudySync® library and this workbook are intended as touchstones to generate interest in an author's work. The excerpts and passages do not substitute for the reading of entire texts, and StudySync® strongly recommends that students seek out and purchase the whole literary or informational work in order to experience it as the author intended. Links to online resellers are available in our digital library. In addition, complete works may be ordered through an authorized reseller by filling out and returning to StudySync® the order form enclosed in this workbook.

Reading & Writing Companion   375

Copyright © BookheadEd Learning, LLC

NOTES

from her job in a separate bank account in her name. It hadn't bothered him. His own mother had fallen to pieces when his father died, abandoning the house he grew up in and moving back to Calcutta, leaving Shukumar to settle it all. He liked that Shoba was different. It astonished him, her **capacity** to think ahead. When she used to do the shopping, the pantry was always stocked with extra bottles of olive and corn oil, depending on whether they were cooking Italian or Indian. There were endless boxes of pasta in all shapes and colors, zippered sacks of basmati rice, whole sides of lambs and goats from the Muslim butchers at Haymarket, chopped up and frozen in endless plastic bags. Every other Saturday they wound through the maze of stalls Shukumar eventually knew by heart. He watched in disbelief as she bought more food, trailing behind her with canvas bags as she pushed through the crowd, arguing under the morning sun with boys too young to shave but already missing teeth, who twisted up brown paper bags of artichokes, plums, gingerroot, and yams, and dropped them on their scales, and tossed them to Shoba one by one. She didn't mind being jostled, even when she was pregnant. She was tall, and broad-shouldered, with hips that her obstetrician assured her were made for childbearing. During the drive back home, as the car curved along the Charles, they **invariably** marveled at how much food they'd bought.

20 It never went to waste. When friends dropped by, Shoba would throw together meals that appeared to have taken half a day to prepare, from things she had frozen and bottled, not cheap things in tins but peppers she had marinated herself with rosemary, and chutneys that she cooked on Sundays, stirring boiling pots of tomatoes and prunes. Her labeled mason jars lined the shelves of the kitchen, in endless sealed pyramids, enough, they'd agreed, to last for their grandchildren to taste. They'd eaten it all by now. Shukumar had been going through their supplies steadily, preparing meals for the two of them, measuring out cupfuls of rice, defrosting bags of meat day after day. He combed through her cookbooks every afternoon, following her penciled instructions to use two teaspoons of ground coriander seeds instead of one, or red lentils instead of yellow. Each of the recipes was dated, telling the first time they had eaten the dish together. April 2, cauliflower with fennel. January 14, chicken with almonds and sultanas. He had no memory of eating those meals, and yet there they were, recorded in her neat proofreader's hand. Shukumar enjoyed cooking now. It was the one thing that made him feel productive. If it weren't for him, he knew, Shoba would eat a bowl of cereal for her dinner.

21 Tonight, with no lights, they would have to eat together. For months now they'd served themselves from the stove, and he'd taken his plate into his study, letting the meal grow cold on his desk before shoving it into his mouth without pause, while Shoba took her plate to the living room and watched game shows, or proofread files with her arsenal of colored pencils at hand.

Skill:
Theme

The characters live in modern-day Boston during a week of nightly blackouts on their street. This forces them to stop avoiding each other, building suspense and suggesting a theme having to do with how relationships change.

22   At some point in the evening she visited him. When he heard her approach he would put away his novel and begin typing sentences. She would rest her hands on his shoulders and stare with him into the blue glow of the computer screen. "Don't work too hard," she would say after a minute or two, and head off to bed. It was the one time in the day she sought him out, and yet he'd come to dread it. He knew it was something she forced herself to do. She would look around the walls of the room, which they had decorated together last summer with a border of marching ducks and rabbits playing trumpets and drums. By the end of August there was a cherry crib under the window, a white changing table with mint-green knobs, and a rocking chair with checkered cushions. Shukumar had disassembled it all before bringing Shoba back from the hospital, scraping off the rabbits and ducks with a spatula. For some reason the room did not haunt him the way it haunted Shoba. In January, when he stopped working at his carrel[3] in the library, he set up his desk there deliberately, partly because the room soothed him, and partly because it was a place Shoba avoided.

23   Shukumar returned to the kitchen and began to open drawers. He tried to locate a candle among the scissors, the eggbeaters and whisks, the mortar and pestle she'd bought in a bazaar in Calcutta, and used to pound garlic cloves and cardamom pods, back when she used to cook. He found a flashlight, but no batteries, and a half-empty box of birthday candles. Shoba had thrown him a surprise birthday party last May. One hundred and twenty people had crammed into the house — all the friends and the friends of friends they now systematically avoided. Bottles of vinho verde had nested in a bed of ice in the bathtub. Shoba was in her fifth month, drinking ginger ale from a martini glass. She had made a vanilla cream cake with custard and spun sugar. All night she kept Shukumar's long fingers linked with hers as they walked among the guests at the party.

24   Since September their only guest had been Shoba's mother. She came from Arizona and stayed with them for two months after Shoba returned from the hospital. She cooked dinner every night, drove herself to the supermarket, washed their clothes, put them away. She was a religious woman. She set up a small shrine, a framed picture of a lavender-faced goddess and a plate of marigold petals, on the bedside table in the guest room, and prayed twice a day for healthy grandchildren in the future. She was polite to Shukumar without being friendly. She folded his sweaters with an expertise she had learned from her job in a department store. She replaced a missing button on his winter coat and knit him a beige and brown scarf, presenting it to him without the least bit of ceremony, as if he had only dropped it and hadn't noticed. She never talked to him about Shoba; once, when he mentioned the baby's death, she looked up from her knitting, and said, "But you weren't even there."

---

3. **carrel** a small cubicle or study area in a library

25   It struck him as odd that there were no real candles in the house. That Shoba hadn't prepared for such an ordinary emergency. He looked now for something to put the birthday candles in and settled on the soil of a potted ivy that normally sat on the windowsill over the sink. Even though the plant was inches from the tap, the soil was so dry that he had to water it first before the candles would stand straight. He pushed aside the things on the kitchen table, the piles of mail, the unread library books. He remembered their first meals there, when they were so thrilled to be married, to be living together in the same house at last, that they would just reach for each other foolishly, more eager to make love than to eat. He put down two embroidered place mats, a wedding gift from an uncle in Lucknow, and set out the plates and wineglasses they usually saved for guests. He put the ivy in the middle, the white-edged, star-shaped leaves girded by ten little candles. He switched on the digital clock radio and tuned it to a jazz station.

26   "What's all this?" Shoba said when she came downstairs. Her hair was wrapped in a thick white towel. She undid the towel and draped it over a chair, allowing her hair, damp and dark, to fall across her back. As she walked absently toward the stove she took out a few tangles with her fingers. She wore a clean pair of sweatpants, a T-shirt, an old flannel robe. Her stomach was flat again, her waist narrow before the flare of her hips, the belt of the robe tied in a floppy knot.

27   It was nearly eight. Shukumar put the rice on the table and the lentils from the night before into the microwave oven, punching the numbers on the timer.

28   "You made *rogan josh,*" Shoba observed, looking through the glass lid at the bright paprika stew.

29   Shukumar took out a piece of lamb, pinching it quickly between his fingers so as not to scald himself. He prodded a larger piece with a serving spoon to make sure the meat slipped easily from the bone. "It's ready," he announced.

30   The microwave had just beeped when the lights went out, and the music disappeared.

31   "Perfect timing," Shoba said.

32   "All I could find were birthday candles." He lit up the ivy, keeping the rest of the candles and a book of matches by his plate.

33   "It doesn't matter," she said, running a finger along the stem of her wineglass. "It looks lovely."

34   In the dimness, he knew how she sat, a bit forward in her chair, ankles crossed against the lowest rung, left elbow on the table. During his search for the candles, Shukumar had found a bottle of wine in a crate he had thought was empty. He clamped the bottle between his knees while he turned in the corkscrew. He worried about spilling, and so he picked up the glasses and held them close to his lap while he filled them. They served themselves, stirring the rice with their forks, squinting as they **extracted** bay leaves and cloves from the stew. Every few minutes Shukumar lit a few more birthday candles and drove them into the soil of the pot.

35   "It's like India," Shoba said, watching him tend his makeshift candelabra. "Sometimes the current disappears for hours at a stretch. I once had to attend an entire rice ceremony[4] in the dark. The baby just cried and cried. It must have been so hot."

36   Their baby had never cried, Shukumar considered. Their baby would never have a rice ceremony, even though Shoba had already made the guest list, and decided on which of her three brothers she was going to ask to feed the child its first taste of solid food, at six months if it was a boy, seven if it was a girl.

37   "Are you hot?" he asked her. He pushed the blazing ivy pot to the other end of the table, closer to the piles of books and mail, making it even more difficult for them to see each other. He was suddenly irritated that he couldn't go upstairs and sit in front of the computer.

38   "No. It's delicious," she said, tapping her plate with her fork. "It really is."

39   He refilled the wine in her glass. She thanked him.

40   They weren't like this before. Now he had to struggle to say something that interested her, something that made her look up from her plate, or from her proofreading files. Eventually he gave up trying to amuse her. He learned not to mind the silences.

41   "I remember during power failures at my grandmother's house, we all had to say something," Shoba continued. He could barely see her face, but from her tone he knew her eyes were narrowed, as if trying to focus on a distant object. It was a habit of hers.

42   "Like what?"

43   "I don't know. A little poem. A joke. A fact about the world. For some reason my relatives always wanted me to tell them the names of my friends in

---

4. **rice ceremony** Annaprashan, the Indian ritual of a baby's first feeding with rice

America. I don't know why the information was so interesting to them. The last time I saw my aunt she asked after four girls I went to elementary school with in Tucson. I barely remember them now."

44　Shukumar hadn't spent as much time in India as Shoba had. His parents, who settled in New Hampshire, used to go back without him. The first time he'd gone as an infant he'd nearly died of amoebic dysentery. His father, a nervous type, was afraid to take him again, in case something were to happen, and left him with his aunt and uncle in Concord. As a teenager he preferred sailing camp or scooping ice cream during the summers to going to Calcutta. It wasn't until after his father died, in his last year of college, that the country began to interest him, and he studied its history from course books as if it were any other subject. He wished now that he had his own childhood story of India.

45　"Let's do that," she said suddenly.

46　"Do what?"

47　"Say something to each other in the dark."

48　"Like what? I don't know any jokes."

49　"No, no jokes." She thought for a minute. "How about telling each other something we've never told before."

50　"I used to play this game in high school," Shukumar recalled. "When I got drunk."

51　"You're thinking of truth or dare. This is different. Okay, I'll start." She took a sip of wine. "The first time I was alone in your apartment, I looked in your address book to see if you'd written me in. I think we'd known each other two weeks."

52　"Where was I?"

53　"You went to answer the telephone in the other room. It was your mother, and I figured it would be a long call. I wanted to know if you'd promoted me from the margins of your newspaper."

54　"Had I?"

55　"No. But I didn't give up on you. Now it's your turn."

56　He couldn't think of anything, but Shoba was waiting for him to speak. She hadn't appeared so determined in months. What was there left to say to her?

NOTES

He thought back to their first meeting, four years earlier at a lecture hall in Cambridge, where a group of Bengali poets were giving a recital. They'd ended up side by side, on folding wooden chairs. Shukumar was soon bored; he was unable to decipher the literary diction, and couldn't join the rest of the audience as they sighed and nodded solemnly after certain phrases. Peering at the newspaper folded in his lap, he studied the temperatures of cities around the world. Ninety-one degrees in Singapore yesterday, fifty-one in Stockholm. When he turned his head to the left, he saw a woman next to him making a grocery list on the back of a folder, and was startled to find that she was beautiful.

57   "Okay" he said, remembering. "The first time we went out to dinner, to the Portuguese place, I forgot to tip the waiter. I went back the next morning, found out his name, left money with the manager."

58   "You went all the way back to Somerville just to tip a waiter?"

59   "I took a cab."

60   "Why did you forget to tip the waiter?"

61   The birthday candles had burned out, but he pictured her face clearly in the dark, the wide tilting eyes, the full grape-toned lips, the fall at age two from her high chair still visible as a comma on her chin. Each day, Shukumar noticed, her beauty, which had once overwhelmed him, seemed to fade. The cosmetics that had seemed superfluous were necessary now, not to improve her but to define her somehow.

62   "By the end of the meal I had a funny feeling that I might marry you," he said, admitting it to himself as well as to her for the first time. "It must have distracted me."

63   The next night Shoba came home earlier than usual. There was lamb left over from the evening before, and Shukumar heated it up so that they were able to eat by seven. He'd gone out that day, through the melting snow, and bought a packet of taper candles from the corner store, and batteries to fit the flashlight. He had the candles ready on the countertop, standing in brass holders shaped like lotuses, but they ate under the glow of the copper-shaded ceiling lamp that hung over the table.

64   When they had finished eating, Shukumar was surprised to see that Shoba was stacking her plate on top of his, and then carrying them over to the sink. He had assumed she would retreat to the living room, behind her barricade of files.

Skill:
Theme

The story is told in third-person point of view, but the narrator reveals Shukumar's thoughts. He "felt good" reflecting on memories. Sharing secrets changed him, suggesting that minor revelations can have a big impact.

65   "Don't worry about the dishes," he said, taking them from her hands.

66   "It seems silly not to," she replied, pouring a drop of detergent onto a sponge. "It's nearly eight o'clock."

67   His heart quickened. All day Shukumar had looked forward to the lights going out. He thought about what Shoba had said the night before, about looking in his address book. It felt good to remember her as she was then, how bold yet nervous she'd been when they first met, how hopeful. They stood side by side at the sink, their reflections fitting together in the frame of the window. It made him shy, the way he felt the first time they stood together in a mirror. He couldn't recall the last time they'd been photographed. They had stopped attending parties, went nowhere together. The film in his camera still contained pictures of Shoba, in the yard, when she was pregnant.

68   After finishing the dishes, they leaned against the counter, drying their hands on either end of a towel. At eight o'clock the house went black. Shukumar lit the wicks of the candles, impressed by their long, steady flames.

69   "Let's sit outside," Shoba said. "I think it's warm still."

70   They each took a candle and sat down on the steps. It seemed strange to be sitting outside with patches of snow still on the ground. But everyone was out of their houses tonight, the air fresh enough to make people restless. Screen doors opened and closed. A small parade of neighbors passed by with flashlights.

71   "We're going to the bookstore to browse," a silver-haired man called out. He was walking with his wife, a thin woman in a windbreaker, and holding a dog on a leash. They were the Bradfords, and they had tucked a sympathy card into Shoba and Shukumar's mailbox back in September. "I hear they've got their power."

72   "They'd better," Shukumar said. "Or you'll be browsing in the dark."

73   The woman laughed, slipping her arm through the crook of her husband's elbow. "Want to join us?"

74   "No thanks," Shoba and Shukumar called out together. It surprised Shukumar that his words matched hers.

75   He wondered what Shoba would tell him in the dark. The worst possibilities had already run through his head. That she'd had an affair. That she didn't respect him for being thirty-five and still a student. That she blamed him for being in Baltimore the way her mother did. But he knew those things weren't

true. She'd been faithful, as had he. She believed in him. It was she who had insisted he go to Baltimore. What didn't they know about each other? He knew she curled her fingers tightly when she slept, that her body twitched during bad dreams. He knew it was honeydew she favored over cantaloupe. He knew that when they returned from the hospital the first thing she did when she walked into the house was pick out objects of theirs and toss them into a pile in the hallway: books from the shelves, plants from the windowsills, paintings from walls, photos from tables, pots and pans that hung from the hooks over the stove. Shukumar had stepped out of her way, watching as she moved **methodically** from room to room. When she was satisfied, she stood there staring at the pile she'd made, her lips drawn back in such distaste that Shukumar had thought she would spit. Then she'd started to cry.

76 He began to feel cold as he sat there on the steps. He felt that he needed her to talk first, in order to reciprocate.

77 "That time when your mother came to visit us," she said finally. "When I said one night that I had to stay late at work, I went out with Gillian and had a martini."

78 He looked at her profile, the slender nose, the slightly masculine set of her jaw. He remembered that night well; eating with his mother, tired from teaching two classes back to back, wishing Shoba were there to say more of the right things because he came up with only the wrong ones. It had been twelve years since his father had died, and his mother had come to spend two weeks with him and Shoba, so they could honor his father's memory together. Each night his mother cooked something his father had liked, but she was too upset to eat the dishes herself, and her eyes would well up as Shoba stroked her hand. "It's so touching," Shoba had said to him at the time. Now he pictured Shoba with Gillian, in a bar with striped velvet sofas, the one they used to go to after the movies, making sure she got her extra olive, asking Gillian for a cigarette. He imagined her complaining, and Gillian sympathizing about visits from in-laws. It was Gillian who had driven Shoba to the hospital.

79 "Your turn," she said, stopping his thoughts.

80 At the end of their street Shukumar heard sounds of a drill and the electricians shouting over it. He looked at the darkened facades of the houses lining the street. Candles glowed in the windows of one. In spite of the warmth, smoke rose from the chimney.

81 "I cheated on my Oriental Civilization exam in college," he said. "It was my last semester, my last set of exams. My father had died a few months before. I could see the blue book of the guy next to me. He was an American guy, a

maniac. He knew Urdu and Sanskrit. I couldn't remember if the verse we had to identify was an example of a *ghazal* or not. I looked at his answer and copied it down."

82 It had happened over fifteen years ago. He felt relief now, having told her.

83 She turned to him, looking not at his face, but at his shoes — old moccasins he wore as if they were slippers, the leather at the back permanently flattened. He wondered if it bothered her, what he'd said. She took his hand and pressed it. "You didn't have to tell me why you did it," she said, moving closer to him.

84 They sat together until nine o'clock, when the lights came on. They heard some people across the street clapping from their porch, and televisions being turned on. The Bradfords walked back down the street, eating ice-cream cones and waving. Shoba and Shukumar waved back. Then they stood up, his hand still in hers, and went inside.

85 Somehow, without saying anything, it had turned into this. Into an exchange of confessions — the little ways they'd hurt or disappointed each other, and themselves. The following day Shukumar thought for hours about what to say to her. He was torn between admitting that he once ripped out a photo of a woman in one of the fashion magazines she used to subscribe to and carried it in his books for a week, or saying that he really hadn't lost the sweater-vest she bought him for their third wedding anniversary but had exchanged it for cash at Filene's, and that he had gotten drunk alone in the middle of the day at a hotel bar. For their first anniversary, Shoba had cooked a ten-course dinner just for him. The vest depressed him. "My wife gave me a sweater-vest for our anniversary," he complained to the bartender, his head heavy with cognac. "What do you expect?" the bartender had replied. "You're married."

Skill:
Story Elements

Shukumar feels disconnected from Shoba, but instead of talking to her about it, he fixates on a picture from a magazine. This dilemma shows that the conflict between the characters had already been brewing before the baby's death.

86 As for the picture of the woman, he didn't know why he'd ripped it out. She wasn't as pretty as Shoba. She wore a white sequined dress, and had a sullen face and lean, mannish legs. Her bare arms were raised, her fists around her head, as if she were about to punch herself in the ears. It was an advertisement for stockings. Shoba had been pregnant at the time, her stomach suddenly immense, to the point where Shukumar no longer wanted to touch her. The first time he saw the picture he was lying in bed next to her, watching her as she read. When he noticed the magazine in the recycling pile he found the woman and tore out the page as carefully as he could. For about a week he allowed himself a glimpse each day. He felt an intense desire for the woman, but it was a desire that turned to disgust after a minute or two. It was the closest he'd come to infidelity.

87   He told Shoba about the sweater on the third night, the picture on the fourth. She said nothing as he spoke, expressed no protest or reproach. She simply listened, and then she took his hand, pressing it as she had before. On the third night, she told him that once after a lecture they'd attended, she let him speak to the chairman of his department without telling him that he had a dab of pâté on his chin. She'd been irritated with him for some reason, and so she'd let him go on and on, about securing his fellowship for the following semester, without putting a finger to her own chin as a signal. The fourth night, she said that she never liked the one poem he'd ever published in his life, in a literary magazine in Utah. He'd written the poem after meeting Shoba. She added that she found the poem sentimental.

88   Something happened when the house was dark. They were able to talk to each other again. The third night after supper they'd sat together on the sofa, and once it was dark he began kissing her awkwardly on her forehead and her face, though it was dark he closed his eyes, and knew that she did, too. The fourth night they walked carefully upstairs, to bed, feeling together for the final step with their feet before the landing, and making love with a desperation they had forgotten. She wept without sound, and whispered his name, and traced his eyebrows with her finger in the dark. As he made love to her he wondered what he would say to her the next night, and what she would say, the thought of it exciting him. "Hold me," he said, "hold me in your arms." By the time the lights came back on downstairs, they'd fallen asleep.

89   The morning of the fifth night Shukumar found another notice from the electric company in the mailbox. The line had been repaired ahead of schedule, it said. He was disappointed. He had planned on making shrimp *malai* for Shoba, but when he arrived at the store he didn't feel like cooking anymore. It wasn't the same, he thought, knowing that the lights wouldn't go out. In the store the shrimp looked gray and thin. The coconut milk tin was dusty and overpriced. Still, he bought them, along with a beeswax candle and two bottles of wine.

90   She came home at seven-thirty. "I suppose this is the end of our game," he said when he saw her reading the notice.

91   She looked at him. "You can still light candles if you want." She hadn't been to the gym tonight. She wore a suit beneath the raincoat. Her makeup had been retouched recently.

92   When she went upstairs to change, Shukumar poured himself some wine and put on a record, a Thelonious Monk album he knew she liked.

93 When she came downstairs they ate together. She didn't thank him or compliment him. They simply ate in a darkened room, in the glow of a beeswax candle. They had survived a difficult time. They finished off the shrimp. They finished off the first bottle of wine and moved on to the second. They sat together until the candle had nearly burned away. She shifted in her chair, and Shukumar thought that she was about to say something. But instead she blew out the candle, stood up, turned on the light switch, and sat down again.

94 "Shouldn't we keep the lights off?" Shukumar asked. She set her plate aside and clasped her hands on the table. "I want you to see my face when I tell you this," she said gently.

95 His heart began to pound. The day she told him she was pregnant, she had used the very same words, saying them in the same gentle way, turning off the basketball game he'd been watching on television. He hadn't been prepared then. Now he was.

96 Only he didn't want her to be pregnant again. He didn't want to have to pretend to be happy.

97 "I've been looking for an apartment and I've found one," she said, narrowing her eyes on something, it seemed, behind his left shoulder. It was nobody's fault, she continued. They'd been through enough. She needed some time alone. She had money saved up for a security deposit. The apartment was on Beacon Hill, so she could walk to work. She had signed the lease that night before coming home.

98 She wouldn't look at him, but he stared at her. It was obvious that she'd rehearsed the lines. All this time she'd been looking for an apartment, testing the water pressure, asking a Realtor if heat and hot water were included in the rent. It sickened Shukumar, knowing that she had spent these past evenings preparing for a life without him. He was relieved and yet he was sickened. This was what she'd been trying to tell him for the past four evenings. This was the point of her game.

99 Now it was his turn to speak. There was something he'd sworn he would never tell her, and for six months he had done his best to block it from his mind. Before the ultrasound she had asked the doctor not to tell her the sex of their child, and Shukumar had agreed. She had wanted it to be a surprise.

100 Later, those few times they talked about what had happened, she said at least they'd been spared that knowledge. In a way she almost took pride in her decision, for it enabled her to seek refuge in a mystery. He knew that she assumed it was a mystery for him, too. He'd arrived too late from Baltimore — when it was all over and she was lying on the hospital bed. But

Skill:
Story Elements

Shukumar has to decide whether or not to tell Shoba the sex of their baby. He wanted to protect Shoba, but now that she has hurt him, he wants to hurt her back. The motivation to cause Shoba pain leads to the climax of the story.

he hadn't. He'd arrived early enough to see their baby, and to hold him before they cremated him. At first he had recoiled at the suggestion, but the doctor said holding the baby might help him with the process of grieving. Shoba was asleep. The baby had been cleaned off, his bulbous lids shut tight to the world.

101 "Our baby was a boy," he said. "His skin was more red than brown. He had black hair on his head. He weighed almost five pounds. His fingers were curled shut, just like yours in the night."

102 Shoba looked at him now, her face contorted with sorrow. He had cheated on a college exam, ripped a picture of a woman out of a magazine. He had returned a sweater and got drunk in the middle of the day instead. These were the things he had told her. He had held his son, who had known life only within her, against his chest in a darkened room in an unknown wing of the hospital. He had held him until a nurse knocked and took him away, and he promised himself that day that he would never tell Shoba, because he still loved her then, and it was the one thing in her life that she had wanted to be a surprise.

103 Shukumar stood up and stacked his plate on top of hers. He carried the plates to the sink, but instead of running the tap he looked out the window. Outside the evening was still warm, and the Bradfords were walking arm in arm. As he watched the couple the room went dark, and he spun around. Shoba had turned the lights off. She came back to the table and sat down, and after a moment Shukumar joined her. They wept together, for the things they now knew.

"A Temporary Matter" from INTERPRETER OF MALADIES by Jhumpa Lahiri. Copyright © 1999 by Jhumpa Lahiri. Reprinted by permission of Houghton Mifflin Harcourt Publishing Company. All rights reserved.

First Read

Read the short story "A Temporary Matter." After you read, complete the Think Questions below.

☁ THINK QUESTIONS

1. How does Shukumar feel about himself? Why? Cite evidence from the story to support your answer.

2. What new habits do Shoba and Shukumar develop after the death of their baby, and what do these habits reveal about their relationship? Cite evidence from the story to support your answer.

3. How did Shukumar feel about Shoba before the death of their baby? What evidence from the text leads you to this conclusion?

4. Use context clues to determine the meaning of the word **diligent** as it is used in "A Temporary Matter." Write your definition of *diligent* here and explain which clues helped you figure it out.

5. Keeping in mind that the Latin prefix *ex-* means "from" and that the Latin root *-tract-* means "to draw or pull," determine the meaning of the word **extracted** as it is used in "A Temporary Matter." Write your definition of *extract* here and explain which clues helped you figure it out.

Skill:
Theme

Use the Checklist to analyze Theme in "A Temporary Matter." Refer to the sample student annotations about Theme in the text.

••• CHECKLIST FOR THEME

In order to identify two or more themes or central ideas of a text, note the following:

- ✓ the subject and how it relates to the themes in the text

- ✓ if one or more themes is stated directly in the text

- ✓ details in the text that help to reveal each theme:

  - the title and chapter headings
  - details about the setting
  - the narrator's or speaker's tone
  - characters' thoughts, actions, and dialogue
  - the central conflict, climax, and resolution of the conflict
  - shifts in characters, setting, or plot events

- ✓ when the themes interact with each other

To determine two or more themes or central ideas of a text and analyze their development over the course of the text, including how they interact and build on one another to produce a complex account, consider the following questions:

- ✓ What are the themes in the text? When do they emerge?

- ✓ How does each theme develop over the course of the text?

- ✓ How do the themes interact and build on one another?

Please note that excerpts and passages in the StudySync® library and this workbook are intended as touchstones to generate interest in an author's work. The excerpts and passages do not substitute for the reading of entire texts, and StudySync® strongly recommends that students seek out and purchase the whole literary or informational work in order to experience it as the author intended. Links to online resellers are available in our digital library. In addition, complete works may be ordered through an authorized reseller by filling out and returning to StudySync® the order form enclosed in this workbook.

Reading & Writing Companion **389**

Skill: Theme

Reread paragraphs 94–99 of "A Temporary Matter." Then, using the Checklist on the previous page, answer the multiple-choice questions below.

↻ YOUR TURN

1. Which statement best analyzes the theme that is revealed by details like characters' thoughts, setting, and narrator's tone in this passage?

   ○ A. The change in the setting creates a homey feeling that becomes a safe space for Shoba to reveal her subjective point of view and prepares readers for the story's happy ending.

   ○ B. The shift in point of view from Shukumar's thoughts to Shoba's point of view jars the reader, mirroring the abrupt change in focus from present to past events.

   ○ C. The story's surprise ending is foreshadowed by the narrator's revelation of Shukumar's secret, which takes readers from the couple's home to a hospital.

   ○ D. The third-person limited point of view helps readers understand Shukumar's reaction to learning the truth, which is heightened by the sudden change from darkness to light.

2. This question has two parts. First, answer Part A. Then, answer Part B.

   Part A: What theme is strongly suggested by details like characterization, setting, point of view, and plot events in this passage?

   ○ A. People rarely keep secrets.
   ○ B. You cannot hide from the truth.
   ○ C. Bad news hurts less when revealed slowly.
   ○ D. Spouses sometimes need to lie to each other.

   Part B: Which evidence best supports the answer chosen in Part A?

   ○ A. Before the ultrasound she had asked the doctor not to tell her the sex of their child . . .

   ○ B. "Shouldn't we keep the lights off?" Shukumar asked. She set her plate aside and clasped her hands on the table. "I want you to see my face when I tell you this," she said gently.

   ○ C. He was relieved and yet he was sickened. This was what she'd been trying to tell him for the past four evenings.

   ○ D. " . . . and for six months he had done his best to block it from his mind."

Skill:
Story Elements

Use the Checklist to analyze Story Elements in "A Temporary Matter." Refer to the sample student annotations about Story Elements in the text.

In order to identify the impact of the author's choices regarding how to develop and relate elements of a story or drama, note the following:

- ✓ where and when the story takes place, who the main characters are, and the main conflict, or problem, in the plot

- ✓ the order of the action

- ✓ how the characters are introduced and developed

- ✓ the impact that the author's choice of setting has on the characters and their attempt to solve the problem

- ✓ the point of view the author uses, and how this shapes what readers know about the characters in the story

To analyze the impact of the author's choices regarding how to develop and relate elements of a story or drama, consider the following questions:

- ✓ How does the author's choices affect the story elements? The development of the plot?

- ✓ How does the setting influence the characters?

- ✓ Which elements of the setting impact the plot, and in particular the problem the characters face and must solve?

- ✓ Are there any flashbacks or other story elements that have an effect on the development of events in the plot? How does the author's choice of utilizing a flashback affect this development?

- ✓ How does the author introduce and develop characters in the story? Why do you think they made these choices?

Skill:
Story Elements

Reread paragraph 84 of "A Temporary Matter." Then, using the Checklist on the previous page, answer the multiple-choice questions below.

⟳ YOUR TURN

1. The narrator reveals that Shukumar originally lies to Shoba about what really happened to the sweater vest because—

   ○ A. he wants Shoba to feel embarrassed about the gift.

   ○ B. he knows that Shoba would want to share the money.

   ○ C. he thinks the truth would make Shoba hurt or angry.

   ○ D. he thinks it is funny to lie to Shoba about small things.

2. How does Shukumar's decision to tell Shoba the truth affect the plot of the story?

   ○ A. It shows that Shukumar is becoming more willing to talk about difficult things with his wife.

   ○ B. It reveals that Shukumar is unloving and does not care how the truth might affect Shoba.

   ○ C. It foreshadows that Shoba may do something that will be hurtful to her husband.

   ○ D. It indicates that Shukumar regrets marrying Shoba and staying married to her.

A Temporary Matter

Close Read

Reread "A Temporary Matter." As you reread, complete the Skills Focus questions below. Then use your answers and annotations from the questions to help you complete the Write activity.

◎ SKILLS FOCUS

1. Identify a passage in which the third-person narrator reveals Shukumar's perspective on how the characters' daily lives have changed after the death of their child. Explain how this passage develops a theme relating to changing relationships.

2. Highlight a section of the text that describes Shoba's behavior before the death of the child. Explain how the description of this behavior contributes to the reader's understanding of Shoba's character and contributes to the plot of the story.

3. Identify details that show how the setting affects characterization. Explain which details you think are particularly effective in developing a character and why.

4. Find a scene in which Shoba tells Shukumar something that she has been keeping from him. Summarize what happens in the scene.

5. What effect does a change in routine have on the characters in "A Temporary Matter"? Does it cause them to change? Or, does it help them realize that change has already happened?

✎ WRITE

LITERARY ANALYSIS: Critic Christopher Tayler once described Jhumpa Lahiri's stories in this way: "Unflashily written, long, almost grave in tone, her new stories patiently accumulate detail, only gradually building up a powerful emotional charge." Do you agree that "A Temporary Matter" is like this? Examine the traits named and find passages of the story that either prove or contradict Tayler's opinion.

Please note that excerpts and passages in the StudySync® library and this workbook are intended as touchstones to generate interest in an author's work. The excerpts and passages do not substitute for the reading of entire texts, and StudySync® strongly recommends that students seek out and purchase the whole literary or informational work in order to experience it as the author intended. Links to online resellers are available in our digital library. In addition, complete works may be ordered through an authorized reseller by filling out and returning to StudySync® the order form enclosed in this workbook.

Reading & Writing Companion   **393**

Tryst with Destiny
Speech on the Eve of India's Independence

INFORMATIONAL TEXT
Jawaharlal Nehru
1947

Introduction

This speech, given to announce India's independence from almost 200 years of British rule, was delivered to Parliament by Jawaharlal Nehru (1889-1964), the man who would become India's first prime minister. After studying law at Cambridge, Nehru returned to India, where he eventually became Mohandas Gandhi's successor. Nehru's daughter, Indira Gandhi, who later became prime minister of India, was the first and only woman to hold the post. In this triumphant address, Jawaharlal Nehru celebrates Indian victory, but also earnestly urges his fellow patriots to consider the kind of future they intend to forge for their country.

"We end today a period of ill fortune and India discovers herself again."

NOTES

I

1   Long years ago we made a tryst with destiny, and now the time comes when we shall redeem our pledge, not wholly or in full measure, but very substantially. At the stroke of the midnight hour, when the world sleeps, India will awake to life and freedom. A moment comes, which comes but rarely in history, when we step out from the old to

School children in front of Red Fort on the 72nd Independence Day, on August 15, 2018 in New Delhi, India.

the new, when an age ends, and when the soul of a nation, long suppressed, finds **utterance**. It is fitting that at this solemn moment we take the pledge of dedication to the service of India and her people and to the still larger cause of humanity.

2   At the dawn of history India started on her unending quest, and trackless centuries are filled with her striving and the grandeur of her success and her failures. Through good and ill fortune alike she has never lost sight of that quest or forgotten the ideals which gave her strength. We end today a period of ill fortune and India discovers herself again. The achievement we celebrate today is but a step, an opening of opportunity, to the greater triumphs and achievements that await us. Are we brave enough and wise enough to grasp this opportunity and accept the challenge of the future?

3   Freedom and power bring responsibility. The responsibility rests upon this Assembly, a **sovereign** body representing the sovereign people of India. Before the birth of freedom we have endured all the pains of labour and our hearts are heavy with the memory of this sorrow. Some of those pains continue even now. Nevertheless, the past is over and it is the future that beckons to us now.

4   That future is not one of ease or resting but of **incessant** striving so that we may fulfil the pledges we have so often taken and the one we shall take

today. The service of India means the service of the millions who suffer. It means the ending of poverty and **ignorance** and disease and inequality of opportunity. The ambition of the greatest man of our generation has been to wipe every tear from every eye. That may be beyond us, but as long as there are tears and suffering, so long our work will not be over.

5   And so we have to labour and to work, and work hard, to give reality to our dreams. Those dreams are for India, but they are also for the world, for all the nations and peoples are too closely knit together today for any one of them to imagine that it can live apart. Peace has been said to be indivisible; so is freedom, so is prosperity now, and so also is disaster in this One World that can no longer be split into isolated fragments.

6   To the people of India, whose representatives we are, we make an appeal to join us with faith and confidence in this great adventure. This is no time for petty and destructive criticism, no time for ill-will or blaming others. We have to build the noble mansion of free India where all her children may dwell.

II

7   The appointed day has come-the day appointed by destiny-and India stands forth again, after long slumber and struggle, awake, vital, free and independent. The past clings on to us still in some measure and we have to do much before we redeem the pledges we have so often taken. Yet the turning-point is past, and history begins anew for us, the history which we shall live and act and others will write about.

8   It is a fateful moment for us in India, for all Asia and for the world. A new star rises, the star of freedom in the East, a new hope comes into being, a vision long cherished materializes. May the star never set and that hope never be betrayed!

9   We rejoice in that freedom, even though clouds surround us, and many of our people are sorrowstricken and difficult problems encompass us. But freedom brings responsibilities and burdens and we have to face them in the spirit of a free and disciplined people.

10   On this day our first thoughts go to the architect of this freedom, the Father of our Nation [Gandhi], who, embodying the old spirit of India, held aloft the torch of freedom and lighted up the darkness that surrounded us. We have often been unworthy followers of his and have strayed from his message, but not only we but succeeding generations will remember this message and bear the imprint in their hearts of this great son of India, magnificent in his faith and strength and courage and humility. We shall never allow that torch of freedom to be blown out, however high the wind or stormy the tempest.

11 Our next thoughts must be of the unknown volunteers and soldiers of freedom who, without praise or reward, have served India even unto death.

12 We think also of our brothers and sisters who have been cut off from us by political boundaries and who unhappily cannot share at present in the freedom that has come. They are of us and will remain of us whatever may happen, and we shall be sharers in their good [or] ill fortune alike.

13 The future beckons to us. Whither do we go and what shall be our endeavour? To bring freedom and opportunity to the common man, to the peasants and workers of India; to fight and end poverty and ignorance and disease; to build up a prosperous, democratic and progressive nation, and to create social, economic and political institutions which will ensure justice and fullness of life to every man and woman.

14 We have hard work ahead. There is no resting for any one of us till we redeem our pledge in full, till we make all the people of India what destiny intended them to be. We are citizens of a great country on the verge of bold advance, and we have to live up to that high standard. All of us, to whatever religion we may belong, are equally the children of India with equal rights, privileges and obligations. We cannot encourage communalism[1] or narrow-mindedness, for no nation can be great whose people are narrow in thought or in action.

15 To the nations and peoples of the world we send greetings and pledge ourselves to cooperate with them in furthering peace, freedom and democracy.

16 And to India, our much-loved motherland, the ancient, the eternal and the ever-new, we pay our **reverent** homage and we bind ourselves afresh to her service.

JAI HIND

✏ WRITE

RHETORICAL ANALYSIS: Write an essay explaining what makes this speech memorable and important. Why is it "recognized as one of the greatest of the 20th century"? Identify the audience and what the speaker wants from them. How do rhetorical devices such as personification and repetition likely affect the crowd's emotions?

---

1. **communalism** a system that encourages loyalty to narrower communities or identities over an allegiance to society writ large

A
Small Place

INFORMATIONAL TEXT
Jamaica Kincaid
1988

Introduction

Jamaica Kincaid (b. 1949) was born Elaine Potter Richardson on the Caribbean island of Antigua. Raised in poverty, she was sent at the age of 17 to work as an au pair in New York. There, she began her writing career, eventually penning short fiction featured in publications like *The Paris Review* and becoming a long-tenured staff writer at *The New Yorker*. Much of her writing centers on themes of colonial legacy, racism, class, and power dynamics. These themes are well evident in *A Small Place*, a work of creative nonfiction that draws heavily on the author's experiences growing up in Antigua.

"You will have to accept that this is mostly your fault."

1 Have you ever wondered to yourself why it is that all people like me seem to have learned from you is how to imprison and murder each other, how to govern badly, and how to take the wealth of our country and place it in Swiss bank accounts[1]? Have you ever wondered why it is that all we seem to have learned from you is how to corrupt our societies and how to be **tyrants**? You will have to accept that this is mostly your fault. Let me just show you how you looked to us. You came. You took things that were not yours, and you did not even, for appearances' sake, ask first. You could have said, "May I have this, please?" and even though it would have been clear to everybody that a yes or no from us would have been of no consequence you might have looked so much better. Believe me, it would have gone a long way. I would have had to admit that at least you were polite. You murdered people. You imprisoned people. You robbed people. You opened your own banks and you put our money in them. The accounts were in your name. The banks were in your name. There must have been some good people among you, but they stayed home. And that is the point. That is why they are good. They stayed home. But still, when you think about it, you must be a little sad. The people like me, finally, after years and years of agitation, made deeply moving and **eloquent** speeches against the wrongness of your domination over us, and then finally, after the mutilated bodies of you, your wife, and your children were found in your beautiful and spacious bungalow[2] at the edge of your rubber plantation[3]— found by one of your many house servants (none of it was ever yours; it was never, ever yours)—you say to me, "Well, I wash my hands of all of you, I am leaving now," and you leave, and from afar you watch as we do to ourselves the very things you used to do to us. And you might feel that there was more to you than that, you might feel that you had understood the meaning of the Age of Enlightenment (though, as far as I can see, it had done you very little good); you loved knowledge, and wherever you went you made sure to build a school, a library (yes, and in both of these places you distorted or erased my history and glorified your own). But then again, perhaps as you observe

---

1. **Swiss bank accounts** authorities have repeatedly found Swiss bank accounts held by criminal enterprises or tax evaders to take advantage of the country's financial secrecy laws
2. **bungalow** a simple, small house or cottage, usually one-story
3. **rubber plantation** a large-scale farm for growing and harvesting rubber from trees

the **debacle** in which I now exist, the utter ruin that I say is my life, perhaps you are remembering that you had always felt people like me cannot run things, people like me will never grasp the idea of Gross National Product[4], people like me will never be able to take command of the thing the most simpleminded among you can master, people like me will never understand the notion of rule by law, people like me cannot really think in **abstractions**, people like me cannot be **objective**, we make everything so personal. You will forget your part in the whole setup, that bureaucracy is one of your inventions, that Gross National Product is one of your inventions, and all the laws that you know mysteriously favour you. Do you know why people like me are shy about being capitalists? Well, it's because we, for as long as we have known you, *were* capital, like bales of cotton and sacks of sugar, and you were the commanding, cruel capitalists, and the memory of this is so strong, the experience is so recent, that we can't quite bring ourselves to embrace this idea that you think so much of.

Excerpted from *A Small Place* by Jamaica Kincaid, published by Farrar, Straus & Giroux.

✏ WRITE

CORRESPONDENCE: Like Jamaica Kincaid, write a letter protesting a great wrong. Direct the letter to the person you hold responsible, such as a government official, a business executive, a criminal, or a bully. You might emulate Kincaid's tone or other techniques she used to make her message effective, or you might deliberately choose different techniques if you think they work better. Be sure your ideas flow logically. You want to make it clear to the person you are writing to why he or she is in the wrong.

4. **Gross National Product** the total economic value generated by a country in one year

Ghosts

FICTION
Chimamanda Ngozi Adichie
2009

Introduction

Many young Americans first learned of award-winning Nigerian writer Chimamanda Ngozi Adichie (b. 1977) from a speech of hers featured in a Beyoncé song, "Flawless." By that point, Adichie's dynamic body of work—three novels, numerous essays, and a collection of short stories—had already earned her a MacArthur fellowship and a spot in *The New Yorker*'s "20 Under 40" series. The daughter of Nigerian academics, Adichie grew up in the same house where renowned author Chinua Achebe used to live. The story presented here, "Ghosts," weaves factual characters and events from her own history into the fictional story of a university professor, James Nwoye (Adichie's own father's name), who encounters an old colleague he'd presumed dead in the Nigerian Civil War— 37 years earlier.

"Two men haunted by war meet again—thirty-seven years after their last encounter."

Skill:
Textual Evidence

James explicitly resists the impulse to make sure Ikenna "is not a ghost." This supports the inference that James's education separates him from "the ways of" his "people." Will the story reveal whether Ikenna is a ghost?

1   Today I saw Ikenna Okoro, a man I had long thought was dead. Perhaps I should have bent down, grabbed a handful of sand, and thrown it at him, in the way my people do to make sure a person is not a ghost. But I am an educated man, a retired professor of seventy-one, and I am supposed to have armed myself with enough science

Nigerian author Chimamanda Ngozi Adichie

to laugh indulgently at the ways of my people. I did not throw sand at him. I could not have done so even if I had wished to, anyway, since we met on the concrete grounds of the university bursary[1].

2   I was there to ask about my pension, yet again. "Good day, Prof," the dried-looking clerk, Ugwuoke, said. "Sorry, the money has not come in."

3   The other clerk, whose name I have now forgotten, nodded and apologized as well, while chewing on a pink lobe of kolanut. They were used to this. I was used to this. So were the tattered men who were clustered under the mango tree, talking loudly. The education minister has stolen the pension money, one fellow said. Another said that it was the vice chancellor, who deposited the money in personal high-interest accounts. When I walked up to them, they greeted me and shook their heads apologetically about the situation as if my professor-level pension is somehow more important than their messenger-level or driver-level pensions. They called me Prof, as most people do, as the hawkers sitting next to their trays under the tree did. "Prof! Prof! Come and buy good banana!"

4   I chatted with Vincent, who was our driver when I was faculty dean in the eighties. "No pension for three years, Prof. This is why people retire and die," he said.

---

1. **bursary** an institution's treasury

NOTES

5   "*O joka*," I said, although he, of course, did not need me to tell him how terrible it was.

6   "How is Nkiru, Prof? I trust she is well in America?" He always asks about our daughter. He often drove my wife, Ebere, and me to visit her at the College of Medicine in Enugu. I remember that when Ebere died, he came with his relatives for *mgbalu*[2] and gave a touching, if rather long, speech about how well Ebere treated him when he was our driver, how she gave him our daughter's old clothes for his children.

7   "Nkiru is well," I said.

8   "Please greet her for me when she calls, Prof."

9   "I will."

10   He talked for a while longer, about ours being a country that has not learned to say thank you, about the students in the hostels not paying him on time for mending their shoes, but it was his Adam's apple that held my attention; it bobbed alarmingly as if just about to pierce the wrinkled skin of his neck and pop out. Vincent must be in his early sixties—since the non-academic staff retire at sixty rather than sixty-five—but he looks older. He has little hair left. I quite remember his **incessant** chatter while he drove me to work in those days; I remember, too, that he was fond of reading my newspapers, a practice I did not encourage.

11   "Prof, won't you buy us banana? Hunger is killing us," one of the men said. He had a familiar face. I think he was Professor Eboh's gardener, next door. His tone had that half-teasing, half-serious quality, but I bought groundnuts and a bunch of bananas for them, although what they really needed was some moisturizer. Their faces and arms looked like ash. It is almost March but the Harmattan[3] is still very much here: the dry winds, the crackling static on my clothes, the gritty dust on my eyelashes. I used more lotion than usual today, and Vaseline on my lips, but still the dryness made my palms and face feel tight. Ebere used to tease me about not moisturizing properly, especially in the Harmattan, and sometimes would stop me and slowly rub her Nivea on my arms, my legs, my back. We have to take care of this lovely skin, she would say with that playful laughter of hers. She always said my complexion was the persuading trait, since I did not have any money like her other suitors. Seamless, she called it. I saw nothing particularly distinct in my dark umber tone, but I did come to preen a little with the passing years, with Ebere's massaging hands.

---

2. ***mgbalu*** a traditional Igbo burial ceremony
3. **the Harmattan** dry wind from the Sahara blowing into West Africa that is also the name of the season when it comes, typically from November to March

Skill:
Story Elements

James listens to the men, noticing his effect on them. Their lives are difficult, but James admires their positive attitudes: they laugh a lot and have "whole" spirits.

Skill:
Story Elements

James is shocked to see Ikenna Okoro because he thought Ikenna had died. The author uses a flashback to give details about James and his family evacuating at the beginning of the war.

12   "Thank you, Prof!" the men said, and then began to mock one another about who would do the dividing.

13   I stood around and listened to their talk. I was aware that they spoke more respectably because I was there: carpentry was not going well, children were ill, more money-lender troubles. They laughed often. Of course they nurse resentment, as they well should, but it has somehow managed to leave their spirits whole. I often wonder whether I would be like them if I did not have money saved from my appointments in the Federal Office of Statistics and if Nkiru did not insist on sending me dollars that I do not need. I doubt it; I would probably have hunched up like a tortoise shell and let my dignity whittle away.

14   Finally I said good-bye to them and walked toward my car, parked near the whistling pine trees that shield the Faculty of Education from the bursary. That was when I saw Ikenna Okoro.

15   He called out to me first. "James? James Nwoye, is it you?" He stood with his mouth open and I could see that his teeth are still complete. I lost one last year. I have refused to have what Nkiru calls "work" done, but I still felt rather sour at Ikenna's full set.

16   "Ikenna? Ikenna Okoro?" I asked in the tentative way one suggests something that cannot be: the coming to life of a man who died thirty-seven years ago.

17   "Yes, yes." Ikenna came closer, uncertainly. We shook hands, and then hugged briefly.

18   We were not good friends, Ikenna and I; I knew him fairly well in those days only because everyone knew him fairly well. It was he who climbed the podium at the Staff Club, he who would speak until he was hoarse and sweating, he who handed out simplified tenets of Nyerere, the type smudgy on cheap paper. The social sciences people had too much time on their hands and worshiped radicals of all sorts who were thought by those of us in the sciences to be empty vessels. We saw Ikenna differently. I'm not sure why, but we forgave his peremptory style and did not discard his pamphlets and rather admired the erudite asperity with which he blazed through issues. He is still a shrunken man with froglike eyes and light skin that has become discolored with age. One heard of him in those days and then struggled to hide great disappointment upon seeing him, because the depth of his rhetoric somehow demanded good looks. But then my people say that a famous animal does not always fill the hunter's basket.

19   "You're alive?" I asked. I was quite shaken. My family and I saw him on the day he died, 6 July, 1967, the day we evacuated in a hurry, with the sun a strange fiery red in the sky and nearby the *boom-boom-boom* of shelling as the federal soldiers advanced. We were in my Peugeot 404. The militia waved us through the campus gates and shouted that we should not worry, that the

vandals—as we called the federal soldiers—would be defeated in a matter of days and we could come back. The local villagers, the same ones who would pick through lecturers' dustbins for food after the war, were walking along, hundreds of them, women with boxes on their heads and babies tied to their backs, barefoot children carrying bundles, men dragging bicycles, holding yams. I remember that Ebere was consoling our daughter, Zik, about the doll left behind in our haste, when we saw Ikenna's green Kadet. He was driving the opposite way, back into campus. I horned and stopped. "You can't go back!" I called. But he waved and said, "I have to get some manuscripts." Or maybe he said, "I have to get some materials." I thought it rather foolhardy of him to go back in since the shelling sounded close and our troops would drive the vandals back in a week or two anyway. But I was also full of a sense of our collective invincibility, of the justness of the Biafran cause[4], and so I did not think much else of it until we heard Nsukka fell on the very day we evacuated and the campus was occupied. The bearer of the news, a relative of Professor Ezike, also told us that two lecturers had been killed. One of them had argued with the federal soldiers before he was shot. We did not need to be told this was Ikenna.

20 Ikenna laughed. "I am, I am!" He seemed to find his own response even funnier because he laughed again. Even his laughter, now that I think of it, seemed discolored, hollow, nothing like the aggressive sound that reverberated all over the Staff Club in those days.

21 "But we saw you," I said. "You remember? That day we evacuated?"

22 "Yes," he said.

23 "They said you did not come out."

24 "I did." He nodded. "I did. I left Biafra the following month."

25 "You left?" It is incredible that I felt, today, a brief flash of that deep disgust that came when we heard of saboteurs—we called them sabos—who betrayed our soldiers, our just cause, our nascent nation, in exchange for a safe passage across to Nigeria, to the salt and meat and cold water that the blockade kept from us.

26 "No, no, it was not like that, not what you think." Ikenna paused and I noticed that his gray shirt sagged at the shoulders. "I went abroad on a Red Cross plane. I went to Sweden." There was an uncertainty about him, a **diffidence** that seemed alien, very unlike the man who so easily got people to *act*. I remember how he organized the rallies after Biafra was declared, all of us

---

4. **the Biafran cause** referring to the political struggle of the breakaway Republic of Biafra, an area of eastern Nigeria which fought in the Nigerian Civil War for independence from 1967 until defeat in 1970

crowded at Freedom Square while Ikenna talked and we cheered and shouted, "Happy Independence!"

27 "You went to Sweden?" I asked.

28 "Yes."

29 He said nothing else and I realized that he would not tell me more, that he would not tell me just how he had come out of the campus alive or how he came to be on that plane; I know of the children airlifted to Gabon later in the war but certainly not of people flown out on Red Cross planes, and so early, too. The silence between us was tense.

30 "Have you been in Sweden since?" I asked.

31 "Yes. My whole family was in Abagana when they bombed it. Nobody left, so there was no reason for me to come back." He stopped to let out a harsh sound that was supposed to be laughter but sounded more like a series of coughs. "I was in touch with Doctor Anya for a while. He told me about rebuilding our campus, and I think he said you left for America after the war."

32 In fact, Ebere and I came back to Nsukka right after the war ended in 1970, but only for a few days. It was too much for us. Our books were in a charred pile in the front garden, under the umbrella tree. The lumps of calcified feces in the bathtub were strewn with pages of my *Mathematical Annals*, used as toilet paper, crusted smears blurring the formulas I had studied and taught. Our piano—Ebere's piano—was gone. My graduation gown, which I had worn to receive my first degree at Ibadan, had been used to wipe something and now lay with ants crawling in and out, busy and oblivious to me watching them. Our photographs were ripped, their frames broken. So we left for America and did not come back until 1976. We were assigned a different house on Ezenweze Avenue and for a long time we avoided driving along Imoke Street, because we did not want to see the old house; we later heard that the new people had cut down the umbrella tree. I told Ikenna all of this, although I said nothing about our time at Berkeley, where my friend Chuck Bell arranged my teaching appointment. Ikenna was silent for a while, and then he said, "How is your little girl, Zik? She must be a grown woman now."

33 He always insisted on paying for Zik's Fanta when we took her to the Staff Club on Family Day because, he said, she was the prettiest of the children. I suspect it was really because we had named her after our president, and Ikenna was an early Zikist before claiming the movement was too tame and leaving.

34 "The war took Zik," I said in Igbo. Speaking of death in English has always had for me a disquieting finality.

35 Ikenna breathed deeply, but all he said was "*Ndo*," nothing more than sorry. I am relieved he did not ask how—there are not many hows anyway—and that he did not look inordinately shocked, as if war deaths are ever really accidents.

36 "We had another child after the war, another daughter," I said. But Ikenna was talking in a rush. "I did what I could," he said. "I did. I left the International Red Cross. It was full of cowards who could not stand up for human beings. They backed down after that plane was shot down at Eket as if they did not know it was exactly what Gowon wanted. But the World Council of Churches kept flying in relief through Uli. At nights! I was there in Uppsala when they met. It was the biggest operation they had done since the Second World War. I organized the fundraising. I organized the Biafran rallies all over the European capitals. You heard about the big one at Trafalgar Square[5]? I was at the top of that. I did what I could."

37 I was not sure that Ikenna was speaking to me. It seemed that he was saying what he had said over and over to many people. I looked toward the mango tree. The men were still clustered there, but I could not tell whether they had finished the bananas and groundnuts. Perhaps it was then that I began to feel submerged in hazy nostalgia, a feeling that has still not left me.

38 "Chris Okigbo died, not so?" Ikenna asked and made me focus once again. For a moment, I wondered if he wanted me to deny that, to make Okigbo a ghost-come-back, too. But Okigbo died, our genius, our star, the man whose poetry moved us all, even those of us in the sciences.

39 "Yes, the war took Okigbo."

40 "We lost a colossus in the making."

41 "True, but at least he was brave enough to fight." As soon as I said that, I was regretful. I had meant it only as a tribute to Chris Okigbo, who could have worked at one of the directorates like the rest of us university people but instead took up a gun to defend Nsukka. I did not want Ikenna to misunderstand my intention and wondered whether to apologize. He looked away. A small dust whirl was building up across the road. The wind whipped dry leaves off the trees. Perhaps because of my discomfort, I began to tell Ikenna about the day we drove back to Nsukka, about the landscape of ruins, the blown-out roofs, the houses riddled with holes that Ebere said were rather like Swiss cheese. When we got to the road that runs through Aguleri, Biafran soldiers stopped us and shoved a wounded soldier into our car; his blood dripped onto the backseat and, because the upholstery had a tear, soaked deep into the stuffing, mingled with the very insides of our car. A stranger's blood. I was not sure why I chose this particular story to tell Ikenna, but to make it seem

5. **Trafalgar Square** public square in the City of Westminster, London that is a site of major political demonstrations

NOTES

worth his while I added that the metallic smell of the soldier's blood reminded me of him, Ikenna, because I had always imagined that the federal soldiers shot him and left him to die, left his blood to stain the street. This is not true; I neither imagined such a thing, nor did that wounded soldier remind me of Ikenna. If he thought my story strange, he did not say so. He nodded and said, "I've heard so many stories, so many."

42 "How is life in Sweden?" I asked.

43 He shrugged. "I retired last year. I decided to come back and see." He said "see" as if it meant something more that what one did with one's eyes.

44 "What about your family?" I asked.

45 "I never married."

46 "Oh," I said.

47 "And how is your wife doing? Nnenna, isn't it?" Ikenna asked.

48 "Ebere."

49 "Oh, yes, of course, Ebere. Lovely woman."

50 "Ebere fell asleep three years ago," I said in Igbo. I was surprised to see the tears that glassed Ikenna's eyes. He had forgotten her name and yet, somehow, he was capable of mourning her, or of mourning a time immersed in possibilities. I realize, now, that Ikenna is a man who carries with him the weight of what could have been.

51 "I'm so sorry," he said. "So sorry."

52 "It's all right," I said. "She visits."

53 "What?" he asked me with a perplexed look, although he, of course, had heard me.

54 "She visits. She visits me."

55 "I see," Ikenna said with that pacifying tone one reserves for the mad.

56 "I mean, she visited America quite often; our daughter is a doctor there."

57 "Oh, is that right?" Ikenna asked too brightly. He looked relieved. I don't blame him. We are the educated ones, taught to keep tightly rigid our boundaries of what is considered real. I was like him until Ebere first visited, three weeks after her funeral. Nkiru and her son had just returned to America. I was alone. When I heard the door downstairs close and open and close again, I thought nothing of it. The evening winds always did that. But there was no rustle of leaves outside my bedroom window, no *swish-swish* of the avocado and

Skill:
Textual Evidence

James says his wife "visits" him. When Ikenna appears "perplexed" and uses a "pacifying tone," James changes the subject. This supports the inference that James is worried about what others think about him seeing his wife's ghost.

cashew trees. There was *no* wind outside. Yet, the door downstairs was opening and closing. In retrospect, I doubt that I was as scared as I should have been. I heard the feet on the stairs, in much the same pattern as Ebere walked, heavier on each third step. I lay still in the darkness of our room. Then I felt my bedcover pulled back, the gently massaging hands on my arms and legs and chest, and a pleasant drowsiness overcame me—a drowsiness that I am still unable to fight off. I woke up, as I still do after her visits, with my skin supple and thick with the scent of Nivea.

58   I often want to tell Nkiru that her mother visits weekly in the Harmattan and less often during the rainy season, but she will finally have reason to come here and bundle me back with her to America and I will be forced to live a life cushioned by so much convenience that it is sterile. A life littered with what we call "opportunities." A life that is not for me. I wonder what would have happened if we had won the war. Perhaps we would not be looking overseas for those opportunities, and I would not need to worry about our grandson who does not speak Igbo, who, the last time he visited, did not understand why he was expected to say "good afternoon" to strangers, because in his world one has to justify simple courtesies. But who can tell? Perhaps nothing would have changed even if we had won.

59   "How does your daughter like America?" Ikenna asked.

60   "She is doing very well."

61   "And you said she is a doctor?"

62   "Yes." I felt that Ikenna deserved to be told more, or maybe that the tension had not quite **abated,** so I said, "She lives in a small town in Connecticut, near Rhode Island. The hospital board had advertised for a doctor, and when she came they took one look at her and said they did not want a foreigner. But she is American-born—you see, we had her while at Berkeley—and so they were forced to let her stay." I chuckled, and hoped Ikenna would laugh along, too. But he did not.

63   "Ah, yes. At least it's not as bad now as it was for us. Remember what it was like schooling in *oyibo*-land[6] in the late fifties?" he asked.

64   I nodded to show I remembered, although Ikenna and I could not have had the same experience as students overseas; he is an Oxford man while I did not school in England at all.

65   "The Staff Club is a shell of what it used to be," Ikenna said. "I went there this morning."

---

6. ***oyibo*-land** country of Western or white people

NOTES

66 "I haven't been there in so long. Even before I retired, it got to the point where I felt too old and out of place there. These greenhorns⁷ are inept. Nobody is teaching. Nobody has fresh ideas. It is university politics, politics, politics, while students buy grades with money or their bodies."

67 "Is that right?"

68 "Oh, yes. Things have fallen. Senate meetings have become personality cult battles. It's terrible. Remember Josephat Udeana?"

69 "The great dancer."

70 I was taken aback for a moment because it had been so long since I thought of Josephat as he was in those days, by far the best ballroom dancer we had on campus. "Yes, yes, he was," I said, and I felt a strange gratitude that Ikenna's memories were frozen at a time when I still thought Josephat to be a man of integrity. "Josephat was vice chancellor for six years and ran this place like his father's chicken coop. Money disappeared and then we would see new cars stamped with the names of foreign foundations that did not exist. Some people went to court, but nothing came of that. He dictated who would be promoted and who would be stagnated. In short, the man acted like a solo University Council. This present vice chancellor is following him faithfully. I have not been paid my pension since I retired, you know."

71 "And why isn't anybody doing something about all this? Why?" Ikenna asked, and for the briefest moment the old Ikenna was there, in the voice, the outrage, and I was reminded again that this was an intrepid man. Perhaps he would pound his fist on a nearby tree.

72 "Well," I shrugged. "Many of the lecturers are changing their official dates of birth. They go to Personnel Services and bribe somebody and add five years. Nobody wants to retire."

73 "It is not right. Not right at all."

74 "It's all over the country, really, not just here." I shook my head in that slow, side-to-side way that my people have perfected when referring to things of this sort, as if to say that the situation is, sadly, **ineluctable.**

75 "I was reading about fake drugs in the papers; it looks serious," Ikenna said, and I immediately thought it too convenient of a coincidence, his bringing up fake drugs. Selling expired medicine is the latest plague of our country, and if Ebere had not died the way she did, I would have found this to be a normal segue in the conversation. But I was suspicious. I wondered if Ikenna had heard how Ebere died and wanted to get me to talk about it, to exhibit a little more of the lunacy that he had already glimpsed.

7. **greenhorns** a newcomer or inexperienced person

76 "Fake drugs are horrible," I said gravely, determined to say nothing else. But I may have been wrong about Ikenna's plot, because he did not pursue the subject. He asked me, "So what do you do these days?" He seemed curious, as if he were wondering just what kind of life I am leading here, alone, in a university town that is now a withered skin of what it used to be, waiting for a pension that never comes. I smiled and said that I am resting; is that not what one does on retiring?

77 Sometimes I drop by to visit my old friend Professor Maduewe. I take walks across the faded field of Freedom Square with the flame trees. Or along Ikejiani Avenue, where the motorcycles speed past, students perched astride, often coming too close to one another as they avoid the gaping potholes. In the rainy season, when I discover a new gully where the rains have eaten at the land, I feel a flush of accomplishment. I read newspapers. I eat well; my househelp, Harrison, comes five days a week and his onugbu soup is unparalleled. I talk to our daughter often, and when my phone goes dead every other week, I hurry to NITEL to bribe somebody to get it repaired. I unearth old, old journals in my dusty, cluttered study. I breathe in deeply the scent of the neem trees that screen my house from Professor Eboh's—a scent that is supposed to be medicinal, although I am no longer sure what it is said to cure. I do not go to church; I stopped going after Ebere first visited, because I was no longer uncertain. It is our diffidence about the afterdeath that leads us to religion. So on Sundays I sit on the veranda and watch the vultures stamp on my roof, and I imagine that they glance down in bemusement. "Is it a good life, Daddy?" Nkiru has taken to asking lately, with that faint, vaguely troubling American accent. It is not good or bad, I tell her, it is simply mine. And that is what matters.

78 I asked Ikenna to come back to my house with me, but he said he was on his way to Enugu, and when I asked if he would come by later, he made a vague motion with his hands that suggested assent. I know he will not come though. I will not see him again. I watched him walk away, this shriveled nut of a man, and I drove home thinking of the lives we might have had and the lives we did have, all of us who went to the Staff Club in those good days before the war.

79 Because of the minor scratch I had as I backed it out last week, I was careful parking my Mercedes in the garage. It is fifteen years old but runs quite well. I remember how excited Nkiru was when it was shipped back from Germany, where I bought it when I went to receive the Science Africana prize. It was the newest model. I did not know this, but her fellow teenagers did and they all came to look at it. Now, of course, everyone drives a Mercedes, imported secondhand from Cotonou. Ebere used to mock them, saying our car is old but much better than all those *tuke-tuke* things people are driving with no seatbelts. She still has that sense of humor. At her burial, when our grandson

read his poem, "Keep Laughing, Grandma," I thought the title perfect, and the childish words almost brought me to tears, despite my suspicion that Nkiru wrote most of them.

80   I looked around the yard as I walked indoors. Harrison does a little gardening, mostly watering in this season. The rose bushes are just dried stalks, but at least the hardy cherry bushes are a dusty green. I turned the TV on. It was still raining on the screen, although Doctor Otagbu's son, the bright young man who is reading electronics engineering, came last week to fix it. My satellite channels went off after the last thunderstorm. One can stay some weeks without BBC and CNN anyway, and the programs on NTA[8] are quite good when they are not showing half-naked, dancing American teenagers. It was NTA, some days ago, that broadcast an interview with yet another man accused of importing fake drugs—typhoid fever medicine in this case. "My drugs don't actually kill people," he said, helpfully, facing the camera as if in an appeal to the masses. "It is only that they will not cure your illness." I turned the TV off because I could no longer bear to see the man's blubbery lips. But I was not offended, not as egregiously as I would have been if Ebere did not visit. I only hoped that he would not be let free to go off once again to China or India or wherever they go to import expired medicine that will not actually kill people, but will only make sure the illness kills them.

81   I am sitting now in my study, where I helped Nkiru with her difficult secondary school math assignments. The armchair leather is solid and worn. The pastel paint above the bookshelves is peeling. I wonder why it never came up, throughout the years, that Ikenna did not die. True, we did sometimes hear stories of men who had been thought dead and who walked into their compounds months, even years, after January 1970; I can only imagine the quantity of sand poured on broken men by family members suspended between disbelief and hope. But we hardly talked about the war. When we did it was with an implacable vagueness, as if what mattered were not that we crouched in muddy bunkers during air raids after which we buried corpses with bits of pink on their charred skin, not that we ate cassava peels and watched our children's bellies swell, but that we survived. It was a **tacit** agreement among all of us, the survivors of Biafra. Even Ebere and I, who had debated our first child's name, Zik, for months, agreed very quickly on Nkiru: what is ahead is better. We will look forward, forward, forward.

"Ghosts" by Chimamanda Adichie. Copyright © 2009 by Chimamanda Ngozi Adichie, used by permission of The Wylie Agency LLC

---

8. **NTA** Nigerian Television Authority

First Read

Read the short story "Ghosts." After you read, complete the Think Questions below.

1. Why did James Nwoye think that Ikenna Okoro was dead? Cite evidence from the text.

2. What did James and his wife see when they visited their old home, and how did it affect them? Support your response with evidence from the text.

3. What is life in Nigeria like in the aftermath of the war? Cite specific examples from the text as support.

4. The narrator says about Ikenna Okoro, "There was an uncertainty about him, a **diffidence** that seemed alien, very unlike the man who so easily got people to *act*." Using contextual clues from this passage, explain what the word *diffidence* means.

5. The adjective *taciturn* is commonly used to describe someone who is quiet or withdrawn. With this in mind, what do you think a "**tacit** agreement" might be? Explain, in your own words, the meaning of this term in the final paragraph of the story.

Please note that excerpts and passages in the StudySync® library and this workbook are intended as touchstones to generate interest in an author's work. The excerpts and passages do not substitute for the reading of entire texts, and StudySync® strongly recommends that students seek out and purchase the whole literary or informational work in order to experience it as the author intended. Links to online resellers are available in our digital library. In addition, complete works may be ordered through an authorized reseller by filling out and returning to StudySync® the order form enclosed in this workbook.

Reading & Writing Companion   **413**

Skill:
Textual Evidence

Use the Checklist to analyze Textual Evidence in "Ghosts." Refer to the sample student annotations about Textual Evidence in the text.

••• CHECKLIST FOR TEXTUAL EVIDENCE

In order to support an analysis by citing evidence that is explicitly stated in the text, do the following:

✓ read the text closely and critically

✓ identify what the text says explicitly

✓ find the most relevant textual evidence that supports your analysis

✓ consider why an author explicitly states specific details and information

✓ cite the specific words, phrases, sentences, or paragraphs from the text that support your analysis

✓ determine where evidence in the text still leaves certain matters uncertain or unresolved

In order to interpret implicit meanings in a text by making inferences, do the following:

✓ combine information directly stated in the text with your own knowledge, experiences, and observations

✓ cite the specific words, phrases, sentences, or paragraphs from the text that led to and support this inference

In order to cite textual evidence to support an analysis of what the text says explicitly as well as inferences drawn from the text, consider the following questions:

✓ Have I read the text closely and critically?

✓ What inferences am I making about the text?

✓ What textual evidence am I using to support these inferences?

✓ Am I quoting the evidence from the text correctly?

✓ Does my textual evidence logically relate to my analysis or the inference I am making?

✓ Does evidence in the text still leave certain matters unanswered or unresolved? In what ways?

Skill:
Textual Evidence

Reread paragraph 58 of "Ghosts." Then, using the Checklist on the previous page, answer the multiple-choice questions below.

⟳ YOUR TURN

1. This question has two parts. First, answer Part A. Then, answer Part B.

   Part A: Which inference is best supported by this paragraph?

   ○ A. More opportunities exist in America than Nigeria.

   ○ B. The narrator does not want to live in America.

   ○ C. The narrator loves Nigeria despite its problems.

   ○ D. Nkiru does not know about her mother's ghost.

   Part B: Which evidence from the paragraph best supports the answer to Part A?

   ○ A. "I often want to tell Nkiru that her mother visits weekly in the Harmattan and less often during the rainy season . . ."

   ○ B. ". . . I will be forced to live a life cushioned by so much convenience that it is sterile."

   ○ C. "I wonder what would have happened if we had won the war."

   ○ D. "Perhaps we would not be looking overseas for those opportunities . . ."

Please note that excerpts and passages in the StudySync® library and this workbook are intended as touchstones to generate interest in an author's work. The excerpts and passages do not substitute for the reading of entire texts, and StudySync® strongly recommends that students seek out and purchase the whole literary or informational work in order to experience it as the author intended. Links to online resellers are available in our digital library. In addition, complete works may be ordered through an authorized reseller by filling out and returning to StudySync® the order form enclosed in this workbook.

Reading & Writing
Companion

415

Skill:
Story Elements

Use the Checklist to analyze Story Elements in "Ghosts." Refer to the sample student annotations about Story Elements in the text.

Copyright © BookheadEd Learning, LLC

••• CHECKLIST FOR STORY ELEMENTS

In order to identify the impact of the author's choices regarding how to develop and relate elements of a story or drama, note the following:

- ✓ where and when the story takes place, who the main characters are, and the main conflict, or problem, in the plot

- ✓ the order of the action

- ✓ how the characters are introduced and developed

- ✓ the impact that the author's choice of setting has on the characters and their attempt to solve the problem

To analyze the impact of the author's choices regarding how to develop and relate elements of a story or drama, consider the following questions:

- ✓ How do the author's choices affect the story elements? The development of the plot?

- ✓ How does the setting influence the characters?

- ✓ Which elements of the setting affect the plot and, in particular, the problem the characters face and must solve?

- ✓ Are there any flashbacks or other story elements that have an effect on the development of events? How does the author's choice of using a flashback affect this development?

- ✓ How does the author introduce and develop characters in the story? Why do you think the author made these choices?

Skill:
Story Elements

Reread paragraph 81 of "Ghosts." Then, using the Checklist on the previous page, answer the multiple-choice questions below.

⟳ YOUR TURN

1. This question has two parts. First, answer Part A. Then, answer Part B.

   Part A: How do the setting details in this paragraph help the reader better understand the characters?

   - ○ A. The details about the horrors of the war help the reader understand why the characters look toward the future instead of the past.
   - ○ B. The details about James's study help the reader understand how much time has passed since James experienced the horrible war.
   - ○ C. The details about dead men returning after the war help the reader understand that James is not the only character who sees ghosts.
   - ○ D. The details about the horrors of the war help the reader understand what killed Zik and how Ikenna survived.

   Part B: Which evidence best supports the answer to Part A?

   - ○ A. "I am sitting now in my study, where I helped Nkiru with her difficult secondary school math assignments."
   - ○ B. "True, we did sometimes hear stories of men who had been thought dead and who walked into their compounds months, even years, after January 1970 . . ."
   - ○ C. "When we did it was with an implacable vagueness, as if what mattered were not that we crouched in muddy bunkers during air raids after which we buried corpses with bits of pink on their charred skin . . .
   - ○ D. Even Ebere and I, who had debated our first child's name, Zik, for months, agreed very quickly on Nkiru . . ."

2. Which statement best explains why the author ends the story with this paragraph?

   - ○ A. The paragraph refers back to the beginning of story when James wants to throw sand at Ikenna.
   - ○ B. The paragraph emphasizes the relationship between Ebere and James that is the focus of the story.
   - ○ C. The paragraph explains that Ikenna is not the only one to return after so many years.
   - ○ D. The paragraph clarifies some of James's past and his outlook on the present.

Reading & Writing Companion

GHOSTS

Close Read

Reread "Ghosts." As you reread, complete the Skills Focus questions below. Then use your answers and annotations from the questions to help you complete the Write activity.

◎ SKILLS FOCUS

1. Identify a detail that introduces the social and economic setting, and explain why this detail is effective in helping readers understand the theme of the story.

2. Identify James's reaction to his interaction with the men he buys groundnuts and bananas from. Infer and explain an implicit meaning evident in the textual evidence. Does anything still remain unresolved?

3. Highlight a passage in which James speaks in Igbo, and explain how the relationship between characterization and point of view in the passage helps develop a theme in the story.

4. Identify an example of vivid sensory language, and explain how it helps shape the reader's perception of characters and events in the story.

5. Reread paragraphs 42–51. In what ways has the change caused by war brought these two men closer together and helped them better understand each other? In what ways has the war separated them and increased their differences?

✎ WRITE

COMPARE AND CONTRAST: In many ways, "Ghosts" has two main characters: James Nwoye, the narrator, and Ikenna Okoru, James's former colleague. How are the personalities and experiences of these two men different? How are they similar? What do their stories, taken together, tell you about the Nigerian Civil War and its inevitable effects on Nigeria? Support your ideas with textual evidence.

ARK

FICTION
Ehud Lavski and Yael Nathan
2006

Introduction

Author Ehud Lavski and artist Yael Nathan of EL Comics tell the tale of one man's determined mission to preserve wildlife as we know it in their graphic story "ARK." In a world plagued by mutation and illness, one man makes a determined effort to preserve wildlife—and the world—as we know it. With his body plagued by illness, will he succeed? Or will the world be irrevocably changed?

"It's a roll of the dice every time. This time it worked."

1

2

Reading & Writing Companion

3

4

5

7

8

✏ WRITE

NARRATIVE: If you are familiar with graphic novels or comics, you know that each panel communicates an idea, even if there are no words on it. The art does most of the work. Create your own narrative in the form of a graphic novel, like "ARK." You don't need to write the whole story, just three panels. Alternatively, you could illustrate a story you read in class or a favorite story you read on your own time. Share your work with the class and see if they understand what is happening on the page.

Introduction

Two experts in the field of psychology, Mahzarin Banaji (b. 1956) and Anthony Greenwald (b. 1939), based their book, *Blindspot: Hidden Biases of Good People*, on "Project Implicit." Project Implicit details their research on how people have implicit biases that affect behavior, whether consciously or not. Their "IAT," or "implicit-association test," was collaboratively created in 1995 and has risen in popularity as people have become more open to exploring their hidden biases of gender, class, race, and culture. Banaji and Greenwald are pioneers in cognition, paving the way for deeper thought into thought itself, as seen in the following excerpt.

"Of course, honesty may be an overrated virtue."

Blue Lies

1   At some time, all of us will give answers that we know are untrue, for the paradoxical and totally strange reason that we actually believe the answer to be *more essentially truthful* than the actual truth. The phrase "true blue" inspired the color for this category of untruths. Some examples:

2   Q8. *Did you vote in last Tuesday's election?*

3   (Survey researcher to regular voter who neglected to vote last Tuesday but who answers yes because—"truth be told"—he or she is a "regular voter")

4   Q9. *Did you do all of the reading for the last test?*

5   (Professor to student who received a low grade on an exam and did not read the assigned texts but who answers yes)

6   Q10. *What radio station do you listen to?*

7   (Asked of a guest at an elite dinner gathering who answers "public radio," but whose car has only two preset stations, one for talk radio, the other for pop music)

8   Those who answer these three questions in known-untrue fashion may intend their answers to communicate a truth deeper than the actual facts would **indicate**, as in: *I am the type of person who votes regularly (even though I was too busy to vote last Tuesday); who always does the assigned work (but didn't last week because I had too many assignments from other courses); who shares the cultural and political values associated with public radio (but listens to it only when what's on the other stations is boring).*

9   We can justify blue lies such as these by observing that they allow others to see us as we (honestly) see ourselves. But this is a charitable view. Less charitably, these blue lies are ploys to produce favorable regard by others.

Social psychologists know this ploy well, and have a telling name for it—*impression management*.

10   Impression management even comes into play when people are answering questions that do not seem to permit much wiggle room. If someone wants to know your age, height, and weight, what would you say? Although many people provide entirely accurate answers, researchers have repeatedly found that **substantial** minorities err when asked about these basic facts on survey questionnaires. And the errors are systematic: With the exception of answers provided by the very young, the very thin, and the very tall, the errors are virtually all in the direction of being younger, lighter in weight, and taller than can be verified with the aid of birth certificates, scales, and rulers.

11   Impression management has become well recognized as a problem in survey research. Survey participants will often produce less-than-true responses even when they know that their answers will just be fed into a computer and no researcher will ever see or hear them—even when they have been further assured that after their responses have been recorded, no one will be able to identify them as the source of their answers.

12   The problem of distortion of survey data by impression management is so great that survey researchers have devised a strategy to identify and weed out those survey participants who appear most likely to give responses shaped by their desire to make a favorable impression. The strategy calls for inserting some true-false catch questions such as the following into a survey.

13   Q11. *I am always courteous, even to people who are disagreeable.*

14   Q12. *I always apologize to others for my mistakes.*

15   Q13. *I would declare everything at customs, even if I knew that I could not possibly be found out.*

16   Researchers assume that many of those who answer "true" to these questions are impression managers because, for most people, full honesty should produce "false" to all three. After all, few people are *always* courteous, few people *always* apologize for mistakes, and few are so **scrupulously** honest that they would make a statement that could cost them money if they could avoid the financial penalty through a minor deception that would remain undetected. It is a more than mildly ironic comment on the **vicissitudes** of self-report survey methods that social scientists credit the person who admits to cheating at customs with greater honesty than the one who claims not to cheat.

17   If you think that you could honestly answer "true" to all three of Q11, Q12, and Q13, it is possible that you are among the very small group of completely

NOTES

Reading & Writing
Companion

honest people on the planet. Of course, honesty may be an overrated virtue. If you decided to report all of your flaws to friends and to apply a similar standard of total honesty when talking to others about their shortcomings, you might soon find that you no longer have friends. Should you have any doubts about this, recall Q2 (*Do I look fat in these jeans?*). The white lie **typically** offered in response to Q2 can also be seen as a reflected blue lie, providing a mirror in which the questioner can find welcome agreement with his or her own too-good-to-be-true perception (that is, *I look just great*). Tamper with that self-regard at your own risk.

18   Our daily social lives demand, and generally receive, repeated lubrication with a certain amount of untruthfulness, which keeps the gears of social interaction meshing smoothly.

Excerpted from *Blindspot: Hidden Biases of Good People* by Mahzarin R. Banaji and Anthony G. Greenwald, published by Delacorte Press.

✏ WRITE

PERSONAL NARRATIVE: Banaji and Greenwald describe lies that people tell because they believe they more wholly represent the truth than the actual truth, even though that sounds illogical. In a narrative, describe a "blue lie" (as defined by the authors) of your own. Your narrative should include the reasoning behind your lie—such as why you believed it to be more "true" than the actual truth— whom you told it to, and what happened as a result.

News Literacy in the Misinformation Age

INFORMATIONAL TEXT
The News Literacy Project
in partnership with StudySync
2018

Introduction

This essay offers insights into the numerous types of misinformation that circulate in today's information ecosystem, and how false or misleading information often tries to exploit our biases. It also offers insight into the practice of journalism, so young people can imagine how stories they read on a daily basis come to fruition. The News Literacy Project is a nonprofit that works with schools, libraries, and media organizations to teach young people about how to navigate news and information in the current digital era. Their resources are nonpartisan and are offered online, in professional development courses, and in their weekly newsletter.

"Why does it matter if people create, share or believe false information?"

NOTES

The Case for News Literacy

1   If you decided to look at every single post by every single person on Facebook on a typical day — spending just one second on each post — how long do you think it would take you?

2   Let's do the math: About 1 billion status updates are made on Facebook every day. Each day is made up of 86,400 seconds — 60 seconds x 60 minutes x 24 hours. So if you did nothing else — no time for eating, no time for sleeping, no time for TV or movies, no time for school — it would take you . . . 11,574 days, or 32 years. *Thirty-two years*, just to glance through *one day's* worth of Facebook posts!

3   Now, add to this pile of status updates everything else that is created and shared in a typical day — every tweet, news report, blog post, meme, comment, photo, video and podcast — and you'd need several lifetimes to see it all. If you tried to actually read, watch, listen to and think about just one day's worth of news and information, you would need several thousand lifetimes.

4   It's not only the amount of information that's challenging; it's also the complexity of what we're reading, watching and hearing. Some of this information is, without question, credible. Some is incomplete, like raw videos, images or documents. Some is often misleading, like strong partisan opinions or branded content. And some of it is just plain fake: fake accounts on social media, faked videos, fake leaked documents, fake tweets, faked pictures, fake quotes and, of course, "fake news."

5   This avalanche of information is hitting us at a time when anyone with internet access can, in a growing number of ways, amplify his or her voice to reach a global audience. Anyone with a smartphone can document an event and share it with the world. More people than ever before have the most powerful tools in human history to search for, evaluate, comment on and spread information.

6   Learning how to manage the challenges of this information landscape and make the most of its opportunities are essential skills for today's citizens — especially when it comes to discerning fact from fiction. After all, citizens hold the power in a democracy. They determine what form their government will take by deciding which issues they think are most important and then voting for the candidates whose ideas and policies best address those issues. To do this effectively — to truly participate — citizens need accurate, reliable information about those issues, those ideas, those policies and those candidates.

7   Here's the good news: Finding news and information has never been easier, and access is expanding to more people every day.

8   But here's the bad news: As we search for what we need, we also encounter a lot of unverified, misleading or inaccurate information — some of which is actually designed to trick us into believing and sharing things that aren't true. Those materials can cause people to make bad decisions about all kinds of things — their health, their education options, their career choices or their vote. If our neighbors or fellow citizens believe a piece of false information, their resulting votes or decisions can indirectly affect us too. And while people have been fighting false information for a long time (after all, rumors, hoaxes and propaganda are nothing new), they now need a new set of skills to help them spot falsehoods and know what's true and what's not.

9   Becoming news literate gives citizens the skills and habits they need to recognize credible information, and to spot misleading or deceptive language or images that could trick them into forming false beliefs. It helps them to evaluate the purpose of information, to understand the signs that a piece of information has been checked, and to identify when something can or cannot be trusted. And, most importantly, it enables them to make informed choices that empower their voices and that strengthen our democracy by helping it meet the needs of its people.

10   What do you think? Think about all the information you consume in a day. Do you know which pieces of information are credible? What are the most exciting — and the most challenging — aspects of today's information landscape? What is the role of credible information in a democracy?

The Misinformation Age

11   A shaky video, taken by a handheld camera, of three friends using their cell phones to pop a pile of popcorn kernels. A report that Pope Francis has endorsed Donald Trump for president. A description in a well-known newspaper of a competitive poodle-clipping event at the 1900 Olympics in Paris.

12   Each of these seemed convincing to thousands of people, but each of them is false:

- The popcorn video was a hoax staged by an internet marketing agency hired by a maker of Bluetooth headsets. Designed to appear raw and authentic, it racked up millions of views on YouTube before it was revealed to be fake.

- The item about the pope and Trump was the most widely shared story on Facebook in the final months of the 2016 presidential campaign. It originated on WTOE5news.com (a self-described "fantasy news website" whose name sounds like it could be a local television news site) and was picked up by EndingtheFed.com, an anonymously-registered website that had several of the most widely shared items on Facebook during the campaign (all of which were fake).

- The article about poodle-clipping at the Olympics was published by The Telegraph, a well-known British news organization, as an April Fool's Day hoax, then shared by others who mistook it as real.

13   These are all examples of misinformation, a phenomenon so common on the internet that people frequently joke about it. In fact, one of the most popular memes about misinformation is the below image. See if you can get the joke:

"YOU CAN'T BELIEVE EVERYTHING YOU HEAR ON THE INTERNET."
- ABE LINCOLN, 1868

14   Despite the fact that just about everyone who uses the internet (about half the world's population) knows how unreliable information found online can be, many people still get fooled every day.

15   Why does misinformation continue to thrive? The primary reason may be this: On the internet, anyone can publish anything. This is beneficial and empowering for the millions of people who have access to more than a million terabytes of information and, potentially, a global audience for their

stories and ideas. It also means that much of the information found online has never been checked for accuracy.

16   Second, misinformation often takes advantage of our cognitive biases — our blind spots as human beings. It frequently causes us to have a strong emotional reaction — such as fear, or curiosity, or anger — that can make us feel or hope that something is true before we've taken the time to determine whether that expectation is reasonable. So we tend to filter the world of information through the biased lens of our own beliefs, noticing only those details and ideas that support what we want to believe.

17   This emotional reaction also makes us act faster than we should: We click, comment and share before we consider the stakes of sharing something we haven't verified — and most of the platforms and tools we use to engage with information make it easy to do this.

18   There's also an increasing number of free or low-cost ways to create convincing (but false) information: screenshot tools, photo- and video-editing software, graphic design tools, website hacking tools, fake tweet generators and thousands of social sharing and discussion sites and online communities where falsehoods, hoaxes and rumors can be released to specific audiences and catch fire.

19   Creating and spreading misinformation can be enormously profitable. Purveyors of "fake news" and other forms of clickbait can make tens of thousands of dollars in ad revenue a month from the traffic to their websites generates. Hoaxers and conspiracy theorists on YouTube can make significant amounts of money in the same way. Other people create or share misinformation to cause chaos, to troll others or for internet "karma" — for likes, upvotes, shares, reactions and new followers.

20   Finally, misinformation is a cheap and effective way for political activists to **alter** debates about controversial issues. And once an idea gets loose in the ether — once it starts to get shared in a variety of places and go viral — it's nearly impossible to stop it. Research even suggests that repeating a false claim as part of a fact check can sometimes strengthen it. (This is due to a cognitive bias known as the illusory truth effect: Things we see or hear enough times stick with us, and start to seem true after a while.)

21   Sometimes false information gets loose because of an innocent mistake, or as a joke. Sometimes it's created to make money. Sometimes it's a deliberate distortion of an issue for political gain. Whatever the reason, misinformation can have very real effects, causing people to form faulty beliefs, lose faith in our institutions and in the very idea that anything is true, or take misguided action that can hurt others.

22 Luckily, as people become more and more aware of misinformation, they can also get better at **detecting** it. Here are some simple guidelines:

- Be aware when a piece of information causes you to have a strong emotional reaction. Pause and reflect on what you're feeling, and why.

- If the photo, claim or video seems too good (too outrageous, too amazing, too shocking, too terrible, or too infuriating) to be true, know that it probably isn't.

- Search for more information from credible sources. Do a quick search for the claim that is being made. Do links from fact-checking sites such as Snopes.com or FactCheck.org turn up? For an item on social media, read the comments (or, on Twitter, subsequent tweets) to see if anyone has verified it or found it to be false, and take a closer look at the account that shared it.

- Help to stop the spread of misinformation by correcting it wherever you see it being shared. Be respectful, be calm and cite high-quality sources that show why the information is false.

23 Think about what you've learned about misinformation. Think about the false information you've experienced firsthand. Why does it matter if people create, share or believe false information?

Standard Practice

24 When you read a news article, do you ever wonder what the reporter thinks or feels about the issue, event or **controversy** they are reporting on? Which political candidate do they support? Which policy do they prefer? Which sports team do they hope will win?

25 If you still have these kinds of questions after reading a news article, it means the writer is doing a good job keeping his or her personal views out of the story. Since the primary purpose of news is to inform, reporters have a duty to share information in as **unbiased** a way as possible. Even though all journalists have their own opinions, they typically strive to be as **neutral** as possible in their reporting — representing all **relevant** sides of a story without placing too much emphasis or authority where it doesn't belong.

26 How do journalists make sure they publish stories that are as neutral and fair as possible? All credible news outlets have a set of standards, or guidelines for how stories should be reported. Every newsroom's standards are different, but they share similar values, telling journalists to seek the truth and be fair and honest in reporting it.

27 When journalists report a story, they should pursue the "best **obtainable** version of the truth," as journalist Carl Bernstein puts it, by finding and verifying

all relevant details for their audience. This means they interview more than just one person — responsible journalists cite multiple credible sources, including documents when necessary, to get the full story.

28   For example, in reporting a workplace accident in which there are details to investigate but no clear indication of who is at fault, good journalists wouldn't just interview the person who got hurt. They would speak to eyewitnesses who saw the accident happen, they would offer the people involved an opportunity to comment on their guilt or innocence and they would contact the police for an official accident report. They would strive to treat every source fairly, giving each person a chance to respond to any allegations of wrongdoing. They would also locate and share any documents associated with the accident, which might include company memos or emails, police reports, independent reports like safety testing, chemical reports or NGO findings, relevant surveys and polls and video footage from the scene.

29   Journalists are also supposed to ensure that there are no conflicts of interest, which happen when a journalist has a strong personal connection with a group or issue that could get in the way of or compromise their ability to be fair in their reporting. In order to avoid conflicts of interest, journalists don't accept favors or gifts from sources. Most journalists also keep their political views private, and avoid participating in most political activities, such as protests or petitions. Some journalists don't even vote as a way of remaining as neutral as possible. Most news organizations also have standards, or guidelines, delineating the limitations on political activities that their journalists are expected to observe. If a conflict of interest is unavoidable, journalists should always be open and transparent about it.

30   How else do professional journalists seek to ensure accuracy and fairness in their work? They get help from other people — after a story is written, editors go through it and verify the story's facts by looking them up or double-checking the sources. These editors will also flag reporting they feel is unfair in some way, identify wording that is unclear or biased, or call attention to any critical sources or details that might be missing. Editors act as a second set of eyes, aiding reporters by showing them how their stories might be read and interpreted by other people.

31   Once an article is published, most news outlets have a way for their audience to contact them to report any errors or problems with the reporting — and credible news organizations will acknowledge their errors and correct them. Editors may read, respond to and publish these letters — whether they come in as mail, or electronically, through email or social media posts. Some news outlets also have public editors — or independent editors who point out ethical issues and problems with the reporting and publish this criticism on behalf of readers.

32 Despite all the standards in place for journalists, it is still important for news consumers to seek news from a variety of high quality sources. That way, they can quickly note which details have been verified by multiple news outlets, and get a more comprehensive understanding of the news of the day.

33 What do you think? How much do you know about the checks and balances journalists go through before they publish a story? How can news consumers tell whether journalism is well-reported or poorly-reported? How can news organizations improve their standards? What journalistic standards are most important? How do you think your local news organizations do in trying to follow these guidelines? What guidelines can journalists follow to help ensure that their reporting is accurate, fair and reliable?

✏ WRITE

PERSONAL RESPONSE: What do you think motivates certain sites or organizations to release fake news and information? What do you think makes individuals susceptible to believing fake news and information? And what measures can one take to avoid being fooled? Remember to support your ideas with textual evidence and your own background knowledge and experiences.

Honesty on Social Media

ARGUMENTATIVE TEXT
2018

Introduction

Social media is increasingly the domain where a larger and larger portion of human interactions take place. However, since online relationships require us to construct profiles or avatars to represent ourselves, they are inherently different from face-to-face relationships. Our online behaviors can easily lean toward deception, using anonymity to weave fantastical versions of our realities. Yet there are also aspects of the internet which hold us accountable to the truth of our offline lives. Both essays present strong opinions about the effects of social media on our interpersonal relationships. Which do you find more persuasive?

"The more we time we spend on social media platforms, the more deceptive we become."

NOTES

Social Media: Does It Make Us More or Less Honest?

Point: Of Course We're More Deceptive on Social Media. It's Easy To Be.

Skill: Media

The author refers to a chart from a reliable source that shows the increase in social media use. This is a good way of supporting the author's purpose of visually showing the growing impact of social media on people's lives.

1   Look up from your device of choice on any bus or train, in any coffee shop, or in any place where people are made to wait, and you will most certainly find someone—and likely many people—also staring at a cell phone, tablet, laptop, or other device. A great deal of our day-to-day lives is spent engaging with technology—increasingly to access social media platforms. A survey by the Pew Research Center reports that social media usage has grown dramatically for users of all age groups, even though around 50% of users do not trust social media companies to protect their data (Rainie). Consequently, the more we time we spend on social media platforms, the more deceptive we become.

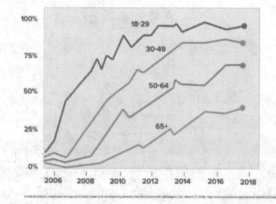

SOCIAL MEDIA USE HAS GROWN DRAMATICALLY

% OF US ADULTS WHO SAY THEY USE SOCIAL MEDIA SITES, BY AGE

Let's Be Honest: We Are All Liars

2   While most people consider themselves to be honest, most of us lie to benefit ourselves. In his book *The (Honest) Truth About Dishonesty*, behavioral economist Dan Ariely explains how people negotiate whether to be honest or dishonest: "This is where our amazing cognitive flexibility comes into play. Thanks to this human skill, as long as we cheat by only a little bit, we can benefit from cheating and still view ourselves as marvelous human beings" (27). Ariely's research shows that even within this framework, an individual's level of dishonesty can be affected by context—whether the reward is money or something that can be exchanged for money, whether there are reminders of moral standards, and whether someone within one's social group is dishonest, amongst many others.

3   People's behavior on social media, predictably, reflects this tendency to lie, but the context encourages dishonesty. In a recent study on dishonesty online, researchers found that while 32% of users on sites like Facebook reported being "always honest" in their posts, the expectations for honesty online are pretty **abysmal**: "Between 55 and 90 percent of participants believed others were lying at least some of the time about their age, gender, activities, interests, and appearance" (Misener). This belief affects users' behavior online: "[W]hen we think other people are lying online, we're more likely to lie ourselves" (Misener). This makes social media platforms spaces in which dishonesty can easily become commonplace.

Fonder Hearts Encouraged: Deception in Dating

4   One of the more common uses of social media is to attract a mate and to communicate with him or her. People often manipulate how they present themselves for both purposes. There are, of course, the smaller lies— exaggerating one's height, posting only flattering or modified photos of oneself, etc. But social media can also lead to more serious deception. In fact, this practice has become so widespread that it has a name—*catfishing*, or creating fake profiles on social media sites to deceive others. One example of this was the case of Manti Te'o, the Notre Dame football player whose long-distance girlfriend—"Lennay Kekua," who apparently died during their courtship—turned out to be the machinations of a young man named Ronaiah Tuiasosopo (Zeman). Through the use of Facebook, Twitter, Instagram, phone calls, and photos of an acquaintance, Tuiasosopo managed to convince Te'o to fall in love with his imaginative creation, a feat that would have been a cumbersome, **formidable** challenge, if not impossible, had it been attempted face-to-face. But through the use of technology, including social media, Tuiasosopo managed to deceive Te'o for more than two years.

NOTES

Skill:
Informational
Text Elements

The author introduces a paradox in the section heading, and then uses the first sentence to explain the paradox. The author then supports this idea and elaborates on it with evidence from an expert.

Skill:
Informational
Text Elements

The author explains how social media pushes usually honest people toward dishonesty. The author also uses data and evidence here to support this idea, and connects back to the section heading.

Please note that excerpts and passages in the StudySync® library and this workbook are intended as touchstones to generate interest in an author's work. The excerpts and passages do not substitute for the reading of entire texts, and StudySync® strongly recommends that students seek out and purchase the whole literary or informational work in order to experience it as the author intended. Links to online resellers are available in our digital library. In addition, complete works may be ordered through an authorized reseller by filling out and returning to StudySync® the order form enclosed in this workbook.

Reading & Writing
Companion

443

Marketing and Social Media: Skilled Deception for Profit

5   The advent of social media has also opened up new ways for people and businesses to manipulate media and the public to their benefit. In his book *Trust Me, I'm Lying: Confessions of a Media Manipulator*, Ryan Holiday explains how he exploits bloggers to promote products and clients. Holiday explains that bloggers depend on traffic to generate profit and attract attention to their blogs, which they hope to use to either secure better jobs or to generate enough income so they can become self-employed. Holiday, aware that the bloggers are willing to do many things to achieve these outcomes, uses these motives to exploit them to his advantage. One way he does this is by providing them with just enough information to produce a provocative headline—and clicks, of course: "If I am giving them an official comment on behalf of a client, I leave room for them to speculate by not fully addressing the issue. . . . I trick the bloggers, and they trick their readers. This arrangement is great for the traffic-hungry bloggers, for me, and for my attention-seeking clients" (71). While this arrangement works for those who stand to make a profit from consumers' attention, it promotes **ambiguity** and scandal at the expense of informative, meaningful communication via social media.

Is It Time to Log Off?

6   While social media offers us opportunities to connect with others near and far for reasons both common and quirky—to share our lives with friends and family, to find love, or to share our love of fan fiction—it is easily manipulated. Whether we tell small lies or big ones on social media, deception does not help us create meaningful connections with one another. That presents us with an urgent and important decision as social media becomes an integral part of our lives and threatens to normalize dishonesty: Do we abandon social media, or do we relinquish our morality.

"[Social media] encourages us to be honest precisely because we are navigating a relationship."

Counterpoint: When Everyone's Watching, It's Too Hard to Lie

8   Thirty years ago, we would have had to ask around—or wait until the next high school reunion—to reconnect with a long-lost friend; now a quick search on Facebook or Instagram will likely do the trick and, in the process, lead us to other acquaintances we used to know but may have forgotten about. Social media, like many advancements, has profoundly changed the way we engage with others, and because it allows us to establish or develop relationships, even if it is not face-to-face, it encourages us to be honest precisely because we are navigating a relationship.

Progress Is Always Imperfect

9   Some argue that social media makes us more dishonest because it establishes a connection that can be easily manipulated. Social media, like any other advancement, is not a perfect tool; some people will surely misuse it, but that does not **negate** its usefulness. People who think that the use of social media makes us more dishonest are simply clinging to romanticized notions of how we ought to engage with one another. They oppose technological advancement and only want to live in the past. Unwilling to accept virtual connections as valid, they are simply not interested in the possibilities that new technologies offer us.

NOTES

When We're Connected, We're More Honest

10 Social media helps us easily connect to more people—family, friends, and colleagues, sometimes on the same platform—and it is a repository of information and exchanges. As each new avenue of communication opens, the pressure to conduct oneself honestly and ethically grows. These connections and exchanges—and their visibility to others—affect our behavior. Psychologist Pamela Routledge explains the significance of this phenomenon: "Social media relationships operate with the same rules as offline ones. They are social contracts that thrive on honesty and are destroyed by deceit. . . . New media does a lot of things. One of them is that it makes it hard to keep secrets a secret. Think of that as making people accountable for their behavior."

11 Facebook is a good example of a social media platform whose popularity can help encourage honesty, at least by its users. In 2018 studies of social media by the Pew Research Center and We Are Social showed that Facebook reigned supreme among social media platforms:

- Facebook is the most popular social media platform in the world, with 2.167 billion users (Kemp).

- In the United States, Facebook is used by 68% of adults, and about 74% of those adults who use Facebook visit the site at least once a day (Smith and Anderson).

- Facebook has seen an increase of 20% in users 65 and older in the year before the study was published (Kemp).

- Of popular social media sites, Facebook has the highest percentage of users who log on at least once a day, with many users visiting several times a day (Smith and Anderson).

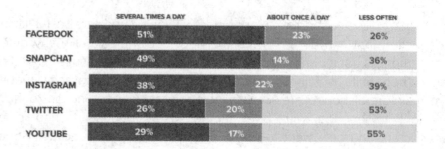

A MAJORITY OF FACEBOOK, SNAPCHAT AND INSTAGRAM USERS VISIT THESE PLATFORMS ON A DAILY BASIS

AMONG US ADULTS WHO SAY THEY USE _____, THE % WHO USE EACH SITE:

	SEVERAL TIMES A DAY	ABOUT ONCE A DAY	LESS OFTEN
FACEBOOK	51%	23%	26%
SNAPCHAT	49%	14%	36%
INSTAGRAM	38%	22%	39%
TWITTER	26%	20%	53%
YOUTUBE	29%	17%	55%

Credit: Social Media in 2018, Pew Research Center, Washington, D.C. (March 1, 2018), http://assets.pewresearch.org/wp-content/uploads/sites/14/2018/03/01105133/PI_2018.03.01_Social-Media_FINAL.pdf

12 This **ubiquity**, both the increasing number of people who use the platform and the frequency of their use, is not without consequence: billions of people are using a platform that connects them to other people who know details about their lives, which creates an increasingly large pool of people who are adept at using the internet, including social media, to fact-check a post and catch users in a lie. This puts pressure on people to be careful about what they say in a space that so many people have access to.

13 LinkedIn, a professional social media platform, has a similar effect. In his research on dishonesty online, Professor Jeffrey Hancock examined people's behavior on LinkedIn and found that "LinkedIn resumes were less deceptive about claims that could be verified by people in a person's social network, such as an applicant's prior work experience and job" (281). While this did not prohibit all deception, it did deter deception about the more important elements of a resume.

When We're Honest, We're More Connected

14 Social media can also provide a space within which sharing a difficult, personal matter is easier, and that opportunity to be open and honest can help us connect with others. PostSecret, for example, allows people to anonymously share their secrets: individuals send in their secrets, and those secrets are anonymously posted on several social media platforms. This act of sharing helps both those who send in the secrets and those who read them on social media platform. Sometimes people write in to reflect upon secrets they have shared, and sometimes others who read the secrets are inspired to share something related. Even if they do not share something themselves, individuals get to connect with an experience, and that can help them feel validated or help them address a problem in their own lives. By creating a space within which people can be honest, these platforms help people connect around authentic experiences.

Social Media Helps Keeps Us Connected and Honest

15 It is easy to dismiss virtual spaces as free-for-alls where people can do their worst with anonymity and no consequences, but that is not an accurate reflection of those sort of spaces. Social media helps foster real, meaningful relationships; dishonesty within those spaces can damage those relationships just as honesty can help strengthen them. Social media is like the ocean. It is vast and deep and teeming with life, giving us opportunities to find meaning if we conduct online relationships with honesty and dependability. Online relationships are too important to risk losing them through dishonesty.

First Read

HONESTY ON SOCIAL MEDIA

Read "Honesty on Social Media." After you read, complete the Think Questions below.

☁ THINK QUESTIONS

1. When it comes to online interactions, the Point essay identifies a significant difference between people's assessments of their own honesty versus the honesty of others. What is this difference, and how might it affect human behavior? Explain.

2. Using information from the Point and Counterpoint essays, briefly describe how both authors believe people are affected by our increased use of social media. Cite specific evidence to support your answer.

3. What does the author of the Counterpoint essay think about the effect of anonymity on our ability to make genuine, deep connections on the internet? Explain briefly, citing evidence.

4. Based on context clues in the fourth paragraph of the Point essay, what do you think the word **formidable** means? Write your best definition of *formidable* here, explaining how you arrived at its meaning.

5. The Latin word *ambo* means "both," and the Latin word *agere* means "act" or "do." The combination of these roots gives us the noun **ambiguity.** With this in mind, try to infer the meaning of the word *ambiguity* as it is used in the fifth paragraph of the Point essay. Write your best definition of the word here, along with as many other words as you can think of that feature these Latin roots.

Skill:
Informational Text Elements

Use the Checklist to analyze Informational Text Elements in "Honesty on Social Media." Refer to the sample student annotations about Informational Text Elements in the text.

••• CHECKLIST FOR INFORMATIONAL TEXT ELEMENTS

In order to identify a complex set of ideas or sequence of events, note the following:

- ✓ key details in the text that provide information about individuals, events, and ideas

- ✓ interactions between specific individuals, ideas, or events

- ✓ important developments over the course of the text

- ✓ transition words and phrases that signal interactions between individuals, events, and ideas, such as *because, as a consequence,* or *as a result.*

- ✓ similarities and differences of types of information in a text

To analyze a complex set of ideas or sequence of events and explain how specific individuals, ideas, or events interact and develop over the course of the text, consider the following questions:

- ✓ How does the author present the information as a sequence of events?

- ✓ How does the order in which ideas or events are presented affect the connections between them?

- ✓ How do specific individuals, ideas, or events interact and develop over the course of the text?

- ✓ What other features, if any, help readers to analyze the events, ideas, or individuals in the text?

Please note that excerpts and passages in the StudySync® library and this workbook are intended as touchstones to generate interest in an author's work. The excerpts and passages do not substitute for the reading of entire texts, and StudySync® strongly recommends that students seek out and purchase the whole literary or informational work in order to experience it as the author intended. Links to online resellers are available in our digital library. In addition, complete works may be ordered through an authorized reseller by filling out and returning to StudySync® the order form enclosed in this workbook.

Reading & Writing Companion   **449**

Skill:
Informational Text Elements

Reread paragraphs 10–11 of "Honesty on Social Media." Then, using the Checklist on the previous page, answer the multiple-choice questions below.

⟳ YOUR TURN

1. Which sentence or phrase most directly supports the topic presented in the heading for this section?

   ○ A. "As each new avenue of communication opens, the pressure to conduct oneself honestly and ethically grows."

   ○ B. "'Social media relationships operate with the same rules as offline ones.'"

   ○ C. "'New media does a lot of things.'"

   ○ D. "In 2018 studies of social media by the Pew Research Center and We Are Social showed that Facebook reigned supreme among social media platforms:"

2. What idea is the evidence presented in the bulleted list intended to support?

   ○ A. More connections between people results in less honesty.

   ○ B. More connections between people results in more honesty.

   ○ C. Facebook is the most popular social media platform in the world.

   ○ D. Facebook has the highest percentage of users who log on at least once a day.

Skill:
Media

Use the Checklist to analyze Media in "Honesty on Social Media." Refer to the sample student annotations about Media in the text.

••• CHECKLIST FOR MEDIA

In order to determine how to integrate and evaluate multiple sources of information presented in different media or formats, note the following:

- ✓ the key elements in each source of information
- ✓ the various elements of a particular medium and how the parts are put together
- ✓ how each media or format, such as visually or quantitatively, presents the sources of information
- ✓ what information is included or excluded in each media presentation
- ✓ the audience of each media presentation and the author's purpose
- ✓ the reliability and credibility of each presentation

To integrate and evaluate multiple sources of information presented in different media or formats as well as in words in order to address a question or solve a problem, consider the following questions:

- ✓ How is each media presentation reliable or credible?
- ✓ How can you use each media presentation?
- ✓ How can you integrate multiple sources of information presented in different media or formats to address a question or solve a problem?

Skill:
Media

sync skills

Reread paragraph 11 of "Honesty on Social Media." Then, using the Checklist on the previous page, answer the multiple-choice questions below.

⟳ YOUR TURN

1. The main purpose of the chart is to show—

    ○ A. which social media platforms are most popular.

    ○ B. which social media platforms have the best fact-checking capabilities.

    ○ C. how often leading social media platforms are used by social media users.

    ○ D. how social media platforms can help detect the percentage of users who are dishonest.

2. The main reason the author includes the chart in the essay is to support the point that—

    ○ A. so many people use Facebook every day that users feel pressured not to lie.

    ○ B. Facebook, Snapchat, and Instagram are the most popular social media platforms.

    ○ C. Facebook and Snapchat have better fact-checking tools than other platforms do.

    ○ D. more than half of the users of the top three platforms use them at least daily.

3. The author's inclusion of this graphic feature is effective because it—

    ○ A. shows how many different social media sites there are.

    ○ B. reveals the different ways people use social media.

    ○ C. attempts to explain why social media sites can be damaging.

    ○ D. reinforces the claim that social media usage is widespread.

HONESTY ON SOCIAL MEDIA

Close Read

Reread "Honesty on Social Media." As you reread, complete the Skills Focus questions below. Then use your answers and annotations from the questions to help you complete the Write activity.

◎ SKILLS FOCUS

1. Identify the thesis in the first paragraph of "Point: Of Course We're More Deceptive on Social Media. It's Easy to Be." Write two reasons that the author offers in paragraphs 2–4 to support the thesis.

2. An appeal to logos is a persuasive method that seeks to convince readers by offering reasonable and sound evidence to support an argument. Such evidence includes quotations from reliable sources. Identify an appeal to logos in "Point: Of Course We're More Deceptive on Social Media. It's Easy to Be," and explain how it affects the way the text is read and understood.

3. Identify a print feature in the first four paragraphs of "Counterpoint: When Everyone's Watching, It's Too Hard to Lie." Explain how this feature helps the reader.

4. Identify a main idea in the last two paragraphs of "Counterpoint: When Everyone's Watching, It's Too Hard to Lie" and analyze how the author makes connections to this idea and develops it.

5. How are we different, now that the world of social media has changed our relationships to one another? Do you agree more with the Point or Counterpoint arguments when it comes to the way we approach honesty on social media? Has our relationship with social media changed the way we are honest in real life?

✏ WRITE

DISCUSSION: Which article did you find the most convincing? Do you believe we suspend our usual honesty when we are on social media? How do the graphs and media influence your opinion? Discuss how the writers' use of evidence and language contribute to the persuasiveness of the text.

Dawn Revisited

POETRY
Rita Dove
1999

Introduction

Rita Dove (b. 1952) is a widely heralded American poet, the second African American to receive the Pulitzer Prize for Poetry and the first African American ever to be named United States Poet Laureate. "Dawn Revisited" was first included in *On the Bus with Rosa Parks*, a finalist for the National Book Critics Circle Award in 1999. While most of her work contains historical elements, she imbues these events and perspectives with her own personal touch.

"How good to rise in sunlight, in the prodigal smell of biscuits"

1 Imagine you wake up
2 with a second chance: The blue jay
3 **hawks** his pretty **wares**
4 and the oak still stands, spreading
5 **glorious** shade. If you don't look back,

6 the future never happens.
7 How good to rise in sunlight,
8 in the **prodigal** smell of biscuits –
9 eggs and sausage on the grill.
10 The whole sky is yours

11 to write on, blown open
12 to a blank page. Come on,
13 shake a leg! You'll never know
14 who's down there, frying those eggs,
15 if you don't get up and see.

From *Collected Poems 1974–2004*, by Rita Dove (W.W. Norton, 2016). Reprinted by permission of the author.

✏ WRITE

NARRATIVE: Imagine you're the speaker, waking up to a new day. Write out the rest of your day as you would if you were starting a new chapter in a book. Use details from the poem to show how your past would affect your present—and your future.

Please note that excerpts and passages in the StudySync® library and this workbook are intended as touchstones to generate interest in an author's work. The excerpts and passages do not substitute for the reading of entire texts, and StudySync® strongly recommends that students seek out and purchase the whole literary or informational work in order to experience it as the author intended. Links to online resellers are available in our digital library. In addition, complete works may be ordered through an authorized reseller by filling out and returning to StudySync® the order form enclosed in this workbook.

Reading & Writing Companion   **455**

Commencement Address at the New School

ARGUMENTATIVE TEXT
Zadie Smith
2014

Introduction

Novelist and essayist Zadie Smith (b. 1975) was born and raised in London, daughter of a Jamaican mother and a white English father. Her first novel, *White Teeth*, published in 2000 when she was just 25 years old, was an international sensation, frequently appearing on lists of the best British novels of the last 50 years. In her commencement address to the 2014 graduates of the New School in New York City, she underlines the power and fulfillment of public participation over private isolation.

"Be thankful you get to walk so close to other humans. It's a privilege."

NOTES

Skill:
Summarizing

1 Welcome graduating class of 2014 and congratulations. You did it! You made it! How do you feel?

2 I guess I can only hazard a guess which means thinking back to my own graduation in England in 1997, and extrapolate from it. Did I feel like you? I should say first that some elements of the day were rather different. I wasn't in a stadium listening to a speech. I was in an eighteenth-century hall, kneeling before the dean who spoke Latin and held one of my fingers. Don't ask me why.

3 Still the essential facts were the same.

4 Like you I was finally with my degree and had made of myself—a graduate. Like you I now had two families, the old boring one that raised me, and an exciting new one consisting of a bunch of freaks I'd met in college.

5 But part of the delightful anxiety of graduation day was trying to find a way to blend these two tribes, with their differing haircuts and political views, and hygiene standards and tastes in music. I felt like a character in two different movies. And so old! I really believed I was ancient. Impossibly distant in experience from the freshmen only three years below. I was as likely to befriend a squirrel as a freshman. Which strange relationship with time is perhaps unique to graduates and toddlers. Nowadays, at age 38, if I meet somebody who's 41, I don't **conclude** that friendship is impossible between us. But when I was 21, the gap between me and an 18-year-old felt insurmountable. Just like my four-year-old daughter, who'd rather eat sand than have a playdate with a one-year-old.

6 And what else? Oh the love dramas. So many love dramas. Mine, other people's. They take up such a large part of college life it seems unfair not to have them properly reflected in the transcript. Any full account of my university years should include the fact that I majored in English literature, with a minor in drunken discussions about the difference between loving someone and being 'in love' with that person. What can I tell you, it was the '90s. We were really into ourselves. We were into self-curation. In the '90s, we even had a thing called 'Year of Trousers' which signified any kind of ethnic or exotic

The notes read: *Zadie Smith speaks to the 2014 graduates of the New School. To understand how they feel, she will rely on how she felt as a recent college graduate 17 years earlier.*

pants one brought back home from a distant (ideally third world) country. And these trousers were meant to alert to a passing stranger the fact that we'd been somewhere fascinating, and thus added further colour to our unique personalities.

7   Personally I couldn't afford the year off but I was very compelled by those trousers.

8   In short, the thing I wanted most in the world was to be an **individual**. I thought that's what my graduation signified, that I had gone from being one of the many, to one of the few. To one of the ones who would have 'choices' in life. After all my father didn't have many choices, his father had none at all. Unlike them, I had gone to university. I was a special individual. Looking back it's easy to diagnose a case of self-love. People are always accusing students of self-love, or self obsession. And this is a bit confusing because college surely encourages the habit. You concentrate on yourself in order to improve yourself. Isn't that the whole idea? And out of this process hopefully emerge strikingly competent individuals, with high self esteem, prepared for personal achievement.

9   When we graduate, though, things can get a little complicated. For how are we meant to think of this fabulous person, we've taken such care of creating? If university made me special did that mean I was worth more than my father, more than his father before him?

10   Did it mean I should expect more from life than them? Did I deserve more?

11   What does it really mean to be one of 'the few'?

12   Are the fruits of our education a sort of gift, to be circulated generously through the world, or are we to think of ourselves as pure **commodity**, on sale to the highest bidder? Well let's be honest, you're probably feeling pulled in several directions right now. And that's perfectly natural.

13   In the '90s, the post-graduation dilemma was usually presented to us as a straight ethical choice, between working for the banks, and doing selfless charitable work. The comic extremity of the choice I now see was perfectly deliberate. It meant you didn't have to take it too seriously. And so we peeled off from each other. Some of us, many of us, joined the banks. But those that didn't had no special cause to pat ourselves on the back. With rare exceptions, we all pursued self interest more or less. It wasn't a surprise. We'd been raised that way. Born in the seventies, we did not live through austerity, did not go to war like my father, or his father. For the most part we did not join large political or ideological movements. We simply inherited the advantages for which a previous generation had fought.

Skill:
Summarizing

Smith explains the choice her generation faced after college: make money by working at a bank or help others. Smith now thinks that choice is funny, which means she no longer believes what she once did.

14 And the thing that so many of us feared was the idea of being subsumed back into the collective from which we'd come. Of being returned to the world of the many. Or doing any work at all in that world.

15 In my case this new attitude was particularly noticeable. My own mother was a social worker, and I had teachers in my rowdy state school who had themselves been educated at precisely the elite institution I would later join. But amongst my college friends, I know of no one who made that choice. For the most part, we were uninterested in what we considered to be 'unglamorous pursuits'. We valued individuality above all things. You can thank my generation for the invention of the word 'supermodel', and the popularisation of 'celebrity' and 'lifestyle', often used in conjunction with each other. Reality TV—that was us. Also televised talent shows. Also Ugg boots—you're welcome, millennials! And when the fussier amongst us detected in these visions of prestigious individuality perhaps something a little crass and commercialized, our solution was to go in some ways further down the same road, to out-individuate the celebrated individuals.

16 We became hipsters. Defined by the ways we weren't like everybody else. One amusing, much commented upon consequence of this was that we all ended up individuals of the same type. Not one-of-a-kind, but one . . . of a kind.

17 But there was another aspect I now find melancholic. We isolated ourselves. It took us the longest time to work out that we needed each other. You may have noticed that even now we seem somewhat stunned by quite ordinary human pursuits, like having children or living in a neighbourhood, or getting ill. We are always writing lifestyle articles about such matters in the Sunday papers. That's because, until very recently, we thought we were going to get through this whole life thing purely on our own steam. Even if we were no fans of the ex-British Prime Minister Margaret Thatcher, we had unwittingly taken her most famous slogan and embedded it deep within our own lives. "There is no such thing as society," she said. We were unique individuals. What did we need with society? But then it turned out that the things that have happened to everybody since the dawn of time also happened to us. Our parents got old and ill. Our children needed schools and somewhere to play. We wanted trains that ran on time. We needed each other. It turned out we were just human—like everybody.

18 Now I may have this completely backward, but I get the sense that something different is going on in your generation. Something hopeful. You seem to be smarter, sooner. Part of these smarts is surely born out of crisis. In the '90s we had high employment and a buoyant economy. We could afford to spend weeks wondering about the exact length and shape of our beards, or whether

Skill:
Language, Style, and Audience

Smith mocks her generation using simple words and non-standard syntax. The sentences are brief, and the punctuation creates humorous pauses. This effectively conveys a lighthearted and informal tone.

Skill:
Textual Evidence

Smith characterizes her generation as people who thought they could always succeed in life on their own. But, as they got older, they realized this wasn't possible. This textual evidence supports one of Smith's main ideas.

Skill:
Textual Evidence

Smith focuses on the major issues faced by the current generation. She argues that these issues can only be solved by people working together. This textual evidence reveals how Smith sees the current generation as different from her own.

Kurt Cobain[1] was a sell-out. Your situation is more **acute**. You have so many large, collective tasks ahead, and you know that. We had them too, but paid little attention, so now I'm afraid it falls to you. The climate, the economy, the sick relationship between the individual prestige of the first world and the anonymity of the third—these are things only many hands can fix working together. You are all individuals but you are also part of a generation and generations are defined by the projects they take on together.

19   Even at the level of slogan you decided to honour the contribution of the many over the few, that now famous '99 Percent'[2]. As far as slogans go, which is not very far, yours still sounds more thoughtful to me than the slogans of my youth which were fatally infected by advertising. Be strong. Be fast. Be bold. Be different. Be you . . . be you, that was always the takeaway. And when my peers grew up, and went into advertising, they spread that message far and wide. "Just be you," screams the label on your shampoo bottle. "Just be you," cries your deodorant. "Because you're worth it." You get about fifty commencement speeches a day, and that's before you've even left the bathroom.

20   I didn't think you'd want any more of that from me. Instead I want to speak in favor of recognizing our place within 'the many'. Not only as a slogan, much less as a personal sacrifice, but rather as a potential source of joy in your life.

21   Here is a perhaps silly example. It happened to me recently at my mother's birthday. Around midnight it came time to divide up the rum cake, and I, not naturally one of life's volunteers, was press-ganged into helping. A small circle of women surrounded me, dressed in West African wraps and headscarves, in imitation of their ancestors. "Many hands make short work," said one, and passed me a stack of paper plates. It was my job to take the plated slices through the crowd. Hardly any words passed between us as we went about our collective task, but each time we set a new round upon a tray, I detected a hum of deep satisfaction at our many hands forming this useful human chain. Occasionally as I gave out a slice of cake, an older person would look up and murmur, "Oh you're Yvonne's daughter," but for the most part it was the cake itself that received the greeting or a little nod or a smile, for it was the duty of the daughter to hand out cake and no further commentary was required. And it was while doing what I hadn't realised was my duty that I felt what might be described as the exact opposite of the sensation I have standing in front of you now. Not puffed up with individual prestige, but immersed in the beauty of the crowd. Connected if only in gesture to an ancient line of practical women working in companionable silence in the

---

1. **Kurt Cobain** composer, singer and guitarist Kurt Cobain (1967–1994) was frontman of the Seattle post-punk band Nirvana
2. **'99 Percent'** a populist term referring to the percentage of the American population who are not extremely wealthy

service of their community. It's such a ludicrously tiny example of the collective action and yet clearly still so rare in my own life that even this minor instance of it struck me.

22 Anyway my point is that it was a beautiful feeling, and it was over too soon. And when I tried to look for a way to put it into this speech, I was surprised how difficult it is to find the right words to describe it. So many of our colloquial terms for this 'work of many hands' are sunk in infamy. 'Human chain' for starters; 'cog in the machine'; 'brick in the wall'. In such phrases we sense the long shadow of the twentieth century, with its brutal collective movements.

23 We do not trust the collective, we've seen what submission to it can do. We believe instead in the individual, here in America, especially. Now I also believe in the individual, I'm so grateful for the three years of college that helped make more or less of an individual out of me—teaching me how to think, and write. You may well ask, who am I to praise the work of many hands, when I myself chose the work of one pair of hands, the most isolated there is.

24 I can't escape that accusation. I can only look at my own habit of self love and ask, "what is the best use I can make of this utterly human habit?" Can I make a gift of myself in some other way? I know for sure I haven't done it half as much as I could or should have. I look at the fine example of my friend, the writer and activist Dave Eggers, and see a man who took his own individual prestige and parlayed it into an extraordinary collective action—826 National[3], in which many hands work to create educational opportunities for disadvantaged kids all over this country.

25 And when you go to one of Dave's not-for-profit tutoring centres, you don't find selfless young people grimly sacrificing themselves for others. What you see is joy. Dave's achievement is neither quite charity nor simple individual philanthropy[4]. It's a collective effort that gets people involved in each other's lives.

26 I don't mean to speak meanly of philanthropy. Generally speaking, philanthropy is always better than no help at all, but it is also in itself a privilege of the few. And I think none of us want communities to rise or fall dependent upon the whims of the very rich. I think we would rather be involved in each other's lives and that what stops us, most often, is fear.

27 We fear that the work of many hands will obscure the beloved outline of our individual selves. But perhaps this self you've been treasuring for so long is

Skill:
Language, Style, and Audience

The repetition of the words "collective" and "individual" draws attention to the choice Smith thinks people must make. Throughout the speech, she posits that people can focus on individual goals or work as part of a group.

---

3. **826 National** a nationwide nonprofit organization founded by the writer Dave Eggers to encourage and help youth ages six to eighteen interested in writing

4. **philanthropy** voluntary promotion of human welfare, usually with money or influence

itself the work of many hands. Speaking personally, I owe so much to the hard work of my parents, to the educational and health care systems in my country, to the love and care of my friends.

28 And even if one's individual prestige, such as it is, represents an entirely solo effort, the result of sheer hard work, does that everywhere and always mean that you deserve the largest possible slice of the pie?

29 These are big questions, and it is collectively that you'll have to decide them. Everything from the remuneration of executives to the idea of the commons itself depends upon it. And, at the core of the question, is what it really means to be 'the few' and 'the many'. Throughout your adult life you're going to have a daily choice to throw your lot in with one or the other. And a lot of people, most people, even people without the luxury of your choices, are going to suggest to you, over and over, that only an idiot chooses to join the many, when he could be one of the few.

30 Only an idiot chooses public over private, shared over gated, communal over unique. Mrs. Thatcher, who was such a genius at witty **aphorism**, once said, "A man who beyond the age of twenty-six, finds himself on a bus, can count himself a failure."

31 I've always been fascinated by that quote. By its dark assumption that even something as natural as sharing a journey with another person represents a form of personal denigration. The best reply to it that I know is that famous line of Terence, the Roman playwright. *Homo sum, humani nihil a me alienum puto.* 'I am a human being. I consider nothing that is human alien to me.'

32 Montaigne liked that so much he had it carved into the beams of his ceiling. Some people interpret it as a call to toleration. I find it stronger than that, I think it's a call to love. Now, full disclosure, most of the time I don't find it easy to love my fellow humans. I'm still that solipsistic 21-year-old. But the times I've been able to get over myself and get involved at whatever level, well what I'm trying to say is those have proved the most valuable moments of my life.

33 And I never would have guessed that back in 1997. Oh, I would have paid lip service to it, as a noble idea, but I wouldn't have believed it. And the thing is, it's not even a question of ethics or self-sacrifice or moral high ground, it's actually totally selfish. Being with people, doing for people, it's going to bring you joy. Unexpectedly, it just feels better.

34 It feels good to give your unique and prestigious selves a slip every now and then and confess your membership in this unwieldy collective called the human race.

35 For one thing, it's far less lonely, and for another, contra to Mrs Thatcher, some of the best conversations you'll ever hear will be on public transport. If it weren't for the New York and London subway systems, my novels would be books of blank pages.

36 But I'm preaching to the converted. I see you, gazing into your phones as you walk down Broadway. And I know solipsism must be a constant danger, as it is for me, as it has been for every human since the dawn of time, but you've also got this tremendous, contrapuntal force propelling you into the world.

37 For aren't you always connecting to each other? Forever communicating, rarely scared of strangers, wildly open, ready to tell anyone everything? Doesn't online anonymity tear at the very idea of a prestige individual? Aren't young artists collapsing the border between themselves and their audience? Aren't young coders determined on an all-access world in which everybody is an equal participant? Are the young activists content just to raise the money and run? No. They want to be local, grassroots, involved. Those are all good instincts. I'm so excited to think of you pursuing them. Hold on to that desire for human connection. Don't let anyone scare you out of it.

38 Walk down these crowded streets with a smile on your face. Be thankful you get to walk so close to other humans. It's a privilege. Don't let your fellow humans be alien to you, and as you get older and perhaps a little less open than you are now, don't assume that exclusive always and everywhere means better. It may only mean lonelier. There will always be folks hard selling you the life of the few: the private schools, private planes, private islands, private life. They are trying to convince you that hell is other people. Don't believe it. We are far more frequently each other's shelter and correction, the antidote to solipsism, and so many windows on this world.

39 Thank you.

"New School Commencement Speech" by Zadie Smith. Published by The New School, 2014. Copyright © Zadie Smith. Reproduced by permission of the author c/o Rogers, Coleridge, & White Ltd., 20 Powis Mews, London W11 1JN

First Read

Read "Commencement Address at the New School." After you read, complete the Think Questions below.

☁ THINK QUESTIONS

1. How does Zadie Smith evaluate her own generation's experiences, as compared to generations before and after? Explain, citing specific examples.

2. Why does Smith quote former British Prime Minister Margaret Thatcher at various points in her speech? What purpose does Thatcher serve in the address? Cite specific evidence from the text to support your answer.

3. What particular small event impressed on Smith the emotional value of shared work and contact with a community? Explain briefly, citing specific evidence from the text to support your response.

4. What is the meaning of the word **commodity** as it is used in the text? Write your best definition here. Then, check an online or print dictionary and compare your answer to the definition you find there.

5. Use context clues to determine the meaning of the word **aphorism** as it is used in the text. Write your definition here, and explain which clues helped you determine its meaning.

Skill:
Language, Style, and Audience

Use the Checklist to analyze Language, Style, and Audience in "Commencement Address at the New School." Refer to the sample student annotations about Language, Style, and Audience in the text.

••• CHECKLIST FOR LANGUAGE, STYLE, AND AUDIENCE

In order to determine an author's style and possible intended audience, do the following:

✓ identify instances where they author uses key terms throughout the course of a text

✓ examine surrounding words and phrases to determine the context, connotation, style, and tone of the term's usage

✓ analyze how the author's treatment of the key term affects the reader's understanding of the text

✓ note the audience—both intended and unintended—and possible reactions to the author's word choice, style, and treatment of key terms

To analyze how an author's treatment of language and key terms affect the reader's understanding of the text, consider the following questions:

✓ How do the author's word choices enhance or change what is being described?

✓ How do the author's word choices affect the reader's understanding of key terms and ideas in the text?

✓ How do choices about language affect the author's style and audience?

✓ How often does the author use this term or terms?

Please note that excerpts and passages in the StudySync® library and this workbook are intended as touchstones to generate interest in an author's work. The excerpts and passages do not substitute for the reading of entire texts, and StudySync® strongly recommends that students seek out and purchase the whole literary or informational work in order to experience it as the author intended. Links to online resellers are available in our digital library. In addition, complete works may be ordered through an authorized reseller by filling out and returning to StudySync® the order form enclosed in this workbook.

Reading & Writing Companion   465

Skill:
Language, Style, and Audience

Reread paragraphs 30–34 of "Commencement Address at the New School." Then, using the Checklist on the previous page, answer the multiple-choice questions below.

⟳ YOUR TURN

1. In paragraph 31, Smith's choice to quote the Roman playwright Terence effectively—

   ○ A. shows off her knowledge of Latin in order to impress her audience with her intelligence.
   ○ B. encourages her listeners to focus on their own accomplishments and ignore others.
   ○ C. provides a counterpoint to Thatcher and emphasizes her own idea of what is truly important.
   ○ D. convinces her listeners that ancient Roman culture represented a high point in world history.

2. Which statement best evaluates how Smith uses language and style to affect the reader's/listener's perception of the relationship between individualism and collectivism?

   ○ A. Smith's repetition of the words "human" and "people" strongly reminds an audience of individuals that they are also part of a large group.
   ○ B. Smith's decision to include a funny quotation by Margaret Thatcher strongly suggests that people should avoid spending too much time with others.
   ○ C. Smith's concession that she does not always like other people strongly encourages the audience to focus on one another's individual faults.
   ○ D. Smith's wit and dismissive tone strongly suggest that the audience should not take her too seriously and should instead make up their own minds.

Skill:
Textual Evidence

Use the Checklist to analyze Textual Evidence in "Commencement Address at the New School." Refer to the sample student annotations about Textual Evidence in the text.

••• CHECKLIST FOR TEXTUAL EVIDENCE

In order to support an analysis by citing evidence that is explicitly stated in the text, do the following:

✓ read the text closely and critically

✓ identify what the text says explicitly

✓ find the most relevant textual evidence that supports your analysis

✓ consider why an author explicitly states specific details and information

✓ cite the specific words, phrases, sentences, or paragraphs from the text that support your analysis

✓ determine where evidence in the text still leaves matters uncertain or unresolved

In order to interpret implicit meanings in a text by making inferences, do the following:

✓ combine information directly stated in the text with your own knowledge, experiences, and observations

✓ cite the specific words, phrases, sentences, or paragraphs from the text that led to and support this inference

In order to cite textual evidence to support an analysis of what the text says explicitly as well as inferences drawn from the text, consider the following questions:

✓ Have I read the text closely and critically?

✓ What inferences am I making about the text?

✓ What textual evidence am I using to support these inferences?

✓ Am I quoting the evidence from the text correctly?

✓ Does my textual evidence logically relate to my analysis or the inference I am making?

✓ Does evidence in the text still leave certain matters unanswered or unresolved? In what ways?

Skill:
Textual Evidence

Reread paragraph 21 of "Commencement Address at the New School." Then, using the Checklist on the previous page, answer the multiple-choice questions below.

⟳ YOUR TURN

1. This question has two parts. First, answer Part A. Then, answer Part B.

   Part A: Which inference is best supported by this paragraph?

   ○ A. It is easy for a grown daughter to forget the duties she has toward her mother, particularly around a parent's birthday.

   ○ B. It is important for people to honor their ancestors by continuing to respect ancient customs, such as serving cake at a birthday party.

   ○ C. Working as part of a community creates something more beautiful and beneficial than working for individual recognition.

   ○ D. Even when the task is seemingly minor, performing a job in honor of one's parents represents an important step in becoming an adult.

   Part B: Which textual evidence from the paragraph best supports the answer to Part A?

   ○ A. "A small circle of women surrounded me, dressed in West African wraps and headscarves, in imitation of their ancestors."

   ○ B. "It was my job to take the plated slices through the crowd."

   ○ C. ". . . but for the most part it was the cake itself that received the greeting or a little nod or a smile, for it was the duty of the daughter to hand out cake and no further commentary was required."

   ○ D. "Connected if only in gesture to an ancient line of practical women working in companionable silence in the service of their community."

Skill:
Summarizing

Use the Checklist to analyze Summarizing in "Commencement Address at the New School." Refer to the sample student annotations about Summarizing in the text.

••• CHECKLIST FOR SUMMARIZING

In order to determine how to write an objective summary of a text, note the following:

✓ answers to the basic questions *who, what, where, when, why,* and *how*

✓ in literature or nonfiction, note how two or more themes or central ideas are developed over the course of the text, and how they interact and build on one another to produce a complex account

✓ stay objective, and do not add your own personal thoughts, judgments, or opinions to the summary

To provide an objective summary of a text, consider the following questions:

✓ What are the answers to basic *who, what, where, when, why,* and *how* questions in literature and works of nonfiction?

✓ Does my summary include how two or more themes or central ideas are developed over the course of the text, and how they interact and build on one another in my summary?

✓ Is my summary objective, or have I added my own thoughts, judgments, and personal opinions?

Please note that excerpts and passages in the StudySync® library and this workbook are intended as touchstones to generate interest in an author's work. The excerpts and passages do not substitute for the reading of entire texts, and StudySync® strongly recommends that students seek out and purchase the whole literary or informational work in order to experience it as the author intended. Links to online resellers are available in our digital library. In addition, complete works may be ordered through an authorized reseller by filling out and returning to StudySync® the order form enclosed in this workbook.

Reading & Writing
Companion

469

Skill:
Summarizing

Reread paragraphs 27–29 of "Commencement Address at the New School." Then, using the Checklist on the previous page, answer the multiple-choice questions below.

⟳ YOUR TURN

1. How does this part of the speech build on main ideas throughout the speech?

   ○ A. Smith argues that we all depend on family, friends, and society, and that group efforts make shared support and community possible.

   ○ B. Smith tells her audience that they face the choice of being part of a community or part of the elite, just like Smith's generation did.

   ○ C. Smith points out that members of the developed world, like her audience, have many more choices and options than members of the developing world.

   ○ D. Smith argues that most people think it is a bad idea to seek to belong to a community when they could become a member of the ruling elite.

2. Which of the following is the most complete and unbiased summary of paragraphs 27–29?

   ○ A. Smith clearly conveys the idea that people cannot rise to the top without any help and so she advocates for the value of community. However, she also recognizes that most people rightly view the choice to reject individuality as a silly one.

   ○ B. Smith argues that we often reject working with others because of the fear of being obscured. But most people are products of collective work, and it is an important choice to strive to be an individual or part of a community, even though many believe rejecting community is best.

   ○ C. Smith argues that successful people do not become successful completely on their own, and they owe a lot to the support of their family, friends, and society.

   ○ D. Smith points out that even if people are able to achieve success completely on their own, it's not clear whether they deserve more than everyone else. Smith tells her audience that they will have to face the difficult choice of being poor and common or a member of the elite.

Close Read

Reread "Commencement Address at the New School." As you reread, complete the Skills Focus questions below. Then use your answers and annotations from the questions to help you complete the Write activity.

◎ SKILLS FOCUS

1. Find a passage in which Smith uses a compare-and-contrast text structure to convey her ideas. Analyze whether the choice to use this structure helps the author make her ideas clear.

2. Highlight a passage in which Smith describes her attitude toward her generation. Summarize how details in the passage you selected develop two of the main ideas in the speech.

3. What can you infer is Zadie Smith's opinion of philanthropy? What are the positives and possible failures she sees in philanthropy? Find textual evidence to support your answer. Note where the textual evidence may leave matters unresolved.

4. Identify an example of vivid sensory language. Explain how Smith's choice to include these details effectively shapes the audience's perception of her main ideas.

5. Why is the generation graduating in 2014 so different from the class Zadie Smith graduated with in 1997? What are some of the causes that Zadie Smith identifies as the reasons things have changed so much between these generations? Cite textual evidence to support your answer.

✏ WRITE

PERSONAL RESPONSE: Most of Smith's commencement speech is about seeing oneself as one of the few or one of the many. React to this speech in a short essay. Use the examples she gives to summarize her central idea about individualism. Tell whether you plan to be one of the few or one of the many when you leave school. Explain your choice, using examples from your own life and textual evidence from Smith's speech.

Extended Oral Project and Grammar

EXTENDED
ORAL
PROJECT

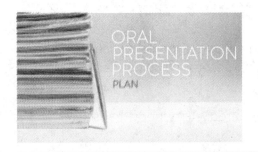

Oral Presentation Process: Plan

PLAN	DRAFT	REVISE	EDIT AND PRESENT

The four years spent in high school undoubtedly change graduates. The experiences they have, the knowledge they gain, and the memories they make will stay with them for a lifetime. Just as high school students change, the world around them changes, too. A common life goal is to leave the world a little better than you found it, whether that world is your high school, your community, or your country, for example.

WRITING PROMPT

What do future students need to know?

As your high school years now come to a close, think back on the last several years and consider the topics you have covered in all of your subjects. Then, consider the world around you now and select a topic, issue, person, or event that is important to you, but that was not covered in your formal studies. Develop an argument to support the claim that this topic, issue, person, or event should be included in future high school instruction so that the details and significance will be heard and remembered. In order to prepare for your presentation, consider how best to meet the needs of the audience, purpose, and occasion by employing the following:

- elements of classical speeches, including an introduction, body, transitions, and a conclusion

- the art of persuasion and rhetorical devices

- the appropriate use of formal or informal language as well as purposeful vocabulary, tone, and voice

- visual aids that support the information presented, including citations and a works cited list for any information obtained from outside sources

- speaking techniques, such as eye contact, an appropriate speaking rate and volume, pauses for effect, enunciation, purposeful gestures, and appropriate conventions of language

Please note that excerpts and passages in the StudySync® library and this workbook are intended as touchstones to generate interest in an author's work. The excerpts and passages do not substitute for the reading of entire texts, and StudySync® strongly recommends that students seek out and purchase the whole literary or informational work in order to experience it as the author intended. Links to online resellers are available in our digital library. In addition, complete works may be ordered through an authorized reseller by filling out and returning to StudySync® the order form enclosed in this workbook.

Reading & Writing Companion

473

Introduction to Oral Presentation

Compelling oral presentations use both effective speaking techniques and engaging writing to express ideas and opinions. Oral presentations can have a variety of purposes, including persuasion. The characteristics of an effective argumentative oral presentation include:

- the organizational elements of classical speeches, including an introduction, body, transitions, and a conclusion

- the art of persuasion and rhetorical devices

- the appropriate use of formal or informal language as well as purposeful vocabulary, tone, and voice

- speaking techniques, such as eye contact, an appropriate speaking rate and volume, pauses for effect, enunciation, purposeful gestures, and appropriate conventions of language

These characteristics can be organized into four major categories: context, structure, style & language, and elements of effective communication. As you continue with this Extended Oral Project, you'll receive more detailed instruction and practice in crafting each of the characteristics of argumentative writing and speaking to create your own oral presentation.

Before you get started on your own oral presentation, read this oral presentation that one student, Josh, wrote in response to the prompt. As you read the Model, highlight and annotate the features of oral presentation writing that Josh included in his presentation.

☰ STUDENT MODEL

Navigating the Digital World

By Josh

Introduction—Opening

My dad often jokes that my cell phone is glued to my hand. I do admit that I use my phone a lot, but almost everything I do is online. In the past 24 hours, I bought my grandmother a birthday present, took a history quiz, streamed three episodes of my favorite television show, ordered dinner, and researched the causes and effects of air pollution—all with a device in the palm of my hand.

NOTES

Introduction—Claim

There are many advantages to living in the digital world, but we need to stop and consider how being online affects individuals and our society. Because a goal of any high school curriculum is to prepare students to enter the world, a contemporary high school education is not complete without lessons on living in a digital world.

Living in a Digital World

- We need to consider the online community's effects on individuals and society, both positive and negative.
- Schools should provide lessons on living in the digital world.

Body—Counterclaim

Some might believe that it is the responsibility of parents to teach their children how to be safe and smart online. I agree that parents should play a key role in teaching children how to navigate the internet, but not all parents are experts on the fast-paced digital world. That's why including formal instruction in media literacy in schools would ensure that all students learn how to be good online citizens.

For instance, if students studied the fact-checking guidelines that journalists use, they could enhance their media literacy. If everyone is going to participate in the digital world, then we should make sure that the digital world is a good place for everyone to be.

Not Everyone Agrees

Some believe parents should be responsible.

• Not all parents are experts.
• Schools can provide formal instruction in media literacy.
• Students can learn how to fact-check what they discover online.

Body—Elaboration

At the click of a button, users can access the thoughts, opinions, and knowledge bases of millions of other people, whether they are located across town or across an ocean. People from all over the world weigh in on a myriad of topics on social media. This all might sound great; however, it is a double-edged sword.

Sometimes it is hard to know whether or not the information you read online is accurate, authoritative, and trustworthy. It should be our duty to make the internet better, safer, and more accurate for future generations.

At the same time, aspects of the internet, such as social media, can help create online communities that help people feel safe and heard and also help them organize social action.

To accomplish this goal, schools need to teach students how to analyze and evaluate online sources and how to be responsible digital citizens. That means contributing to the digital space in a positive way, putting an end to cyberbullying, and stopping the propagation of false information.

The Online World Is a Double-Edged Sword

• How do I know whether or not the information I read online is accurate, authoritative, and trustworthy?
• Can social media help people feel safe and heard and also help them organize social action?
• How can schools help students become responsible digital citizens?

NOTES

Body—Evidence and Analysis #1

While some people use the internet primarily to gain information, others go online to enact change.

Based on data collected by the Pew Research Center, Graph 1 demonstrates that there are various ways an individual can show that they are civically active on social media. The dark blue bar at the bottom of the graph indicates that 53% of U.S. adults have taken these actions, and the light blue bars show the percentage of people who have participated in specific activities on social media.

The most popular of these actions is taking part in a group of similarly minded activists on social media.

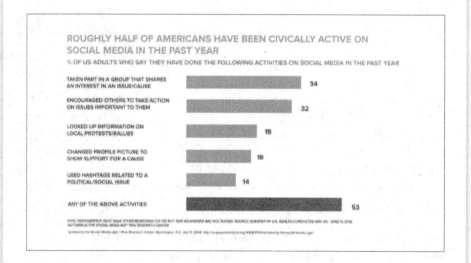

ROUGHLY HALF OF AMERICANS HAVE BEEN CIVICALLY ACTIVE ON SOCIAL MEDIA IN THE PAST YEAR

% OF US ADULTS WHO SAY THEY HAVE DONE THE FOLLOWING ACTIVITIES ON SOCIAL MEDIA IN THE PAST YEAR

TAKEN PART IN A GROUP THAT SHARES AN INTEREST IN AN ISSUE/CAUSE	34
ENCOURAGED OTHERS TO TAKE ACTION ON ISSUES IMPORTANT TO THEM	32
LOOKED UP INFORMATION ON LOCAL PROTESTS/RALLIES	19
CHANGED PROFILE PICTURE TO SHOW SUPPORT FOR A CAUSE	18
USED HASHTAGS RELATED TO A POLITICAL/SOCIAL ISSUE	14
ANY OF THE ABOVE ACTIVITIES	53

Body—Evidence and Analysis #2

My next graph indicates that people believe these actions to be effective in specific ways.

Graph 2 also represents data collected by the Pew Research Center and shows that most Americans believe that social media is important to gain the attention of politicians. If we combine the "Very" (dark blue) and "Somewhat" (blue) bars, we see that around 60% of Americans say social media platforms are at least partly effective for getting politicians to pay attention to issues, creating activist movements, and influencing policy decisions.

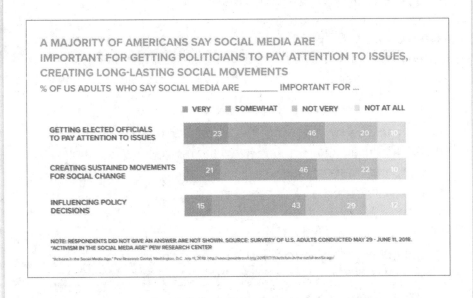

A MAJORITY OF AMERICANS SAY SOCIAL MEDIA ARE
IMPORTANT FOR GETTING POLITICIANS TO PAY ATTENTION TO ISSUES,
CREATING LONG-LASTING SOCIAL MOVEMENTS

% OF US ADULTS WHO SAY SOCIAL MEDIA ARE _____ IMPORTANT FOR ...

■ VERY   ■ SOMEWHAT   ■ NOT VERY   ■ NOT AT ALL

	VERY	SOMEWHAT	NOT VERY	NOT AT ALL
GETTING ELECTED OFFICIALS TO PAY ATTENTION TO ISSUES	23	46	20	10
CREATING SUSTAINED MOVEMENTS FOR SOCIAL CHANGE	21	46	22	10
INFLUENCING POLICY DECISIONS	15	43	29	12

NOTE: RESPONDENTS DID NOT GIVE AN ANSWER ARE NOT SHOWN. SOURCE: SURVERY OF U.S. ADULTS CONDUCTED MAY 29 - JUNE 11, 2018.
"ACTIVISM IN THE SOCIAL MEDIA AGE" PEW RESEARCH CENTER

"Activism In the Social Media Age." Pew Research Center, Washington, D.C. July 11, 2018. http://www.pewinternet.org/2018/07/11/activism-in-the-social-media-age/

Body—Evidence and Analysis #2 (continued)

These are impressive numbers, and even our political leaders agree
(watch the video in the Plan lesson on the StudySync site):

President Obama Urges Public to Use
Social Media to Contact Senators

NBC News Archives Xpress

NOTES

Body—Evidence and Analysis #3

In addition, as Graph 3 demonstrates, social media is enabling citizens who had previously felt marginalized, including Hispanic and African American citizens, to find their voices and express their views.

As we can see by following the legend at the top of the graph, African American and Hispanic users are more likely than their white counterparts to state that social media platforms are effective for their activism.

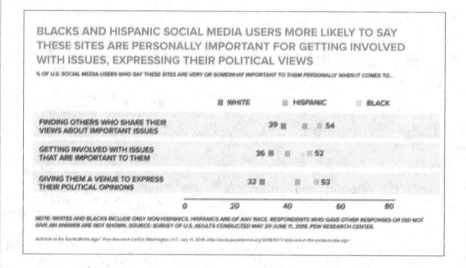

BLACKS AND HISPANIC SOCIAL MEDIA USERS MORE LIKELY TO SAY
THESE SITES ARE PERSONALLY IMPORTANT FOR GETTING INVOLVED
WITH ISSUES, EXPRESSING THEIR POLITICAL VIEWS

% OF U.S. SOCIAL MEDIA USERS WHO SAY THESE SITES ARE VERY OR SOMEWHAT IMPORTANT TO THEM PERSONALLY WHEN IT COMES TO...

	WHITE	HISPANIC	BLACK
FINDING OTHERS WHO SHARE THEIR VIEWS ABOUT IMPORTANT ISSUES	39		54
GETTING INVOLVED WITH ISSUES THAT ARE IMPORTANT TO THEM	36		52
GIVING THEM A VENUE TO EXPRESS THEIR POLITICAL OPINIONS	32		53

NOTE: WHITES AND BLACKS INCLUDE ONLY NON-HISPANICS. HISPANICS ARE OF ANY RACE. RESPONDENTS WHO GAVE OTHER RESPONSES OR DID NOT GIVE AN ANSWER ARE NOT SHOWN. SOURCE: SURVEY OF U.S. ADULTS CONDUCTED MAY 29-JUNE 11, 2018. PEW RESEARCH CENTER

"Activism in the Social Media Age" Pew Research Center, Washington, D.C. July 11, 2018. http://www.pewinternet.org/2018/07/11/activism-in-the-social-media-age/

Body—Review

Although online activism can have positive effects by including a multitude of opinions, raising awareness, and promoting change, there can be many drawbacks, including people verbally attacking others and using dehumanizing speech.

Schools can help by teaching students how to evaluate the claims of online activists and how to participate effectively and respectfully in online activism.

A Brighter Future

- Bullying, hate speech, and misinformation are big challenges in the digital world.
- We can create a better internet by educating students to engage effectively.

Conclusion

As my classmates and I prepare to graduate from high school, we feel like experts on many topics. We've read great literature, memorized essential formulas, and repeated famous lab experiments. As a result, we are ready to move on to the next phases of our lives. While few teenagers would admit that there is something they do not know about social media, we must acknowledge that the digital world has many pitfalls. Formal lessons on living in the digital world will help future graduates become better digital citizens, be more aware of other people's experiences, and maybe even change the world.

Thank you!

Works Cited

"A majority of Americans say social media are important for getting politicians to pay attention to issues, creating long-lasting social movements." Pew Research Center, 10 July 2018, Washington, D.C., www.pewinternet. org/2018/07/11/public-attitudes-toward-political-engagement-on-social-media/pi_2018-07-10_social-activism_0-05/.

"Blacks and Hispanic social media users more likely to say these sites are personally important for getting involved with issues, expressing their political views." Pew Research Center, 10 July 2018, Washington, D.C., www.pewinternet.org/2018/07/11/public-attitudes-toward-political-engagement-on-social-media/pi_2018-07-10_social-activism_0-04/.

"President Obama Urges Public to Use Social Media to Contact Senators." NBC News Archives Xpress, NBC News, 29 July 2011,www.nbcnewsarchivesxpress.com/ contentdetails/214755.

"Roughly half of Americans have been civically active on social media in the past year." Pew Research Center, 10 July 2018, Washington, D.C., www.pewinternet.org/2018/07/11/public-attitudes-toward-political-engagement-on-social-media/pi_2018-07-10_social-activism_0-02/.

WRITE

When you write for an oral presentation, it is important to consider your audience and purpose so you can write appropriately for them. Your purpose is implied in the prompt. Reread the prompt to determine your purpose for writing and presenting.

To begin, review the questions below and then select a strategy, such as brainstorming, journaling, reading, or discussing, to generate ideas.

- **Purpose:** What topic, issue, person, or event will be the focus of your presentation, and what important ideas do you want to convey?

- **Audience:** Who is your audience, and what message do you want to express to your audience?

- **Thesis:** What claim will you communicate about the significance of this topic, issue, person, or event?

- **Evidence:** What facts, evidence, and details might you include to support your ideas? What research might you need to do? What anecdotes from your personal life or what background knowledge is relevant to the topic of your presentation?

- **Organization:** How can you organize your presentation so that it is clear and easy to follow?

- **Clear Communication:** How will you make sure that your audience can hear and understand what you are saying?

- **Gestures and Visual Aids:** What illustrations or other visual aids could you use during your presentation? What effect will they have on your audience? What physical gestures and body language will help you communicate your ideas?

Response Instructions

Use the questions in the bulleted list and the ideas you generated to write a one-paragraph summary. Your summary should describe what you will discuss in your oral presentation.

Don't worry about including all of the details now; focus only on the most essential and important elements. You will refer to this short summary as you continue through the steps of the writing process.

Please note that excerpts and passages in the StudySync® library and this workbook are intended as touchstones to generate interest in an author's work. The excerpts and passages do not substitute for the reading of entire texts, and StudySync® strongly recommends that students seek out and purchase the whole literary or informational work in order to experience it as the author intended. Links to online resellers are available in our digital library. In addition, complete works may be ordered through an authorized reseller by filling out and returning to StudySync® the order form enclosed in this workbook.

Reading & Writing Companion 483

Skill: Organizing an Oral Presentation

••• CHECKLIST FOR ORGANIZING AN ORAL PRESENTATION

In order to present information, findings, and supporting evidence that convey a clear and distinct perspective, do the following:

- choose a style for your oral presentation, either formal or informal

- determine whether the development and organization of your presentation, as well as its substance and style, are appropriate for your purpose, audience, and task

- determine whether your presentation conveys a clear and distinct perspective so listeners can follow your line of reasoning

- make sure you address alternative perspectives that oppose your own in your presentation

- make strategic, or deliberate, use of digital media, such as textual, graphical, audio, visual, and interactive elements, to add interest and enhance your audience's understanding of the findings, reasoning, and evidence in your presentation

To present information, findings, and supporting evidence conveying a clear and distinct perspective, consider the following questions:

- Did I make sure that the information in my presentation conveys a clear and distinct perspective, so listeners can follow my line of reasoning?

- Have I presented opposing or alternative viewpoints in my presentation?

- Are the organization, development, substance, and style appropriate for my purpose and audience?

- Have I made strategic use of media to add interest and enhance my audience's understanding of my presentation?

⟳ YOUR TURN

Read each sentence below. Then, complete the chart on the next page by determining where each sentence belongs in the outline. Write the corresponding letter for each sentence in the appropriate row.

	Sentences
A	I will acknowledge the counterclaim that forming sleep habits is complicated by early start times at school, extracurricular activities in the evening, homework, and maintaining a social life. The school schedule can prevent teenagers from getting adequate sleep, regardless of screen time. However, screens can complicate sleep schedules even more, especially when it's so hard to find the time to rest.
B	I can include a graph that shows the relationship between sleep quality and energy levels.
C	I can use words like *next, thus,* and *additionally* to support the logical flow of ideas in my argument.
D	Everybody sleeps, but some people do it better than others. I can include an anecdote about struggling with getting enough sleep because I keep my phone next to me when I sleep. My thesis will state that students should learn sleep strategies to develop good habits and support their health.
E	I believe that this topic is important because lots of people are unaware of how screen usage affects sleep patterns. I also want to explain how good sleep habits lower your risk for serious health problems and increase your ability to think clearly and get along with others.
F	In the end, I will reiterate the importance of getting solid sleep each day. I will rephrase my thesis and summarize my main points.
G	I want to convince people that students should learn about forming good sleep habits.

Purpose	
Introduction / Thesis	
Alternative/Opposing Viewpoints	
Body	
Visual Aids	
Logical Progression	
Conclusion / Rephrasing of Thesis	

✏ WRITE

Use the questions in the checklist to outline your oral presentation. Be sure to include a clear thesis and a logical progression of valid reasons.

Skill:
Evaluating Sources

••• CHECKLIST FOR EVALUATING SOURCES

As you reread the sources you gathered, identify the following:

- where information seems inaccurate, biased, or outdated
- where information strongly relates to your task, purpose, and audience
- where information helps you make an informed decision or solve a problem

In order to conduct advanced searches to gather relevant, credible, and accurate print and digital sources, use the following questions as a guide:

- Is the material published by a well-established source or expert author?
- Is the material up-to-date or based on the most current information?
- Is the material factual, and can it be verified by another source?
- Are there discrepancies between the information presented in different sources?
- Are there specific terms or phrases that I can use to adjust my search?

Please note that excerpts and passages in the StudySync® library and this workbook are intended as touchstones to generate interest in an author's work. The excerpts and passages do not substitute for the reading of entire texts, and StudySync® strongly recommends that students seek out and purchase the whole literary or informational work in order to experience it as the author intended. Links to online resellers are available in our digital library. In addition, complete works may be ordered through an authorized reseller by filling out and returning to StudySync® the order form enclosed in this workbook.

Reading & Writing Companion   **487**

↻ YOUR TURN

Choose the best answer to each question.

1. Josh finds an article titled "A Look at 2012: How Social Media Will Bring Us Together" that was published on a website that his teacher recommended. What should Josh do to make sure he is reading a reliable source?

    ○ A. Josh should check all the information in the article to confirm that it is still relevant today.

    ○ B. Josh should check if the article contains too many counterclaims from experts on this topic.

    ○ C. Josh should check if he agrees with the arguments and reasons presented by the author.

    ○ D. Josh should check to make sure that any data and evidence presented in the article are unique.

2. Josh finds another article from 2018 titled "Social Media Will Ruin Us" published by *The Simpler Life*, a nationally distributed magazine. What should Josh consider before using this source?

    ○ A. The source may be outdated and contain information that is no longer relevant.

    ○ B. The source may be unreliable because it is printed in a nationally distributed magazine.

    ○ C. The source may be irrelevant to his thesis or presentation because it is about social media.

    ○ D. The source may be biased, given the title of the article and of the magazine in which it is published.

YOUR TURN

Complete the chart by filling in the title and author of a source for your presentation and answering the questions about it.

Source Title and Author:	
Reliability: Has the source material been published in a well-established book or periodical or on a well-established website? Is the source material up-to-date or based on the most current information?	
Accuracy: Is the source based on factual information that can be verified by another source? Are there any discrepancies between this source and others?	
Credibility: Is the source material written by a recognized expert on the topic? Is the source material published by a well-respected author or organization?	
Decision: Should I use this source in my presentation?	

Skill: Considering Audience and Purpose

••• CHECKLIST FOR CONSIDERING AUDIENCE AND PURPOSE

In order to present information so that listeners can follow the line of reasoning and to ensure that the organization, development, substance, and style of your presentation are appropriate, note the following:

- When writing your presentation, convey and maintain a clear and distinct perspective or viewpoint.

- Make sure listeners can follow your line of reasoning, or the set of reasons you have used, so that your perspective is clear.

- Address any opposing or alternative perspectives.

- Check the development and organization of the information in your presentation to see that they are appropriate for your purpose, audience, and task.

- Determine whether the substance, or basis of your presentation, is also appropriate for your purpose, audience, and task.

- Remember to adapt your presentation to your task, and if it is appropriate, use formal English and not language you would use in ordinary conversation.

To better understand how to present information so that listeners can follow the line of reasoning and to ensure that the organization, development, substance, and style of your presentation are appropriate, consider the following questions:

- Have I organized the information in my presentation so that my perspective is clear?

- Did I address any opposing or alternative perspectives?

- Have I developed and organized the information so that it is appropriate for my purpose, audience, and task?

- Are the substance and style suitable?

Copyright © BookheadEd Learning, LLC

⟳ YOUR TURN

Read each statement below. Then, complete the chart by identifying whether the statements are appropriate for a formal presentation. Write the corresponding letter for each statement in the appropriate column.

	Statements
A	Horror movies can be real scary flicks.
B	Knowing basic first aid could help save lives.
C	Sewing not only encourages creativity, but it also improves manual dexterity.
D	My mom thinks that video games are such a waste of time, but she's wrong.
E	The history of American television reflects the values, issues, and ideals of an ever-changing nation.
F	Frank Wills, this guy who helped uncover the Watergate scandal in 1972, is somebody people should know about.

Appropriate	Inappropriate

YOUR TURN

Complete the chart by answering each question about your presentation.

Question	My Response
What is my purpose, and who is my audience?	
Do I plan to use formal or informal language?	
How will I organize information so that my perspective is clear?	
How will I address opposing or alternate perspectives?	
What sort of tone, or attitude, do I want to convey?	
How would I describe the voice I would like to use in my presentation?	
How will I use vocabulary and language to create that particular voice?	

Skill:
Persuasive Techniques

••• CHECKLIST FOR PERSUASIVE TECHNIQUES

In order to compose argumentative texts using genre characteristics and craft, use the following steps:

1. First, consider your audience and purpose. You should ask yourself:

   - What does the audience already know or understand about my topic or argument? What possible biases does the audience hold?

   - What are the strengths and limitations of my argument?

   - What counterclaim(s) have I identified?

   - What are the strengths and limitations of each counterclaim?

2. Next, consider the following persuasive techniques and the ways you might use one or more to reach your audience and achieve your purpose:

   - Appeals to Logic

     > What findings or supporting evidence will I use to support my claim?

     > What is the most effective way to present factual information to persuade my audience that my argument is logically sound and reasonable?

   - Appeals to Emotion

     > What emotions do I want my audience to feel about my topic?

     > What words or phrases should I include to bring about those feelings in my audience?

   - Appeals to Ethics

     > Which experts could I use to establish the credibility of my claims?

     > What words or phrases should I include to remind my audience of our shared values about what is right, good, and fair?

- Rhetorical Devices or Style

  > How can I use language in artful and persuasive ways to persuade my audience to accept my position?

  > What specific rhetorical devices, such as rhetorical questions, repetition, or parallelism, do I want to use to make my argument more persuasive?

- Counterclaim

  > What is an alternative or opposing perspective that my audience might have?

  > How can I rebut that opposing perspective in a way that respects my audience and strengthens my argument?

YOUR TURN

Read the appeals below. Then, complete the chart by placing each appeal in the appropriate category. Write the corresponding letter for each appeal in the appropriate column.

	Appeals
A	If you care about your child's safety, you will buy this car seat.
B	Cell phone use leads to 1.6 million car crashes a year.
C	Drivers have a responsibility to keep everyone safe.
D	No one wants to suffer and have his or her life cut short from a disease caused by poor diet.
E	As a pediatrician, I provide my patients information on healthy eating.
F	Unhealthy eating and inactivity cause 678,000 deaths every year.

Appeal to Logic	Appeal to Emotion	Appeal to Ethics

WRITE

Use the questions in the checklist to think about persuasive techniques that you can use in your presentation. Then, write a few sentences using persuasive techniques that you might be able to include in your presentation.

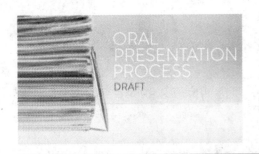

Oral Presentation Process: Draft

| PLAN | DRAFT | REVISE | EDIT AND PRESENT |

You have already made progress toward writing your argumentative oral presentation. Now it is time to draft your argumentative oral presentation.

✏ WRITE

Use your plan and other responses in your Binder to draft your argumentative oral presentation. You may also have new ideas as you begin drafting. Feel free to explore those new ideas as they occur to you. You can also ask yourself these questions to ensure that your writing is focused, organized, and developed with evidence and elaboration:

Draft Checklist:

- **Focus:** Is the topic of my presentation clear to my audience? Have I included only relevant information and details about my topic? Have I avoided extraneous details that might confuse or distract my audience?

- **Organization:** Is the organization of ideas and events in my presentation logical? Have I reinforced this logical structure with transitional words and phrases to help my audience follow the order of ideas? Do the sentences in my presentation flow together naturally? Will the sentences sound choppy or long-winded when I deliver them orally?

- **Evidence and Elaboration:** Do all of my details support my thesis about why this topic, issue, person, or event should be included in high school instruction? Have I elaborated on the evidence to explain how it supports my thesis?

Before you submit your draft, read it over carefully. You want to be sure that you've responded to all aspects of the prompt.

Here is Josh's argumentative oral presentation draft. As you read, notice how Josh develops his draft to be focused, organized, and developed with evidence and elaboration. As he continues to revise and edit his argumentative oral presentation, he will find and improve weak spots in his writing, as well as correct any language or punctuation mistakes.

☰ STUDENT MODEL: FIRST DRAFT

 NOTES

Navigating the Digital World

My dad often jokes that my cell phone is glued to my hand. I do admit that I use my phone a lot, but almost everything I do is online. In the past 24 hours, all with a device in the palm of my hand, I bought my grandmother a birthday present, took a history quiz, streamed three episodes of my favorite television show, ordered dinner, and researched the causes and effects of air pollution. There are many advantages to living in the digital world, but we need to stop and consider how being online affects individuals and our society. Because a goal of any high school curriculum is to prepare students to enter the world, a contemporary high school education is not complete without lessons on living in a digital world.

~~Some might beleive that it is the responsibility of parents to teach their children how to be safe and smart online. I agree that parents should play a key role in teaching children how to navigate the internet. However, they cannot be the only solution. Let's be honest: parents are too out-of-touch to know everything there is to know about the fast-paced digital world. That's why including formal instruction in media literacy in schools would ensure that all students learn how to be good online citizens, for instance, if students studied the fact-checking guidelines that journalists use, they could enhance their media literacy and never fall trap to fake news again.~~

Body—Counterclaim

Some might believe that it is the responsibility of parents to teach their children how to be safe and smart online. I agree that parents should play a key role in teaching children how to navigate the internet, but not all parents are experts on the fast-paced digital world. That's why including formal instruction in media literacy in schools would ensure that all students learn how to be good online citizens.

For instance, if students studied the fact-checking guidelines that journalists use, they could enhance their media literacy. If everyone is going to participate in the digital world, then we should make sure that the digital world is a good place for everyone to be. [Show slide with bullet points.]

 Skill:
Reasons and Evidence

The second paragraph of Josh's draft includes exaggeration and illogical reasoning, which undermine his argument. He revises his points to ensure that his reasoning is sound.

At the click of a button, users can access the thoughts, opinions, and knowledge bases of millions of other people, weather they are located across town or across an ocean. People from all over the world weigh in on a myriad of topics on social media. This all might sound great however, it is both a plus and a minus. Sometimes it is hard to know whether or not the information you read online is accurate, authoritative, and can be trusted. It should be our duty to make the internet better. More accurate for future generations. To accomplish this goal, schools need to teach students how to analyze and evaluate online sources and how to be responsible digital citizens.

~~As graphs 1 and 2 demonstrate, more and more Americans are using social media for the purpose of online activism and believe that social media is important to gain the attention of out-of-touch politicians. In addition, social media is enabling citizens who had previously felt marginalized to find their voices and express their views. Although online activism can have positive effects by including a multitude of opinions, raising awareness, and promoting change, there can be many bad effects, including people verbally attacking others and using dehumanizing speech. Schools can help avoid these disastrous and uncivil behaviors. [Show graphs that provide information about demographics and activities of social media users.]~~

Body—Evidence and Analysis #1
While some people use the internet primarily to gain information, others go online to enact change.

Based on data collected by the Pew Research Center, Graph 1 demonstrates that there are various ways an individual can show that they are civically active on social media. [Show Graph 1.] The dark blue bar at the bottom of the graph indicates that 53% of U.S. adults have taken these actions, and the light blue bars show the percentage of people who have participated in specific activities on social media.

The most popular of these actions is taking part in a group of similarly minded activists on social media.

Body—Evidence and Analysis #2
My next graph indicates that people believe these actions to be effective in specific ways. [Show Graph 2.]

Graph 2 also represents data collected by the Pew Research Center and shows that most Americans believe that social media is important to gain the attention of politicians. If we combine the "Very" (dark blue) and "Somewhat" (blue) bars, we see that around 60% of Americans say social media platforms are at least partly effective for getting politicians to pay attention to issues, creating activist movements, and influencing policy decisions.

Skill: Engaging in Discourse

Josh's partner tells him that the data in the graphs creates a strong logical appeal. He could strengthen the appeal, though, by providing a more detailed explanation of the graphs, which Josh decides to do.

Skill: Communicating Ideas

When Josh delivers his presentation, he'll point to the parts of the graphs that he's discussing. He'll use these gestures to focus the audience's attention on the information and help make the graphs clear.

NOTES

These are impressive numbers, and even our political leaders agree: [Show video of former President Obama.]

Body—Evidence and Analysis #3
In addition, as Graph 3 demonstrates, social media is enabling citizens who had previously felt marginalized, including Hispanic and African American citizens, to find their voices and express their views. [Show graph 3.]

As we can see by following the legend at the top of the graph, African American and Hispanic users are more likely than their white counterparts to state that social media platforms are effective for their activism.

As my classmates and I preparing to gradute from high school. we feel like experts on many topics I personally loved learning about the central nervous system thought learning about how the framers wrote the Constitution was really cool. We've read great literature, memorized formulas, and famous lab experiments. We are ready to move on to the next phases of our lives. Few teenagers would admit that there is something they do not know about social media. We must acknowledge that the digital world has many pitfalls. Formal lessons on living in the digital world will help future graduates a lot.

[Show a works cited slide.]

Sources

- Pew Center Research graphs that show demographics and activities of social media users:

  - http://www.pewinternet.org/2018/07/11/public-attitudes-toward-political-engagement-on-social-media/pi_2018-07-10_social-activism_0-02/

  - http://www.pewinternet.org/2018/07/11/public-attitudes-toward-political-engagement-on-social-media/pi_2018-07-10_social-activism_0-05/

  - http://www.pewinternet.org/2018/07/11/public-attitudes-toward-political-engagement-on-social-media/pi_2018-07-10_social-activism_0-04/

  - https://www.nbcnewsarchivesxpress.com/contentdetails/214755

- **Obama video:**

  - https://www.nbcnewsarchivesxpress.com/contentdetails/214755

Skill:
Sources and
Citations

Josh will include a citation on each slide containing information from an outside source. At the end of his presentation, he'll include a works cited slide, listing all the sources he used.

Skill:
Sources and Citations

••• CHECKLIST FOR SOURCES AND CITATIONS

In your oral presentation, provide citations for any information that you obtained from an outside source. This includes the following:

- direct quotations
- paraphrased information
- tables and data
- images
- videos
- audio files

The citations in your presentation should be as brief and unobtrusive as possible. Follow these general guidelines:

- The citation should indicate the author's last name and the page number(s) on which the information appears (if the source has numbered pages), enclosed in parentheses.
- If the author is not known, the citation should list the title of the work and, if helpful, the publisher.

At the end of your presentation, include your works cited list, which should include all the texts you quote or reference directly in your presentation. Your works cited list should also follow the guidelines of a standard and accepted format, such as MLA. These are the elements and the order in which they should be listed in works cited entries, according to the MLA style:

- author (followed by a period)
- title of source (followed by a period)
- container, or the title of the larger work in which the source is located (followed by a comma)
- other contributors (followed by a comma)
- version (followed by a comma)
- number (followed by a comma)
- publisher (followed by a comma)

- publication date (followed by a comma)

- location (followed by a comma)

- URL, without the "http://" (followed by a period)

Not all of these elements will apply to each citation. Include only the elements that are relevant for the source.

To check that you have gathered and cited sources correctly, consider the following questions:

- Did I cite the information I found using a standard format to avoid plagiarism?

- Did I include all my sources in my works cited list?

↻ YOUR TURN

Read the elements and examples below. Then, complete the chart by placing them in the correct order, according to the MLA style for a works cited list. Write the corresponding letter for each element and example in the appropriate column.

	Elements and Examples
A	publisher
B	"A Theatrical Moscow Trial Draws the Ire of Russia's Cultural Elite."
C	title of source
D	Atlantic Media Company,
E	URL
F	container
G	*The Atlantic,*
H	www.theatlantic.com/international/archive/2019/01/russian-artist-serebrennikov-culture-trial-moscow/580306/.
I	Nemtsova, Anna.
J	author
K	publication date
L	14 Jan. 2019,

Example	Element

WRITE

Use the information in the checklist to create or revise your citations and works cited list. Make sure to identify the source of each piece of researched information in your presentation. This will let your audience know that the information you are presenting is trustworthy. When you have completed your citations, compile a list of all your sources and write out your works cited list. Refer to the *MLA Handbook* as needed.

Skill:
Communicating Ideas

Copyright © BookheadEd Learning, LLC

••• CHECKLIST FOR COMMUNICATING IDEAS

Follow these steps as you rehearse your presentation:

- **Eye Contact:** Practice looking up and making eye contact while you speak. Rehearse your presentation in front of a mirror, making eye contact with yourself. Consider choosing a few audience members to look at during your presentation, but scan the audience from time to time so it doesn't seem as if you're speaking directly to only two or three people.

- **Speaking Rate:** Record yourself so you can judge your speaking rate. If you find yourself speaking too fast, time your presentation and work on slowing down your speech. In addition, you might want to plan pauses in your presentation to achieve a specific effect.

- **Volume:** Be aware of your volume. Make sure that you are speaking at a volume that will be loud enough for everyone to hear you, but not so loud that it will be uncomfortable for your audience.

- **Enunciation:** Decide which words you want to emphasize, and then enunciate them with particular clarity. Emphasizing certain words or terms can help you communicate more effectively and drive home your message.

- **Purposeful Gestures:** Rehearse your presentation with your arms relaxed at your sides. If you want to include a specific gesture, decide where in your presentation it will be most effective, and practice making that gesture until it feels natural.

- **Conventions of Language:** Make sure that you are using appropriate conventions of language for your audience and purpose.

⟳ YOUR TURN

Read the examples of students who are communicating their ideas below. Then, complete the chart by first identifying the appropriate category for each example and then deciding whether the example illustrates effective or ineffective communication. Write the corresponding letter for each example in the appropriate place in the chart.

	Examples
A	A student stands up straight in clear view of his or her audience.
B	A student speaks very softly and rushes through the presentation, using a monotone voice.
C	A student does not look up from his or her notecards.
D	A student uses his or her hands to emphasize a particularly important point.
E	A student slouches and stands with his or her arms crossed.
F	A student begins her formal presentation by saying, "Hello. Today I will talk about rainforests."
G	A student allows his or her arms to hang limply and does not move at all.
H	A student makes eye contact with various members of the audience.
I	A student projects his or her voice, but does not shout. He or she pronounces words carefully and speaks at a slightly slower rate than used in normal conversation.
J	A student begins her formal presentation by saying, "Yo. I'mma talk about some trees."

Category	Example of Effective Communication	Example of Ineffective Communication
Posture		
Eye Contact		
Volume/Rate/Enunciation		
Gestures		
Language Conventions		

✎ WRITE

Practice delivering your presentation by yourself or in front of a partner.

As you present, do the following:

- Employ steady eye contact.
- Use an appropriate speaking rate and volume to clearly communicate your ideas.
- Use pauses and enunciation for clarity and effect.
- Use purposeful gestures to add interest and meaning as you speak.
- Maintain a comfortable, confident posture to engage your audience.
- Use language conventions appropriate for an argumentative presentation, and avoid slang or inappropriate speech.

If you are working with a partner, use the checklist to evaluate your partner's communication of ideas.

When you finish giving your argumentative oral presentation, write a brief but honest reflection about your experience of communicating your ideas. Did you make good eye contact? Did you speak too quickly or too softly? Did you maintain a comfortable, confident posture? Did you use appropriate language? Did you struggle to incorporate gestures that looked and felt natural? How can you better communicate your ideas in the future?

Skill:
Reasons and Evidence

In order to identify a speaker's point of view, reasoning, and use of evidence and rhetoric, note the following:

- the stance, or position, the speaker takes on a topic
- whether the premise, or the basis of the speech or talk, is based on logical reasoning
- whether the ideas follow one another in a way that shows clear, sound thinking
- whether the speaker employs the use of exaggeration, especially when citing facts or statistics
- the speaker's choice of words, the points he or she chooses to emphasize, and the tone, or general attitude

In order to evaluate a speaker's point of view, reasoning, and use of evidence and rhetoric, consider the following questions:

- What stance, or position, does the speaker take? Is the premise based on sound, logical reasoning? Why or why not?
- Does the speaker use facts and statistics to make a point? Are they exaggerated?
- What points does the speaker choose to emphasize?
- How does the speaker's choice of words match the tone he or she wants to establish?

Please note that excerpts and passages in the StudySync® library and this workbook are intended as touchstones to generate interest in an author's work. The excerpts and passages do not substitute for the reading of entire texts, and StudySync® strongly recommends that students seek out and purchase the whole literary or informational work in order to experience it as the author intended. Links to online resellers are available in our digital library. In addition, complete works may be ordered through an authorized reseller by filling out and returning to StudySync® the order form enclosed in this workbook.

Reading & Writing Companion 507

YOUR TURN

Read each example of reasoning from a draft of Josh's oral presentation below. Then, complete the chart by sorting the examples into two categories: those that are logical and those that are illogical. Write the corresponding letter for each example in the appropriate column.

Examples	
A	As students' access to all forms of media increases, so does their ability to navigate it responsibly.
B	A student's access to technology does not mean that the student uses it appropriately or is a good digital citizen.
C	Becoming media literacy savvy is complicated because it requires time, resources, and training.
D	We can always tell teachers to become more media literacy savvy because they use technology each day in their classrooms.
E	Living in a digital world means being inundated with both fake and legitimate news on a daily basis, but discerning fact from fiction can be tricky.
F	If a person doesn't know how to distinguish fake news from legitimate information, he or she is not trying.

Logical Reasoning	Illogical Reasoning

YOUR TURN

Below are three examples of an ineffective use of evidence from a previous draft of Josh's oral presentation. In the second column, rewrite the sentences to use the evidence effectively, without exaggeration or faulty reasoning. The first row has been completed for you as an example.

Ineffective Use of Evidence	Effective Use of Evidence
Technology has made things like home security systems possible. We know that thanks to technology the world is a safer place.	There are many advantages to living in the digital world, including technological advances that make us safer, such as home security systems.
According to Nonprofit Tech for Good, 51% of wealthy donors prefer to give online. This shows that social media is so powerful that it could ensure Americans vote in every election.	
Studies show that most people are skeptical of the information they read on the internet. According to my father, past generations believed everything they read, heard, or saw.	

Skill:
Engaging in Discourse

sync skills

••• CHECKLIST FOR ENGAGING IN DISCOURSE

You and a partner will take turns practicing your argumentative oral presentations and giving feedback. The feedback you provide should be meaningful and respectful. That is, you should offer an honest assessment as well as specific tips for improvement, while using kind and considerate language.

In your feedback, make sure to evaluate and critique the speaker using these categories. Remember to always start by telling the speaker what he or she did particularly well.

Positive Points:

- What is most effective about the oral presentation?
- What strong points does the speaker make?
- Which particular phrases are well written and memorable?

Clarity:

- Does the speaker express his or her ideas in a clear, understandable way?
- What changes can the speaker make to improve the clarity of his or her message?

Evidence and Elaboration:

- Does the speaker offer a range of positions on his or her topic or issue?
- Is there an opportunity to clarify, verify, or challenge ideas and conclusions made in the argument?
- Does the speaker resolve contradictions in his or her argument?
- Does the speaker use transitions and explanations effectively to show the relationship between ideas?
- Where can the speaker add transitions or explanations to improve the logical flow of his or her message?
- What additional information or research is required to deepen his or her message?

Diction:

- Does the speaker's choice of words have an impact, or a strong effect?
- Where can the speaker improve his or her word choice to create a stronger impact?

Syntax:

- Does the speaker use sentence construction to create a strong impact?

- Where can the speaker use sentence-construction techniques, such as ending a sentence with the most important idea, to improve the impact of his or her syntax?

Rhetorical Strategies:

- Does the speaker use language persuasively?

- Where can the speaker employ specific techniques, such as appeals to logic, emotion, and ethics, to improve the impact of his or her presentation?

YOUR TURN

Read each example of feedback below. Then, complete the chart by placing the examples in the appropriate category. Write the corresponding letter for each example of feedback in the appropriate row. Some examples may belong in more than one category.

	Feedback
A	I'm not sure what you mean by "these strategies." Can you elaborate?
B	I think this sentence would be stronger if you moved the most important phrase to the end.
C	The wording of this sentence is a little vague. You might consider using more topic-specific vocabulary.
D	You make a good point here, but it would be stronger if you added a quote from a credible source.
E	I liked how you used an anecdote to make your opening more memorable.
F	The word *however* shows a strong connection between your ideas and evidence in this paragraph.

Category	Feedback
Positive Points	
Clarity	
Evidence and Elaboration	
Diction	
Syntax	
Rhetorical Strategy	

✎ WRITE

Take turns reading your presentation aloud to a partner. When you finish, write a reflection about your experience of giving feedback. How did you ensure that your feedback was both meaningful and respectful? What did you do well? How can you improve in the future?

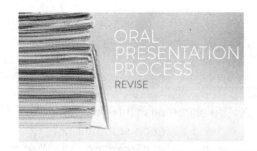

Oral Presentation
Process: Revise

PLAN	DRAFT	REVISE	EDIT AND PRESENT

You have written a draft of your argumentative oral presentation. You have also received input from your peers about how to improve it. Now you are going to revise your draft and prepare your presentation by creating or revising slides and visuals to support your argument.

◀◀ REVISION GUIDE

Examine your draft to find areas for revision. Keep in mind your purpose and audience as you revise for clarity, development, organization, and style. Also, examine your draft to find slides that might need additional clarification or revision. For example, when Josh revised his presentation, he paid careful attention to how the content of each slide supported his thesis and message. Use the guide below to help you review:

Review	Revise	Example
Clarity		
Highlight each sentence that connects to your thesis statement.	Make sure the claim is clear for your audience in both your introduction and conclusion. Add headings to your presentation slides to clarify your ideas and claims for your audience, and simplify your ideas by turning them into brief bullet points.	Formal lessons on living in the digital world will help future graduates a lot. become better digital citizens, be more aware of other people's experiences, and maybe even change the world.

Please note that excerpts and passages in the StudySync® library and this workbook are intended as touchstones to generate interest in an author's work. The excerpts and passages do not substitute for the reading of entire texts, and StudySync® strongly recommends that students seek out and purchase the whole literary or informational work in order to experience it as the author intended. Links to online resellers are available in our digital library. In addition, complete works may be ordered through an authorized reseller by filling out and returning to StudySync® the order form enclosed in this workbook.

Reading & Writing Companion 513

Review	Revise	Example
Development		
Identify and annotate places in your presentation where your thesis is not supported by details.	Add details that strongly support the reasons for your claim. Include images, graphs, videos, and other visual elements that support your argument in your presentation. Think about places where a visual aid might replace text.	To accomplish this goal, schools need to teach students how to analyze and evaluate online sources and how to be responsible digital citizens. That means contributing to the digital space in a positive way, putting an end to cyberbullying, and stopping the propagation of false information.
Organization		
Syntax can help you emphasize ideas. Identify strong words and phrases that show your main ideas, and place them strategically.	Revise sentences so that the most important word or phrase comes at the end. Think about places where a visual aid might enhance a section of the presentation.	In the past 24 hours, ~~all with a device in the palm of my hand,~~ I bought my grandmother a birthday present, took a history quiz, streamed three episodes of my favorite television show, ordered dinner, and researched the causes and effects of air pollution~~:~~—all with a device in the palm of my hand.
Style: Word Choice		
Identify key words and phrases that connect ideas across sentences. Annotate places where more precise language would strengthen the connection.	Replace vague or awkward words and phrases with precise ones that emphasize the connections between your ideas.	Although online activism can have positive effects by including a multitude of opinions, raising awareness, and promoting change, there can be many drawbacks ~~bad effects~~, including people verbally attacking others and using dehumanizing speech.

Review	Revise	Example
Style: Sentence Fluency		
Read your presentation aloud, and listen to the way the text sounds. Does it sound choppy? Or does it flow smoothly with rhythm, movement, and emphasis on important details and events?	Shorten a group of long sentences, or join shorter sentences together using conjunctions and/or dependent clauses.	~~We~~ As a result, we are ready to move on to the next phases of our lives. ~~Few~~ While few teenagers would admit that there is something they do not know about social ~~media. We~~ media, we must acknowledge that the digital world has many pitfalls.

✏ WRITE

Use the revision guide, as well as your peer reviews, to help you evaluate your argumentative oral presentation to determine places that should be revised.

Please note that excerpts and passages in the StudySync® library and this workbook are intended as touchstones to generate interest in an author's work. The excerpts and passages do not substitute for the reading of entire texts, and StudySync® strongly recommends that students seek out and purchase the whole literary or informational work in order to experience it as the author intended. Links to online resellers are available in our digital library. In addition, complete works may be ordered through an authorized reseller by filling out and returning to StudySync® the order form enclosed in this workbook.

Reading & Writing Companion   **515**

Grammar: Parallel Structure

Parallel Structure

Parallel structure, or parallelism, is the deliberate repetition of words, phrases, or other grammatical structures of equal weight or importance.

Not Parallel	Parallel
The soup was hot, wholesome, and **tasted delicious**.	The soup was hot, wholesome, and **delicious**.
After dinner, Kevin completed his Spanish homework, wrote his English essay, and **has studied** for his math test.	After dinner, Kevin completed his Spanish homework, wrote his English essay, and **studied** for his math test.
Peter opened the world almanac, **checking the index**, and identified the capital of Rwanda.	Peter opened the world almanac, **checked the index**, and identified the capital of Rwanda.

Parallelism is a rhetorical device that helps emphasize ideas, establish rhythm, and make a text or speech more memorable. The examples below are from "Be Ye Men of Valour," a speech British Prime Minister Winston Churchill delivered in 1940 at a critical time during World War II.

Text	Explanation
I speak to you for the first time as Prime Minister in a solemn hour for the life **of our country, of our empire, of our allies, and**, above all, **of the cause of freedom**. . . . I am sure I speak for all when I say we are ready **to face it, to endure it, and to retaliate against it** to any extent that the unwritten laws of war permit. . . . We must have, and have quickly, **more aeroplanes, more tanks, more shells, more guns**. Be Ye Men of Valour	Churchill uses parallelism in lists for its rhetorical effect. • Parallel prepositional phrases emphasize the gravity of the *solemn hour* Churchill cites. • The parallel series of infinitive phrases emphasizes the readiness of Churchill and the people to whom he speaks. • The deliberate repetition of *more* in the list of elements needed emphasizes the immediacy of the country's need for equipment and ammunition.

⟳ YOUR TURN

1. How should this sentence be changed to achieve parallel structure?

> He regretted staying up past midnight, eating too much pizza, and then getting up early in the morning to go running.

○ A. Replace **he regretted** with **regretting**.
○ B. Replace **staying** with **stayed**.
○ C. Replace **getting** with **got**.
○ D. No change needs to be made to this sentence.

2. How should this sentence be changed to achieve parallel structure?

> Sarah set the table, lit the candles, and waiting for her date to arrive.

○ A. Insert **and** after **table**.
○ B. Delete **lit the candles**.
○ C. Replace **waiting** with **waited**.
○ D. No change needs to be made to this sentence.

3. How should this sentence be changed to achieve parallel structure?

> David couldn't fall asleep because the TV was blaring, the shouting children, and the dog was barking.

○ A. Replace **TV was blaring** with **blaring TV**.
○ B. Replace **shouting children** with **children were shouting**.
○ C. Replace **dog was barking** with **barking dog**.
○ D. No change needs to be made to this sentence.

4. How should this sentence be changed to achieve parallel structure?

> She watched how the wind shifted, parting clouds, and streaming sunlight.

○ A. Change **how the wind shifted** to **how the shifting wind**.
○ B. Change **how the wind shifted** to **the shifting wind**.
○ C. Replace **and** with **with**.
○ D. No change needs to be made to this sentence.

Grammar:
Sentence Variety - Openings

Sentence Openers

Varying your syntax is one way to help a reader remain engaged. One way to vary your syntax is to use a variety of sentence openers, which help a reader more clearly understand the connection between sentences. The following strategies can help you vary the types of sentence openers you use:

Strategies	Text
Use a prepositional phrase to begin a sentence.	On the enclosed porch at the back of the house, a crisp white bag still sat on the wicker chaise, filled with lace she had once planned to turn into curtains. A Temporary Matter
Use an adverb to begin a sentence.	Generally speaking, philanthropy is always better than no help at all, but it is also in itself a privilege of the few. Commencement Address at the New School
Use a verb ending in *-ed* or *-ing* to begin a sentence.	Finding news and information has never been easier, and access is expanding to more people every day. News Literacy in the Misinformation Age
Use a very short sentence, which can help emphasize an important point or create excitement.	He looked relieved. Ghosts
Use transitional words (showing cause and effect, similarities or differences, etc.) to begin a sentence.	Consequently, the more time we spend on social media platforms, the more deceptive we become. Honesty on Social Media
Use words that indicate time or a sequence of events to begin a sentence.	At the stroke of the midnight hour, when the world sleeps, India will awake to life and freedom. Tryst with Destiny

↻ YOUR TURN

1. How should this sentence be edited to use transitional words showing cause and effect as a sentence opener?

> The new CEO took over and began to make many necessary changes.

- ○ A. Frighteningly, the new CEO took over and began to make many necessary changes.
- ○ B. As a result, the new CEO took over and began to make many necessary changes.
- ○ C. Behind closed doors, the new CEO took over and began to make many necessary changes.
- ○ D. No change needs to be made to this sentence.

2. How should this sentence be edited to use an adverb as a sentence opener?

> Luckily, I made it to the meeting on time.

- ○ A. I made it to the meeting on time, luckily.
- ○ B. I am lucky that I made it to the meeting on time.
- ○ C. I luckily made it to the meeting on time.
- ○ D. No change needs to be made to this sentence.

3. How should this sentence be edited to make the sentence opener clearer?

> People live in cities.

- ○ A. Cities are places where people live.
- ○ B. The people live in cities.
- ○ C. Many people live in cities.
- ○ D. No change needs to be made to this sentence.

4. How should this sentence be edited to use a sentence opener that indicates time?

> The first scholar to edit Emily Dickinson's poems collected all of them into a single edition.

- ○ A. The poems of Emily Dickinson were all collected into a single edition by a scholar.
- ○ B. Surprisingly, the first scholar to edit Emily Dickinson's poems collected all of them into a single edition.
- ○ C. Several decades later, the first scholar to edit Emily Dickinson's poems collected all of them into a single edition.
- ○ D. No change needs to be made to this sentence.

Oral Presentation Process:
Edit and Present

PLAN	DRAFT	REVISE	EDIT AND PRESENT

You have revised your oral presentation based on your peer feedback and your own examination.

Now, it is time to edit your argumentative oral presentation. When you revised, you focused on the content of your oral presentation. You practiced strategies for citing your sources, communicating your ideas, presenting strong reasons and evidence, and engaging in discourse. When you edit, you focus on the mechanics of your oral presentation, paying close attention to language, syntax, and rhetorical devices that can be heard by your audience while you are talking.

Use the checklist below to guide you as you edit:

☐ Have I included a variety of sentence openers in my presentation?

☐ Have I used parallel structure to emphasize ideas, establish rhythm, and make my text or presentation more memorable?

☐ Have I used any language that is too informal for my presentation?

☐ Have I added digital media strategically to enhance my presentation?

☐ Do I have any sentence fragments or run-on sentences?

☐ Have I spelled everything correctly?

Notice some edits Josh has made:

- Edited a sentence to correct a sentence fragment and use transitional words as a sentence opener

- Fixed a misspelled word

- Deleted a run-on sentence

- Changed a sentence to achieve parallel structure

As my classmates and I ~~preparing~~ prepare to ~~gradute~~ graduate from high school~~,~~ we feel like experts on many topics. ~~I personally loved learning about the central nervous system I thought learning about how the framers wrote the Constitution was really cool.~~ We've read great literature, memorized essential formulas, and repeated famous lab experiments. As a result, we are ready to move on to the next phases of our lives.

✎ WRITE

Use the checklist, as well as your peer reviews, to help you evaluate your oral presentation to determine places that need editing. Then, edit your presentation to correct those errors. Finally, rehearse your presentation, including both the delivery of your written work and the strategic use of the digital media you plan to incorporate.

Once you have made all your corrections and rehearsed with your digital media selections, you are ready to present your work. You may present to your class or to a group of your peers. You can record your presentation to share with family and friends or post it on your blog. If you publish online, share the link with your family, friends, and classmates.

Hope

FICTION

Introduction

In this short story, a young girl deals with the grief she feels after a hurricane blows through her town.

V VOCABULARY

anticipate
to think of or predict what will happen in the future

enormous
very large

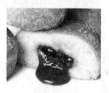

infuse
to cause to be filled with something

maybe
perhaps; possibly

draw
to create an image by making lines and marks

≡ READ

NOTES

1   Today I woke up before it was light out because of the nightmare I've had every night since the storm. It's about Gus drowning in the flood.

Television reporters and meteorologists track Hurricane Frances at the National Hurricane Center.

2   It's all gone—most of our furniture, our clothes, even Darrell's lucky baseball mitt. It's funny, even though so much of our stuff was ruined or lost, I only really care about losing Gus. It sounds crazy, but sometimes I still wander outside asking, "Where are you?" I remember how he used to **anticipate** my thoughts and movements. He followed me everywhere, and he didn't even need a leash. He slept under my bed every night; every morning I'd wake up, look down, and see his front paws sticking out. When I rubbed his belly, he'd stretch out as long as possible so that the fur between his paws would open up like a flower blooming. Then, *crash*, another nightmare. I wake up from this nightmare, drenched in sweat, and Mom is there smoothing my hair. She is reminding me that Darrell's birthday is in a few days and that we need to plan a party.

Islamic Circle of North America Relief USA volunteer Shaza Cheema, right, fills bags of canned foods for Liberty City, FL residents affected by Hurricane Irma.

3   "It's important to keep celebrating our lives," Mom says, trying to **infuse** some cheer in her tone, which is heavy with melancholy. Her eyes are kind, but fill with concern when they look at me now. I know it has something to do with Mrs. Lane telling her about my drawings. They're all worried about what I **draw**, but drawing makes me happiest right now. It's the only time lately when I'm not anxious, or thinking about anything except following my hand around the sketch pad. But I get where they're coming from: the drawings *do* look kind of bad, or as they would say, *unsettling*, or sometimes even *disquieting*. Like there's one where all the trees and telephone poles are knocked down, and huge blue and black waves are so high they cover our whole house. Unfortunately, in that drawing, I drew Gus underwater like in the dream. His white curls pointing straight in different directions. Then another one is just an all black background with one jagged, skinny bolt of lightning cutting through the black sky. The lightning hits my head and splits it open like a pumpkin smashing open on the sidewalk. But I swear drawing makes me feel better.

4   Darrell walked home from school with me today. As we raced through the backyard, we both saw it at the same time: a big, shaking black dog with one white paw like it had been dipped in white paint. Darrell told me to be careful

because it looked like a potentially aggressive dog. He quickly went inside, but I stayed outside. I could tell the dog was afraid, but harmless. It looked how I feel when I wake up from one of those nightmares. So I took off my backpack and sat down on the ground, took out my pad and started drawing. I didn't want to frighten the dog, so I didn't try to move closer. I simply drew in my sketch pad.

5 That night, I told Mom all about the dog in the yard. She seemed a little worried. Dad said he wasn't sure if he was ready to replace Gus.

6 "Can I at least leave some food and water out?"

7 "How do we know it won't bite?" Mom asked. I could hear the trepidation in her voice.

8 "We don't. But he's probably really hungry. If Gus is out there, I'd want someone to make sure he's okay, too."

Rescue flights bring animal victims of Hurricane Katrina out of the flooded Gulf Coast.

9 Mom sighed, but I knew she thought I might be right. I scraped all the leftovers into Gus's old bowl and then went outside and left it right where the dog was that afternoon. I didn't see it, but I said out loud to the trees, "This could be your new home."

10 That night, I drew the black dog dipped in white paint. It was playing with a new toy, on a new bed, and there was new furniture. Darrell was playing baseball outside with his lucky mitt, and flowers and trees were exploding in the yard with color. There were tulips, **enormous** oak trees, rose bushes, and even a hammock. The sun was out, and the sky was blue. I drew Mom gardening with her peculiar-looking straw hat and Dad reading in his favorite chair. I didn't put myself in the drawing. It made me happier to look in from the outside.

NOTES

11 The next day was Darrell's birthday. Mom was busy making a cake for that night before she had to leave for work.

12 "No bad dreams, honey?"

13 But I was too busy running outside to answer. I looked in the dog bowl. It was empty. I looked up the hill and saw the black dog staring at me from behind a tree. I crouched down and held my hand out. The dog inched towards me, peeking from behind trees like a turtle coming out of its shell. She was nervous, so I waited for as long as it took to build her trust. It got close enough that I could see she was a girl dog. Her tail was wagging, but she still seemed terrified. She finally sniffed my hand and then gave it a lick. Then she licked my ear over and over, which was sort of gross because I was covered in slobber, but I understood that to be a good sign.

14 "You're going to be ok. You're home. I hope you like it here." I scratched behind her floppy ear.

15 That night, the black dog celebrated with us! It wasn't a big party and I knew Mom and Dad were really anxious that Darrell would be disappointed because they couldn't buy many presents or anything. But I think we had even more fun than last year. It was a special day for everyone. My heart was still broken because I missed Gus. And I was still sad about the house and everyone's possessions. But there was a new feeling along with the sadness, a warm feeling in my chest and belly, like two very different feelings swirled together to make something new, something better than happiness **maybe**.

16 Dad gave Darrell a new mitt. We ate too much chocolate cake and played with the new dog. Dad belly laughed when the dog skidded across the floor to fetch one of Gus's old squeaky toys. I only realized then that it had been so long since I'd heard a real, big laugh from Dad. I couldn't remember the last time Mom or Dad were so elated. I gave Darrell my drawing, and I could tell he liked it because he hugged me tight. At the end of the night, the black dog was curled up sound asleep on a bunch of blankets I used to make her own bed. Her white paw was folded over her other one. She looked tender, untroubled, and really, really tired.

17 "She can finally sleep because she knows she's safe." Dad said. Mom was sitting on Dad's lap, and Darrell was on his millionth piece of cake when he asked, "So, what's her name?" We were all quiet. Then I said, "Hope. Her name is Hope."

First Read

Read "Hope." After you read, complete the Think Questions below.

1. What event did the narrator and her family experience before the start of the story?

   Before the start of the story, the narrator and her family experienced _____

   _____.

2. Write two or three sentences to describe the plot of the story.

   The plot of the story is about _____

   _____.

3. At the end of the story, how do the narrator and her family feel? Why? Include a line from the text to support your response.

   At the end of the story, the narrator and her family feel _____

   because _____.

4. Use context to confirm the meaning of the word *infuse* as it is used in "Hope." Write your definition of *infuse* here.

   Infuse means _____.

   A context clue is _____.

5. What is another way to say that something is *enormous*?

   Something is _____.

Please note that excerpts and passages in the StudySync® library and this workbook are intended as touchstones to generate interest in an author's work. The excerpts and passages do not substitute for the reading of entire texts, and StudySync® strongly recommends that students seek out and purchase the whole literary or informational work in order to experience it as the author intended. Links to online resellers are available in our digital library. In addition, complete works may be ordered through an authorized reseller by filling out and returning to StudySync® the order form enclosed in this workbook.

Reading & Writing Companion

527

Skill:
Analyzing Expressions

★ DEFINE

When you read, you may find English expressions that you do not know. An **expression** is a group of words that communicates an idea. Three types of expressions are idioms, sayings, and figurative language. They can be difficult to understand because the meanings of the words are different from their **literal,** or usual, meanings.

An **idiom** is an expression that is commonly known among a group of people. For example, "It's raining cats and dogs" means it is raining heavily. **Sayings** are short expressions that contain advice or wisdom. For instance, "Don't count your chickens before they hatch" means do not plan on something good happening before it happens. **Figurative** language is when you describe something by comparing it with something else, either directly (using the words *like* or *as*) or indirectly. For example, "I'm as hungry as a horse" means I'm very hungry. None of the expressions are about actual animals.

••• CHECKLIST FOR ANALYZING EXPRESSIONS

To determine the meaning of an expression, remember the following:

✓ If you find a confusing group of words, it may be an expression. The meaning of words in expressions may not be their literal meaning.

- Ask yourself: Is this confusing because the words are new? Or because the words do not make sense together?

✓ Determining the overall meaning may require that you use one or more of the following:

- context clues

- a dictionary or other resource

- teacher or peer support

✓ Highlight important information before and after the expression to look for clues.

↻ YOUR TURN

Choose the best answer to each question.

1. The sentence "The dog inched towards me, peeking from behind trees like a turtle coming out of its shell" suggests a comparison between—

    ○ A.   the trees and the dog.

    ○ B.   an inch and a turtle.

    ○ C.   the dog and a turtle.

    ○ D.   a turtle and its shell.

2. Which sentence contains an example of figurative language?

    ○ A.   "But I think we had even more fun."

    ○ B.   "My heart was still broken because I missed Gus."

    ○ C.   "Dad gave Darrell a new mitt."

    ○ D.   "We ate too much chocolate cake and played with the new dog."

3. Which sentence contains an example of figurative language?

    ○ A.   "I couldn't remember the last time Mom or Dad were so elated."

    ○ B.   "At the end of the night, the black dog was curled up sound asleep on a bunch of blankets I used to make her own bed."

    ○ C.   "Her white paw was folded over her other one, and she looked tender, untroubled and really, really tired. "

    ○ D.   "Mom was sitting on Dad's lap, and Darrell was on his millionth piece of cake when he asked, 'So, what's her name?'"

Please note that excerpts and passages in the StudySync® library and this workbook are intended as touchstones to generate interest in an author's work. The excerpts and passages do not substitute for the reading of entire texts, and StudySync® strongly recommends that students seek out and purchase the whole literary or informational work in order to experience it as the author intended. Links to online resellers are available in our digital library. In addition, complete works may be ordered through an authorized reseller by filling out and returning to StudySync® the order form enclosed in this workbook.

Reading & Writing
Companion

529

Skill: Visual and Contextual Support

★ DEFINE

Visual support is an image or an object that helps you understand a text. **Contextual support** is a **feature** that helps you understand a text. By using visual and contextual supports, you can develop your vocabulary so you can better understand a variety of texts.

First, preview the text to identify any visual supports. These might include illustrations, graphics, charts, or other objects in a text. Then, identify any contextual supports. Examples of contextual supports are titles, headers, captions, and boldface terms. Write down your **observations**.

Then, write down what those visual and contextual supports tell you about the meaning of the text. Note any new vocabulary that you see in those supports. Ask your peers and your teacher to **confirm** your understanding of the text.

••• CHECKLIST FOR VISUAL AND CONTEXTUAL SUPPORT

To use Visual and Contextual Support to understand texts, do the following:

✓ Preview the text. Read the title, headers, and other features. Look at any images and graphics.

- Write down the visual and contextual supports in the text.

- Write down what those supports tell you about the text.

- Note any new vocabulary that you see in those supports.

- Create an illustration for the reading and write a descriptive caption.

- Confirm your observations with your peers and teacher.

YOUR TURN

Read paragraphs 5–8 from "Hope." Then, complete the multiple-choice questions below.

from "Hope"

That night, I told Mom all about the dog in the yard. She seemed a little worried, and Dad said he wasn't sure if he was ready to replace Gus.

"Can I at least leave some food and water out?"

"How do we know it won't bite?" Mom asked. I could hear the trepidation in her voice.

"We don't. But he's probably really hungry. If Gus is out there, I'd want someone to make sure he's okay, too."

1. The visual support helps readers to—

    ○ A. visualize what a hurricane looks like.

    ○ B. learn about aircraft carriers.

    ○ C. visualize how many animals are rescued after storms.

    ○ D. learn about a lesser-known recovery effort.

2. What background information does the image provide?

    ○ A. Many pets are killed in hurricanes.

    ○ B. It is dangerous for dogs to fly.

    ○ C. Some animals are rescued after storms.

    ○ D. Families are notified when their pets are rescued.

3. Based on the image and its caption, which of the following statements about the characters in the story might be true?

    ○ A. Gus is alive and well because he was rescued and brought to a safe location.

    ○ B. The narrator gave Gus away to a new family.

    ○ C. The black dog in the narrator's yard has been there the whole time.

    ○ D. The narrator's brother rescued the black dog from a shelter.

Close Read

✏ WRITE

NARRATIVE: The short story "Hope" gives the reader a look at how one young girl moves on with her life after a natural disaster. Use your background knowledge about preparation and recovery efforts to write a first-person narrative from her brother's point of view. How has his life changed? How does his experience differ from his sister's experience? Include details from the short story in your writing. Pay attention to and edit for pronouns and antecedents.

Use the checklist below to guide you as you write.

☐ How is Darrell's experience of the hurricane different than his sister's experience?

☐ What happens to Darrell during the story?

☐ How does Darrell feel? How do you know?

Use the sentence frames to organize and write your narrative.

My birthday is in a few days but (I / we) _____ am _____

instead of happy. My family is recovering from a _____.

(We / They) _____ lost most of our belongings and our dog, Gus. We had to evacuate

quickly and _____.

Sometimes I wish I could _____.

My sister has been _____

since the storm. (She / He) _____ misses our dog, Gus. Yesterday, we found a new dog and volunteers

gave my mom _____.

Maybe my birthday will be happy after all.

When the World Sleeps

FICTION

Introduction

On June 15th, 1947, the British House of Commons passed the Indian Independence Act which divided the country into two, India and Pakistan. Their independence was to be granted by August 15th of that same year. In this short drama, a family travels through the night to find safety as India claims its independence from the British.

VOCABULARY

suffocate
to die from lack of oxygen

erupt
to burst suddenly

desperately
in a distressed or severe manner

progress
to move forward toward a better outcome

illusion
an incorrect or false idea

NOTES

READ

1   *It is late at night on August 14th, 1947, the night before India becomes independent from the British. A family is traveling from their old home in Lyallpur, now renamed Faisalabad, headed to the safety of India.*

2   CHARACTERS:
Santosh Singh, 19
Niranjan Singh, 15, her brother
Anjali Singh, 40, their mother

3   *Santosh, Niranjan, and Anjali are crammed in the back of a military truck. They can hear sounds but see nothing outside. Everyone is tense, hungry, and thirsty. They are aware this is a very dangerous journey to safety. Throughout the scene, the actors should be facing out, pressed shoulder to shoulder, as if there were people on all sides of them. They are talking quietly to each other, trying not to draw attention. Anjali, the mother, is seated between Santosh and Niranjan. She is perched on a small box that contains her few remaining possessions. She clutches a small framed photo in her hands.*

4   SANTOSH: I can hardly breathe or move. I feel as if I'm **suffocating**.

NOTES

5   ANJALI: Be patient. There is nothing left to do but pray to Lord Ganesha that we reach the safety of India.

6   SANTOSH: But us poor children are so thirsty!

7   NIRANJAN: How can you bellyache at a time like this? Yes, this journey may be dangerous, or uncomfortable, but these feelings are temporary. In the morning, we will be in a new, wonderful world. A free India.

8   SANTOSH: *(sharp)* How can you know that? And what if we're stopped by the rioters before we get there? What if we're killed as Ram was?

9   ANJALI: Shhh, shhh. Please, let's just pray for your father's safety, for our own.

10 NIRANJAN: Of course we can't know, but millions have risked far more than you have. And you still can complain, no matter what.

11 SANTOSH: I'm sorry, but our life was good before this need for Independence, in case you forgot. We ran and played in the streets without fear as little children. I was able to go to school with my friends and wear gold. What do we have now? I **desperately** miss my friends. We are crammed like animals to slaughter in the back of a military truck, praying not to be massacred. And this is freedom? This is the new India? You can have it.

12 ANJALI: Santosh, you have gone too far!

13 SANTOSH: I don't care.

14 *(Niranjan snorts.)*

15 NIRANJAN: Yes, sister, it was nice and comfortable for *you*, for us, perhaps. But what about the lower castes? Or do you ever think of anyone but yourself and which gold earrings to wear?

16 SANTOSH: *(tears in her eyes, soft)* You've always been so cruel to me.

17 ANJALI: Stop it, children! This is not a time for fighting! This is a time to pray for safety, hope that we make it intact across the border, and to hold each other in the light. We need to stay close, more than ever. For your father, for me, for Ram. Please! You arguing only adds to the destruction. Be sensible.

18 SANTOSH: I'm sorry, Mother. But he's being horrible!

Please note that excerpts and passages in the StudySync® library and this workbook are intended as touchstones to generate interest in an author's work. The excerpts and passages do not substitute for the reading of entire texts, and StudySync® strongly recommends that students seek out and purchase the whole literary or informational work in order to experience it as the author intended. Links to online resellers are available in our digital library. In addition, complete works may be ordered through an authorized reseller by filling out and returning to StudySync® the order form enclosed in this workbook.

Reading & Writing Companion   **535**

19 NIRANJAN: I believe in Jawaharlal Nehru. If we didn't get the chance to cross over by caravan, I would have ridden over the border on horseback all by myself!

20 *(A beat. Santosh suddenly starts laughing through tears. Then they all begin to laugh.)*

21 NIRANJAN: We can have a good laugh, but it's true. I believe in Jawaharlal Nehru. I believe in the new India. You talk of how we were free to play in the streets as children. But so what? At what cost? Without independence, there is no true freedom, just the **illusion** of freedom—but the British owned us, make no mistake. The entire soul of our nation was suppressed. And you talk of wearing gold and missing your friends!

22 ANJALI: Don't be so harsh with your sister. Try to have some compassion. I am so grateful for both of your childhoods, and I always will be. It was a peaceful time.

23 NIRANJAN: If we had cared to look, we would have noticed that it was not a peaceful time for many others. Our sisters, our brothers.

24 SANTOSH: You know, for all of your self-righteousness, Mother is the one who got us a place in this caravan, while Father has stayed behind in great danger to gather our affairs! What do you do except endlessly pontificate?!

25 *(Suddenly, the caravan screeches to a stop. They hear an **eruption** of violence outside of the tent. Shouting, screaming, crying, gun shots. They huddle together, suddenly silent. Anjali prays, holding her children close to her. Niranjan embraces both his mother and sister with his arms, protecting them.)*

25 SANTOSH: *(whispering)* Let us not panic; let us pray together.

26 *(They wait and pray, huddled together. After a few moments, the truck begins to move again, slow and steady. The sounds of the riots slowly fade away. They all let out a big sigh of relief. Anjali clutches the small frame to her chest, her eyes closed.)*

27 ANJALI: I know he is with us; your brother is with us. For now, we are safe.

28 SANTOSH: Yes. For now we are headed to India. To the new world, to the future. Unfortunately, we don't know when we will become the victim of a bullet! Sure, you protect your relatives. But, I can't believe that this is the life we are committing to. I guess you are right, Niranjan. Because, at this point, you must be right.

29   NIRANJAN: Of course I'm right.

30   SANTOSH: Impossible, as always.

31   NIRANJAN: I wouldn't want to disappoint you.

32   *(They laugh.)*

33   ANJALI: I see a bright, new future for us! As long as I have my children, and your father . . . I am home. We will create a beautiful life in India.

34   SANTOSH: I want to have faith in the new India, in Jawaharlal Nehru. I do, we've just lost so much . . .

35   NIRANJAN: But sometimes those sacrifices are necessary, for **progress**. Letting go is an important step to becoming truly free. Look, we are all connected. Place your personal suffering on hold while we work together to end suffering for our people. Can you help this movement to end the violence so that India is a better place for all?

36   SANTOSH: *(quietly, to herself)* Yes. I can and I will.

37   *(Suddenly they hear shouts, but not of violence. Finally, shouts of joy, jubilation! All three look at each other, with light and tears in their eyes.)*

38   SANTOSH: It must be midnight; it has come.

39   NIRANJAN: India is now free. It has finally happened. We are sovereign.

40   ANJALI: The world sleeps still, but we have awakened. When the sun rises, what will we find?

41   *(Santosh takes her mother's hand. They all look out.)*

(BLACKOUT.)

WHEN THE WORLD SLEEPS

First Read

Read "When the World Sleeps." After you read, complete the Think Questions below.

☁ THINK QUESTIONS

1. Who are the main characters in the story? What is their relationship?

   The main characters are _____.

   They are _____.

2. Write two or three sentences describing the setting of the story.

   The setting of the story is _____

   _____.

3. Why are the characters traveling? Include a line from the text to support your response.

   The characters are traveling because _____

   _____.

4. Use context to confirm the meaning of the word *illusion* as it is used in "When the World Sleeps."
   Write your definition of *illusion* here.

   Illusion means _____.

   A context clue is _____.

5. What is another way to say that something *erupted*?

   Something _____.

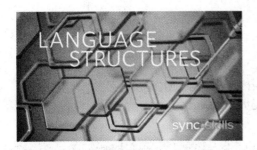

Skill:
Language Structures

★ DEFINE

In every language, there are rules that tell how to **structure** sentences. These rules define the correct order of words. In the English language, for example, a **basic** structure for sentences is subject, verb, and object. Some sentences have more **complicated** structures.

You will encounter both basic and complicated **language structures** in the classroom materials you read. Being familiar with language structures will help you better understand the text.

••• CHECKLIST FOR LANGUAGE STRUCTURES

To improve your comprehension of language structures, do the following:

✓ Monitor your understanding.

- Ask yourself: Why do I not understand this sentence? Is it because I do not understand some of the words? Or is it because I do not understand the way the words are ordered in the sentence?

✓ Pay attention to **perfect tenses** as you read. There are three perfect tenses in the English language: the present perfect, past perfect, and future perfect.

- **Present perfect tense** can be used to indicate a situation that began at a prior point in time and continues into the present.

  > Combine *have* or *has* with the past participle of the main verb.
  > Example: I **have played** basketball for three years.

- **Past perfect tense** can describe an action that happened before another action or event in the past.

  > Combine *had* with the past participle of the main verb.
  > Example: I **had learned** how to dribble a ball before I could walk!

Please note that excerpts and passages in the StudySync® library and this workbook are intended as touchstones to generate interest in an author's work. The excerpts and passages do not substitute for the reading of entire texts, and StudySync® strongly recommends that students seek out and purchase the whole literary or informational work in order to experience it as the author intended. Links to online resellers are available in our digital library. In addition, complete works may be ordered through an authorized reseller by filling out and returning to StudySync® the order form enclosed in this workbook.

Reading & Writing Companion **539**

- **Future perfect tense** expresses one future action that will begin and end before another future event begins or before a certain time.

  > Use *will have* or *shall have* with the past participle of a verb.
  > Example: Before the end of the year, I **will have played** more than 100 games!
  > Example: By the time you play your first game, I **will have played** 100 games!

✓ Break down the sentence into its parts.

- Ask yourself: What actions are expressed in this sentence? Are they completed or are they ongoing? What words give me clues about when an action is taking place?

✓ Confirm your understanding with a peer or teacher.

⟳ YOUR TURN

Read each sentence and notice the perfect tense in each one. Then, sort each sentence into the correct category by writing the letter in the Present Perfect, Past Perfect, or Future Perfect column.

	Sentences
A	My aunt has read that book.
B	They have visited Berlin.
C	The series finale will have aired by the end of the year.
D	Before next week, the student will have prepared for the exam.
E	My brother had washed the dishes before going to bed.
F	We got a sandwich after the movie had ended.

Present Perfect	Past Perfect	Future Perfect

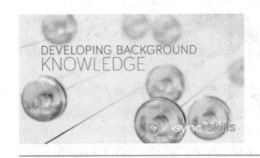

Skill: Developing Background Knowledge

★ DEFINE

Developing background knowledge is the process of gaining information about different topics. By developing your background knowledge, you will be able to better understand a wider variety of texts.

First, preview the text to determine what the text is about. To **preview** the text, read the title, headers, and other text features and look at any images or graphics. As you are previewing, identify anything that is unfamiliar to you and that seems important.

While you are reading, you can look for clues that will help you learn more about any unfamiliar words, phrases, or topics. You can also look up information in another resource to increase your background knowledge.

••• CHECKLIST FOR DEVELOPING BACKGROUND KNOWLEDGE

To develop your background knowledge, do the following:

✓ Preview the text. Read the title, headers, and other features. Look at any images and graphics.

✓ Identify any words, phrases, or topics that you do not know a lot about.

✓ As you are reading, try to find clues in the text that give you information about any unfamiliar words, phrases, or topics.

✓ If necessary, look up information in other sources to learn more about any unfamiliar words, phrases, or topics. You can also ask a peer or teacher for information or support.

✓ Think about how the background knowledge you have gained helps you better understand the text.

Please note that excerpts and passages in the StudySync® library and this workbook are intended as touchstones to generate interest in an author's work. The excerpts and passages do not substitute for the reading of entire texts, and StudySync® strongly recommends that students seek out and purchase the whole literary or informational work in order to experience it as the author intended. Links to online resellers are available in our digital library. In addition, complete works may be ordered through an authorized reseller by filling out and returning to StudySync® the order form enclosed in this workbook.

Reading & Writing Companion   **541**

↻ YOUR TURN

Read each quotation from "When the World Sleeps" below. Then, complete the chart by identifying the background knowledge that helps you understand each quotation.

Background Knowledge Options	
A	Areas formerly controlled by the British were divided into two countries: Pakistan and India.
B	The transition to independence for India was not entirely peaceful.
C	Starting in the Middle Ages, Indian society was divided into different classes called castes.

Quotation	Background Knowledge
"A family is traveling from their old home in Lyallpur, now renamed Faisalabad, headed to the safety of India."	
"But what about the lower castes?"	
"Suddenly, the caravan screeches to a stop. They hear an eruption of violence outside of the tent. Shouting, screaming, crying, gun shots."	

WHEN THE WORLD SLEEPS

Close Read

✏ WRITE

LITERARY ANALYSIS: Santosh and her brother Niranjan view the experience of fleeing their hometown very differently. Choose one of the characters, and write a paragraph in which you explain his or her perspective and why he or she looks at this event this way. Include textual evidence to support your analysis. Pay attention to and edit for homophones.

Use the checklist below to guide you as you write.

☐ How does the character refer to real-life people, places, or events?

☐ How does the character feel about fleeing Pakistan for India?

☐ Why does the character feel this way?

Use the sentence frames to organize and write your literary analysis.

The character I chose is _____.

This character is _____ about Indian independence.

_____ thinks (they're / their / there) _____

lives under British rule were _____.

This character believes that traveling to India is _____.

In the play, the character states, _____.

This line shows _____.

studysync®

Text Fulfillment Through StudySync

If you are interested in specific titles, please fill out the form below and we will check availability through our partners.

ORDER DETAILS

Date:

TITLE	AUTHOR	Paperback/ Hardcover	Specific Edition *If Applicable*	Quantity

SHIPPING INFORMATION	BILLING INFORMATION ☐ *SAME AS SHIPPING*
Contact:	Contact:
Title:	Title:
School/District:	School/District:
Address Line 1:	Address Line 1:
Address Line 2:	Address Line 2:
Zip or Postal Code:	Zip or Postal Code:
Phone:	Phone:
Mobile:	Mobile:
Email:	Email:

PAYMENT INFORMATION

☐ CREDIT CARD   Name on Card:

Card Number: Expiration Date: Security Code:

☐ PO   Purchase Order Number:

StudySync Text Fulfillment, BookheadEd Learning, LLC
610 Daniel Young Drive | Sonoma, CA 95476